THE LIFE AND TIMES OF A GERMAN METHODIST CIRCUIT RIDER ON THE FRONTIER OF TEXAS

CONRAD PLUENNEKE
(1819-1897)

BY

ROBERT LAMAR FEUGE, PhD
2014

ISBN: 978-1494400996

Printed in the United States by Createspace.

Library of Congress Control Number: 2014900856

"We of the present generation, living in well organized cities and communities, surrounded by all the comfort and luxury, seemingly indispensable in modern life, can hardly conceive or properly appreciate the hardships and privations of the early Texas pioneers, struggling with iron difficulties and dangers of frontier life, but we have every reason to hold these men in cherished and revered remembrance. Their noble work should not fall into oblivion."

Moritz Tiling (1913)

DEDICATION

This book is dedicated to the Pluenneke family and to the many other pioneering German Methodist families who settled on the frontier in Mason County, particularly along Beaver Creek and Willow Creek.

TABLE OF CONTENTS

ACKNOWLEDGEMENTS

A number of people have contributed mightily to the publication of this book and I wish to offer my heartfelt thanks to all of them. Foremost, I wish to thank the members of the Pluenneke family, particularly Jan Appleby, Gerry Daniel, Don Daniel, Trey Nelson, and Charles Pluenneke who reside in Texas as well as Friedrich Pluenneke, who lives in Klein-Lafferde, Germany. All of them have provided me with invaluable documents, photographs, books, and other highly useful information about the history of the Pluenneke, Leifeste, and Kothmann families in Mason County. I am particularly grateful to Charles Pluenneke, Don Daniel, and Gerry Daniel for getting me beyond two locked gates to visit the Conrad Pluenneke homestead at Lower Willow. I especially thank Don Daniel for using GPS technology to locate the old Pluenneke house accurately and plot it on a map.

I could not have written this book without the assistance of several Methodist historians. First, I wish to acknowledge the contributions of my friend Wilbur Crenwelge, M.D. whom I regard as the *de facto* Methodist historian in Fredericksburg (Texas) as well as a valuable source for old Methodist Church documents and gaining access to them. Most importantly, he helped me get in touch with *my Inner Methodist*. In a similar vein, I owe a huge debt of gratitude to William (Bill) Hardt, former Chair of the Texas Conference's Commission on Archives and History. He and his father, John Wesley Hardt, have literally written the book about the history of Methodism in Texas. Over the past four years, Bill has generously shared his knowledge of the Methodist organization and history with me, particularly parts that pertain to the German Methodist Conferences and missions. In addition, he has always patiently answered my many, many questions about the faith and its complicated organization. I also want to express appreciation to archivist Timothy Binkley at the Bridwell Library at Southern Methodist University who dug out many old records of German Methodism for me. In that same vein, thanks are owed to Professor Ted Campbell of Southern Methodist University for accessing Methodist Conference records on my behalf. Finally, thanks to

Dale Patterson who found the front cover image in the archives of Drew University.

Thanks to John Molleston at the Texas General Land Office and to Donaly Brice of the Texas State Library in Austin for retrieving information from their archives. Thanks to Cindy Kothmann in the Mason County Clerk's office for locating obscure land documents in its files.

Graciously, Gary and Margaret Kraisinger have provided me with much information about cattle trailing in the 19th century, including maps of the Goodnight-Loving Trail as well as other information about moving cattle across the Llano Estacado and the Pecos River. Thanks!

To my longtime classmate and friend Mark Wieser from Fredericksburg, I say danke for sharing his vast collection of history books and translating German documents into English for my benefit.

Last, many thanks go to Jan Appleby, Gregg Eckhardt, Bill Hardt, Fran Hoerster, and Csaba Martonyi for their careful reviews and many thoughtful suggestions that led to this book's improvement.

PROLOGUE

In his brief biography about Conrad Pluenneke written in 1986, Julius E. DeVos wrote, "He (Conrad) – was not an ordinary man. In other times or other places, he would have probably been a great leader of his fellow men." After almost four years of painstaking research on the life of Conrad Pluenneke, I heartily concur with that conclusion. Conrad Pluenneke was indeed an exceptionally versatile, determined, and capable man. Throughout his life, he repeatedly exhibited courage, intelligence, energy, ambition, confidence, resilience, and an adventurous spirit – all traits of a successful immigrant. It is easy to see why people might follow him.

Conrad, like so many other German immigrants who came to Texas between 1844 and 1847 under the inept leadership of the Adelsverein, soon found himself stranded in a very different country without protection, support, or resources. He came in quest of land but a wide range of events carried him well beyond his boyhood dreams to a different future.

The following quotation was written by C.H. Doering and submitted to Wilhelm Nast who published it in *Der Christliche Apologete* in 1849. It seems apt here because It could have just as well have been written by Conrad Pluenneke as he neared the end of life:

"My native land is Germany. Why I was induced to leave my Fatherland affectionate friends and go to a strange land, I begin now to understand. I see in it the finger of God. It was his inscrutable providence that inspired me. The infinite grace of our Lord opened my eyes, under the preaching of Methodist ministers, to see the bottomless abyss, at the edge of which I unconsciously stood; and this mercy pointed out the way and the means by which I should escape the wrath to come – faith in the Lamb."

A quote from Horace Walpole [1] might have served just as appropriately as the one by Doering. Like the three Princes of Serendip,

---

[1] Walpole, Horace. *The Three Princes of Serendip*. 1854.

Conrad Pluenneke went to a strange place, in this case Texas, and there discovered things either by accident or by sagacity for which he was not searching when he left Germany.

Before I begin the story, I feel compelled to say a few words about my approach to writing this biography. The type of books that I write are generally categorized as either *historical fiction* or *biographical fiction*. Authors who work in this genre generally take a historical subject and write a fictionalized story about it. That I have done herein. Because of the way that I write such books, however, the genre might be better described as **historical** *fiction* because I tend to emphasize historical aspects over more fictional ones. In this book. I am writing about Conrad Pluenneke and the era in which he lived. In a few places, I have included much historical detail about that era, maybe too much, to provide the reader with a thorough understanding of his temporal and geographical context. But, I must hasten to add, what you are about to read is not entirely a history book. It contains some fiction which I have added to round out the story and provide a sense of what Conrad Pluenneke was really like. While I have used fiction, I have discarded unsubstantiated family lore and anecdotes that I could not verify.

Writing an accurate biography about a man who lived and died more than a century ago, while simultaneously trying to make it interesting to a modern reader, has been a challenge to me. In a way, writing this story has been like trying to assemble a picture puzzle with little or no knowledge of what the completed puzzle looks like. No one alive today knew Conrad Pluenneke so I have had no firsthand accounts on which to draw to arrive at an understanding of his personality. I have deduced the details of Conrad's life and his personality, therefore, through careful research as well as rigorous analyses of both documents and photos that he left behind. To identify the many achievements of Conrad Pluenneke has involved delving into a variety of archives that pertain to his emigration, army service, real estate transactions, census data, naturalization records, tax records, religion, communications, cemetery plots, etcetera. Together, that research has yielded a vast amount of information about him but some of that data was found to be incorrect or in conflict with other confirmed data. I have culled out or resolved those portions during a rigorous validation effort.

Once I had the factual details of Conrad's life before me (i.e., the pieces of the puzzle), I had to somehow make sense of that information. To do that, I placed his accomplishments on a time line and looked for trends or patterns that might suggest what he might be doing at each step of his life. I also looked closely at his photographs and his signature for clues about his personality. What I saw, particularly in the latter, was a very neat, literate, organized, and deliberate man. [2] To those patterns and traits, I applied logical *if-then deduction* to develop a crude *word portrait* about him and his life, one that hopefully resembles the actual man.

The analytic process produced a factual structure, or skeleton, for the story but one that was somewhat dry and devoid of life. To that skeleton, I added fictional details to flesh out and complete the story. Slowly, the resolution of Conrad's portrait improved and I began to see the man but still in dim light. When my research had exhausted all leads and uncovered what I thought was all knowable facts about him, I stepped back figuratively, looked at the mosaic pattern of those details, and made a final interpretation of how I saw Conrad Pluenneke. In that final step, I used my imagination as well as my own personal experiences to fill in and complete Conrad's story. Thus, this book is a little autobiographical and my own unique interpretation of the assembled facts. It is how I alone see Conrad Pluenneke. Is my narrative the final word on him? No, absolutely not! Will everyone agree with my story? There too, the answer is no! Very likely, every one of my readers will see the pattern slightly differently and come to view Conrad Pluenneke through their own lens of experience and creativity. However, that is part of biography and explains why multiple biographies have been written about the same subject.[3] What you are about to read is my biography of Conrad Pluenneke.

As I implied earlier, my aim throughout has been to carefully assemble the puzzle and provide the reader with a reasonably good portrait of Conrad Pluenneke that is largely based on fact. While most of the pieces to the Conrad Pluenneke picture puzzle are factual and logical, a few parts of it are entirely fictional. For example, I have very little knowledge of old-style Methodism but I do know that Conrad Pluenneke's conversion to Methodism had to be very dramatic because it had a such a powerful and lasting effect on his life. Especially in reli-

---

[2] See Conrad Pluenneke's photograph and signature on the Dedication Page.

[3] For example, there have been over 200 books written about the life of George Washington.

gion, I have tried not to stray too far from what I know but I had to deal with his conversion to Methodism, which I imagine to be every bit as powerful as that of Saul on the Road to Damascus. As I have written about it, Conrad's conversion is entirely fictional but typical of religious conversions in that era. Where I have added such fictional details to the story, I have based them either on someone's expert knowledge, on what other immigrants wrote in their diaries about pioneer events, or what I have determined to be a reasonable and logical course of action that any immigrant in that era might have taken in a similar situations.

Of course, the dialog in this book is entirely fictional but the characters are as real as I could imagine them. As in the life of *Christoph Feuge*, [4] Heinrich Stiehl is an influential character in this story. He too is another of my great great grandfathers and was one of the early ardent Methodists in Fredericksburg. In this book, I have made him a sort of Methodist prophet in the wilds of central Texas, spreading the Word and leading others in the right direction.

In a different vein, I have always wondered why my pioneering German ancestors seemed to be so Hell-bent on acquiring land. Many of them, like Conrad Pluenneke and Christoph Feuge, grew up in very modest German farming communities, working on small family patches of land. Somehow, most of the immigrants from Germany in that era seemed to have big dreams about owning an estate. Why? To answer that question, I had to try to understand the German mindset about land in the 19th century. I was forced to step back and consider that in 1840, Germany and most of Europe had just emerged from the Feudal era. [5] The last anti-feudal law was passed by the Kingdom of Hanover in 1831, just 14 years before most of them left Germany. During the thousand year span of the feudalism era, wealthy Lords owned most of the land and commoners (such as the Pluenneke family) served their Lord's interests by working their fields and fighting their wars, with few or no civil rights. In return, the Lords were obligated to protect their servants and provide for them but many abused their people and forced them to serve as little more than slaves. For the serfs, there was no escape and that sense of bondage was unconsciously passed on from generation to generation to generation. [6] When the

---

[4] Feuge, Robert L. *Christoph Feuge*. Llumina Press, Coral Springs, FL. 2009.
[5] Simms, Brendan. *The Struggle for Master in Germany*, 1998.
[6] Shils. Edward. *Traditions*. 1981.

feudal system ended early in the 19th century, commoners gained limited freedom, a small voice in government, and, perhaps most importantly, the right to own land. Even after the land was redistributed, however, the Lords managed to retain the best lands for themselves and continued to control German society. While in servitude, the lower class envied the power that their Lords wielded. The basis of their power began with ownership of land on a grand scale. As Seidman (2007) has pointed out, land ownership was then (and still is) a zero-sum game. In other words: If I own the land, you don't and that gives me an advantage over you. After Feudalism ended, it was very difficult for former serfs to obtain good land in Germany. It was not only scarce but very expensive and the descendants of serfs lacked the resources and political connections to acquire the best tracts so they bought what they could afford. Now free and living on their own small patches of ground, commoners were left to practice subsistence farming, barely eking out a living for their families. However, they were stuck in a class-oriented society. If they had wished to become Lord-like and own large tracts of land, the only avenue open to them was to leave Germany. Leaving the Fatherland was almost unthinkable to many Germans in that era. Yet, conditions were bad and the American frontier beckoned, partly because of glowing letters from people like Friedrich Ernst in Texas. It offered not only cheap land but freedom and self governance. Texas, in particular, was very attractive but it was also thought to be untamed and risky. It took a near total collapse of the German economy to force German citizens to consider emigrating to other countries.

It is my assertion that the Pluenneke family was typical of those post-feudal families that soured on the status quo in Germany in 1845 and chose to emigrate to Texas. With but a small patch of farm land, they and their offspring were condemned to a future working as impoverished subsistence farmers or maybe even as paupers. It is my belief that the Pluennekes, particularly Conrad, seized on what they must have felt like was their one and only opportunity to forge a better future for the family but they surely must have had some reservations about leaving their homeland.

Why did I undertake to write this story? Several Reasons: First, I began just wanting to know something about my great great grandfather. When Jan Appleby (also a Pluenneke descendant) sent me a copy of the so called *Pluenneke Book*, I was ecstatic because it contained what I consider the single most valuable piece of what would become the Conrad Pluenneke puzzle: a letter written by Conrad Pluenneke to a cousin back in Germany in 1861. The original four page letter, written in longhand German, had somehow been preserved by the Pluenneke family in Germany for over 150 years. Around 1975, it was translated into English by Friedrich Pluenneke [7] and sent to Texas. In the letter, Conrad describes almost every detail of his life in Texas, including his religion; his ranch; his livestock; market conditions for his produce, weather; his Pluenneke relatives in Texas, and his own family. Through its expressive narrative, the letter provides a tremendous insight into both Conrad's personality and his life in early 1861. He was a literate man. To a biographer, such a letter is a treasure trove of information and it, more than anything, was what motivated me to write this biography. As I looked at Conrad Pluenneke's life, I saw that it spanned four of the most eventful and consequential decades of U.S. and Texas history. He not only lived through those decades but actively participated in them. Second, I want Conrad Pluenneke to be remembered. Most of the Germans who chose to emigrate to Texas in the 1840s (like the Pluennekes) and who managed to survive after gallantly fighting to tame the land, are today in danger of being forgotten, *swept into oblivion* as Tiling put it. In our modern era of convenience and high tech gadgets, it is difficult to comprehend the hardships our ancestors endured to establish their families on these shores. We of today owe them and cannot allow them to just fade away and become forgotten. Last, Conrad Pluenneke is a wonderful role model for anyone in future generations who dares to risk pursuing success when the outcome is far from being certain.

Robert Lamar Feuge
2014

---

[7] Friedrich Pluenneke currently lives in Klein-Lafferde, Germany

Chapter 1

GERMANY AND 19TH CENTURY EMIGRATION

Had it all been a dream? Had the old man been mesmerized and somehow made to believe that he had really accomplished what he had dreamt of for so very, very long? On his deathbed, Conrad Pluenneke struggled to hang onto life while simultaneously trying to remember his past, a life's story that now seemed distant and vague to him. Occasionally, discrete memories from that past came into focus and he fleetingly recalled events – crossing the Atlantic or marching off to Mexico or becoming a Methodist or acquiring thousands of acres of land, or trailing cattle –. Had he really left Germany as a young man and achieved so much success in Texas? To him, it seemed so but in his present deteriorating mental state, it seemed more like a dream and he just could not be sure. The precious details of a life full of accomplishment, of which he was so very proud, were now locked in his brain and shrouded in a gossamer-like mental fog, largely inaccessible. As he tried to sort through that mental haze, however, he dimly recalled that his future had begun with a simple insight that he had when he was but a 16 year old boy, plowing the field for his father back in Germany. That epiphany had put him on a different trajectory through life. To him, it felt as though he had been lured along each step of that path by an unseen beckoning finger, even when it had not been obvious to him.

In the spring of 1835, a 16 year old boy of medium height and wiry build, stood silently at the end of a newly furrowed row on his father's farm and scanned the field around him, admiring his work in the dimming light of late afternoon. Only a small fraction of the field had been plowed but the six long rows that Conrad Pluenneke had just finished were very straight and absolutely parallel with one another, just as his father had taught him. As he thought about the next day, he knew his father would be very pleased when the elder Pluenneke came out to the field to inspect his son's work. The knowledge of that impending approval brought a wisp of a smile to the boy's face. He had been plowing since early morning and was extremely tired but he knew that tomorrow and for many days to come, he would be back in that field to plow row after row until the entire field had been turned over and readied for planting. His aged father was no longer able to help with fieldwork so it was all up to Conrad, the eldest son of the family.

It was now early March and he was very aware that the field had to be fully plowed by the end of the month. In April, the new crop of sugar beets[8] would be put into the ground and it was extremely vital to his family's future. If timely rains fell and all went well, the crop would mature and be harvested in the summer. Much of that sugar beet crop would be sold into the local market to generate spendable income for the Pluenneke family. It was their best, if not only, opportunity to earn money for the coming year so nothing dared be left to chance. Everything had to be done perfectly to ensure a good crop and a good harvest. After carefully planting seeds, Conrad knew that the rows of sugar beets would require much weeding and care before harvest. Those were also chores he would have to perform. After that crop was harvested, the fields would have to be plowed again and readied for another crop. In the fall, winter wheat would be planted, nurtured, and harvested. Unlike sugar beets, wheat was a household staple and, therefore, only a small portion of that crop would be sold at local markets. Most of it would be used to make bread for the family. At other times, alternative crops, such as Turkish Corn, would be rotated into their farm cycle to help replenish the soil.

Plowing, planting, and harvesting were all parts of the cyclic ritual of farm life in Germany and that cycle had been drummed into him for most of his 16 years. Conrad Pluenneke knew that if he continued to farm for a living, his life would revolve around that cycle and it would be repeated year after year for the rest of his life. In the rigid class structure of German society, he had been born into farming and it was preordained that he would be a subsistence farmer and poor all of his life. In that unchanging social structure of Germany, he was, therefore, effectively trapped and without means to alter his destiny. Even at his young age, when he dared to think about it, the idea of being trapped in that position was very unsettling to him.

---

[8] Sugar beets were developed in Germany around 1747 and as a result of Napoleon's influence, flourished into a major crop there and in France.

Plowing in the manner that Johann Pluenneke expected it to be done was an art form. Walking behind a pair of yoked oxen while forcing the plow deep into the earth and yet keeping it and the oxen on a straight path was slow, tedious, and strenuous work. Doing it so rigorously drained one both physically and mentally. While it might be tempting for a young boy to become lax and deviate from such rigidly straight plowing, young Conrad took pride in what he did and so he exerted the extra effort to make the rows perfect. That was just his nature but he also wanted to please his father. In all aspects of his young life, Conrad had been taught to do the job well or not at all, and he had taken that litany to heart.

Although tired and now toiling late into the afternoon, he decided that he needed to plow one more row before quitting. Afterward, he would feed the oxen and put them away before retiring to the house for the night. Like him, they were hungry and in need of a good rest but a little more needed to be done that day. Before Conrad Pluenneke turned the oxen around to plow that one last row, he paused briefly to survey the family farm and though in a weary state, allowed his mind to drift to thoughts about the farm and its history in the context of the surrounding area. From his earliest days in Volkschule,[9] history interested him, particularly that of his home state, the Duchy of Braunsweig. He had read avidly about events that had affected it and the rest of Europe. To his amazement, many of those great events had transpired in their vicinity and just decades before 1819, the year of his birth.

The place was Klein-Lafferde, a tiny village about 200 miles west of the Rhine River in what was then known as the German Confederation (now Germany). The Pluenneke farmland was situated on ancient land just outside of Klein-Lafferde but their rock house was nestled within the compact village. Klein-Lafferde was (and still is) a tight cluster of buildings, surrounded entirely by fields. Many of the homes in Klein-Lafferde shared walls with other houses and often had barns or animal pens attached to their walls as well. The compact arrangement of houses provided a strong social context for the farming community.

The land surrounding the village had been occupied at various times by invading Volks, Goths, Vandals, Saxons, Angles, Lombards,

---

[9] Mandatory education regimen instituted by Prussians in the early 19th century.

and Franks after the fall of the Roman Empire around 800 AD. From the Middle Ages onward, it had been owned by feudal Lords who wielded power in the Duchy of Braunsweig, which had once been part of the Duchy of Saxony. As the feudal system began to crumble at the very end of the 18th century, and as former serfs gained limited rights, some of the land in the Duchy had been opened to commoners. Sometime in that era or perhaps a generation earlier, some of its land had been acquired by his ancestors. After the elder Pluenneke passed away in 1815, the land had passed to his oldest son, Johann Heinrich Conrad Pluenneke by way of the Law of Primogeniture, an inheritance law that required property be passed to the oldest son.

As Conrad's gaze wandered across the fields and the gentle rolling terrain to the forest beyond, he thought about the many earth-shattering events that had transpired in their region in just the past half century. Major Napoleonic battles, such as the Jena-Auerstadt Campaign, had occurred south of Klein-Lafferde and had changed the political landscape in Germany. In 1835, those events were still vivid memories for many people who lived through the recent history of Europe, including his father, Johann Heinrich Pluenneke.

After France's bloody revolution in 1792, which occurred 16 years after the American Revolution, brutal wars had been waged by Napoleon to gain French hegemony in Europe. Those wars, initiated by Prussia and its ally Russia, had been fought largely on soils of the Holy Roman Empire for German-speaking people, or simply, *The Reich*. In such battles, countless men of Germanic heritage had been conscripted into different military forces and had died ingloriously for issues in which they had little or no stake. In those fierce battles, farms were overrun and destroyed by marching forces and also by cannon fire. Innocent bystanders became collateral damage in the lengthy and destructive campaigns and the land of German-speaking people in northern Europe lay in ruin. When Napoleon was finally defeated in 1814, it ended over 20 years of continuous warfare in Europe and resulted in the Congress of Vienna (1814-1815). That representative body sought to restore order in Europe by establishing a balance of power between France, Great Britain, Russia, Prussia, Austria, and what was loosely called the *Third Germany* or *Little Germany,* the aggregate of many small states that composed *The Reich*. Peace was to be achieved by creating a German Confederacy and redefining the proper spheres of influence between the European powers. That peace accord ended *The Reich*, redefined national boundaries, and left indelible marks on German-speaking people across the continent.

During the war, France occupied much of northern Europe and its occupation allowed ideas of modernization and democratic ideals to spread and those seeds took root. As a consequence, feudalism ended in the second decade of the 19th century and that allowed poorer families, such as the Pluennekes, to own land. Such a degree of land ownership for commoners had not been possible since sometime in the Middle Ages, if ever.

Coincident with the end of *The Reich* and the end of feudalism came the end of the ecclesiastical Holy Roman Empire, lessening the stranglehold that Catholicism had held over German-speaking people, particularly those with different religious views. As a result, German-speaking people who were Protestant (e.g., the Pluennekes) had more religious freedom and more voice in an increasingly secular society.

Events of the previous 50 years had also forced the German society to begin to modernize, however begrudgingly. Its stolid middle class seemed to prefer retention of the rigid class structure that had defined its society for centuries. German society also became more democratic. The Pluennekes, while still poor rural farmers, gained the right to vote for representatives in *The Bund*, the body that governed the German Confederacy. At the same time, industrial modernization began. Farming methods were improved although poorer citizens such as the Pluennekes continued to plow their fields without any mechanization.

During the previous two decades, a move toward the establishment of a German Nation-State had also been initiated and some German-speaking people were headily embracing the idea of a unified German nation and the possibilities it might bring. Common folk, such as the Pluennekes, began to refer to themselves increasingly as Germans, not Prussians, not Austrians, but Germans.

Still, there were problems in the emerging German nation during the first half of the turbulent 19th century. As a result of the end of warfare and increasing modernization, improvements to their health occurred. More food (such as potatoes and sugar beets) became available and sanitation practices became commonplace. As a result, infant mortality went down and the life span of Germans increased. Those two factors led to a population explosion. In the stratified society, there were too few jobs in Guilds to support a burgeoning population and that led to widespread unemployment, poverty, and eventually, unrest. In parallel, German citizens were heavily taxed to help pay for the country's recovery from decades of war and to provide for future defense.

With that historical context in mind, Conrad's thoughts drifted to his own life and what directions it might take in the future. From the days of his earliest childhood, he had dreamed of owning land and being wealthy but never fully understood why. [10] He had not known his grandfather but he had heard wishful stories in the Pluenneke family about how both his grandfather and other Pluennekes had yearned to own vast tracts of good land and live the life of a feudal Baron. Would his future include land in Germany? Now just 16 years of age, he had doubts that owing an estate was possible but somehow he still clung to those dreams and wanted to change his family's destiny. He wanted the Pluenneke name to be held in honor and respect. Moreover, he desperately wanted control over his future. He didn't want to settle for the life of a subsistence farmer, he wanted more.

At the time, however, Conrad's vision of what his future might hold in store for him was limited to what he was familiar with, mainly agricultural Germany. He had been born and raised on the family farm. All of his immediate kin were farmers and they had seen to it that agriculture was ingrained in him from his birth to his present state. That subtle familial pressure and the existing mores of German society determined that he would dutifully follow his family's tradition and therefore, earn his living by framing. The Pluenneke family had long ago accepted their place in society and he was honor-bound to farm. Thus, it was preordained that he would follow in their footsteps and take his place in the Klein-Lafferde agricultural society.

That fate, however, did not suit Conrad Pluenneke at all. As he thought deeply about his life on that summer day in 1835, he suddenly came to the stark realization that he had no future in Klein-Lafferde or even in the whole of Germany, except to farm on a very small scale.

---

[10] Shils (1981) "The past does have to be remembered by all who reenact it, the deposit is carried forward to the next generation by a chain of assertion and reception."

Because of its repetitive and largely uncontrollable nature, he had come to loathe farming life, possibly because he had been trained to perform it with great rigor. In the Germany of that era, farming was a sure path to poverty and even at 16 years of age, he was already weary of subsistence living. It was a dramatic moment for such a young man but in that instant of insight, he felt a strange warming of his heart like nothing he had ever experienced in his brief existence on Earth. The truth and the clarity of that epiphany resonated within his very soul and registered deeply in his brain. Eerily, it was as though he was being guided to think about another place and another life, one with more promise.

If he was going to succeed in life, and he felt certain that he was meant to succeed, Conrad had to find an alternative occupation. "If only I could find a way to get control of my own personal circumstances," he thought, "I might be able to reshape my own destiny." In reality, he had neither money or political influence. In that era, wresting control of one's fate in Germany was exceedingly difficult, especially when everything about the country was dedicated to maintaining the status quo. Everywhere, the German people were locked into an antiquated guild system that regulated much of their lives and thwarted their upward social mobility. Somehow, despite cultural pressure and obvious futility of the idea, that epiphany stuck in Conrad's mind. If he could not break through in Germany and elevate his status, then he would go where there was more freedom and more social mobility. With that simple insight came the possibilities of a much larger world and he vowed to remain open to it.

From that day onward, he had a growing sense that he was different, not at all like the rest of his family or his friends. They, like others in Klein-Lafferde, were content with the status quo, content to plod along through life, but he wasn't. They accepted their places in the rigid German society with its limited opportunities and were thankful for them but he didn't. He wanted more from life and began to seek opportunities to escape the invisible bonds that promised to hold him on the family farm.

On that day, a young Conrad Pluenneke could have scarcely imagined, even in his wildest, most far-fetched dreams, how far that epiphany would take him. In just two decades or so, his life would be completely different. A decade or so later, he would no longer be a German, he would no longer be Lutheran, and he would no longer be without hope for a better future. To get to that place, though, he would have to take risks, work very hard, shoulder more responsibility, and dream higher than he had ever dreamt before. On that day, he silently vowed that if an opportunity arose that would allow him to take charge of his future, he would pursue it with a vengeance. All he needed was opportunity.

Ah, dreams! In a blink, Conrad Pluenneke's mind came back to his here and now existence in Klein-Lafferde. The sun was setting and he still felt that he needed to finish another row before quitting. He urged the yoke of mildly protesting oxen to the start of another row and began to plow, shoving the blade deep into the earth. At last, he reached the end of the row and took the pair of oxen back to the barn where he unyoked them and fed them. When all was in proper order, he wearily walked back to their house in Klein-Lafferde in semidarkness, knowing that his mother Sophie would have dinner on the table for him.

That night, he would think ahead to Sunday afternoon when he could slip away from farm chores for a while and go hiking deep into the forest land that lay just north of Klein-Lafferde. He loved the adventure of exploring the wilderness and was not at all intimidated by what he came across there. After dwelling on those pleasant thoughts, he fell into a sound sleep and dream large dreams about his future.

A few days later and perhaps quite by chance, Conrad came across a copy of a letter that Friedrich Ernst had sent to Herr Schwartz in Oldenburg back in 1832. Ernst, a former German citizen, had emigrated to Texas, which was a state of Mexico in 1831. In North America, Ernst had done well and wrote to encourage other Germans to follow him. The letter had created quite a sensation throughout Germany where it was widely copied and distributed. The copy of Ernst's letter that he now held had been posted on the wall of a grocery market in Klein-Lafferde. In the letter, Ernst described his seemingly idyllic life and related how each single man who applied to the Austin Colony was given a quarter of a league (roughly 1,100 acres) of very fertile Texas land but had to pay $160 in installments to cover costs, such as surveying. The fee was payable through sale of crops. The letter went on to state that Europeans were especially welcome. The land, while free to immigrants, was being resold for as much as $1 per acre. The climate was described as Mediterranean. It sounded almost utopian to a young man who was desperately seeking a different path in life. After reading the four page letter twice, Conrad Pluenneke dashed home, grabbed a pencil and some paper, and returned to town where, for the next hour, he copied Ernst's letter word for word. In coming years, he read and reread the content of that copied letter until he knew it by heart. It was like a sign from Heaven. But, as always, his dream was stymied by the lack of money. How could a subsistence farmer afford to emigrate and pay $160 in fees?

Fast forward almost 10 years to 1844. The most important part of the story about Johann Julius Conrad Pluenneke begins in the summer of that year on his father's farm in central Germany. Known in the family as Conrad, he is now nearly 25 years old, the oldest son of Johann Heinrich Conrad and Sophie (nee Schmidt) Pluenneke, and is a newly married man. He is a farmer and has now worked the family fields for a dozen years under the supervision of his elderly and increasingly decrepit father. All the while, he and his wife continue to live under the elder's roof. With 10 people in the small house, living conditions border on claustrophobic. The small family farm, just outside of Klein-Lafferde, consists of three fields that amount to just over 30 acres. The Pluenneke farm is located approximately 60 miles south southeast of the city of Hanover.[11] The Pluenneke's extended family is both Christian and Protestant in faith. They routinely attend the local German Evangelical Lutheran church at Klein-Lafferde on the Sabbath, their only day of respite from farm chores. While they attend church regularly and observe Lutheran rites, they are not part of the so-called Piety Movement that is sweeping Germany and the rest of Europe. To them, religion is important but it is just one strand in the fabric of their everyday agricultural lives. Much as with other families in the community, the Pluennekes observe Christian rituals such as marriages, births, as well as baptisms and have done so for many decades.

As a youngster, Conrad had eagerly and easily completed Volkschule in nearby Langede where it became evident that he was a conscientious and able student, perhaps even precocious. As a result of his solid education, he had morphed into a young man who read avidly

---

[11] At that time, Klein-Lafferde was located very near the border of Braunsweig with The Kingdom of Hanover and that boundary shifted often because of changes in regional geopolitics.

about a wide array of topics when he had time away from farm chores. By nature, he was serious and extremely curious about every aspect of German life, including politics. He avidly read newspapers when he could get access to them and he fully understood how geopolitical events in Europe and the German Confederation affected his life as well as his future but he knew there was little he could do about it. He was still a poor farmer, trapped in a world made by his ancestors, and at times, that reality depressed him because it dimmed his future prospects. When that happened, he would reread Ernst's letter and wonder about life in Texas. Now married, he would be entitled to a full league of land in Texas - 4,400 plus acres! He could scarcely comprehend that amount of land. Those thoughts briefly brightened his life but he still saw no way to afford emigration to that distant place. He would need help from an organization or a benefactor to enable he and his young wife to emigrate to Texas.

On that summer day in 1844, Conrad stood in the field and surveyed their crop of Turkish corn and then slowly shook his head in disbelief. Although the crop only was raised to feed their farm animals, its quality and yield were far below what the family had hoped for. The stalks were small and the ears of corn were brown and distorted – they would yield very little useable corn. To get through the year, they would have to buy grain to feed the few animals they owned. He shook his head again and then slowly knelt down. Using his right hand, Conrad scooped up a handful of soil from the field and slowly but deliberately, opened his fist to allow the soil to trickle down through his fingers. As it tumbled out, he rubbed some of it between his forefinger and his thumb, carefully scrutinizing its contents. To him, the soil seemed somehow ancient. It was spent and lacking in vital nutrients. It had been worn out through centuries of overuse and poor management. His sample also had a gritty quality about it, not at all like loam. He thought about soil for a moment. From his schooling, he knew that the soil in central Germany was indeed very old, having been deposited there during the retreat of massive glaciers during the last major ice age, some 12,000 years earlier. The area had been occupied and farmed by a number of cultures after that retreat. Since he had begun to farm it with his father some 12 years earlier, the land had become increasingly unproductive year. Now, in 1844, it was barely producing enough to feed their family and their animals.

Conrad Pluenneke's soil sample was also very dry but that was partly because of recent climatic changes in the region. For three consecutive years, they had experienced erratic weather patterns that had resulted in poor crop yields and blights. At times, farmers had experienced droughts and at other times, deluges of rain and unseasonable cold spells. Those drastic changes in climate weakened the plants and made them susceptible to fungi and other diseases that created blights on certain crops. As a result, a blight affected German potato production and the country suffered precipitous declines in their food supply. While it was not affected as much as Ireland was, the blight was devastating to a nation that had come to be heavily dependent on potatoes.

Part of the problem had to do with global climate change. For more than a century, the northern part of the planet had been affected by extreme coldness and variable conditions, stemming from what scientists would later refer to as a *Little Ice Age*. In that era, glacial masses of ice moved south, well into Scandinavia and extreme northern Europe. As a result of those shifts, winters in Klein-Lafferde were prolonged and, conversely, summers became much shorter and cooler. Those changes adversely affected the already short growing season in Europe. By the middle of the 19th century, the *Little Ice Age* finally began to dissipate but in the changing climatic era that ensued, there were still wild swings in local weather. As a result of such erratic weather, farmers in Braunsweig suffered bad harvests for several consecutive years and it affected them, both financially and emotionally.

Around the turn of the 19th century, the countryside around Klein-Lafferde had also borne the ravages of the Napoleonic Wars. All of that damage affected soil in the fields and reduced its ability to sustain crops. Since taking it over, his father had worked diligently for more than three decades to restore his land to a point where he could wring a decent living from it. That goal had required much hard work on his part and he had barely managed to turn the family farm around in his lifetime.

After inheriting the family farm from his father in 1815, Johann Heinrich Conrad Pluenneke was allowed to marry in 1819 by the officialdom of Braunsweig. On January 30th of that year, he took Sophie Schmidt as his bride at the local German Evangelical Lutheran church. Their first child, Johann Julius Conrad Pluenneke, was born on the family farm 11 months later and duly christened in the same Lutheran church in Klein-Lafferde. As a youngster, Conrad had worked the fields with his father and learned to farm from him. Over time, his father instilled a love for the land, just as he and other ancestors had before him, but not the job of farming. Within a decade, six more siblings would be welcomed into the Pluenneke family, including Friedrich, Conrad's younger and only brother.

Under the prevailing Law of Primogeniture, Conrad Pluenneke and his siblings knew that he would inherit the family farm after their father's death because he was the oldest son. While he would benefit from that inheritance, the law did not seem fair to Conrad or to his siblings, particularly Friedrich. As a result of it, Conrad's brother and five sisters would inherit little more than livestock. But, that was the law of the land in 1845. If Conrad harbored any ideas about dividing ownership of the family farm between his brother and five sisters, it's small size made that impractical. Dividing 30 acres into seven parcels would mean that each child would receive roughly four acres, far too few to farm. It was well established that at least 10 acres were required in that locale for a family to survive by subsistence farming. Thus, none of the seven Pluenneke children had decent prospects for the future except, perhaps, Conrad. As he thought about the land and its increasing infertility, Conrad knew that the old order had to be changed. The Law of Primogeniture was wrong and no longer viable or relevant in the new era of global freedom. Their lives had to adjust to the changing times or they would quickly become paupers.

Across the Atlantic, the British colonies in North America had revolted in 1776 and formed a democratic society that rejected old European laws like Primogeniture. Within two generations, the spirit of self-rule and democracy had spread from American across the Atlantic to the European continent. In that enlightened era, France took America's lead and overthrew its monarchy in 1792 but it established a slightly different form of democracy. Those events were not lost on the average German citizen. They followed the business cycles, food prices, and wages in those democracies. By comparison, their autocratic form of government and stratified society seemed trite. The *Zeitgeist* (spirit of the times) seemed to call for democracy, not autocracy.

In 1844, many German citizens like the Pluennekes were beginning to discover that there was much wrong with their country and their culture. The country's economy was in shambles. The onset of the

Industrial Revolution had begun to unleash mechanical devices and processes that partially or fully replaced many menial workers. As a result, those laborers became unemployed. Some of them tried to adapt by moving into occupations held by lower classes of citizens who, in turn, displaced others. That repetitive replacement set into motion a powerful downward spiral that displaced many, many workers in all classes of society. That domino effect rippled down the rigid status society and created massive unemployment, particularly at the bottom of the hierarchy. At the same time, Germany was contending with overpopulation. An antiquated set of laws, modernization, and an overabundance of workers coupled with massive unemployment, very high taxes, and strictly regulated markets, led to an economic crisis of epic proportions. For the average citizen, the national economic situation was a nightmare and many Germans feared for their future. The worsening situation kept farmers, such as Conrad Pluenneke, locked in poverty and trapped in the underclass of German society with little or no hope of ever having a better life. The prospects for their children were even bleaker. That stark fact made an indelible impression on Conrad Pluenneke.

At the time when the underclasses were suffering, Prince Metternich and those in power at the highest levels of German society were fighting modernization while attempting to restore the lavish German courts of the 18th century. They were hopelessly out of touch with the sensibilities of their countrymen but the royalty alone had the wealth and the power. As a result, the gap between the wealthiest and the poorest citizens widened significantly in that era. Prince Metternich, the tyrannical head of the German Confederation, cracked down hard on those who dared to dissent. His repressive efforts led to widespread civil unrest, protest, and a demand for change but that dissent was either ignored or suppressed.

Besides the Law of Primogeniture, the various German states had other laws that average German citizens could barely tolerate. One such law required young men above the age of 17 to serve lengthy stints in the army. After decades of combat in their area and throughout Europe, the German citizens in Klein-Lafferde and elsewhere in Europe were tired of war. If there was going to be war again, they wanted a voice in it because it had been devastating to their lives and their economy. Further, they did not want their younger generation to be affected by armed strife as they themselves had been for most of their lives. Lower echelons of citizenry in the Duchy of Braunsweig were also angered because the sons of wealthy families were often spared from military duty or community labor because they were able to hire substitutes. All those factors wore mightily on the psyches of the Pluenneke family and other Germans.

Around 1840, a group of about 160 tenant farmers sent a written plea to the Duke of Braunsweig asking him to:

1. Provide relief from their heavy tax burden;
2. Eliminate the practice of hiring substitutes for military service;
3. Provide more representation for farmers in the state assembly;
4. Provide relief from uncompensated but mandatory road work;
5. Regulate property rental rates; and
6. Establish a state institution to care for the old, poor, sick, and invalid farm tenants and their families.

There is no record of how the Duke received their plea but it informed him of pressing problems that were affecting farmers in his state.

While the country's economy was deteriorating, thereby causing widespread unemployment as well as dire poverty, the structured German society did not allow mobility within the framework. Those safely ensconced in trade guilds were actively resisting change and democratization of society for fear that they would lose their cozy niche. The laws of the guild system prevented one born into a particular class, such as farming, from quickly switching into another higher class, say merchant or craftsman. To switch, the applicant had to pay stiff fees and wait for openings that were highly regulated. The stratified class system, therefore, kept Conrad Pluenneke locked into the farming class but it also protected his niche in the hierarchy by regulating the number of farms and who could own farms.

With the present state of affairs in Germany, Conrad was again confronted with the fact that he had a bleak future as a farmer. His children, should he and his wife have a family, would also become farmers. If their offspring could not arrange to own enough land to support a family, they would likely slide into poverty and become charity cases. To elevate oneself in that social hierarchy, one had to have money, time, and political influence - all of which most farmers generally lacked. While the Pluennekes had time, they lacked money or political clout in the Duchy of Braunsweig. Thus, Conrad Pluenneke was effectively trapped in one of the lowest rungs of German Society, with no simple way out.

The slow demise of the German economy had already unsettled many of its poorer citizens and forced some of them into homeless poverty. For those who were barely afloat in the economy, it caused them to worry about the ultimate fate of the German nation. What would happen to them if the German economy collapsed completely? The government, it seemed, was indifferent to their collective plight and they fretted about their future. Some dissenters openly advocated other forms of government, such as Communism, or a return to Monarchy. By 1844, the society seemed on the brink of anarchy and many began to look for alternatives, an act that would have been unthinkable just a generation before. To Germans, who were just becoming unified, their country was beginning to lose its meaning.

One solution to overpopulation and the lack of jobs was emigration. Other countries in the wider world with market economies had jobs and welcomed German citizens. If enough citizens left their country, unemployment at home would ease and jobs would become available for the jobless who stayed behind. Seizing the initiative from the government, emigration entrepreneurs began to organize companies that touted schemes to transport some German citizens to other countries. Stories swirled around the country about how wonderful life was in Argentina, Brazil, New Zealand, and America.

As result of the emigration mania that ensued, Germans increasingly departed on their own for other places but generally speaking, they were not prepared or well enough equipped to cope with the hardships they would find in those new countries. Differences in language, customs, and climate were just some problems those emigrants faced overseas. A few did manage to succeed on their own but many did not, partly because they were ill prepared to exert the effort required to compete and succeed in a competitive, market-oriented, capitalistic society. While the economies of those democratic countries were better than that of Germany in 1845, they were not utopias. They too had national issues of their own to deal with. America, for example, had border disputes with Mexico, problems quelling indigenous natives, and it was contending with the issue of human slavery. In the ensuing emigration mania, those important issues were glossed over or brushed aside and the stampede was on to other places. If emigration was going to solve Germany's economic problems, then someone had to step in and do something to facilitate the process. That is where the Adelsverein entered the picture.

In 1842, a group of German nobles met to form a society to do something about German cultural problems, using emigration as a tool. While helping Germans to emigrate, they also intended to make a profit from the venture. The nobles created a legal entity called the *Gesellschaft zum Schutz deutscher Einwanderer* to not only promote emigration abroad but also serve to guide and protect German emigrants in foreign places such as Texas. Over the course of several years, the aims of the society and its membership changed several times. By 1844, it had become just another of several emigration companies that, with little analytical or management skill, made bold promises to emigrants that its founders could never live up to. The Noble's League, or Adelsverein, with no emigration experience, somehow managed to secure the settlement rights to more than three million acres of land in central Texas that had been granted to Henry Fischer and Burchard Miller. Only three of its members had first hand knowledge of Texas and one of them retreated from the Society because he deemed its colonization plan to be unworkable. Nonetheless, the Adelsverein jumped at the opportunity to acquire a grant and began to lease ships, recruit Germans for emigration to Texas, and put them as well as their families on ships bound for Galveston.

They bought the rights to the grant from Henry Fisher and Burchard Miller, both of whom turned out to be shady entrepreneurs. Neither of them had set foot in the grant area and yet touted it to the Adelsverein as almost paradise. Their grant document had provisions inserted by the Republic of Texas that required the duo to settle thousands of Germans in just 18 months and in 1845, that clock was already winding down. In their haste to form overseas colonies, get emigrants to Texas, and settle them by the deadline, the Adelsverein failed to comprehend that their land grant, known as the *Fisher-Miller Grant*, was over 300 miles inland, was very rugged, lacked access roads, and was inhabited by hostile Comanche Indians who would fiercely resist settlement by white people. In addition, a brewing dispute between the U.S. and Mexico over their mutual border threatened to become an all-out shooting war and that would not help colonization matters either.

The Adelsverein badly needed wagons and teamsters to get their clients inland and they were being siphoned off to support the U.S. Army in its preparation for war with Mexico.

To scout the land and oversee the initial colonization of the Grant, the Adelsverein sent one of its Nobles to Texas, Prince Karl Solms-Braunfels. He was a Royal with grand ideas, very little management savvy, and no taste for frontier life. When Prince Solms-Braunfels realized that he would be unable to get colonists to the Grant in time to meet contractual requirements, he bought a league of land on the Comal River about 100 miles south of the Grant for the Adelsverein and founded its first colony, New Braunfels. After spending the Society into deep financial trouble, the Prince abruptly resigned and returned to Germany. His hastily named successor, Baron Otfreid von Meusebach (later known in Texas as John O. Meusebach), came from Germany and arrived early in 1845, determined to right the Adelsverein's financial ship and colonize the grant area.

Undeterred by its financial woes in Texas, the Adelsverein in Germany continued to push its emigration program. It published glowing articles in local newspapers about its emigration society and what it would provide to those who chose to emigrate with them. In one particular ad placed in the Mainzer *Zeitung*, Texas was touted as an idyllic place to live. It was said by them that Texas had fertile soil, warm weather, and picturesque land.

One day, Conrad went into Langede to buy seed and while there, have some coffee. In the market, he happened to spot a copy of the regional newspaper and bought it. On its front page, a reprinted article by the Adelsverein dominated the sheet and it immediately caught his attention. While sipping coffee, he read the ad with great interest. The article described how German couples like he and his young wife [12] would be shepherded to Texas, protected, and provided 320 acres of prime land to farm in a colony composed entirely of German-speaking immigrants. Not only would the Adelsverein transport them across the ocean to Texas, It would also provide them with good land, a cabin, and farm implements to work their land. Best of all, the Verein promised to provide all of that for a fixed fee, which amounted to roughly

---

[12] Despite research in Germany and in Texas, the author has been unable to learn the identity of Conrad's first wife.

$245 per person. That price was more than Ernst's letter had quoted for land in Austin's Colony and it fetched much less land for the price but it included costly transportation across the Atlantic Ocean and overland transportation to the Grant. As Conrad thought about the article, he concluded the Adelsverein's emigration program might offer he and his wife the means to escape their situation in Germany. Such a move would likely still involve farming but he would have the freedom not to farm if he found another occupation there.

From his reading, he knew that much had changed in Texas since Ernst wrote his now famous letter. Texas had successfully revolted against Mexico and won its independence. The Republic of Texas, much like its neighbor country America, valued free enterprise, free speech, freedom of religion, and democratic rule. For several years, rumors had swirled around the world that the United States of American might annex Texas as part of *Manifest Destiny*, its drive westward to the Pacific Ocean. Those rumors made Texas even more attractive to potential emigrants but they were abhorred by members of the Adelsverein because the nobles knew that the United States would never tolerate German colonies in one of its states, especially if that colony attempted to maintain allegiance to an Old World country.

After finishing his coffee, Conrad stood up, very carefully folded the newspaper under his arm, and went home. Several days after reading the article several times, Conrad enthusiastically shared it with his wife and eventually with the rest of the Pluenneke family. Upon hearing his account of what the Adelsverein might do for them, his wife and elderly parents immediately expressed deep reservations about emigration because that would mean they would leave family and friends behind, make a dangerous crossing over a vast ocean, and settle in a strange new land where people spoke in English or Spanish, not German. For a few weeks, the topic of emigration was tabled because of those concerns but Conrad continued to mull the idea over in his head. Would it be possible for he and his wife to emigrate and leave his family behind? Even at the reasonable price of $245 per person, he did not have that much money. The only asset that the family possessed that might cover those costs was the Pluenneke farm. He would have to find a way to persuade all of them to join them willingly or give up the idea forever. At one time, the elder Pluenneke would have never considered leaving Klein-Lafferde – it was all he knew – but some things had changed that loosened his ties to the family land.

Back in January of 1842, the unmarried oldest daughter of the Pluenneke family, Karoline, had greeted the family with some unwanted and rather shocking news: she was pregnant. In the sensibility of 19th century Germany, bearing a child out of wedlock was a major scandal. In the small town of Klein-Lafferde, her condition was duly noticed as her abdomen swelled over the course of the spring and shortly thereafter, gossip ensued in town about the "loose morals" of the Pluenneke family. At the Lutheran church, where one might have expected some forgiveness, the ostracism silently rained down on the family when they attended Sunday services. While little was said directly to Karoline or the family about the scandal, the silent actions of the congregation spoke volumes. With only one church in town, the Pluennekes had no alternative that would meet their religious needs. On the streets, people that the family had known for decades gradually became distant. The hushed ostracism grew almost in correlation with Karoline's girth. In time, the family slowly withdrew from the church although they did send their youngest daughters and granddaughter (Henriette) to the Lutheran church for confirmation. Now increasingly isolated in the small, close-knit community, they found conditions so intolerable that they began to think more favorably about the idea of moving away. Emigration offered them a viable way out of their predicament in the community and it also offered them an opportunity for a better life.

When the topic of emigration was initially raised, Karoline had strongly demurred because she was single and had a three year old daughter. Understandably, she had grave concerns about crossing the Atlantic with a young child. Conrad, however, was still enamored with the idea and would not be easily dissuaded from the notion of emigrating to Texas. He saw it as a personal opportunity for all of them to gain more freedom, get a large amount of fertile land on which to farm, and prosper in the free market economy of America. With his young wife, he could foresee a bright future in America where their children, should they be so blessed, would eventually inherit large tracts of land from them, something that was not possible in the German Confederacy of 1845. As Conrad saw it, his younger brother, Friedrich, would also benefit because he would be eligible to inherit part of the family land in Texas and would be free to acquire land of his own. In Texas, Friedrich's prospects would be much brighter.

Faced with a negative response from his family, Conrad reconsidered emigrating with his wife and leaving the rest of the family behind. His departure, however, would leave the rest of the family in a difficult position. His parents were elderly (55 and 47, respectively) [13] and depended heavily on Conrad's brawn to make the farm productive enough to satisfy their needs. His young brother, Johann Friedrich, was only 10 years old and not nearly ready to take over the family farm. His four sisters, whose ages ranged from 23 to 12, were healthy but could not offer much assistance because farming was a brawn-intensive occupation. Because of the age of their youngest children, the senior Pluennekes could not consider emigration unless they took the entire family with them. Despite all those limitations, Conrad was adamant about emigration and continued to lobby hard for his viewpoint. The only viable solution he could envision that would provide a good future for the Pluenneke family was to emigrate to Texas.

After considerable debate within the family, Conrad and his father decided to learn more about the possibility of emigrating to Texas with the Adelsverein. In the spring of 1845, they left the farm and drove the family's ox cart to Bremen to meet with agents from the Adelsverein. To get there, they followed a primitive dirt road to Peine and from it to Hanover. In the large city, they took another road that led north and continued on it until they entered the valley that funneled the Weser River towards the North Sea. In that valley, they intersected an improved road that paralleled the river and led to Bremen, a port city near the mouth of the Weser.

In past centuries, Bremen had been a thriving port city but its harbor up the Weser River had begun to silt up, making it difficult for ships with deeper draws to reach the port. In response to its plight, Bremen acquired land from the Kingdom of Hanover at the mouth of the Weser River and built a deep-water port facility there, which they named Bremerhaven. The new port handled most of the traffic between Bremen and the rest of the international commercial world. To connect the two ports, Bremen provided daily steam-powered vessels to ferry passengers and their baggage to Bremerhaven for a small fee.

When the two arrived in Bremen, Conrad and his father were surprised at the number of people in who were crowding into Bremen.

---

[13] In 1845, the life expectancy of a male in Germany was about 62 years.

The town was swarming with German citizens from many inland towns, all seeking to emigrate to America or elsewhere. Mixed in with those emigrating from Germany were immigrants from other countries and others, many of whom were doing business in Germany. With some difficulty, they found the Adelsverein office at Bremen that was conveniently located near the docks. Inside the office, they met Dr. Hill, the Society's chief emigration officer and agent.

At once, Dr. Hill began to explain their program to the Pluennekes. He stated that the Society was looking for industrious, reliable, and upstanding members of Germany to join their program. Dr. Hill went on to say that the Adelsverein had acquired 3.5 million acres of fertile land in central Texas and needed some six or seven thousand citizens to settle there in the next year. His voice on this matter belied some urgency. For those families who opted to join them, he said they would contractually guarantee 320 acres of land at one of several colonies they planned to build. Those colonies would have churches, schools, military protection, and other civic amenities. As a further inducement, Dr. Hill said that the society would erect cabins for emigrants and would help them establish fields and produce crops. The colonies would have well stocked warehouses with seed, farm implements, and other tools. For all of that support, clients would only have to pay about 1800 Guldens per person ($245 US dollars at the time).[14]

With some quick math, Conrad figured that the family would need at least 22,000 Guldens to emigrate. Since they only had a few thousand Guldens that had been saved over the past decade, they would be forced to sell the family farm that he quickly reckoned might earn them between 20,000 and 25,000 Guldens. That stark fact made emigration an all or none proposition for the family. If they sold the farm and used the money to emigrate, they would never be able to return to Germany and resume farming. If they did emigrate, they would be put into a situation where they would be forced to succeed in Texas or perish trying. Emigration, thus, had great risks attached to it.

Dr. Hill went on to say that the Verein had many ships scheduled to depart from Bremen on a regular basis for the rest of 1845 and well into 1846. To secure spots on one of those ships, the family would have to choose a departure date and then deposit money with the Ger-

---

[14] The exchange rate in 1846 was about 7.5 Guldens per U.S. dollar.

man Emigration Company. Dr. Hill checked his files and announced the Verein had plenty of vacant spaces on ships, particularly those departing in October and November of 1845 from Bremerhaven. Other ships were scheduled to depart from Antwerp in Belgium. With that information, Conrad and his father returned to the farm where they discussed their findings over a period of several weeks.

Again, Karoline declined to consider emigration. To her, it was out of the question with a young daughter. As for herself, she felt the venture was too risky to consider seriously. She would stay and live out her life ignobly in Klein-Lafferde.

Conrad's wife also had concerns about crossing the Atlantic. The ocean was a huge expanse where almost anything could happen and she had heard there were hurricanes in the Atlantic that could easily sink sailing ships. She asked, "Has the Adelsverein lost any ships at sea?" Conrad replied that Dr. Hill had mentioned that one of their ships, the *Nahant*, had been driven onto rocks in the English Channel during a storm but none of their ships had been lost to hurricanes in the Atlantic or the Gulf of Mexico. He also recalled that Dr. Hill had gone on to postulate that there were few hurricanes during winter months in the Atlantic. If they left in November or December, they would likely avoid being affected by such huge storms.

Conrad's mother, Sophie, inquired about food and water on the ship. Conrad replied that Dr. Hill had assured them that the food would be plentiful and sumptuous but he had emphasized that the family could choose to bring their own food if they were concerned that shipboard fare might not be to their liking. Eating food provided by the Verein would be more convenient but it would also be more costly. If they did choose to provide their own food, they would have to spend much time preparing and storing it in spoil-proof containers, plus they would have to amass enough to last them for three months. They could not risk running out of food in the middle of the ocean. Conrad asserted that taking their own food would give them more control over their diet and that maintaining their health during the trip was imperative. In the end, they decided to provide their own food and save money. However, water was a different issue. Potable water would be taken onboard at Bremerhaven in large wooden casks and rationed out to families for cooking and drinking during the voyage. Should the ship's supply run low and require replenishment, Dr. Hill had assured them it could be easily obtained at islands such as the Azores or the Bahamas while enroute to Texas.

The younger children wanted to know how long it would take for the boat to get to Texas from Bremerhaven. Johann Pluenneke said that the Verein's agent, Dr. Hill, had told them that the time at sea depended on weather but that most crossings took about 75 days.

Conrad's mother, Sophie, wanted to know about medical care on the ship and at the colonies in Texas. Again, Dr. Hill had told the men that each ship would have medical personnel onboard and that they could treat almost any injury or illness. He also told them that they would have to pay one additional U.S. dollar for health care in Galveston. Such coverage was mandated by the state laws of Texas.

In time, all pertinent questions were addressed and answered. If they intended to go before the end of the year (1845), they had to make a firm decision in the coming days. Carefully, they weighed their options, pro and con. They all agreed there was no future for any of them in Germany where social and economic conditions were going to continue to deteriorate. Leaving made sense but there were many risks involved in emigration to Texas. While it was described as a beautiful place, there were obstacles to starting new lives there. They would live in a country that spoke English or Spanish but not German. In time, they would have to learn a new language. Additionally, they would be forced to establish a new farm that would entail much hard work for Conrad and his father. Conrad stated that he would commit to that amount of effort. He and his father would have to work hard to start a successful farm but they felt they could rely on the Adelsverein for guidance and assistance. In time, young Friedrich would be able to help with farm work and that would lessen their load. What about the Indians? They had heard that the natives who occupied the Grant land in Texas were hostile to white people but Conrad had been assured that the Adelsverein would deal with them, either militarily or by negotiating a peace treaty with them. "They were no match for German might," Dr. Hill had boldly stated.

After much discussion, the family decided to accept the risks and emigrate to Texas. In September, Conrad and his father went back to

Bremen to sign a contract with the Adelsverein. [15] After signing it and making a down payment for eight people, they were given a little red account book with credit for half of their fees. They were told that the credits could be used in Texas to buy tools, seeds, and other supplies for their new farm. They selected a departure date of November 3rd to avoid hurricanes. If the voyage took 75 days, they would arrive in Texas near the middle of January in 1846. Their ship was identified by Dr. Hill as the *brig Apollo* and was to be captained by a man named Feldhausen. To save money, they opted to take their own food.

With the decision to emigrate firmly made, Conrad's father turned to the task of selling their family farm while Conrad's mother and wife began to identify belongings to take with them as well as to stockpile food for the transoceanic trip. While they performed those tasks, Conrad addressed the issue of getting all of their credentials together. The Adelsverein had strict requirements for its clients and therefore all applicants had to submit their papers for critical review. That documentation included the following:

- Birth certificates;
- Marriage licenses;
- Letters from local ministers attesting to their character;
- Financial statements that showed the family had resources necessary to pay for emigration and survival in Texas.

Despite its claim to help the poor, the Adelsverein refused to select paupers or people who were known to be either dishonest or slothful. It only chose the most solid and dependable citizens for its emigration program because the Verein would have to depend on them to work hard and persevere under adverse conditions in Texas if its colonization effort was to succeed. Character mattered.

A month later, Johann Heinrich Pluenneke found a buyer for his farm. Christian Meyer and his wife Fredericke (nee Pluenneke) had relatives in Langede and wanted to relocate so that they could farm near their kin. The farm, with its three fields and sturdy rock house, brought Johann Pluenneke about 24,000 Guldens or roughly $3,200

---

[15] See Appendix 1. Johann Heinrich Conrad Pluenneke's contract which guaranteed him 320 acres of land, provided that he stayed on the land for three years, built a house, farmed at least 15 acres, and paid for survey costs.

U.S. dollars. That amount would cover their emigration fees ($2450) and leave them with about 5,625 Guldens (or $750 U.S.) to meet other emigration expenses and get started in America.

In September, the oldest daughter Karoline changed her mind at the last moment and decided to emigrate rather than remain alone in Klein-Lafferde. Her father, Johann Heinrich, wrote to the Adelsverein to inquire whether it was still possible for Karoline and her young daughter Henriette to join their family on the *Apollo*. After an affirmative response from the Verein, she and Conrad hurriedly gathered her credentials and submitted them to Dr. Hill in Bremen. At almost the last second, she and little Henriette were accepted.[16] The Pluennekes had to scramble to find $490 to pay their fees but they managed to do that. Thus, all ten members of Johann Heinrich Pluenneke's branch of the Pluenneke family would leave Germany and emigrate to the New World together, united in their quest for a new life. [17]

As the departure date neared, the Pluennekes said tearful goodbyes to family and friends. They packed all their belongings, including household furniture, utensils, clothing, bedding, rifles, and ammunition in wooden crates, not fully knowing how useful those wooden crates would become, and shipped them to Bremen, in care of Captain Feldhausen/*brig Apollo*. On November 1st, with the farm securely sold, belongings packed up, and with money in hand, the family went to Bremen to await their departure to America, which now was but three days away. As a final gesture before leaving on the wagon, Conrad took whitewash and painted "Hin Nach Texas" (Gone to Texas) on their barn in Klein-Lafferde.

After a long wagon trip over a rough road, the family arrived in Bremen and spent their only night there at the Vorwerks Hotel, huddled into a single room. The cost for that room was 600 Guldens ($80 U.S.). Early the next day, Sophie Pluenneke went to H. H. Meier's store to buy milk for their granddaughter while Conrad and her husband went to pay their final installment to the Verein for their emigra-

---

[16] Internal Adelsverein communications, dated September 22,1845.

[17] In 1845, the Pluenneke family consisted of 10 people: the parents (Johann and Sophie) plus six children: Johann Julius (Conrad), Karoline, Conradina, Fredericke, Dorothea, and Johann Heinrich Friedrich Pluenneke. In addition, there was Conrad's wife and Henriette, the three year old daughter of Karoline, The author has been unable to establish the identity of Conrad's wife.

tion. That afternoon, they paid 300 Guldens ($40 U.S.) to be ferried down the Weser River to Bremerhaven by steamboat. Several hours later, they arrived at the docks and located the Verein office where they verified that they had paid their fees, obtained the contract, [18] and were officially registered by Verein agents. They were instructed to return to the wharf at sunrise the next day and be prepared to depart shortly thereafter. Slowly, reality began to set in they were really leaving Germany. At that point, they had less than $3.000 Guldens ($400) which was kept in a pocket of Johann Heinrich' pants.

Early on November 3rd, the 10 members of the Johann Pluenneke family trundled to the wharf and boarded the *brig Apollo*.[19] Their group included the senior Pluennekes, their five children, and their young granddaughter, Henriette, as well as Conrad and his wife. After they were logged in by Captain Feldhausen, they found their way below decks to steerage. It was a dark and dank place, already filled with other German emigrants. Most of them were strangers to the Pluennekes. In a short time, they met a number of them, including Ludolph Meyer, Ferdinand Gellerman, and Carl Rode. Eventually, they located a space that would accommodate their large family and settled in for a lengthy voyage.

Their accommodations in the ship's steerage section were dank and dismal. Their space amounted to about a 64 square feet which now contained 10 crudely constructed small straw mattresses, a shallow box filled with sand on which to cook, two pots for their excrement, and a whale oil lantern. The entire steerage area was already filling with smoke as several emigrants tried to build fires to keep warm. As best as Conrad could determine, the hold of the ship only had four small vents so little could be done to eliminate or reduce the smoky conditions.

After a short adjustment period in which they arranged their carry-on belongings in their space, the Pluenneke family climbed the stairs to the main deck to get their last views of Germany. As they looked out over the array of ships in the harbor of Bremerhaven and the green

---

[18] See Appendix 1 Johann Pluenneke's contract with the Adelsverein.

[19] The *brig Apollo* was built by Heinrich Bosse in Berg (Germany) and launched in 1835. It had made one previous trip to Galveston, that in 1844 and landed on December 20th of that year. (Morgenthaler, 2007).

landscape, Conrad's mother began to weep openly. For her, it suddenly all became very real. She would likely never see her Schmidt relatives again. Conrad's young wife was similarly overcome with emotion. It was evident that the impending departure of the *Apollo* would change their lives forever and quite naturally, there were a few regrets and second thoughts among the family but no one dared give voice to them. They were on the ship and committed to move to America. Conrad, always the optimist, tried to console his wife and family by reminding them what they would be getting in Texas. The Adelsverein had promised them much.

After all emigrants were thought to be on board, Captain Feldhausen ordered all of them to come to the main deck for a roll call. As each family name was shouted out by the Bosun's Mate, a family shouted "hier" or "yah" and their name was checked off. When the Pluennekes name was called, Johann answered for the members of his family. They were 1 of 22 families and 10 of 95 total passengers on the *brig Apollo*. [20] When all had been accounted for, the Captain dismissed the passengers and ordered the crew to prepare to go to sea. Quickly, the crew scattered to assume their assigned departure posts.

At anchor, the hull of the brig creaked and groaned as it wallowed aimlessly in the tiding estuary of the Weser River. With the tide now fully in, the crew scrambled to unfurl small sails and weigh the anchor. As the breeze stiffened, the sails briefly caught wind, fluttered, and then billowed. The wooden-hulled *brig Apollo* began to move down the Weser River towards its estuary and the North Sea, with Captain Feldhausen at the helm.

The emigrants flocked to the rails of the brig to catch fleeting glimpses of the Fatherland fading into their collective pasts. One of them shouted "auf wiedersehn" and waved furiously as though saying goodbye to an old friend. That comment and gesture brought many sighs from the ninety or so passengers who craned their necks to look back upstream.

At first, cruising down the Weser was enjoyable. There was no rolling or pitching or yawing. "It was like wafting along on a cloud," one passenger said. The ship was steady and there was very little sen-

---

[20] Kleineke, C. W. Jr. Fischer-Miller and G.E.C. Forever. Corsicana, TX, 1996.

sation of movement, unless one looked out at fixed objects on the banks. Occasionally, they saw other ships going upstream and they seemed to race past the *Apollo*. One astute passenger pointed out that the "extra speed" was due to the relative speed of the two vessels approaching one another.

In an hour or so, the brig sailed within sight of the Weser's estuary and the riven widened to encompass much of the space before the ship. When the *brig Apollo* left the Weser estuary and sailed into open waters, the North Sea immediately became choppy, causing the brig to wallow on all three of its axes. It began to pitch up and down as waves were met and it began to roll from side to side. In choppy water, it yawed left and right as well. For many passengers who had little or no at-sea experience, the fun ceased within an hour and they began to experience nausea and were quickly overcome with seasickness. Some ran to the rails and heaved into the sea while others went below and laid their bodies down on the straw mattresses. Conrad's wife and his younger siblings spent much time during that first day at the ship's rails, vomiting into the sea. They became dehydrated and lost their appetite. Somehow, Conrad was less affected. For the rest of that day and several more, all the passengers learned to adjust to the *Apollo*'s motion at sea.

After about four hours of sailing, the vessel neared the Helgoland Islands, an archipelago in the North Sea, and Captain Feldhausen gave orders to reconfigure the sails. At the same time, he swung the helm to the port and tacked across the prevailing north wind towards the eastern mouth of the English Channel. For the next two days, he would use dead-reckoning navigation techniques to direct his ship to the center of the channel. The captain was well aware that other emigration ships had difficulty when high winds drove them perilously near the rocky coast in the channel. His intent was to keep the Apollo in the center of the channel.

On the fourth day of sailing, the ship entered the English Channel and the passengers were treated to views of the White Cliffs of Dover off the starboard side. The emigrants lined the rail to catch a glimpse of the famous cliffs and the country of England. That night, lights were spotted off their port side which some said were from lighthouses on the shore near the French town of Calais. Again, passengers came on deck to catch a quick view of France. Two days later, they saw Land's End and from there on, it was all Atlantic Ocean.

One night in the following week, about two weeks removed from Bremerhaven, the ship sailed into a violent storm in the Atlantic. Huge waves battered the ship as lightning flashed about, followed by sharp cracks of thunder. As a result of the waves, the ship was tossed about like a tiny leaf trapped in white water rapids. In steerage, the passengers were slammed into the bulkheads and rolled about. They and their children became alarmed, making the younger children cry. They had no experience to inform them that such storms at sea were routine. By the next morning, the sea was calm again and the passengers took their places on the deck to converse, enjoy the sunshine, and watch for marine life.

For the next two months or so, the *brig Apollo* would ply the waters of the Atlantic Ocean and the Gulf of Mexico before landing at Galveston. It would travel from very frigid waters in the northern latitudes to much warmer, tropical waters far to the south. Its passengers would migrate more than 1,320 miles towards the equator or, said another way, they would move to a place that was more than 12 degrees of latitude south of Germany. In all, the trip would cover roughly 7,000 miles of water in 78 days (see Figure 1-1). It promised to be a great adventure, especially for a family that had not gone to sea before.

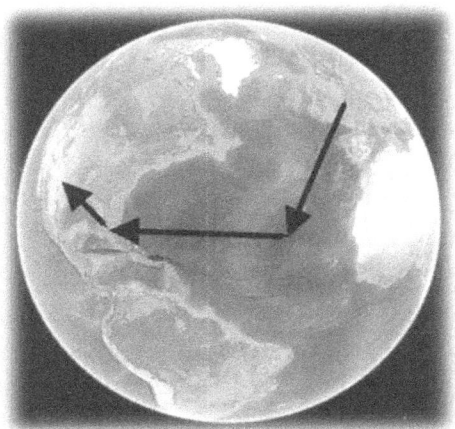

Figure 1-1 The *brig Apollo's* Approximate Path Across the Atlantic

Chapter 2

LANDING IN GALVESTON

At noon on Monday, January 19th 1846, Captain Feldhausen went to his cabin, took his brass sextant from its teak case that was normally stored in a large trunk, and then walked out onto the main deck of the ship. His intent was to make celestial readings of the winter sun, which, now in winter, lay low in the southern sky. Overhead, atmospheric conditions were clear but a crisp, steady breeze from the north buffeted him from behind as he aimed the instrument skyward. He took three readings and after each one, jotted down his observations in a little log book that he kept in a side pocket of his heavy jacket. After the last shot, he carefully surveyed the horizon of the Gulf of Mexico one last time, noted the wind conditions, stroked his beard, and then retired to his cabin. He seated himself at a plotting table that was bolted to the bulkhead of the ship. On it, navigation charts and tools were strewn about. Using his observations and tabled data from a navigation book, he meticulously converted the three celestial readings to a single, fairly precise estimate of the vessel's position, which he carefully plotted on his navigation chart. As he stroked his beard and gazed at the chart, a faint smile spread across his face. He double-checked his figures and confirmed that his ship's position in the Gulf of Mexico was about 96 nautical miles south southeast of Galveston, Texas. The brig had been at sea for over 75 days and now it was nearing the port of Galveston, its final destination. Clamoring back onto deck, he pointed aft and shouted, "LOG!" to the crew. At that command, a sailor dropped his line and raced towards the stern. At the rear of the ship, the seaman opened a wooden chest and grasped the large log that was attached to a very long length of rope that was neatly folded on itself in the box. On the Captain's command and with a short windup, he tossed the log aft into the waters that were receding behind the ship. The rope had knots tied at equal spaces along its length. Each knot corresponded to a meter of length. After the log was tossed overboard, the sailor began counting knots as he played the rope out of the chest. At the same time, Captain Feldhausen monitored time as it elapsed on the ship's clock. After five minutes, the Captain shouted "TIME" and the sailor stopped playing rope out of the wooden chest. At the Captain's call, the crewman shouted out his final count of knots and laboriously began to haul the rope back in, neatly folding it in the process, and storing it in the box with the log resting on top of the folds. The Captain made a record of how many knots had played out in that interval of time and returned to his cabin where he computed his ship's speed of advance. As he calculated it, the ship was presently moving through the water at four nautical miles per hour. With 96 miles to go and with favorable winds, the *brig Apollo* would be in port approximately 24 hours later, 78 days after it left the German port of Bremerhaven. The Captain directed the First Mate to inform the crew and passengers that the *brig Apollo* would arrive in Galveston tomorrow around noon if all went well. So far, it hadn't.

It had been a difficult ocean crossing for almost everyone aboard the *Apollo*. Trouble had begun shortly after the brig cleared the Weser River estuary and entered the North Sea. A violent storm hit the ship and caused seasickness and dehydration among almost all the emigrants. That misery lasted for most of the first week. Later, in the calmer waters of the English Channel, those stricken with seasickness had managed to recover a bit of their strength and had begun to eat solid food again. They had even managed to line up along the gunwales on the main deck to see part of the English coast as they moved by it. That visual experience combined with solid food had lifted the spirits of the weakened passengers but only temporarily. The quality of the food aboard the vessel was very poor and so offered little nutrition to the passengers weakened by prolonged seasickness. For the passengers who had paid for meals, the food had often consisted of rancid meat, very thin soup, and hard tack biscuits plus weak coffee. Those meals, combined with the miseries the passengers had endured, left many of them malnourished, weak, and vulnerable. The Pluennekes, who had opted to bring their own provisions, fared much better for most of the trip. However, Conrad's young wife and his father were severely tested by the ordeal of seasickness.

Beginning a few weeks after leaving the English Channel when the Apollo entered a much warmer climate, outbreaks of disease had begun to plague the ship, particularly in steerage where most of the 95 passengers dwelt. One elderly male emigrant complained of being dizzy, began to vomit, and then had suffered violent diarrhea. Within a few hours, he had died a painful death. Shortly thereafter, a few of the other passengers had begun to complain of the same symptoms. Among the crew, it was thought that the most severe cases had been contracted in steerage where conditions were crowded and most grimy.

After the first and most dire cases had been reported, Captain Feld-hausen had consulted the ship's doctor about the problem and his medical diagnosis was cholera. That very word sent shivers down the spine of the Captain, as it would have any man of that era. In his many voyages back and forth across the Atlantic, Feldhausen had heard of cholera and knew how such an outbreak of the illness could be devastating at sea where everyone was confined to close quarters on the ship by necessity. In the world of 1846, very little was known about the causes of cholera or how to treat it but there were many theories. All that the Captain could get from the ship's doctor was that, "*Cholera was the disease that walks in darkness,*" a cliché but an accurate one. Cholera popped up suddenly, had extremely dire effects on humans, and then often disappeared just as rapidly. The doctor knew that cholera was a deadly disease that had the potential to kill everyone on board the brig in a short amount of time. His medical officer's cliché, however, was of little help to the Captain who had responsibility for the safety and well-being of the passengers and his crew.

As a first measure, Captain Feldhausen had ordered the medical staff and crew to quarantine the families affected by cholera. In the crowded steerage space, that was difficult. A special place of quarantine had been created in the far aft part of steerage, as far removed from other passengers as was possible. That area was off limits to everyone except the victims, the Captain and his medical staff. In addition, Captain Feldhausen had instructed the medical staff to apply whatever remedies they thought might help those afflicted and those now in quarantine. With the initial victims, the doctor had attempted bloodletting as a cure but that treatment had not worked at all. Those patients, now with less blood flowing through their bodies, had died quickly and painfully from blood clotting.

Upon hearing the bad news of a failed treatment, the Captain had felt pressure to take additional measures because he knew that if the disease was not in check, more passengers would fall ill in coming days and most of them would die within a day or two. At that point, he would have an epidemic on his hands.

While trying various solutions, the medical crew had also studied the problem from various aspects. Oddly, the crew had discovered that some of those who contracted cholera did not live in steerage but lived in much better quarters. A few of those who came down with cholera somehow managed to survive and that was very puzzling to the doctor. He had noted that in some cases, the newly affected patients came from families that were otherwise unaffected by the disease. In other cases, the reverse had happened individuals had remained healthy while the rest of their family had died. Given that paradox, the doctor had puzzled over what caused cholera's spread but, in the end, had failed to arrive at a conclusive answer. As an additional measure, the Captain had ordered a complete cleaning and scrubbing of the ship's quarters, particularly steerage but that too had produced little effect. The outbreak unsettled Captain Feldhausen who was astounded by how rapidly the disease had struck, how seemingly random it had occurred, and how quickly it became fatal.

Cholera had affected the Pluenneke family as well as several others on the *brig Apollo*. The first Pluenneke family member to contract cholera was little Henriette, just over three years of age. When it hit, her first symptom was a feeling of being weak and lethargic. She asked her mother (Karoline) for permission to lie go below decks and lie down on their straw mattress bed. Karoline, thinking it was just another bout of seasickness, did not take her daughter's complaint very seriously and assented. Henriette's aunt, Fredericke, went down into steerage to check on her and had complied with her niece's wishes by fetching a pitcher of water from the barrel up on the main deck. Henriette had consumed quite a bit of water and, for a while, felt a little better. At the time, Fredericke also drank some of the water. Shortly after drinking the water, however, little Henriette had sprawled out on the mattress and then began to feel lightheaded. She had also begun to experience tremors in her arms and legs, followed by numbness in all of her extremities. She had difficulty explaining just what she was experiencing. "I don't feel good and I have a tummy ache," she had murmured weakly. In just a few minutes, however, she complained of a severe headache and her skin had taken on a pallid color that seemed almost translucent to the human eye. Seeing the abrupt change in her little niece's condition, Fredericke quickly summoned their parents. Henriette's grandmother, Sophie, had tried to comfort her by applying wet cloths to her forehead while her grandfather, Johann Heinrich, sang hymns to her but none of that had seemed to help. Her discomfort had grown markedly worse. Her mother, Karoline Pluenneke, sent Fredericke to summon the ship's doctor and after he arrived, he gave Henriette large doses of Calomel but that only seemed to make her condition worse. It caused her stomach and intestines to begin discharging mucus and fluids, making her increasingly dehydrated. As a result, her thirst became unquenchable and that caused her to drink more water. Within an hour, her stomach began to rumble and she had begun to vomit violently and then retched repeatedly without discharging anything. What came out of her mouth was mostly watery and very thin. That misery had been soon accompanied by another symptom: violent and explosive diarrhea. Her mother and her older cousin had tried in vain to keep her clean and comfortable but their efforts were futile. The two symptoms collectively made tiny Henriette become even more dehydrated and more emaciated. As the illness progressed, she had grown weaker and weaker by the minute. The violent discharges continued until her emissions appeared rice-colored, a sure indication of cholera.

From the onset of symptoms, it had been evident to the doctor that Henriette had contracted cholera but neither he or anyone else knew how that could have happened. Nor had anyone, including the doctor, known what could be done for her. In a short time, her pulse had slowed dramatically and her body temperature had begun to drop to a dangerously low level. In response, Henriette's body had shivered and she mentally teetered on the edge of delirium. Within an hour, she had gone into convulsive fits and then had lapsed into unconsciousness. Within 24 hours, Henriette Pluenneke had died and her body had turned a vivid blue, a result of severe dehydration. In death, her face appeared hollow and aged, well beyond her mere three years.

Upon her death, the doctor had quickly notified Captain Feldhausen. As with others who had died of cholera, the Captain had ordered that Henriette's little body be quickly wrapped in canvas and readied for burial at sea. Since the cause of cholera on the ship was unknown and because passengers on the ship were terrified of contagion, getting the body off the ship quickly had seemed the prudent course of action. The family had asked for time to conduct a religious ceremony but the Captain had demurred. As a consequence, the family had hastily gathered on the aft deck and said a quick prayer for Henriette before her body was placed on a plank and slid into the ocean. Despite the earlier death, other passengers had offered condolences but had generally shunned contact with the Pluenneke family for a while because they feared contagion. Their behavior had shocked and demoralized the Pluennekes, who were made to feel as though they were tainted and somehow were the cause of the disease. In their hearts, they felt certain they had not caused the onset of cholera on the ship but could not prove that to anyone's satisfaction.

Unfortunately, Henriette's death had not been the end of misery for the Pluennekes. Within two days of Henriette's death, her aunt Fredericke went through the same sequence of symptoms, languished in bed, and had died three days later. Somehow, her body had resisted the disease longer than her niece had but in the end, she too succumbed to cholera. A few had thought that she lasted longer because she was older than her niece but that was an unfounded theory. Everyone on board had been certain that she had contracted the disease from her niece and were convinced that the disease was contagious and therefore on a rampage. Again, there was a quick burial at sea, with little ceremony. At the time of her death, Fredericke had only been 21 years of age. Her death left the whole family in deep sorrow and depression but no one person took the two deaths harder than Conrad Pluenneke. Emigration had been his idea and now his family was dying around him. He had felt deep and gut-wrenching anguish over the deaths and those feelings lapsed into guilt.

After the two deaths in the family, the Pluennekes did what other emigrants normally did on the ship. They tried to divert their attention from their misery to their surroundings. They watched marine life cavorting in the ocean, watched the crew at work, and they talked to other families but nothing took away the pain of their loss. At night, they anguished over their loss and prayed for a miracle.

Occasionally, one of the passengers would play a musical instrument or sing for the benefit of the others and that lightened the mood of the Pluenneke family members but the thought of cholera lurked everywhere on the ship. To block out the painful memories, they cooked, cleaned, and did chores just as they had on the farm in a futile attempt to mask their pain and avoid facing the truth.

For a short while, the Pluenneke family had been spared from more misery. Although sorrowful, they had desperately tried to go about their daily lives on the Apollo and forget. Mysteriously, the number of new cases of cholera on the ship had decreased over the course of several weeks and life on the ship had returned to a semblance of normalcy. Everyone in the family had seemed healthy and, although depressed about their lost children, the elder Pluennekes had been thankful that their other children had been spared. Oddly, It had seemed as though Conrad, his wife, and the others who had survived the outbreak, had gained some measure of immunity against the disease.

That hiatus had lasted for only two weeks. In the warmer waters of the southern latitudes, cholera had returned to the *brig Apollo* and with a vengeance. In the renewed wave, young Friedrich Pluenneke was struck down. He, the youngest sibling of Conrad, had been only 12 years old. It was noted by the ship's doctor that Friedrich had no direct contact with either his sister or his niece while they were ill nor had he come into contact with others who had contracted the disease. That made him doubt contagion but he had no real proof for that assertion. Henriette and Fredericke had been treated in quarantine and the medical staff had kept Friedrich, Karoline, Johann Julius Conrad, and his wife well away from the earliest outbreaks. Those facts had made many passengers on the ship question whether cholera was really contagious and a few changed their minds. If it was not contagious, what was causing the outbreak? With no concrete answers, panic had set in among the passengers and they had pressed the medical staff for answers. The staff had tried to think through the various cases and distill from them a pattern that would point at a viable cause and solution but they had derived nothing but more questions and no answers.

From the outbreak, the doctor had tried to contain the disease by cleaning the sleeping quarters but that had no discernible effect. They had kept the victims warm by wrapping them in blankets but that too had not stemmed the spread of cholera. They had tried quarantining affected families and that had not eliminated the problem. In desperation, the medical staff had administered large doses of opium to a few patients, but that treatment also had proven ineffective. In desperation, they resorted to administering whiskey to victims, even to young children and to older generations, but that treatment was equally ineffective. In all of those attempts to stem the disease, however, not one person had ever questioned the drinking water on the ship as the disease's source. It had been ignored because everyone drank water drawn from the same large cask of potable water that was kept on the main deck and not all had come down with cholera.

The epidemic of cholera on the sailing vessel had presented another mystery to the Pluennekes: why were their youngest children stricken by the pestilence while they and the older children were spared? All of them had eaten the same food and all drank from the ship's cask of potable water. Decades later, it would be learned that because the adults had acquired a taste for strong, hot coffee or hot tea, they had unwittingly killed the cholera bacteria in the water supply by boiling water for such brews. Whereas the adults drank hot coffee or hot tea, the children generally drank water. Had the adults boiled water for the children's drinks, the cholera bacteria might have been killed and the younger members of the family would have been spared.

Much later, it would be discovered that cholera outbreaks on the ships at sea (such as the Apollo) occurred because germs of the disease were contained in the water supply or food supply that was loaded onto the ship at the dock. In colder climes, cholera bacteria remain dormant for long periods of time but when introduced to warmer climates, come to life. They likely roused from dormancy when the ship moved into the warmer climate of the tropics. Alternatively, the tainted water may have been taken onboard when supplies were replenished in the Azores. Later it became known that cholera lives mostly in untreated water, particularly that which has become tainted with human waste. Better sanitation practices very likely would have helped curb the disease on the *brig Apollo*.

Regardless of its origin, cholera had claimed the lives of four Pluenneke children on the way to Texas. As devastating as its effect had been on the family, its rampage was not over. It would surface again in their lives but the next time, it would arise on land. Yes, it had been a very difficult and devastating ocean crossing for the Pluennekes.

No one in the family took the deaths harder than Conrad. After all, emigration to Texas had been his idea and he had pushed everyone to join him. Now four of his relatives were dead and he could not avoid feeling the guilt that came with those losses. It brought an ugly feeling that he would remember for the rest of his life.

As the ship neared the Texas coast, the Pluennekes were elated that their long and sorrowful ocean crossing would soon be over. They, like most of the other passengers, wanted to get off the ship and put their misery behind them. Although a bit premature, the family stood en masse on deck with other emigrants and strained for a first sighting of American land. Any joy they felt in arriving, however, was muted by the loss of dear children during the transit. In the deeper recesses of their minds, a single dark question lurked: maybe Texas was not going to be the utopian place that they dreamt of?

The next morning, land was spotted off the starboard side and the passengers aboard the *brig Apollo* began to prepare for debarkation. The Pluennekes gathered all of their possessions, neatly stored them in their bags and trunks, and then went up on deck to get their first glimpse of Texas. At first, all they could see was a long horizontal strip of white sand through the coastal haze but as the ship neared Galveston, they could see more detail and a few buildings along the shore emerged into view. This was Texas. In a few minutes, they could see the opening between Galveston Island to the left and Bolivar Peninsula on the right. That opening was the estuary of the Trinity and San Jacinto Rivers, both of which emptied into Galveston Bay and flowed on into the Gulf of Mexico. The depth of the estuary channel varied but generally averaged about eight feet. A shifting tongue of silt from the estuary extended well into the Gulf and occasionally affected navigation. Inside the estuary area and on the north side of Galveston Island lay the port of Galveston, in what is today called West Bay. Captain Feldhausen expertly sailed the brig through the estuary and anchored the ship several hundred yards from the docks.

With his ship securely at anchor, Captain Feldhausen called the passengers and crew together one last time. He explained that each family would be ferried to the docks in a dory rowed by his crew. At the docks, they would be met by an agent of the Adelsverein, D. H. Klaener. It was explained that he would interview each family and each single man to collect information about them. His log would provide the Society with a record of immigrants brought to Texas by their organization on each ship.[21]

When the Pluenneke's time came, the six remaining members of Conrad's family were boarded on the wooden dory and rowed to the docks. When they arrived, they were elated to see the Stars and Stripes of the United States flying overhead. When they left Germany in November of 1845, Galveston was a port in the Republic of Texas. In those 78 days, Texas had become the 28th state of the union. That wav-

---

[21] See Appendix 2. D. H. Klaener's log for the *brig Apollo* in Galveston TX. The odd mark in the log's columns should be interpreted as *ditto*, i.e., same as the above.

ing symbol of America meant the Pluennekes would become citizens of a democratic society.

Shortly, they were ushered to an office where they met Herr D. H. Klaener who was seated behind a large desk. Before him was an open registry book. As they filed in, he rose, greeted them in their native tongue, and asked them to take a seat, gesturing towards several leather chairs in front of his desk. Klaener began by addressing the senior member of the family, Johann Pluenneke, in German, asking him to provide his name.

"Johann Heinrich Conrad Pluenneke" was the reply "but I am called Conrad by people who know me."

"Wife, Conrad?"

"Yes" Johann Heinrich Conrad Pluenneke answered and gestured towards Sophie who smiled shyly and kept her eyes averted from his gaze.

"Children?"

"Yes, two plus my oldest son and his wife," again gesturing towards his family and specifically at Conrad.

"Two children? Herr Pluenneke, I will treat your son and his wife separately after I have concluded my interview with you."

"Yes, two children–Karoline and Conradina."

"Where are you from, Herr Pluenneke?"

"Germany, Herr Klaener, I am from Klein-Lafferde, a city in the Duchy of Braunsweig in Germany."

"What was your former occupation?", Klaener asked.

Conrad answered "Farmer."

As he gathered the information from Conrad's father, Klaener recorded it on line 27 of the registry book that was before him on the desk. The desk, Conrad noted, appeared to be solid, quite old, and made very well.

Klaener then turned to Johann Julius Conrad Pluenneke, the oldest child, and asked for his name.

"Conrad Pluenneke" was the reply.

"Wife?"

"Yes, Herr Klaener," and Conrad turned to gesture towards his young wife seated behind him. She smiled demurely and nodded to Mr. Klaener.

"Children?"

"None," they both said in almost perfect unison.

"Occupation?"

"Farmer, same as my father, Herr Klaener."

"Are you also from Klein-Lafferde?"

"Yes, Herr Klaener," Conrad answered, " we are both from there."

Using his quill pen, Klaener recorded Conrad's information on line 28 of his log, occasionally dipping it in ink and then writing rapidly. At several points, he attempted to blot the ledger to prevent it from smudging but failed.

He identified the Pluennekes as settlers with the German Emigration Company headed for the Fisher-Miller Grant. His log, after all passengers on the ship had been interviewed, would become the official list of emigrants that arrived on the *brig Apollo* from Bremen, Germany on January 20th, 1846. It would be signed by himself, D. H. Klaener, as agent for the German Emigration Company.

After failing to blot his newest log entries [22] with another piece of paper, Klaener closed his log and informed the Pluennekes that they

---

[22] Failure to blot entries accounts for the cluttered appearance of Klaener's log.

would have to pass through the U. S. Customs office before entering into the city of Galveston and the state of Texas. Since the Pluennekes had never left Germany, much less traveled to the New World, getting through U.S. customs in Texas was a novel experience for them.

After their session, Klaener escorted the Pluennecke family next door to the U. S. Customs office where there was a short line. Before returning to his office, he told the family that when they had cleared customs, they would be taken to a hotel in Galveston where they would reside until they could be transported down the coast to Karlshafen. After bidding them good fortunes, he returned to his office where the next group of immigrants, three people also named Pluenneke, were waiting patiently. Those Pluennekes were likely distant relatives but Johann Heinrich's part of the family was not acquainted with them. They were Charles Pluenneke and his wife plus Hermann Pluenneke. [23] On Klaener's log, Hermann was listed as being 18 years of age and single. Their information was duly taken and recorded in the log as numbers 29 and 30, following that of Johann Julius Conrad Pluenneke and his wife.

At the U. S. Customs office on the Galveston wharf, the bags and trunks of Johann Heinrich Pluenneke's family were thoroughly inspected by agents of the U. S. Government and were found to contain nothing that was contraband or taxable. The family was then directed to a place further down the wharf, near a walled-off area that was punctuated by a large gate. Other immigrants had already congregated there and formed yet another line. That wall represented the limit of Customs control beyond it was America, freedom, and a new life. Among the gathering crowd of immigrants, they recognized Friedrich Haas and his family as well as Wilhelm Hagemann and his family. They also saw Henry Fisher and his large family plus Ferdinand Gellermann. As they mingled with their fellow passengers and talked about the adventure ahead of them, the Pluennekes were soon joined by the other Pluennekes. When he had processed all the passengers from the *brig Apollo*, D. H. Klaener emerged from his office and strode purposefully down the wharf to address the group as a whole.

---

[23] Information about the other Pluennekes does not match data about Johann Heinrich Pluenneke's branch of the family. For example, there were no siblings that were male and 18 years of age nor were any of them married, except for Johann Julius Conrad Pluenneke.

With a strong voice, he told them that outside of the gate, which he gestured to, the German Emigration Company had wagons lined up to take them to the Washington Hotel, which was near the Gulf shore in Galveston. He said another German Emigration Company ship, the Gerhard Hermann, had just arrived and he had to return to his office to begin processing those clients. He did promise the group, however, that he would come to the Washington Hotel the next day and inform everyone about what to expect in coming days. After speaking, he opened the gate, gestured towards the waiting wagons, and then abruptly pivoted to hurry back to his office.

Outside the gates, the latest immigrants were startled to be met by an angry mob of protesters who were carrying signs and placards hand-lettered in German.[24] At the sight of the first German immigrants emerging through the gate, the protesters pressed towards the wall and began shouting, waving their fists, and making menacing gestures. All of their signs strongly urged the new immigrants to return home at once. The citizens of Galveston came to the docks to protest at foreign ship arrivals because they believed that immigrant ships, and even the immigrants themselves, brought cholera and other diseases to their city. They were terrified of epidemics. Had the immigrants been able to respond in English, the passengers of the Apollo would have explained that cholera had existed on their ship but they would have denied that they were the ones who caused the outbreak or spread it. They too were victims. The new immigrants were stung by the harsh protests which made them feel like pariahs and forced them to become ashamed of being foreign born. It was their first instance of being unfairly and falsely accused of something that was not true. It was unfair but it would not be last time that would happen to them.

They were puzzled. Some of their contingent, and four of the Pluenneke's children, had died from the disease on the way to Texas. Why did the Americans not understand that cholera was also their enemy. They had fought the disease on the ship and had failed to eliminate it or stop it. The ship's medical staff had failed as well. The tumult

---

[24] In a letter written by D.H. Klaener which was published in the Weser-Zeitung on July 17, 1846, it was stated that he was being pressured by authorities in Galveston to remove immigrants from the island to prevent another epidemic. Cited in Biesele (1930), page 130.

created by the protesters stunned the immigrants and left them with an unsettled feeling about Americans and what the future might hold for them in Texas.

Conrad deeply felt the sting of being ostracized as an alien, an outsider, and a disease carrier. He tried to hurry his family by the crowd while silently vowing to demonstrate to Americans that he and the others belonged in their country. He could not prove it that day but he vowed to make a contribution to his new homeland in the future. Others felt the same way. To a person, the angry protestors in front of them were not how they had pictured Americans when they left the Fatherland for Texas.

Agents of the Adelsverein quickly shepherded the rest of the new immigrants through the angry mob and loaded them in wagons as rapidly as possible. From the wharf, they were driven directly to the Washington Hotel where they were met at the entrance to the hotel by its manager, Hans Beissner, also an immigrant from Germany. The group was pleased to be greeted in their native language, especially by someone who understood what they had just been through, and one who also understood their situation back in the old country. One by one, he showed families to their small, plain but very clean rooms. He then briefly explained the few rules of the hotel: no fires in the rooms, rooms had to be kept clean, and they were not to engage in violence.

Shortly after the immigrants arrived, agents of the Society had brought their luggage to the hotel and stacked it in the lobby. When one of them asked about the schedule, one of the agents said that a schooner was being sent up the coast from Indian Point to ferry them down to the Matagorda Bay area. He added that the schooner was expected in Galveston the next day or two.

In their small, plain hotel room, the Pluennekes partially unpacked their bags and worked out a living arrangement for six people. They made plans for that evening and for the next day. After being on a ship for 78 days, they were eager to walk around on land and see what Galveston had to offer. They also wanted to find a source for fresh food since they had exhausted most of their own supply and had been existing on what the German Emigration Company offered them on the Apollo. Much of that food had been awful, stale, and poorly prepared. Since they were now in America, Conrad and his son also wanted to exchange their German Guldens for U.S. dollars. Much had to be done in a short time.

Later that afternoon, after getting directions from Herr Beissner, the family bundled up in coats and set out to find the nearest market where they could buy fresh food for the next two days. Within a few blocks, they found the market he had recommended and were pleasantly surprised that the grocer's shelves contained an abundance of fresh vegetables, fruit, and various types of meat. They were also pleased to learn that the market would accept German currency but at a ten to one exchange rate. Since they had few viable options, they reluctantly accepted the merchant's inflated exchange rate and bought an ample amount of food that they expected to last for two days.

After shopping, the family decided to look around Galveston and walked south towards the Gulf shore. In late January, a cold wind blew from the north. Now late in the afternoon, the daylight was waning which made the humid coastal air crisp but delightful. Despite the climate, they were pleased at what they saw. Tropical trees, such as date palms, lined part of the sandy shore beyond tide level. Strange birds, such as great egrets and pelicans, circled overhead near the shore in search of fish on the surface. Compared to their part of Germany, this was a tropical paradise and that beauty helped restore their attitude about leaving Germany. For a while, they forgot about their losses and about the rude reception they had received at the wharf. They reveled in the fact that they would soon be citizens in this beautiful country. After walking up and down the sandy beach for a mile or so, they headed back to their quarters at the Washington Hotel. In their room, they prepared and consumed a sumptuous meal and then retired early. Although the space was cramped, it was far more comfortable than steerage on the brig and they slept peacefully, on solid land at last.

Early the next day, Conrad and his father set out to find a bank where they could exchange their German money for American dollars. Before they departed, they consulted Herr Beissner about banks in the area. He recommended the McKinney, Williams, and Company Bank as a financial institution in Galveston that was known to be fair to immigrants of all nationalities. He also told them the exchange rate should be about seven and a half to one and cautioned them not to accept less. At the bank, they conducted their business and returned to the hotel with about $200 American dollars. Not having a place to stash money, they stuffed the dollars in their pillows.

With the prospect of another day or two at sea, the family decided to walk about the city again, see the more of the shoreline, and get some exercise. While walking, they met a man of German ancestry named Heinz Getz who had lived in Galveston for nearly three years. He had left Hanover in 1842 with the intention of settling in the western part of the state but had become enthralled with Galveston's coastal scenery and decided to live there, partly because it had a German language newspaper and a developing cultural scene. During their brief conversation, Heinz relayed a little of what he knew of the history of the Galveston area to the Pluenneke family.

The land had been originally occupied by fierce natives of the Karankawa tribe, cannibals some thought but without proof. It had been discovered, rediscovered, and explored for centuries by both the French and the Spanish. In the 18th century, the Spanish explorer Jose de Evia charted the area and named the island Galveston in honor of Bernardo de Galvez y Madrid, Count of Galvez. For a time, it was occupied by the pirate Jean Lafitte and his motley crew. The pirate band marauded in the Gulf of Mexico and then retreated to the obscurity of the bay between Galveston Island and what is now called Pelican Island. The island was also once part of Stephen F. Austin's colony but was bought and developed into a city by an entrepreneur named Michel Menard. In 1846, it was the main port of Texas and one of its largest cities, with a population of nearly 4,000 people. Many Germans had arrived in Galveston during the previous two years and some of them had decided to settle in the scenic coastal town rather than forge ahead into the interior of Texas. Herr Getz was one of them.

In return, Conrad told Heinz a little of what was going on in northern Germany - the slumping economy, overpopulation, the decline of trade guilds, high taxation, and the social unrest caused by unemployment and homelessness. All that had caused the Pluennekes to decide to leave Germany. They also inquired about the angry mob that had met their ship at the docks yesterday. "Do Americans dislike Germans?" they asked. "No," Getz said with a matter-of-fact tone, "the local citizens are extremely afraid of diseases because it seems as though no one knows how to eradicate or control them and some Americans falsely believe that immigrants spread such diseases.

Americans (Texians) also worried that immigrants might claim land and take jobs that they felt were rightfully theirs as Americans. Beyond those irrational fears," Getz said, "Americans are good people."

Shortly, they all shook hands with Heinz Getz and headed in the direction of the shoreline. After wading in the chilly waves that broke and then backwashed into the Gulf, the family headed back to the hotel. They ate lunch in their room, rested a little bit, and then left the hotel for another walk.

At the hotel's entrance, they met D. H. Klaener who asked that all immigrants in his charge assemble in the hotel's lobby. He had come to the hotel to deliver a message to all of them; their schooner, the *Tom Jack*, was in Galveston Bay and would depart the next day. In his message, he emphasized that all immigrants destined for an inland colony of the German Emigration Company were to be at the entrance of the hotel at 7 am the next morning with their luggage packed. He added that wagons would be there to transport them and their belongings back to the Port of Galveston. If all went according to schedule, they would be back on the Gulf the next morning and in Karlshafen by tomorrow night. That was possible because it was only about 120 miles from Galveston to the docks at Indian Point and the *Tom Jack* was a fast ship. After some deliberation, a few of the German immigrants who had arrived at Galveston on the *brig Apollo* chose to settle near the Gulf coast and notified Klaener of their decision. To the rest, Klaener said he would see them off the next day, bid them a good night, and departed. With that news, the family went up to their room and began to repack their belongings.

The Pluennekes rose very early the next morning and dragged their baggage to an area outside of the hotel. There, other familiar faces were milling around, talking mostly about the lovely Galveston seacoast they had seen. Shortly, the wagons arrived and the immigrants, along with their possessions, were driven back to the wharf where they were promptly placed in dories and rowed out to the waiting schooner. By 8:00 am, the *Tom Jack* weighed anchor and sailed for the estuarial opening of Galveston Bay into the Gulf of Mexico. After clearing the estuary, the ship tacked hard to starboard and sailed for the mouth of Matagorda Bay. As they sailed southwest, the weather changed abruptly for the worse. Winds, which had been light and variable, perked up and rose to speeds upward of 30 miles per hour. Winds from a Texas

"Blue Norther" buffeted the schooner and created large waves in the Gulf waters. In the rocking schooner, a few passengers experienced nausea and bouts of seasickness again. In the high wind and amidst choppy seas, heavy rain began to fall, reducing visibility considerably. The coastline, which some passengers had been watching, disappeared in the downpour. On the main deck, Captain Behr resorted to dead reckoning navigation and plotted a course on his navigation chart for the mouth of Matagorda Bay. He announced to his passengers that it was going to be difficult to locate the entrance to the Bay under those conditions so he decided to anchor off shore and ride out the northerly wind until the next day. "Tomorrow" he said, "visibility will be better and we will be able to would sail through the mouth to Indian Point without risk." With that news, the Pluennekes settled below decks as best they could and prepared for what they expected to be a long, difficult night at sea. They had been through this on the transatlantic voyage so most of the new immigrants just shrugged and coped with the situation as best they could.

After a stormy and turbulent night at sea, the *Tom Jack* weighed anchor and set sail early the next morning. While the offshore winds had calmed, the coastal area was now enshrouded in a heavy fog that severely limited visibility. The spit of land which separates the Gulf of Mexico from the bay, known as Matagorda Island, lacked navigation aids such as lighthouses or buoys, resources which would help seafarers such as Captain Behr find Cavallo Pass, the mouth of Matagorda Bay, in a heavy fog. In the shrouded atmosphere, there was great risk of running aground on a sand bar or a submerged rock. As a result, the Captain had no choice but drop anchor again and drift, biding his time, and waiting for the fog to lift. At about 11 o'clock, sunshine broke through the fog and it began to lift. Wisps of fog that resembled feathers wafted in the air and danced their way across the Gulf towards the *Tom Jack*. As a result, the opening to Matagorda Bay became sporadically and faintly visible off the port bow. The Captain weighed anchor, set his smaller sails, and began to move cautiously towards the opening. Shortly, it began to rain softly but steadily, again limiting visibility but now the *Tom Jack* was into the pass where land could be spotted dimly on both sides of the ship. With a facing wind, Captain Behr tacked gently right and then left until he was safely through Cavallo Pass and into the Bay. The docks at Indian Point were now off their port side, less than a mile away. The Captain set a heading of 345 degrees and nudged the schooner closer and closer to the docks until he could at last drop anchor. The *Tom Jack* had arrived safely at Indian Point with its load of German immigrants. Aboard the schooner, there was great relief and joy as the emigrants realized the at-sea portion of their trip was over. At last, the newcomers would be on solid ground for good.

Chapter 3

KARLSHAFEN

When Conrad Pluenneke and five other members of the Pluenneke clan arrived at Indian Point aboard the schooner *Tom Jack* on the 23rd of January, it was raining hard and had been for several days. The heavy precipitation severely limited their visibility. Standing near the bow of the schooner, Conrad could barely make out a large wharf that jutted out into the bay from Indian Point, even though it was a scant 300 yards away. Matagorda Bay, where the *Tom Jack* was now wallowing, was a huge expanse of swirling water that was being fed by four swollen streams, coloring it a muddy greenish-brown. Because of the heavy run-off and an incoming tide from the gulf, the floodwater was stalled in the channel and that was causing a gradual rise in the bay's water level.

With rainwater pouring off the brim of his hat, Conrad scanned the bay which seemed to surround him in all directions. Standing beside him was his young wife and his father, who now looked weary and depressed. In the leaden light of a rainy day, the place had a dreary appearance. Indian Point was not at all like Galveston and what they saw before them was not at all what they had expected to see in coastal Texas. To Conrad, what little of the landscape he could see appeared tangled and overgrown.

Among the passengers, however, there was a hubbub of excitement as the schooner neared its final destination. In spite of the steady drizzle, a crowd of curious German immigrants milled about on deck and watched as the crew went through the last steps of securing the sails and anchoring the ship. Among the crowd, Conrad spotted a Verein agent and managed to collar him briefly. Like many others, Conrad wondered about what was going to happen now that they were nearing their destination.

"What are we expected to do?" Conrad asked.

Others crowded around and listened intently to the agent's answer. The man explained that dories were being sent out from the pier to the *Tom Jack*. Shortly he and the other newly arriving immigrants would be put on them and rowed to the wharf. From there, they would be shuttled by way of ox cart to Karlshafen where they would have to find shelter.

"What about our belongings?", Conrad asked. Many in the soaked crowd murmured at the question and nodded.

The agent replied there was no place in Karlshafen [25] to store their belongings but if families were willing to pay a fee of $1, their family possessions could be stored temporarily in a warehouse near the wharf.

Conrad frowned at the answer and initially dissented but finally agreed—what other option did they have?

The agent threaded his way through the milling crowd on the main deck and went downstairs to a lower deck. Shortly he reappeared with a standard German Emigration Society form and thrust it into Conrad's hands. Conrad signed at the appropriate place and thereby agreed to pay $1 to the Adelsverein to store Pluenneke family's belongings in the Society's warehouse. The fee, they assumed, would be deducted from their little account books that the Adelsverein had issued back in Bremen. In turn, others also signed the form and agreed to pay the fee.

Within minutes, silhouettes of dories emerged from within the gloom that hung over the bay and the dark forms of men could be seen rowing furiously against the tide. They were moving towards the *Tom Jack* from the general direction of the wharf. At first, the passengers could barely make out the forms of the crew as they labored to row in unison but as the dories neared the schooner, four men could be clearly discerned in each boat. The immigrants followed the dories visually until they were along side the schooner and tied up to it. In all, there were seven dories. The Captain of the *Tom Jack* told the assembled passengers that each dory could accommodate as many as 15 people plus their light bags. The six remaining members of the Johann Heinrich Pluenneke family, with their personal effects, were placed in the third dory along with the Karl Rode family, plus Ludolph Meyer, and rowed through the swirling murky water to the wharf. There, a member of the crew helped Conrad's father and mother climb the rope ladder which extended from the wharf down to the dory, a height of about six feet. Conrad, his wife, and his two sisters (Karoline and Conradina)

---

[25] Later, Karlshafen would be renamed Indianola.

followed quickly on their heels. The Rode family came next and then Ludolph Meyer. When they all stood on the platform, an agent of the Adelsverein greeted them and then directed them to go to the far end of the wharf where wagons were lined up to take them to Karlshafen.

As a result of recent deluges, the area around the pier was a sloppy quagmire of mud. Slowly, two ox carts slowly slogged their way down a crude path to the pier's landing. A Verein agent loaded the Pluennekes and Ludolph Meyer into one of them, along with their baggage, and then began to ply the muddy road north towards the fledgling community of Karlshafen. During the short drive to Karlshafen, the teamster told the emigrants about events that had taken place in Texas since they left Germany.

"As of last month, Texas is now a state of the United States of America," he said proudly.

The agent went on to say that annexation of the Republic of Texas by the United States had angered its neighbor to the south, Mexico, which was now threatening to invade Texas and reclaim at least part of its former province. The newcomers were thrilled by the first bit of news but alarmed by the second. Having been embroiled in the Napoleonic Wars for decades, they understandably did not want to be involved in another war.

During the short but tedious ride to Karlshafen, Conrad sadly reflected back on their lengthy trip from Bremen to this place. It had not gone as he and his father had planned. The elder Pluennekes, particularly Conrad's father, had been badly affected by seasickness and were now in a weakened state. His young wife had also suffered and was now malnourished, barely able to hold her head up. During his reflection, he looked down at her by his side. She looked pale and obviously very weary. At sea, cholera had claimed the lives of three of his young sisters and the stress of those deaths continued to weigh heavily on him and the others.

In Galveston, the family had begun to learn about the financial disarray of the Adelsverein on which they now so desperately had to depend. That caused Conrad great concern. In the past day or so, they had also gleaned that Texas might become embroiled in a war with Mexico. It seemed as though every bit of news was extremely worrisome. Trying to brighten his own spirits, Conrad consoled himself by recognizing that they had arrived in the new state of Texas and were committed to settling on its land. If he or other members of the family harbored any ideas about giving up and going back to Germany, they were baseless because the family lacked the resources to pay for six return trips to Germany. For better or worse, they were in Texas to stay. Like so many things before, they had to find a way to overcome all the bad that had happened and move forward with their new lives.

When they rolled into the tiny enclave of Karlshafen, they were shocked to see that it consisted of only two or three substantial log buildings and an assortment of crude shelters. Most of them had been constructed from shipping crates and remnants of other wooden objects. Other immigrants, unable to find wood with which to build a hut, were sheltered in canvas tents while some, lacking either tents or wooden structures, simply dug holes in the mud and covered them with blankets. Here and there, the Pluennekes saw people who looked like they were near death and they were. It was a terrible sight for the newly arriving settlers who had already suffered so much just to get to Karlshafen.

When the wagons bearing the Pluennekes and Ludolph Meyer arrived in front of the German Emigration Company's office in Karlshafen, they were met by the Verein agent on duty. He came out to the wagon, helped the new immigrants down, and then ushered the group through ankle-deep mud to the office. As other wagons arrived, the agent performed the same duties. One by one, they all filed in and filled the small room to capacity.

As the agent nervously glanced around the packed room, he could see by the look on their faces that the new immigrants could barely fathom their present situation. All around him were looks of disbelief and disillusionment at the conditions of the town. Until that day, nothing had been said to them that would have led them to expect such awful and dire conditions.

The expressions on their faces plainly said, "This is not what we were promised in our contracts." [26]

---

[26] Karlshafen had been laid out with streets and organized town lots but the sheer number of immigrants that went there between 1845-1847 overwhelmed the planned community. (Biesele, 1930, appendix C.

The agent had witnessed this state of affairs every time a new group of immigrants, fresh from Galveston, arrived in Karlshafen. He dreaded the speech he now had to deliver. In his own mind, he silently questioned why D. H. Klaener in Galveston couldn't forewarn these people about the bad conditions they would face in Karlshafen and keep them in that larger city where there were more and better accommodations. Of course, he also knew the answer to that question. If told, the clients of the German Emigration Company would defect from the program and then it would be unable to meet its contractual obligations to the state of Texas. In a rippling effect, it would thus lose the Fisher-Miller Grant for which it had paid $19,000. Business trumped morality and agents stayed quiet!

The agent too was German and hated to see his fellow compatriots treated so poorly but he had a job to do and so he proceeded to talk.

"As you know by now," he began, "the Republic of Texas has been annexed by the United States of America. Texas is now the newest state in the Union. That means all of you will become American citizens when you make application in your colony."

That remark, bearing good news, was met with a loud cheer and much murmuring among the throng of immigrants. The agent held up his hand to get attention before continuing.

"While the news of annexation is good news for you and me, that news has not been received well by America's neighbor to the south, Mexico. Tension now exists between the two countries over their common border. As I speak, General Zachary Taylor and his army are on the move towards the Nueces River and possibly the Rio Grande River to counter any attempt by Mexico to forcibly retake Texas. Volunteer militias from Texas and other states are also forming and moving south to join him in southern Texas. Those forces will require supplies at the border. As a result of that military situation, all available wagons, drivers, and draft animals have been commandeered by the U.S. Army to move its resources and its troops to the vicinity of the Rio Grande River quickly."

He paused a moment before continuing

"Those assets, wagons, oxen, and teamsters, are also needed by the Verein to transport all of you inland to our Grant area. Until we find a way to acquire other wagons, teams, and drivers, you will be forced to live here in Karlshafen. Without them, we have no means to transport you inland. Further, the areas north of Karlshafen along the Guadalupe River are presently inundated with water and mud as a result of recent rains. Under those conditions, it is nearly impossible to move north on horse or on foot. Let me assure you that Herr Meusebach and all of us are working diligently to get this problem resolved. Meanwhile, what provisions we can find are being brought in to feed you and clothe you. When we have procured transportation, we will notify you immediately. Until then, try to stay calm."

One older man slowly raised his hand and then shouted loudly "How are we to live here? There appears to be no housing and we have no construction materials with us, only a few tools."

The agent shrugged his shoulders and said, "You will just have to find a way to create shelter for yourself and your family. Some previous immigrants have disassembled the wooden crates that housed their belongings and used that wood to build small huts. Others have attempted to make tents from different types of cloth. We agents of the German Emigration Company will do what we can to help you but we are only three men and more ships are expected shortly."

Another immigrant spoke up and asked "What about the credits in the little account books that were issued to all of us back in Bremen? Can't we use them to buy lumber to build houses?"

The agent, clearly uncomfortable, said, "I dislike being the one to tell you this but the money in those accounts has been used to pay creditors here in Texas. The society is experiencing financial difficulty and may be unable to provide all of what was promised to you in Germany, or at least, not a this time. John O. Meusebach, our Commissioner, hopes to get more funding from Germany soon. If he's successful, everything will improve quickly."

In response to that statement, there was a large commotion in the room. The immigrants were at first shocked and then became angry and disillusioned with the Verein. They had relied on the money in those accounts to settle in Texas and now they were being told that it had evaporated. Conrad looked at his father who looked stunned and hurt by the news. He lowered his head and pawed the floor with his boot, trying to make the best of what they had just heard but could not. Johann Pluenneke still had some of the money that they brought with them from Germany but it would not be nearly enough to get them settled, especially since the Verein itself was faltering.

Some in the crowd yelled angry demands to see the Commissioner General but they were told he was in New Braunfels. Others wanted the Verein to send their families back to Germany on the next ship but were rebuffed. Other immigrants just seemed lost, dazed, not able to handle the bad news. All of them had one question in mind: "What will we do now?"

Anticipating their unspoken question, the lead agent blurted out "All of you can stay in this building tonight. It will be crowded but crowdedness will be better than sleeping outside in the rain. Tomorrow, I advise all of you to begin to construct shelter in whatever way you can."

With that, the meeting ended and the group of new immigrants was faced with a dire situation. They were going to be marooned in Karlshafen for the foreseeable future, maybe weeks or even a month. Outside, it was cold, wet, and dreary. The Norther that they had endured in the gulf was slowly moving south and bringing a numbingly cold drizzle with it. The new arrivals had been led to believe that Texas would be warm and dry, not cold and clammy like northern Europe during the winter.

One by one, families and single men unloaded their baggage from the wagon and opened portions of it, searching through it for bedding, warmer clothing, and other means of keeping warm. Back inside the building, each family organized their space to be comfortable, given the number of people in the room. The Pluennekes found a place on the wooden floor of the German Emigration Company building that was near its southwestern corner and tried to make it comfortable for six people. The room was packed, even more crowded than steerage had been on the sailing vessel Apollo.

"At least," Conrad noted to his father, "the floor isn't pitching and rolling."

The night proved to be very uncomfortable for all of them. The stillness of the night was frequently broken by whispers in the dark, loud snoring, and the sobbing of young children who were afraid of their new surroundings. Conrad tried to sleep but he kept thinking about what he and his father had to do the next day and that made his slumber fitful. His young wife, although weakened by illness during the voyage and badly in need of sleep, was also awake most of the night. She fretted about their future in this new strange country but also tried to console her husband. In turn, he tried vainly to comfort her but she couldn't refrain from wishing that the Pluennekes had never agreed to emigrate. At last, she was comforted by the notion that Conrad would take care of her and dozed off for a few hours.

Rising early the next morning and walking outside, the newcomers were pleased to see that the rain had stopped and sunshine was pouring through the trees east of Karlshafen. The Norther, which had dogged them for two days, had passed and left them with a cold but clearing sky. The patches of blue sky overhead lifted their spirits and gave them the needed resolve to overcome their woes temporarily. Inside, the agents made a roaring fire in the large stone fireplace and prepared a breakfast of coffee and hard biscuits for the group.

After eating, the men were taken back to the warehouse at Indian Point where their larger belongings had been stored in a warehouse. With some searching, Conrad and his father found their belongings. After considering different options, they decided to dismantle the wooden crates that housed the furniture they had brought from Germany and use the crate material to construct a crude shelter for the family. With some effort, they managed to drag their larger crates out of the warehouse and onto the wharf. Rummaging through other chests, they found their carpentry tools and began to disassemble the containers, carefully preserving them. After several hours, they had enough wooden sidings to build a modest hut. They took their furniture back into the warehouse, stacked it in a corner, and covered it with old blankets. With the help of an agent, they loaded their wooden crate material onto an ox cart and the agent set about driving them back to Karlshafen. With the cart full of lumber, Conrad and his father had no choice but to slog through the mud on foot beside the cart.

At the small colony, they searched for a decent spot on which to erect their hut. They started with an area that still had trees. Much of the vicinity was a morass of water puddles and mud but they did manage to find a slightly elevated spot of ground near a large, distinctive tree. It was some distance from the German Emigration Building but that spot was much better than many areas that were nearer the office and the large crooked tree might serve as a landmark to locate their hut.

The first step was to try to level off the spot. With shovels, they flattened an area and then stomped on the mud to make the base firm enough to build on. Later, they would try to find stones or something else to form a solid floor that would separate family members from the cold, damp ground but found nothing. With their site prepared, they began to nail the crate sides together to form a simple rectangular box. When they had the box solidly pinned together, they used the remaining wood to form a slightly pitched shed roof that hung over the walls. With saws, they cut out a doorway and used leather laces from old boots to hinge the door in place. It wasn't at all fancy but it was capable of withstanding moderate foul weather. Where there were gaps in the structure, they stuffed rags, paper, and bits of clothing into the holes to prevent cold wind and rain from penetrating to its interior. That crude structure became the Pluenneke's first home in Texas.

The building effort had taken nearly all day. Weary from hard work, the two men returned to the Verein Building late in the afternoon to reunite with their family. Agents had prepared a scanty meal of roasted corn, biscuits, and some very tough venison that barely fed everyone. After eating, the Pluennekes collected their humble belongings, carried them to their new shack, and moved in. Since a quick late afternoon search had failed to reveal useable stones in the area, a few remnants of wood planks were used to create a temporary floor under their bedding. In the tiny space with their baggage, there was barely enough room for six people to lie down so the men volunteered to sleep sitting against the wall but on opposite sides. Although the tiny hut was very crowded, they slept better during their second night in Texas because they were exhausted but mostly because there were fewer people in the space to bother them.

When they arose early the next day, they were pleased to see blue skies again, although the air temperature was downright frigid. In the crisp January atmosphere, the family set out to walk to the Verein Building for provisions. As they walked at a fast and purposeful clip, they noticed shelters that other newly arrived immigrants had built. Some were haphazardly constructed with little or no regard for stability or resistance to weather. Others were variations of tents, made from fabrics brought from Germany.

"Those," Conrad whispered to his wife, "will not suffice in bad weather."

Here and there, crude log cabins had been built with a palisade wall style of building. Obviously, those structures had taken quite an effort and were built by occupants who obviously planned to be there for some time to come. For their efforts, they were rewarded with more comfort against the elements than most of the other families in Karlshafen. Among the huts were a few cabins that were very well built and Conrad's father speculated that those must be the living quarters of Adelsverein agents.

At the building, the immigrants were again treated to a simple breakfast but were warned by the agents that from that day forward, they would only be given provisions by the Verein when they became available. The Society had contracts with farmers in the Houston who were hired to provide meat and vegetables but those goods had to be moved by wagons and they were scarce. From that day until they departed for New Braunfels, they had to find their own firewood and prepare their own meals. When provisions did arrive from Houston, Galveston, or The Plantation at Industry, the new colonists were instructed to come to the Verein Building to get their family's allotment of food. Their full ration of food for coming weeks would be issued sometime later. With that announcement, the newcomers were subtly forewarned that they would likely have to fend for themselves until they settled on their land and began to farm. That took more of Johann Heinrich's money.

Several days after their arrival, another group meeting was held in the German Immigration Company building. It was announced that the Fisher-Miller Grant was not open to settlement, as had been promised. That statement created a loud commotion in the room. The land, it was explained, was still occupied by the fierce Comanche tribe and they had to be dealt with, either militarily or by negotiation and treaty. Further, it had not been surveyed nor had roads to it been established. The Verein hoped that the Grant would be opened early in 1847. It was rumored that Meusebach was planning a foray into Comanche country to negotiate peace with them and that would change everything.

Someone in the group stood up and shouted, "If the Fisher-Miller Grant is not open, where will we all go? How are we to survive here in Texas until it opens?"

The agent replied that when transportation became available, they would be moved to the new colony of New Braunfels in "west Texas" and there, each family would be given land in the colony plus acreage to farm. When the grant did open, they would still receive their full entitlement to 320 acres in it. Immediately, the immigrants realized that things were not going to unfold as they had been led to believe when they signed up for emigration to Texas. How many people could the colony of New Braunfels hold?

Again, a loud tumult arose from the crowd that was now bordering on becoming unruly. Some of them waved their fists angrily at the agents and demanded that they be returned to Germany but only a few managed to arrange that. Those who returned had to use their own funds. Others wanted their fees refunded. Others threatened to file suit against the Verein and some eventually did. Yet others plotted to desert their relatives and to walk to the interior but most of those who tried to walk inland never made it. The blunt announcements had caused great concern among the immigrants about what their future was going to be like in this new world. The agents pleaded for patience and counseled the crowd to wait and see what changes the future might bring. The Pluennekes were among those who chose to wait.

Over the course of a few weeks, life in Karlshafen took on a certain tedious rhythm. Marooned in dire surroundings and living in very cramped quarters, daily life for the family became one of trying to make time pass more quickly and trying to think positively about their future. They pondered what their land in the Fisher-Miller Grant might look like and what type of house the Adelsverein would build for them, that is, if it was still capable of providing housing for its clients.

Living in those primitive conditions was extremely difficult. There was no source for fresh water except for what fell from the skies. Pots and pans were set outside of the huts during storms to catch falling rain which was used strictly for cooking, drinking, and very light bathing. Sanitation in those conditions was nearly impossible. It took extreme effort to walk far enough from camp to defecate or urinate in privacy. A few chose not to make that effort nor did they attempt to bury it. As a result, human waste came in contact with groundwater and with mud, which stuck to boots. When the footwear was removed, the contaminated mud found its way from the boots onto hands and into mouths. It was a filthy miserable existence and the potential for disease was everywhere around them but in that era, no one knew that contaminated water could lead to cholera.

All around the Pluenneke's hut, unfortunate German immigrants from other families were dying of malnutrition, exhaustion, and disease. [27]Almost daily, it seemed that one family or another had to bury one of their own. It was obvious that many, many immigrants were dying in Karlshafen.[28]

With mud that clung tenaciously to shovels, it was very challenging to dig a grave deep enough to bury an adult. As a result, graves were shallower than they should have been. Bodies were occasionally unearthed by wolves, coyotes, and other scavenging animals. They ate the corpses and left bones strewn about the area, which gave Karlshafen's surroundings a macabre appearance. Those decaying human carcasses also made conditions even less sanitary as rotting tissues became mixed with ground water and exacerbated an already bad situation. In that mess, diseases such as cholera and dysentery went unchecked. Cholera, *the disease that walks in darkness* was on the move again.

For an ambitious, energetic young man like Conrad Pluenneke, life at Karlshafen was extremely dismal and boring. He yearned for the family to get out of Karlshafen and get on with their lives. Many days, he was trapped with his family inside their crude makeshift shelter, waiting out what seemed like an endless parade of storm squalls and inclement weather. To pass time, the family sang or read from the *Bible*. Sometimes, they talked about their dream property in Texas and what it might look like. With six people jammed into a tiny cramped space, there was no room to move around nor was there privacy. Dur-

---

[27] The other three Pluennekes who arrived on the *Apollo*. were apparently among those who died at Karlshafen.

[28] Later, a medical doctor (Keister) who had been employed by the Adelsverein and a reporter (Frederick Kapp) estimated that less than half of the 5,347 immigrants who arrived in 1845 and early 1846 survived to live in one of its colonies. Conrad Pluenneke was one the fortunate survivors.

ing rainstorms, they often sat on planks or on the earthen floor with their backs against the crude walls. Those frequent freshets left the area in and around Karlshafen even more inundated with water and deep mud. When the weather did allow them to wander outside the hut, the deep sucking mud and ooze made getting around in the tiny enclave very difficult. Boots sometimes came off feet and were lost in the deep mire.

Within a few weeks of arriving at Karlshafen, Conrad's wife began to grow weaker and weaker. She lost her appetite and slept very poorly in their crude shelter. She began to lose weight and could not seem to stay warm for very long. In despair, her spirits sagged. Conrad tried to coax her to eat, talked to her about maintaining her strength, and generally tried to comfort her in every way he could think of but his efforts were all for naught, -- futile. Her health steadily declined and she became morose. He made coffee for her, piled his blankets on top of her, and even placed his own coat over her to keep her warm but she continued to shiver. She felt thirsty so Conrad gave her water.

"I want to go home," she said over and over, meaning Klein-Lafferde but there was no way to escape from their plight in Karlshafen.

On February 17th, she began to exhibit symptoms that were now all too familiar to the Pluenneke family. At first, she began to feel nauseous and faint. To make her more comfortable, the family created more space in the cramped hut in which she could stretch out. Conrad tried to keep her warm by covering her with blankets and giving her hot drinks, even adding a bit of schnapps to it. Within an hour, she then began to have stomach cramps followed by prolonged vomiting. The family, now knowing what to expect, summoned the colony's only medical person who checked her and gave a preliminary diagnosis of cholera. The entire family shuddered because they instantly knew how this would play out. Conrad tended to her, making warm drinks, cleaning away her vomit, comforting her as best he could, and encouraging her to fight for her life. He tried to pray for her deliverance, offering a bargain to God if he would but spare her from death. Nothing had an effect and she continued to decline. Within a matter of hours, Conrad's wife died while he cradled her head in his arms. He was devastated and screamed at the heavens! Why had God not intervened and saved her?

The family summoned the doctor who checked for a pulse and finding none, pronounced her dead. He encouraged the family to bury her quickly to avoid spread of the disease. His pronouncement was a crushing blow to Conrad and to his dreams about what life was going to be like in Texas. He had brought her here to this Godforsaken place and she was dead. He sat, tears running down his face, muttering inaudibly.

As he looked at his wife's lifeless body, he went into a state of denial. "This cannot be happening," he thought. "She cannot be dead - she just cannot be dead! This must be a bad dream. I'll wake up in a moment and she will be alive and healthy," he sobbed plaintively. But she didn't stir!

He stared at her now blue, gaunt, and vacant face, hoping for a sign of life but there was none. For a moment, he thought he detected a slight twitch but that was just a figment of his imagination. It was difficult for him to absorb in that moment but her lifeless body before him was more than enough tangible proof that she was dead. His wife was gone forever and he was powerless to do anything about it.

At that point, the absolute nature of death hit him like a heavy blow to the gut. He stood up abruptly, felt faint, and his knees buckled slightly. Her death was final! His head reeled and he felt dizzy but he had to face the awful truth that his dear, loving wife was dead and nothing, absolutely nothing, he could do or say would bring her back to life. He would never see her beautiful smile again nor would he ever hear her laugh again. She was gone from his life.

Slowly, his deep sadness and distress turned to anger towards the Adelsverein and then to guilt. Her death was his fault. If he had only been content to stay in Germany and farm, none of these deaths would have occurred.

"Why could I not have been content to lead the simple life of a farmer?", he asked. "Why?"

His father tried to comfort him by saying, "All of us agreed to emigrate to America and we all knew there would be risks. For all we know, she might have died in Germany or somewhere else. It is not your fault, Conrad."

Embracing his son, he whispered in his ear, "Death is a part of life that we have to experience. When you have lived as long as I have, you will realize that bad things happen in life, even to good people and for no apparent reason. We don't know what God has planned for us. Discovering that is just part of human life." That whispered statement caused Conrad to pause and really confront the idea of a real God in the universe for the first time in his life. A being that might control human destiny.

If there is a God, why had that Omnipotent Being allowed his young wife to die? She, nor he, were evil; a little vain perhaps but not bad. As best as he could recall, they had committed no major sins or at least, none that would require such a huge atonement. While the Pluennekes were not deeply religious, they had gone to church regularly and had generally led good, productive lives in Klein-Lafferde. They were good people. Why had God chosen to harm them or, at least, not protect them when obviously bad, sinful people had been left untouched? It just didn't make sense.

At that point, Conrad's overwhelming grief morphed into anger and then outright contempt.

"What value is there in having a Shepherd who does not protect his flock, particularly the good ones?" he flashed sharply.

Those thoughts raised more questions in his mind. Was God absent, off somewhere tending to a flock in another universe? Or was God distracted by something else or preoccupied with someone else at the time of his wife's death? Or was God simply a Creator who, having created the world, vanished forever. Or more simply, was there no God at all?

In books that he had read back in Germany, philosophers had contemplated the possibility that the universe is just a random development, without design and without purpose, a place where things can occur by chance? "Maybe they were right," Conrad thought.

In his current state, he had to admit to himself that he had never truly felt the presence of God, at least not one that communicated with him in any direct or personal way. Maybe God simply does not exist and the universe is just a huge random, chaotic mirage created by hu-

man beings to bring the illusion of order where none exists? Maybe
Earth is just a place where things are determined by the roll of dice? If
that was the case, did accidents and death occur simply because everything changes constantly?

To rid himself of overwhelming guilt, he tried to focus his hatred
on something else. If not on a real God, then the concept of a God.
Mentally, he went on to rationalize that if death is random, then her
death was not anyone's fault it was just another in a long line of capricious events in the lives of human beings.

That line of thinking sent shivers down Conrad's spine. If the universe was not orderly and predictable, then such awful random events
like his wife's untimely death could and likely would occur repeatedly
at unpredictable times throughout his life. If that was the case, it was
impossible for him or anyone else to avoid them. It was like standing
on the tracks in front of a runaway train. It ends in doom. With the
new realization that he was now extremely vulnerable, he clenched his
fist, gestured at the sky, and uttered a long, painful scream. After that
futile gesture, he turned and tried to face reality. All that mattered now
was how he dealt with events that would occur in his life in coming
days.

In a state of deep depression, Conrad walked out into the tangled
brush around Karlshafen with a shovel on his shoulder, searching for
an appropriate burial spot for his young wife. In time, he found a suitable place where a grave might be dug near a pair of tall trees. With a
great deal of effort, he dug a hole three feet down in the sucking mud.
With much searching, he found a pair of logs that he lugged to the
grave site and then returned to the family hut. While he had been dig-
ging the grave, his mother had prepared his wife's body for burial by
wrapping it in one of their old blankets. Now, he hoisted her wrapped,
limp body on his shoulders and trudged through the muck to place her
gently in her final resting place. With tears forming in his eyes, he
could not dispel his feeling that her life was not supposed to end this
way. She had so much to look forward to in the future: a new home
and a family, perhaps. He had wanted children and now there would be
none. His grief was overwhelming and soon, hot bitter tears welled up
in his eyes and rolled down his cheeks. At the gravesite, he lowered
her body gently into the hole, patted it through the old blanket, placed
a piece of her favorite jewelry in the blanket with her, and said his sor-

rowful goodbye to her. After a moment of anguish, he laboriously covered her body with mud and then piled the logs on the grave.

For a while afterward, he sat on his haunches near the grave and thought about the life they had lived together. They had been happy in Germany and he now felt sadness and deep regret that he had dragged her to this awful place and especially to an early death. True, it wasn't entirely his fault but--! As he stood to leave the gravesite, he wasn't completely sure how he could survive in coming days without her. She meant so much to him and his world had revolved around her. His future now seemed so bleak and he was certain he would never meet someone like her again. In an hour or so, he pulled himself together, stood up, and returned to the hut only to sit in silence while his family tried to console him, but nothing helped salve the wound! He knew his pain would lessen over time but in that moment, it was awful and unbearable.

"If only I could just leap forward in time and skip the long painful recovery period," he said wistfully to himself but he knew that was impossible. He just had to endure the pain until time lessened it.

The pain was intense for days and weeks after her death. In the darkness of night, her quiet voice seemed to reach out to him from her grave and assure him by whispering "Conrad, allez gute" but that didn't help. He couldn't sleep and he couldn't eat. Memories of her randomly popped up in his consciousness. The lack of sleep wore on him and he began to grow listless and very depressed.

During lulls in the storms that continued to drench Karlshafen, Conrad put on his boots and overcoat to venture out with his father to talk to other men and at times, with Society employees. Socializing with them became a form of escape. Some of the men who collected under trees in the camp were going through what he was experiencing now. They too had lost loved ones in Karlshafen and were openly sad. Those sessions allowed the bereaved to vent and to alleviate boredom but they also became a means to obtain and pass along news that affected the immigrants.

During these conversations, many of the men talked about the new state of Texas that had officially become the newest state in the United States. As they had been told by Verein agents, statehood had occurred in December of 1845, while the *brig Apollo* was still at sea. From men who had contact with people in Galveston, they confirmed that the admission of Texas to the U.S., however, had greatly displeased its southern neighbor, Mexico. Mexicans living in southern Texas had always felt their nation would reclaim Texas one day and return it to their national fold. Now, their hopes had been dashed forever because Texas had become part of the United States and it was never going to be part of Mexico again. The men further learned that tensions between Mexico and the United States were increasing daily. Troops from both countries were heading for the Rio Grande area and it seemed certain both countries intended to fight over the border issue.[29] There were rumors of minor skirmishes as both sides jockeyed across the big river for position in southern Texas.

For some of the older immigrants, war was an old adversary, something to be dreaded and avoided where possible because of the devastation it left behind. But for others, it offered them an opportunity to prove to dubious Americans that the German immigrants could contribute to America's cause and that they mattered. In their discussions, the question increasingly seemed to be how they, as non-English speaking and foreign-born men, could find a way to help their new state. In time, one of them would summon his Prussian heritage and step forward to offer an answer to the rest of them. They would join the fight!

---

[29] *Report on the Army of Occupation* in The Civilian and Galveston Gazette, Volume 8, February 26, 1846.

Chapter 4

THE MEXICAN-AMERICAN WAR

In Karlshafen, the men's daily conversations became increasingly about the state of Texas and the possibility of an armed conflict with Mexico. To the German men who had come to maturity during the Napoleonic Wars or on the heels of them, all the signs seemed to point towards an all-out war between Mexico and the United States of America. After a diplomatic effort by the United States had failed to resolve its border issue with Mexico, President Polk had ordered troops and supporting materiel towards the Rio Grande to check the northward movement of the Mexican army in that region. Mexico mirrored that movement. If war did erupt, even more wagons, draft animals, and teamsters would be required by the U.S. Army to move its men and supplies to south Texas and possibly deeper into the interior of Mexico. War meant that even fewer wagons and teams would be available to move German immigrants, who were now stranded in Karlshafen, north to Adelsverein colonies. As a consequence, they might be forced to remain at Karlshafen for a lengthy time, possibly months or maybe even a year, in their miserable condition. That fate was intolerable to settlers who needed desperately to get to their land, create farms out of raw land, and begin to feed their families.

Every visitor to Karlshafen brought news of military moves on both sides of the conflict and that information filtered into meetings at the enclave where perhaps a hundred young men were idling away time, waiting for transportation inland. Among those men was Augustus Buchel, a young man of Prussian descent and in whose 33 years of life, had military experience in both France and Turkey. It was his opinion that the U.S. was going to fight Mexico, not only for the southern part of Texas that lay between the Nueces and Rio Grande rivers but also for the land that stretched from Texas to California. As a military man, he wanted to be part of that action. As he made his way around the village of Karlshafen, he talked to other idle young men and began to make the case for raising a militia in Karlshafen that could help their newly adopted country fight the Mexicans. If war did break out, and if they could obtain Volunteer status from the state of Texas, it was said that the U.S. would pay as much as $8 per month to those who joined the Texas militia and officially become part of the

U.S. Army. For those with little or no money, this was an opportunity. With this added information, more young men began to support the idea, especially since they would be paid for their service. Going off to war beat sitting around Karlshafen, waiting for wagons.

At first, Conrad Pluenneke was indifferent, and maybe even a little opposed, to the idea of joining a German immigrant militia. He had left Germany partly because he wished to avoid conscription into the military. Further, going off to fight in Mexico where he would have an uncertain future was a radical departure from his purpose of settling in Texas. Indeed, it was a deviation from his plan but those aspirations now seemed so distant in the wake of his wife's death and all the tragic events that had beset his family enroute to Texas. Along with his own issues, he had family matters to think about. His elderly parents as well as his two remaining siblings needed his help and support now more than ever and he felt that he owed them some responsibility. Of the remaining family members, he alone had the strength and stamina to shepherd them to their new home and establish a farm. As the eldest son, his brawn and his intellect would be needed in coming days to keep the family functioning in the difficult times that likely lay ahead.

While the Society was able to provide meager provisions sporadically for all of its clients, their delay in getting to their land and starting a farm was entirely unforeseen. Most of the immigrants had planned to farm in the first year as a means to support their families. With that plan gone awry, they lacked money to sustain their families for a lengthy period. With the Adelsverein in financial straits, the immigrants were forced to pay for more of their own expenses, mostly food and some clothing, or do without. Those unplanned expenses, even small ones, caused a slow and steady drain on the resources they brought with them from Germany. Over a few weeks, Conrad's attitude about joining the Texas militia began to reverse. The Pluennekes needed money. His father now had less than $50. After his wife's death, dark thoughts often flooded into his mind and possessed him. He had unwittingly slid into a depression and desperately needed to have a purpose in life again. Now widowed, he began to feel that serving in the Texas militia might provide a new purpose for him or somehow revitalize his original plan. Along with the possibility of renewed motivation, he would also receive some income and that would help his family. Perhaps what is more important, Conrad also felt a need to do something to demonstrate to his newly adopted country that he had something to offer it. Symbolically, he wanted to show Texians like those protestors in Galveston that the German immigrants were worthy of citizenship in their state and their country. He was new to America but not to the concept of Nationalism.

Slowly, Conrad's attitude softened and then changed completely. He discussed the idea of enlisting with his father who plainly did not want to risk losing his only remaining son to another war in which the family had no stake. They had left Germany in part so that Conrad and Friedrich would never have to serve in the Prussian army. In the end, however, father and son came to an arrangement. The father, who was far too elderly to enlist, would consent, however uneasily, to Conrad's enlistment in the Texas volunteers while he, Johann Heinrich, would stay in Karlshafen to protect the family. [30] It was understood that Conrad would write frequently and send some of his army pay back to the family. It was planned that after his stint in the Texas militia, Conrad would return to Karlshafen where the family would reunite and then he would help escort the Pluenneke family to New Braunfels or to the Fisher-Miller Grant, if it was open by then. That was an arrangement to which they both could agree.

In early April, it was learned in Karlshafen that John O. Meusebach, the Commissioner General of the Society, was going to establish another colony between New Braunfels and the most southern region of the Fisher-Miller Grant. Not only was the new colony planned to be another stepping stone to the Grant area, immigrants were piling up in New Braunfels and thus overcrowding that colony. Those conditions forced Meusebach to act. In addition, he had to begin moving people north towards the Grant to meet contractual deadlines for settling the land. In Karlshafen, it was learned that Meusebach had bought 10,000 acres of land near the junction of several permanent rivers about 90 miles northwest of New Braunfels and had already dispatched surveyors to lay out a township there. Work was already underway to build a road from New Braunfels to the new colony, using parts of the old historic Pinta Trail. When transportation became available, the new settlers could look forward to going beyond New Braunfels to the newest Adelsverein colony and from there, into the Fisher-Miller Grant when it opened. That news brought with it some optimism.

---

[30] The author has assumed that Conrad would not have enlisted unless he was certain that his father was healthy and able to care for the rest of the family.

At about the same time, more rumors about General Taylor and his army's movements filtered into Karlshafen. The immigrants learned that he had built a large camp near Galveston and then had recently had struck camp to move southwestward to St. Joseph's Island, near the mouth of the Nueces River (near modern day Corpus Christi). Wagons, teamsters, and draft animals were rapidly being sent there to support Taylor's anticipated move to a position even further south. From there, it was thought that General Taylor planned to advance to Point Isabel at the mouth of the Rio Grande River and create a permanent base somewhere along the north bank of the Rio Grande River. To the immigrants in Karlshafen, those moves meant that war was almost certainly coming.

During April, August Buchel slowly began to enlist men in his informal quasi-military company. During lulls in the rain, he began to instruct the men about serving in the military. About a mile north of Karlshafen, Buchel located a flat piece of land that was slightly higher and a little dryer than the surrounding land. With some work, the site could be made into a place that could be used for military drills. In a few days, he and a few volunteers cleared the land of overgrown brush and drained away some of the standing water. Back in the village, Buchel announced that drills would begin the next day for those who wished to join his company. The young men who wished to enlist were told to report to the drill field by shortly after sunrise and bring their knapsacks as well as their long rifles with them. Conrad's army career in Texas had begun.

When they reported to the crude parade grounds at Karlshafen, the men were a heterogeneous lot with little or no organization. Many were still weak from months of idleness, malnutrition, and mild bouts with disease. Some wore pieces of old Prussian uniforms while others wore cottonelle pants and tattered shirts. Some had hats while others did not. Their clothing was wrinkled and dirty, not neat like the uniforms of professional soldiers. In the drills that followed, Buchel taught his recruits the basics of army life: how to march as a unit, how to salute superior officers, and how to fight. To help with command of the unit, Buchel made Emil Kriewitz his First Sergeant of the unit. Day after day, Kriewitz marched his troops in reasonably straight columns, pivoting right and then pivoting left on command, as "Colonel" Buchel looked on. In time, they learned about command structure and the necessity to always follow orders. Slowly, the ragtag outfit began to look and behave in a more organized military manner on the parade field. When they had mastered the art of marching, Augustus Buchel marched them to Port Lavaca and back, a distance of 20 miles, to build their stamina.

While training in Buchel's Company, Conrad met a young man who was just a few months older than himself and from the same general area of Germany. With much in common, they quickly became good friends. Heinrich Leifeste [31] was from the vicinity of Klein-Lafferde and fully understood socio-economic conditions in that part of the country. He too had been a farmer but under the Law of Primogeniture, he had come to realize very early in life that he was not going to inherit the family farm. His family situation was complex and unhappy so he, along with a younger brother and a younger sister, had decided to emigrate to Texas. In their family arrangement, it was decided that Friedrich would not enlist. Instead, he would accompany their sister to a colony inland, most likely Fredericksburg, when wagons began to roll again. There, he would build a log cabin and start their farm while awaiting Heinrich's arrival.

While his troops were being shaped up on the parade grounds by Emil Kriewitz, Augustus Buchel privately met with Meusebach and requested his aid in contacting the Governor of Texas about official recognition for his new German militia. Immediately, Meusebach grasped the merit of creating an all-German company of immigrants to fight against Mexico alongside other Texas volunteer units. As Commissioner General, he knew the Verein would continually need assistance from the state of Texas in the future and its elected officials might be more receptive to those pleas if unsolicited help was offered at the state's moment of need. Meusebach interceded on behalf of Augustus Buchel and shortly thereafter, the Governor issued his approval. The company became a part of the First Regiment of Texas Foot Rifles, with Augustus Buchel as its Captain.

Shortly after border tensions became a shooting war, the Texas Foot Rifle regiment was mustered into the U.S. Army on May 28 of 1846 as Company H of the First Texas Rifle volunteer regiment,

---

[31] Heinrich Leifeste has been described as being 5'3" tall, with light hair, and blue eyes. In *Look Unto the Hills: the Leifeste Family in the United States* by Ruby and Julius DeVos (1985).

commanded by Colonel Albert Sidney Johnston. By enlisting, they agreed to serve six months, from May until November, and were to be paid $8 per month for their duty. As part of the U.S. military, they also qualified to receive a pension.[32]

General Johnston was a colorful military figure and a true warrior at heart. Trained at West Point, he had served ably in Indian Wars on the southwest frontier of the U.S. in the early 1840s. Those wars forcibly removed indigenous Indian tribes from their ancestral home in Mississippi and forced them westward to Arkansas and Oklahoma. Subsequently, he received a commission to be an officer in the Army of the Republic of Texas and moved to Galveston but when Texas was annexed by the U.S. in December of 1845, his commission was lost. At the outbreak of the Mexican-American War in the spring of 1846, Johnston was in Galveston at the home of a friend, Colonel Love, and without a command. He had expected an appointment as Colonel in a new U.S. regiment that was being formed for duty in Texas, but that appointment became mired down in politics because of his outspoken Whiggish views. As a result of those political views, he had a poor standing with Sam Houston, who was not only the hero of Texas's War of independence and the first president of the Texas Republic but was now one of the state's U.S. Senators. Houston used his influence to block al potential assignments for Johnston in Texas and so the General was languishing at Love's home when the War with Mexico began. His wife actively opposed his service in wars but he longed to be in the fray and lobbied his friends to help get him involved in Texas. Fortunately, he was well remembered by General Zachary Taylor from the Black Hawk campaign along the Mississippi River. In April of 1846, Taylor sent a message inviting Albert Sidney Johnston to join his forces in Texas. He jumped at the opportunity and prepared to go, over objections from Mrs. Johnston.

Unable to get transport by sea, he and a group of volunteers hurriedly left Galveston for Point Isabel on horseback, a journey of more than 300 miles. Enroute, his party was joined by other volunteers, including Colonel Buchel's Company H, which joined up with it at the military camp on St. Joseph's Island, near the modern day city of Corpus Christi. The party also included a notable reporter from the New Orleans Picayune newspaper, George Wilkins Kendall, who would

---

[32] See Appendix 3 Conrad Pluenneke's Army Pension document.

chronicle their trip and later write a book about the war. Johnston had no official command or rank until Governor Henderson appeared and took command of the volunteers. By Texas law, the regiment had to conduct a vote to elect their commanding officers. They overwhelmingly approved Johnston for the rank of Colonel and accepted him as the commander of their regiment. A month after leaving Galveston, Johnston's volunteer forces were joined into a much larger command led by Major Jack Hays, a noted Texas Ranger. Kendall reported that on June 6th, "the entire company of Hays, more three hundred strong, rode into Taylor's lines at Point Isabel." They stayed at Point Isabel over a month, drilling and training for combat.

According to Roland (2001), Johnston's regiment found an abundance of sand, heat, and confusion at Point Isabel which was located on the Gulf of Mexico. At the center of the point was Ft. Polk, a hastily erected earthwork located on a 30 foot bluff overlooking the gulf. Inside it, a few score of tents and a half dozen Sutler's huts stood in the midst of a wide array of army supplies and the booty of war, including captured Mexican guns, lances, drums, saddles, and other artifacts. Around the fortress were the encamped volunteers.

The Texas volunteers were without organization, having straggled into service from various towns around the large state. In short order, Colonel Johnston set about shaping them into an integrated fighting unit, a task he was good at. In sweltering heat and amidst occasional heavy downpours, General Johnston whipped his unit into readiness. It was a vexing job but he performed it well, by all accounts.

Johnston's regiment had arrived in south Texas too late to participate in the initial battles of the war, first at Palo Alto and then at Resaca de la Palmas, all of which happened in early May. When Mexican towns were taken, Johnson's unit performed garrison duty and defended Point Isabel, Matamoros, and Camargo in succession. Their longest deployment was at the Mexican city of Matamoros, a place that many American soldiers found very different and very interesting.

In early June, Company H packed up its gear at Point Isabel and marched 27 miles to Matamoros, taking three days to cover the distance. Their route generally traced the northern side of the Rio Grande. Near Matamoros, the regiment was ferried across the big river on a steamboat, Big Hatchee, and immediately took up residence in the finest buildings at the center of town. In Matamoros, Johnston's men were issued Colt "Walker Special" revolvers and tin-encased bullets.[33]

For the soldiers of Company H, the march to Matamoros was grueling in the hot and humid climate. Having lived in a cold climate as recently as six months before duty, most of them were unaccustomed to the sultry weather of southern Texas. In addition, they had lived on a boat for nearly three months. Many of them were in a somewhat weakened state, despite Kriewitz's marches at Karlshafen. Their altered diet had also affected their health. At sea, many had become malnourished because the food on the Verein's ships was putrid and the food at Karlshafen was only slightly better. Some of the men had also suffered through mild bouts with various diseases during the voyage and were understandably weaker and more frail than normal. None the less, they bravely marched westward to Mexico.

As the members of Company H saw it, Matamoros was an old Spanish city situated on the southern side of a large horseshoe bend in the Rio Grande River. In that position, it was bounded on three sides by water.

An American soldier, Thomas Tennery (1970) saw it both from directly across the Rio Grande at Fort Brown and then from within the city itself as part of the occupying force in May of 1846. He described Matamoros in his diary as having "every appearance of being an American town. The streets intersect one another at right angles and are lined by a variety of shade trees, which give the town an air of coolness and renders its appearance very inviting. Many of the buildings are made of brick (adobe) and in the modern style of architecture. The cathedral and market on the central plaza are among the finest (buildings). The dwellings of the poorer classes are constructed with canes, brush, mud, and the like. The town has about 7,000 inhabitants but (once) contained double that number and was a place of importance. Its rapid decline is owing to their internal commotions and growing indolence of the people. The citizens are under the rule of the (Mexican) military which is obligated to provide for them. The vicinity of Matamoros is peopled on both sides of the Rio Grande by Mexicans–who have actively carried on the war against Texas since its beginning."

---

[33] In 1847, the Texas Rangers ordered 2,000 such pistols from Colt's company for use in the Mexican-American War.

Another American soldier noted in his diary that the sidewalks of the city were paved with adobe bricks and that shops in the city were open and conducting business as usual, even though occupied by a foreign power. He also noted that a large adobe wall surrounded it.

The citizens seemed to regard the foreigners as good for business. Some soldiers bought food and other goods from the shops, paying with U.S. dollars that were preferred by the shopkeepers over Mexican currency. Some of the items bought by American soldiers were culture-specific art objects that they packaged up and sent home to wives or other loved ones. Some of the soldiers attended Mass on Sundays at the large Catholic Church that was situated in the central plaza, a massive adobe building that they noted was still unfinished. They attended Catholic services because there were no Protestant churches in Matamoros. Mexican law at the time required that its citizens belong to the Catholic Church. Being Protestant, the diaries of American soldiers recorded observations of what the men saw as odd Catholic religious practices. For example, the Mexican Priests conducted the masses in Latin and faced away from the congregation (as they would have in the U.S.). Further, members of the Parish were observed praying to statues (particularly the Virgin Mary), reciting *The Lord's Prayer* using the beads of their rosaries, making the sign of the cross, and attending confession. These practices were very different from what Protestant men were accustomed to back home.

To the soldiers, the Mexican people overtly seemed proper but other behaviors seemed to betray that piety. Several soldiers noted in their diaries that the local senoritas, rather than shunning the foreign warriors, made extra efforts to flirt with them and often invited some of the men to attend dances held on Saturday nights in the central plaza. They also bared their bodies freely. The men were exhilarated to dance the Spanish Fandango with the young senoritas and often seemed to forget that a war was going on with Mexico. When Mexican women went to the river naked to bathe, the troops crowded around the river and watched. Brothels were common and some men availed themselves of those services, but at a high risk. Sexually transmitted diseases were rampant in the towns along the Rio Grande and American soldiers were infected regularly. Liquor was also plentiful and available at relatively cheap prices. Many of the young men, including Conrad Pluenneke, found a taste for tequila and often drank themselves into a delirium. For young single men in the military, Matamoros was a good duty station.

In diaries and in letters to relatives back home, several soldiers wrote that there were many Hispanic citizens on both sides of the Rio Grande whose allegiance was to Mexico and that a large militia could be raised quickly from their number, should they be induced to serve on the Mexican side. For that and other reasons, the men in the garrison did not trust the Mexican populace. Despite their overt hospitality and their pandering to an occupying force, the soldiers felt that many of the Mexicans were always ready to kill American soldiers and plunder U.S. property whenever they had the opportunity. A dangerous guerrilla band, headed by General Antonio Canales, constantly marauded the weaker and more isolated U.S. positions on the flanks of Matamoros, causing great uneasiness for sentries. His forces would suddenly charge into town on horseback, kill soldiers, and seemingly evaporate into the very air of the countryside. Because of such unpredictable incursions, garrisoning, while not strictly in the combat zone, was considered dangerous duty. Those violent and unexpected guerilla raids often infuriated members of the regular U.S. army and in particular, the Texas Rangers. When they were given the opportunity, they brutally and excessively avenged those atrocities.

Along with Company H volunteers, units of the Texas Rangers were stationed at Matamoros and later at Camargo. Their duty was to protect the American troops and those who were performing garrison duty from Mexican guerillas operating in the countryside. They also served as the rear guard for troops marching towards Monterrey. The Mexican army, as well as the local Mexican citizenry, feared the Texas Rangers. They referred to them as "devils" because they seemed to lack fear and always retaliated harshly for what they described as Mexican atrocities, harking back to the Thornton Affair, Goliad, or the Alamo. No question, their retaliation was brutal and final. One ranger In particular, Captain McCulloch, was a renowned marksman who openly hated Mexicans and relished using them for target practice. It was said about him: "One bullet, one dead Mexican." That seems to have been his motto during the war in Mexico.

General Johnston also had a low regard for Mexicans. "As a race, the inhabitants are — inferior," he was quoted as saying, "resembling in color Indians of the US and not much superior to some of them in civilization."

It was into this milieu that Company H and other volunteer units landed in June of 1846. Their job was to occupy Matamoros and thus prevent Mexican forces from retaking it or from cutting off supply lines between Point Isabel and the forward operating stations, such as Carmargo, which was upriver from Matamoros.

Conrad Pluenneke, serious-minded, Lutheran, and recently widowed, generally refrained from the wild dancing and late night carousing that other soldiers engaged in at Matamoros but did swill Tequila on occasion. Still bereft and grieving over the loss of his wife and family members, he needed time to heal and sometimes took refuge in his military duties He frequently volunteered for extra assignments. In that mindset, he felt uncomfortable with immoral behavior that might seriously degrade his performance or that of the unit. Yet, he was intrigued by Mexican liquor. Back in Germany, he had occasionally sipped schnapps on holidays or drank wine now and then with a meal but they had little effect on him. Mexican liquor, especially Tequila, had a unique flavor and exerted a very powerful effect on him. It was smooth on the tongue but had a bite with an interesting aftertaste. After drinking a few shots of Tequila, he could escape his grief for a while and enjoy life again, if only briefly. Gradually, he came to acquire a dependency on it and drank more. He was convinced that Tequila helped him deal with his grief and bouts of depression. He ignored its bad side effects (i.e., hangovers) so long as they did not degrade his military performance.

Besides consuming Tequila, Conrad fell into other bad habits in the army. He was surrounded by men, mostly back-woodsy, coarse Americans who frequently cursed, bragged, spit, gambled, and lied. He could not help but absorb and inculcate some of those behaviors. It was part of army life. Unfortunately, those were the very qualities that American women, who were attempting to bring civility to the frontier, detested. Most women of that time were looking for men with gentle and more sophisticated habits. Later, Conrad Pluenneke would learn just how strong that sentiment was among women.

At Karlshafen and on the march from Karlshafen to Point Isabel, he became acquainted with Wilhelm Victor Keidel, the unit's medical doctor. A recent German immigrant from Hildescheim, a village not far removed from Klein-Lafferde, Dr. Keidel had attended the Georg Augustus Universitat in Gottingen from 1841 until 1845. Shortly after medical school, he had boarded the *brig Margaretha* and arrived in Galveston in December of 1845, only a month before Conrad's family arrived there. From all accounts, Doctor Keidel was also a serious-minded individual and worked diligently in the makeshift hospital at Matamoros and later at Carmargo, treating wounded soldiers and Mexican citizens alike. Upon learning that the hospital was short-handed, Conrad volunteered to assist Doctor Keidel as a collateral duty. He found work in the hospital, although a crude environment, interesting and soon learned to treat some of the more common medical cases. In Conrad Pluenneke, Doctor Keidel found a willing student, tutored him, and offered him medical books to read in his leisure time. While treating battlefield casualties, Keidel taught him to set broken bones, extract broken teeth, and stitch up minor wounds as well as administer doses of medicine. He also performed other small medical procedures that freed Doctor Keidel to concentrate on the difficult medical cases, such as amputation of limbs or dealing with various diseases.

Conrad's primary duty, however, was soldiering. Under the command of its immediate officer, Colonel Buchel, Company H drilled regularly in the plaza. Sometimes, the unit drilled alone and at other times, they drilled with volunteer units from other states. Represented in such drills were the states of Louisiana, Indiana, Mississippi, and Kentucky. Taken together, the volunteer units from other states were a ragtag army. They did not have regular or matching uniforms and they had no particular style that distinguished them from the regular army. For example, the volunteer company from Mississippi wore white duck pants, red shirts, and broad-brimmed straw hats. The volunteers from Texas were described as having the least military appearance of all the volunteer forces. Besides their appearance, Company H also suffered in that most of the men in that unit spoke only German and therefore had difficulty communicating with other volunteer units. They were often called "the Dutch" and ridiculed as foreigners, even though they were all in the U.S. Army. Always watching drills from the sidelines, General Albert Sidney Johnston wanted his troops to perform smartly but they often managed to disappoint him.

One of Conrad's main tasks in the Army was sentry duty. Regularly, he stood atop the walls of Matamoros and watched for suspicious behavior along the Rio Grande. He and his new friend Heinrich Leifeste were often assigned to night shifts and that gave them a chance to talk openly about their private lives while scanning the countryside. In those talks, Conrad confided to his friend about the loss of his wife and other members of his family. He revealed his mental anguish and how guilty he felt about his role in their death. In return, Heinrich Liefeste told Conrad about his family and their family's history in Boistedt. As a result such talks, a strong bond developed between the two men, one that would last a lifetime.

Much of the garrison duty came in June and July when the heat and humidity at Matamoros was overpowering. Along with high summer temperatures, monsoonal rains pounded the area almost every afternoon, inundating flat terrain around the town. That moisture, combined with already hot conditions, made the environment around Matamoros extremely sultry and almost unbearable. During some days, it was difficult to breathe the heavy air. To avoid the effects of high temperatures, drills were often slated for early in the morning or late in the afternoon. As a result of the sweltering heat and accumulating pools of stagnant water, viral diseases began to pop up amongst Company H soldiers. Mosquitos bred in the stagnant pools and spread malaria, yellow fever, and other diseases. With daily heavy rains, it became difficult to keep human waste out of the army's drinking water and cholera also began to spread through the unit. Those diseases had a debilitating effect on the troops of Company H. A few died and many soldiers became unable to report for daily drills or perform their collateral duties. As a result, the unit became unreliable in the eyes of Colonel Albert Sidney Johnston and he began to consider the idea of dismissing Company H as well as some of the other volunteer units in his command.

By the end of July, orders came down for General Johnston's men to pack up and move from Matamoros to Camargo and perform garrison duty there. It was hoped that the move from the quagmire that surrounded Matamoros might eliminate some of illnesses that Company H and other units had endured. Emil Kriewitz, the First Sergeant, helped organize the move and urged the men on through sweltering heat. As the men prepared to move out, more monsoonal rain fell in the Rio Grande valley and caused the big river to overflow its banks. Because of flooded lowlands and sweltering heat, the disease-ridden men slogged very slowly along a route that paralleled the Rio Grande River, passing though the town of Reynosa. At Reynosa, the unit stopped, rested for a day, and then resumed the march at night. It took Company H and the other volunteer companies nearly two weeks to slog 98 miles to Camargo, most often traveling at night or early morning to avoid the heat.

Almost every day on the march, they began to march well after sundown and plodded forward by torch light until midnight. After sleeping fitfully by the trail, they resumed the march at four in the morning and marched to mid morning, all to avoid the oppressive heat. As they neared midday, the soldiers sought refuge from the sun under the scant shade of mesquite trees, creosote bushes, or whatever place offered a little relief from the sun. Stinging insects, particularly mosquitos, were vicious and added to the misery of the march as did a variety of snakes. When the troops finally arrived at Carmargo, they discovered that the rampaging Rio Grande River had flooded the central area of the small town, leaving its streets covered with deep mud and debris. It was not habitable. Most of the residents of Camargo had already fled southward to higher ground where it was drier and cooler. Sizing up the situation, Colonel Albert Sidney Johnston ordered his troop to move on and occupy a dry dusty valley about three miles south of Carmargo, along the San Juan River. Lacking an understanding of how diseases were spread, the men used the waters of the San Juan for cooking, drinking, and bathing. As a result, disease once again ran rampant through the camp of Company H, even worse than at Matamoros. The diseases seemed to affect Company H more than other volunteer units. Colonel Albert Sidney Johnston attributed their susceptibility to disease to their poorly acclimated state, having only recently arrived from Europe. Volunteers in the regiment regularly came down with dysentery, measles, and light bouts of cholera. As before, those diseases badly affected Company H, causing at least 3 of the 88 men to die and others to become so weak that they could not report to perform their military drills. More than a few were sent to the makeshift hospital for medical treatment. Their unit was no longer effective but there was little that either Buchel or Kriewitz could do about the disease or the climate in Mexico.

General Johnston took a lot of pride in his regiment. He wanted superior performance from his forces to enhance his own reputation and was unhappy about the present state of affairs.

For weeks, Company H continued to try to function in their garrison role but soon after their arrival at Camargo, dissension began to occur in its ranks. The immigrant soldiers, tired from marching in miserable conditions, and wracked by disease, spoke out about the conditions they had to endure. They had not enlisted to serve in garrisons, especially in the awful climate that now existed in northern Mexico. They had enlisted to fight and prove that Germans were worthy of citizenship. In August, the heat became even more oppressive and it compounded the misery of the weary men. The high temperatures and high humidity sapped the men of any desire to perform rigorous duty. As a result, their daily drills became sloppy and rather unbecoming of military men. The German volunteers became targets of even more ridicule, often hurled by members of the regular U.S. Army who, by deriding the foreigners, sought to elevate their own status in the military.

Some officers in Johnson's command began to question the value of retaining the volunteers and proposed to the Colonel that those volunteers who had signed up for a six month tour of duty should be released from their obligation unless they willingly signed on for six more months. It was a way of separating those who really wanted to serve from who did not or could not continue. That stance floated around Camargo and gained traction in Company H.

According to William Preston Johnston (1878), who wrote a biography of his father's life, a delegation of the men from Johnston's command approached General Zachary Taylor about getting out early. The old man brusquely dismissed them, saying, "I don't want anybody around me that doesn't want to stay and fight." The men took that sentiment back to Colonel Johnston, who had just arrived from Matamoros. Upon hearing the facts of the case, he assembled his regiment and put the issue to a vote. The issue was "Do the men want to reenlist for another six months after their present tour of duty or do they want to go home?" The men voted 318 to 224 to disband and thus go home. According to William Preston Johnston (1878), "The majority (of the negative vote) was due in part to the German company (H), which had been on detached service and had suffered repeatedly from sickness, and which voted as a unit to disband." Johnson appealed to the men to reverse their decision but they stood firm. Colonel Johnston was thus compelled to see his labor of months undone in a single hour. His personal hopes of honor and distinction were now severely dissipated. Given the vote, he had no choice but to disband his regiment, which he stoically carried out. In having to do that, he was deeply chagrined but managed to persuade General Taylor to attach himself and Captain Buchel to another division under General Butler. From Camargo, he went on to fight in Monterrey and marched deep into Mexico. Buchel also got attached to another unit and stayed in the U.S. Army until the end of the war but all of his men left the army.

After the vote, the German unit was mustered out of the Army on August 24th in Camargo, Mexico. Unattached, they were on their own in a foreign land and without direction. Sensing their situation and the dangers that 80 plus former soldiers might face moving back to Texas through the war zone in Mexico without support, Emil Kriewitz immediately assumed command of the bedraggled outfit and again organized the men into a semblance of a unit. For their defense, he interceded with the Army to allow them to keep some of the Colt Walker Special six-shooters that had been issued to them earlier. With only small arms and a few rifles, Kriewitz decided that their best chance of surviving in hostile southern Texas was to move together and return to Karlshafen in a manner that did not draw attention to their presence or their prior military service.

Late in August, the remaining 82 men of Company H packed up their gear and began an unorganized trek back to Karlshafen, a trip that took several weeks. From Camargo, they hitched transportation down the Rio Grande on empty supply boats that were returning to the base at Point Isabel. From there, they moved up Padre Island on foot. As the lightly armed men traveled through the countryside, they moved slowly and stealthily, often at night, to avoid contact with Mexican guerillas, outlaws, and Mexican sympathizers. As they trudged along, they scavenged the country side for food and potable water.

In six weeks, Emil Kriewitz led the weakened remnants of Company H back to Karlshafen where their military stint had begun. At the shoddy little village, the 80 or so men hoped to pick up the pieces of their lives that they had left at Karlshafen and complete the emigration process to their Texas land but for some, it would not be that simple. In their absence, life had gone on and they would have to deal with a new reality.

Chapter 5

RETURN TO KARLSHAFEN

When the bedraggled and tired soldiers returned to Karlshafen in early October of 1846, they were surprised to learn that very little had changed about the shanty town during their five month absence. Many of the immigrants were still stuck there and some had died of disease in the interim. The men were further surprised to learn that only a few of the present residents of Karlshafen were aware that they had marched off to Mexico to serve their new country in the Mexican-American War. The current residents were desperate - much more concerned about their own survival and about getting inland than they were about volunteers who had fought in what seemed to them to be a irrelevant war.

With regard to transportation, there was a little more room for optimism in Karlshafen. In the past month, Meusebach had been able to secure a note from the Adelsverein in Germany for $60,000 or roughly 450,000 Guldens. At the present, he was actively scouring the Texas countryside for wagons, oxen, mules, and drivers, but with only modest success. By late October or early November, it was known that Meusebach intended to start sending wagon trains north again on a regular basis.

Upon arriving in Karlshafen, Conrad Pluenneke went directly to the spot where he and his father had erected their crude cabin back in January. It was there that he fervently hoped to reunite with the remaining members of his family, as he and his father had planned. To his chagrin, the rustic hut that he and his father had built was gone. In it's place, another family had built another primitive structure and were presently occupying it. When he approached the hut and inquired about his family, the occupants had no idea of who the Pluennekes were nor where they might have gone. Nor did the occupants have any idea of what might have happened to them. They did, however, tell Conrad how dire their circumstances had become in the tiny village and pleaded for his assistance but he had little to offer them. From that filthy hovel, Conrad went to another hut nearby and inquired within. The German immigrants in that shack also knew nothing of the Pluennekes. They had arrived in Karlshafen in July and had not met anyone named Pluenneke during their three month tenure. It was obvious to Conrad that all of those families were suffering and in a very weakened state of health. They needed medical help. From his recent medical experience in the Army, he knew that some of them had been affected by disease such as yellow fever or malaria and also suffered from malnutrition. He had seen similar symptoms in Mexico.

From there, Conrad strode purposefully towards the German Emigration Company's building which looked roughly the same as it did when he had left back in May. The agents, however, were all new and unrecognizable to him. They too had no knowledge of the Pluenneke family and that bothered him greatly! Although his father and mother were generally quiet people, they would have been known to a few people in the area because of their pleasant demeanor and willingness to help others in need. However, one agent did mention in passing that another agent who had previously worked in Karlshafen now worked at the warehouse at Indian Point. It was possible that he would know about them and where they had gone. With that news, Conrad set out on foot for Indian Point, a mile or so away. After what he had just endured, walking another mile was nothing although his boots were nearly worn out from drills and marching back to Karlshafen.

As he walked at a brisk pace, dark thoughts began to emerge. The agents had told him that the community of Karlshafen had been ravaged by various diseases since April and especially by the now dreaded cholera. That news had sent shivers down his spine. From the transatlantic voyage on the *brig Apollo*, Conrad had developed a great fear of cholera, *the disease that walks in darkness*. He morbidly recalled what that disease had already done to his little niece, three of his younger siblings, and his wife. He shuddered and felt the gloom returning. He also recalled how painfully they had died from it on the boat. In an attempt to erase those dark thoughts from his head, he walked faster and tried to focus on what he would see of Matagorda Bay ahead. Soon, he was at the familiar dock.

At the large warehouse of log-cabin construction, he inquired about the agent who had served at Karlshafen back in the spring. The agent pointed in the direction of a large, burly man who was stacking boxes at the rear of the building, one Fritz Stein. Following the lead, he approached the man and introduced himself.

"Herr, Stein, I am Private Conrad Pluenneke–just back from serving with Company H in the Mexican-American War. My father is Johann Heinrich Conrad Pluenneke, from Klein-Lafferde in Braunschweig."

The man smiled in recognition of the name but then his smile slowly faded to a frown, causing Conrad to swallow hard.

"You came to learn of the whereabouts of your family, no?", Stein said solemnly and turned back toward his work.

Conrad replied "Yes, that is my quest. I need to find them as soon as possible. Do you know where they might be living now?"

Stein turned back, studied Conrad for a moment, and then said slowly and deliberately "I'm afraid I have bad news for you." He motioned for Conrad to sit down on a nearby crate and then continued.

"I did know your father quite well–he was a very good and kind man–but he died from cholera in late May." Stein said. "He was buried outside of Karlshafen to prevent the disease from spreading to others in the village. He and many, many others are buried out there in the wilderness."

Conrad was stunned by the news and sat silently for a few seconds, thinking of his dear father and their life back in Germany. He slowly averted his head and blinked back tears. Again, he felt as though someone had punched him in the stomach, hard and unexpectedly. He could hardly believe the bad news.

"First my niece then my sisters, my brother, and my dear wife! And now my father -- this cannot be happening to me," he thought silently. "Surely this is a bad dream and I will awake to find them all alive." Darkness arose and enveloped him again.

Conrad asked, "Are you sure of what you tell me?" But in a brief moment of reflection, he knew that his question was just denial. Just as it had been with his wife's death, the death of his father was real and could not be denied. At that instant, the guilt and anguish flooded in again.

"This horrendous situation was caused by me and my desire for cheap land in Texas," he said blurted aloud.

Stein lowered his head and stared at the ground a moment before continuing. "Shortly after your father died, your mother also suffered a mild bout with cholera but she survived the disease and regained her health. She most likely contracted the disease while caring for your father. I am sorry to have to tell you all of this bad news." Stein swallowed hard, realizing that he had just delivered a hard blow to the young man in front of him.

Conrad Pluenneke fought back more tears and then asked in a voice broken by emotion "What about my mother and two sisters? Where are they now?"

"There, I have better news for you," Stein said in an upbeat tone. "Your sister Conradina met a teamster named Balthazar Hoffman who drives a wagon between Karlshafen and Houston. They fell in love with one another and decided to marry. He used his wagon to take Conradina, your mother, and her sister, whose name I believe is Karoline, to his hometown in Austin County. Hoffmann is a good man and I believe he will take good care of your family members."

Scratching his brow for a moment, he went on to say, "If I remember correctly, the town where Hoffmann lives is called Buckhorn, perhaps sixty miles northwest of Houston. I think that Hoffmann probably saved their lives by getting them away from Karlshafen. As far as I know, they made it to Buckhorn safely."

That news gave Conrad a little relief and he managed a weak smile. Inwardly, he allowed to himself to be a bit joyful that at least some of the Pluenneke family had survived the ordeal of emigration. "Buckhorn, I must remember that name," he uttered to himself. "Buckhorn! Oh, if we all had just stayed in Germany---!", he said regretfully.

He thanked Fritz Stein for the information and then walked slowly down to the wharf that projected well out into Matagorda Bay. At the end of the huge wooden wharf, he sat down and allowed his feet to dangle off the end of it. For a long while, he stared out at the vast expanse of greenish-brown water in front of him, contemplating his fate. The smell of salty seawater wafted up and around him. Graceful pelicans flew low near the end of the wharf, in search of fish on the surface of the bay. He took all that in and then bowed his head. In Ger-

many, he had been a regular church-goer, one who had mastered the
Evangelical Lutheran prayers and rituals through rote learning. While
he had participated in the liturgy, he never truly felt close to God. He
just went through the motions of appearing to worship God as a ver-
sion of conformity. When he had tried earnestly to experience the deity, it had seemed as though his prayers had gone out into empty space
- a void - darkness. He never sensed any kind of response in return that
he could clearly and objectively link with the voice of a powerful God.
With the events of the past year and recent news, he felt that for the
first time in his life that he really needed to reach that deity and plead
for divine intervention. He ached inside and he desperately needed
help. Everything in his life seemed to be crumbling into ruination.
Without warning, troubling memories of his deceased relatives
whelmed up and percolated into his memory. For brief instances, he
could vividly recall his wife's smile, Fredericke's dainty laugh, and his
father's stern voice. No matter what he did, those memories came and
went, leaving him filled with angst. Gloom! Warm tears rolled down
his cheeks and he choked up. After all, he had been the one who had
pushed the family to emigrate and now six of them were dead, including his young wife. Suddenly, the finality and the permanence of their
deaths struck him hard—very hard. Their collective loss created a huge
void in his life and took away all of his previous sources of happiness.
If only he could reach God and make some sort of grand bargain with
Him that would bring them back to life. His prayer went unanswered.
Then it sunk in—they were dead and death on Earth is final. There was
absolutely nothing he could do to bring them back. Maybe he would
see them again in heaven? He hoped so but the idea that he might see
them in an afterlife was a chimera, without basis. He would never see
them or talk to them again—they were lost forever! Tears flooded his
eyes and he pounded the wharf with his clenched fist repeatedly in anguish.

"Why me?", he asked silently. "Why is this happening to me?"

On the wharf, he tried to pray but his mumbled plea seemed to be
just so many empty words and he doubted that God or any other deity
had heard his request for deliverance from the pain of such losses.
Alas, there would be no magical recovery. That God, if there was a
God, apparently did not care about his fate or was preoccupied elsewhere. For a fleeting moment, he felt like jumping off the wharf, sinking into those murky swirling waters, and ending his agony. His own

death would end the pain and allow him to perhaps rejoin his lost kin in the afterlife, if there was one. He had doubts about that.

As he wallowed in self-pity, Conrad began to faintly and then more lucidly remember words from the *Bible*, words about the many trials that Job went through. He had literally endured Hell on earth and dealt with it. At that point, it came to him that he, Conrad Pluenneke, was not the first human to suffer greatly nor was he likely to be the last. He recalled a sermon that Reverend Kleingeist had delivered about God and self-reliance back in Klein-Lafferde. It was based on the theological notion that God helps those who help themselves. That message was now another epiphany to Conrad! He could not change the past and there was no way to bring back his dead relatives but he could do something about the future. He came to the realization that his future was solely up to him and how he responded from that day forward. While he was still suffering mightily, he realized that he had to stand up, metaphorically dust himself off, and get back to the business of living in reality, of pursuing a good life. If he did that, God might help him and he, in turn, might help others someday. That lesson, learned on the wharf at Indian Point, would stay with him and guide him throughout his life.

With that lesson in mind, he stood up, straightened his back, and walked back down the long wharf until he at last stepped onto solid ground that also served as a metaphor for reality that day. With that initial step off the wharf, he began to live his future.

Since he had no place in which to dwell in Karlshafen, Conrad decided to test the possibility of staying at Indian Point for a while and trying to get himself reoriented to his new reality. After some further mulling about his life, he returned to the German Emigration Company's warehouse and approached Fritz Stein again. He explained that he had no money, no place to stay, no material from which to make a hut, and few prospects for a better life but was capable of performing manual labor. Was there a job for him here? Stein, impressed that Conrad Pluenneke had volunteered to serve in the Texas militia and fought against Mexico, went to the lead agent and interceded on Conrad's behalf. The Verein had had many such requests from new immigrants over the past year, all in dire situations, but Conrad's case was somehow different. He had suffered huge losses in his life, which was not that unusual in Karlshafen, but he had also marched off to the aid of his newly adopted state and risked his life serving in a combat zone–was that not worthy of some special consideration? After some private deliberations, the agents agreed to create a job for him. In return for his labor, the Adelsverein agents would allow Conrad Pluenneke to sleep in the warehouse at night and take meals with them but he had to help provide food by hunting and fishing. They cautioned, however, that this was not a permanent arrangement. He readily accepted their charity and was greatly relieved. He vowed to work hard and without complaint. It was his first good break in life since landing in the New World. His time at Indian Point, however long, would give him a chance to reevaluate his life and make decisions about what to do in the future.

Over the course of nearly two months, he toiled away at the warehouse, moving huge crates and making repairs to the facility. Fritz Stein took Conrad under his tutelage and taught him some basic carpentry skills. In a short time, the former farmer and former Private came to realize that he enjoyed building things.

All the while, he continued to think about his life and his future. Where would he go? What would he do for a living? Over time, he came to realize that he did have a few options. While most of his alternate courses of action were poor choices, a few of them had merit. In his deliberate way, he knew he had to analyze those options and find a way to help himself, with the assurance that by doing so, he might gain God's assistance. He needed a plan. Oh Lord, show me the Way!

As he toiled away in the warehouse, he consciously mulled over his options one by one. One option was to find work somewhere around Matagorda Bay, perhaps at Port Lavaca, and there accumulate enough money to pay for transportation back to Germany. That path would put him back in the German culture, which he had attempted to escape. Once back in the old country, however, he would not be able to resume farming immediately because he had no land. He and his father had sold their property before they emigrated and that was not reversible. Besides that, Germany's national economy had not improved from what he knew of the situation and that meant he would face an uncertain future there. Even if the German economy improved, he also knew that he could not afford to buy good land back in the Fatherland. On balance, that was a poor option and he rejected it without much further thought. He would stay in Texas.

Another option was to reenlist and serve in the U.S. Army that had already trained him for combat. If he took that path, perhaps he could find a way to serve in another locale or in another capacity, possibly in California? As he thought about his recent experiences in the army, however, he quickly recalled that he disliked the rigidity of military life. He did not like marching and he hated taking orders. Also, his continuing reliance on the German language would be a liability in an American military force that communicated only in English. That too was a bad option and he rejected it outrightly.

As he saw it, his only viable option was to stay within the Adelsverein organization's realm and go with it to its inland colonies and thereby escape the coastal miseries and diseases. Once inland, he could claim land in one of its colonies and settle down on land that the Adelsverein had promised his father. That path kept him within the framework of his German culture and in alignment with his original dream of owning a large tract of land. To him, that option had the most merit and he adopted it.

From what he had learned since returning from Camargo, the Adelsverein now had two colonies: the original one at New Braunfels (which was overcrowded) and a second newly established one in Fredericksburg, which was closer to the Fisher-Miller Grant. Maybe in the colony of Fredericksburg he could find his true calling? Slowly, a rudimentary plan began to emerge in Conrad's thinking.

The colony of Fredericksburg had just been established in May of that year (1846) and, from all accounts, good land was still available to be claimed around there. In it, he might also be able to use his father's contract to get land in that village or in the Fisher-Miller Grant, when and if it opened to settlement. With land, he could start a new life as a farmer but that thought brought him upright mentally! Something inside of him shuddered when he thought of farming for the rest of his life. At Fredericksburg, he could keep his German culture and communicate in his native tongue but if he went there, he wanted to pursue a new occupation. In Karlshafen, he would find a way to pursue that idea in coming days.

In the middle of December, he notified Klein that he would be leaving shortly and thanked him for his assistance. "You have helped to turn my life around," Conrad said, "thank you!" To that, Klein merely lowed his head and nodded. On the subsequent crisp but sunny Sunday morning, Conrad Pluenneke left Indian Point early and began to walk the short distance back to Karlshafen with no thought of ever returning to the wharf or the warehouse. His first intent was to attend a German Evangelistic Lutheran church service that morning at which he hoped to meet Heinrich Leifeste and other men he served with in the Mexican-American War. He needed to reconnect with his old friends.

As he walked along the muddy road, Conrad continued to ponder what lay ahead in his future. Would he find suitable land in Fredericksburg? Would he perhaps meet another single woman that he might marry? What would he do to earn money? For the first time in his young life, he felt entirely alone but while alone in a strange new world, he also sensed that he now had real freedom. There were no constraints on what he might choose to do, unlike back in Germany. He, not someone else, would determine his new future in America but he needed a firmer, more tangible plan.

During his brief stint in the Army and at the German Emigration Company's warehouse, Conrad had managed to learn a few words of English but he was nowhere near fluent in that language. He now existed alone in a world that spoke almost exclusively in English, or Spanish. Being of German descent in Texas (and on a larger scale, in America), he was completely out of his element and for the moment, without responsibility or commitment. Whatever he decided to do from this point onward, he sensed that his best chances were within the extended realm of his German culture. He hoped that Fredericksburg would provide that realm but he sensed that he also had to make some accommodations to his new world. Texas was so very different from what he known in Germany.

Since leaving Germany a year earlier, his plan had been to farm a large tract of fertile land in Texas alongside his father and on it, build a life with his young wife. Now without the support of either his father or his wife, he was having doubts about his original plan. Somehow, he sensed that what he might decide or do in coming days might take him down a completely different path. It was just an unsubstantiated feeling that he had, perhaps intuition, but it had the feeling of validity.

As he walked along the rutted and often puddled road, he began to sense that his entire future might hinge on what he might be able to arrange in Karlshafen. He knew that he could no longer languish and mope around aimlessly, content to do menial work. Living in a warehouse alone and apart from the world had not suited him at all. He became aware that His unique future was out there somewhere in the larger world. That insight gave him hope, strength, and resolve, all of which caused him to quicken his pace. He was now in a hurry to learn about his future.

After two months of more or less self-imposed exile at Indian Point, Conrad was returning to Karlshafen to become reconnected with life. Many thoughts swirled in his head as he walked back along the muddy road. He recalled his family's first trip down that road and how disappointed they were when they arrived at Karlshafen. The Adelsverein had been ill prepared for their arrival and it had showed. He thought about how Company H had marched on that road enroute to Point Isabel. Now, he desperately needed to get back to Karlshafen and speak to someone there with authority, someone like John O. Meusebach, about going to Fredericksburg and claiming land. At church in Karlshafen, he hoped to see Meusebach or another high-ranking Verein official where he could plead his case after the service. After an hour of walking, Karlshafen came into view. It was the same dilapidated hodgepodge of poorly constructed huts that it had always been and he was reminded that a few things in life never change.

In the tiny crude village, the first person that he met was Emil Kriewitz, his former First Sergeant of Company H and he was elated to see him again. In the army, Conrad had always respected Kriewitz and found him to be an interesting and colorful man. Upon greeting him and inquiring about his life, Conrad sadly recounted all the bad news he had learned during his first days back in Karlshafen. He told Emil about working and living in the warehouse at Indian Point for the past two months–about all his soul searching, too. To his friend, he also confided that after much thought, he was now planning to go to Fredericksburg and settle there, hoping to find a new calling. Klein had taught him carpentry and maybe he would try that trade.

Kriewitz related that he had spoken to Meusebach recently and that as a result of a large infusion of money from the Verein back in Germany, wagon trains were about to roll northward again. There was renewed hope that the Fisher-Miller Grant might be opened in the coming year because Meusebach had determined to make peace with the

Comanche tribe that lived north of the Llano River. To Conrad, that news meant he might not have to wait long to put his plan into motion.

Conrad asked about housing in Karlshafen, explaining that the hut that he and his father had built before their military duty was now gone. Consequently, he had no place in Karlshafen in which to stay nor did he have material from which to construct a hut. Emil Kriewitz, a single man, readily invited him to share his small, crude quarters until the wagon trains began to roll. Emil explained that he too was heading for Fredericksburg and he would divulge more about what he was doing later that day but for the moment, he had an urgent task that needed his attention. Conrad readily accepted his generous offer. Kriewitz led Conrad to his home where he stashed his duty bag in Kriewitz's rustic hovel and settled in.

That evening, as they ate roasted venison that Kriewitz had shot earlier in the day, Conrad elaborated on his intention to go to Fredericksburg where he felt he might try his hand at carpentry or, if he was forced to, resume farming. During their conversation that evening, Kriewitz intimated to him that John O. Meusebach was coming to Karlshafen the next day. He (Kriewitz) had been given orders to organize and assemble a company of men with military experience to escort Meusebach's surveyors [34] to the Fisher-Miller Grant.

Kriewitz addressed Conrad directly, "Since you are going to Fredericksburg anyway, why not volunteer for escort duty with my unit and earn some money at the same time?"

Conrad thought about that idea for a moment. It had merit and there was no downside to Kriewitz's offer. After a few seconds of internal deliberation, Conrad readily agreed to the idea. He desperately needed money and he needed a way to get to Fredericksburg. All he had in his pocket was a few dollars pay that he had managed to save from his Army pay but it was not enough to sustain him for very long. Kriewitz mentioned that he had also approached several other members of their former company about joining his escort detail. Among the men already enlisted was his friend, Heinrich Leifeste, and his presence in Kriewitz's corp made joining it even more attractive to

---

[34] Kriewitz, Emil. *Recollections From Indian Times* (pages 48 and 49) In Pennniger, R. *Fredericksburg, Texas The First Fifty Years*, 1896.

Conrad. As it were, Emil Kriewitz had also approached Doctor Keidel, whom Conrad knew well and under whom he had worked at Camargo, but Keidel was already committed to go to Fredericksburg independently as the town's physician.

Of the 82 soldiers[35] that had returned from Camargo, Kriewitz managed to recruit enough to make a credible case to Meusebach the next day. The Commissioner-General, upon viewing the list of volunteers, agreed to hire all of them as escorts for his surveyor corps that would move into the Fisher-Miller Grant in coming months. He cautioned that their work would be difficult and very risky at times since the area was still inhabited by hostile Comanches and other tribes. Meusebach also told Kriewitz that the Verein would pay $1 per week and supply his recruits with arms, ammunition, and clothing as well as with provisions while on duty. To that, he added that their work would begin sometime in the next two weeks. Their first job would be to provide an armed escort for the next wagon train leaving for New Braunfels and from there, march on to Fredericksburg to rendezvous with his surveyors.

The following day, Kriewitz assembled his men and relayed those terms to them. They readily assented and began to prepare for duty. With difficulty, the Verein hastily procured a pair of riding horses for the escort detail. Prior to their departure, agents of the Verein outfitted the men with some of the necessities to survive in winter weather as well as to ward off attacks by hostile Indians. It had been reported that a number of tribes were operating between Karlshafen and New Braunfels, including the Karankawas. The escort had to be prepared to deal with them and Kriewitz encouraged them to recall and employ their recent military training in coming days. According to Kriewitz's own written account, [36] his unit left Karlshafen on the first day of January in 1847, destined for New Braunfels.

In Mexico, their regiment had used advance scouts to detect and counter enemy presence near army positions. Kriewitz opted to employ the same approach and began to organize his escort detail accordingly. Conrad recalled some of the Texas Rangers that performed scout duty,

---

[35] Captain Buchel stayed in Mexico and was reassigned to another unit.
[36] *Fredericksburg, Texas---The First Fifty Years*. Penninger, Robert. 1896, pages 48-49.

men such as Hays, Gillespie, and McCulloch, and how they had moved stealthily through the countryside, ahead of their force's advances, often surprising and then preemptively attacking and routing potential Mexican guerilla forces. On escort duty, the armed unit would employ those same tactical techniques. Daily, Kriewitz intended to send advance scouts ahead of the wagon train to survey the terrain and provide early notice of dangerous conditions ahead. Operating with only a pair of men, scouting duty would be very risky. Immediately, Conrad volunteered for scout duty. To him, moving ahead of the wagon train was much more exciting than simply marching along side the 10 wagons plus it offered him the freedom to roam about and see more of the countryside that they passed through. Kriewitz vouched for him as a brave and reliable man, both good qualities for a scout. The other scout, Heinrich Habenicht, was also readily accepted.

A collateral duty of the scouts was to hunt, particularly deer or turkey, to provide meat for the unit's evening meals. In that regard, Conrad also was an asset because he had been known in the Army as highly accurate with a rifle. To increase their range, the two scouts were provided horses and a member of their detail, a former Texas Ranger, was ordered to train the two scouts in basic riding skills and how to care for their mounts. In the intense equestrian training, Conrad discovered that he had the knack when it came to horses and he quickly became a proficient rider. Little did he know that horses would one day play a very large role in his life. Oh Lord, show me the Way.

On the appointed day, Kriewitz's band and the wagon train set out for New Braunfels. Although their route was but a pair of ruts through the wilderness, the route had been improved markedly in the past year. It was relatively dry and the streams that they crossed were well within their banks, making their fords quite easy. As a result, the wagon train made good progress through the coastal area, tracing the eastern bank of the Guadalupe River. Whenever possible, the wagon train stopped overnight in small villages such as Victoria, Cuero, Gonzales, and Seguin along the way to New Braunfels. In those towns, they often took up residence in abandoned buildings. Between such towns, they camped along the trail at designated sites such as Agua Dulce, McCoy's Creek, Colonel North's plantation, Natchez Creek, and Guadalupe Ford, as well as other impromptu places that circumstances occasionally dictated. As the wagon train passed through the countryside, the immigrants and the escort detail bought produce from local farmers and to that food, the escort detail added venison and other meat. On the way to New Braunfels, the wagon train forded a number of small tributaries that drained into the Guadalupe from the east. Those were generally small creeks and quite readily fordable. In the rare occasion that a wagon got mired down, the escort unit helped extricate it and the passengers from the muck.

Along the way, they learned that they would have to cross the large Guadalupe River, which they had been paralleling and which now, in January, was running well above its normal level. The prospect of a large river crossing in wagons caused anxiety among some of the immigrants in the wagon train. To that point, they had not forded a major stream and such an endeavor gave them a great deal of angst. To ease their tension, the lead agent spread the word that there was a ferry at the crossing site but he was unsure whether it would be operating because the river was running high.

When the scouts arrived at the bluff overlooking the Guadalupe crossing, however, they were relieved to see that the ferry was in operation. Its operator was in the act of landing several riders on the far side of the river. As the advance party looked at the crossing, they noted a taut cable stretched from one side of the river to the other. The ferryboat, operated by Adolph von Wedemeyer, was connected to the cable at a capstan on its deck. By cranking that capstan in one direction or another, its operator was able to use the force of the water to propel the ferry across the river, one wagon at a time. Conrad found that to be an ingenious idea. He had seen ferries operate in Germany but never imagined that one would exist in the unsettled portions of Texas. Assured that it was operating safely, Heinrich Habenicht rode back to inform the wagon train that it would be able to cross the Guadalupe River on the ferry and ride into New Braunfels that night. Conrad, meanwhile, rode slowly down the slope to the river.

When the wagon train got to the bluff above the ferry site, the Agent located a horn hanging in a nearby tree and blew three short blasts on it. That signal alerted von Wedemeyer, who had retreated to his nearby cabin on Comal Creek. Shortly he emerged into view near the river's edge, waved at the wagons, and then began to move the ferry across the river. At its east bank, he hopped off the craft and tethered it to a large post. Once the ferry was secure, he beckoned for the train to begin making its descent down the bluff to the landing site.

At the river, Emil Kriewitz divided his military escort in half to protect both sides of the river while the wagons crossed. Half of the escort unit plus one mounted scout would be taken across first and once there, provide protection against a raid on the far bank. Conrad Pluenneke was ordered to cross with the first unit and five wagons while Habenicht was ordered to cross with the last five wagons.

On von Wedemeyer's signal, the first half of the escort detail marched to the ferry landing and boarded it, accompanied by Conrad and his mount. Gesturing, von Wedemeyer directed Conrad to hold his horse under tight rein all the way across the river, thereby preventing it from spooking during the crossing. When the contingent was onboard, Adolph von Wedemeyer loosened the tether, stepped onto the craft, and went to the capstan that he cranked in the opposite direction. Almost immediately, the ferry began to move westward, across the river. On the way over, the ferry occasionally bobbed as the raging current fluctuated horizontally in places. When the ferry reached the far bank, the operator hopped off and tethered the ferry to a large piling. Kriewitz motioned for Conrad to lead his horse off the ferry, remount, and then ride up the bank a short distance to scout the locale. Shortly thereafter, the escort detail walked off the ferry and took up defensive positions higher up the bank. When the first contingent was up the slope a bit and positioned, von Wedemeyer guided his ferry across the river to fetch the first wagon. One at a time, drivers led their teams and wagons onto the ferry, secured them, and were then ferried across the Guadalupe River. That process continued until all wagons and all the military escort was on the west side of the river. The agent in charge then paid von Wedemeyer for his services, thanked him, and then reorganized the wagon train into a line for procession into New Braunfels. At that point on January 10th, they were about a mile away from the colony.

By the time the entire wagon train had crossed the Guadalupe, it was late afternoon and the immigrants in the wagons were weary as was the military unit. They eagerly looked forward to a restful stop in the colony of New Braunfels where they hoped to sleep in a real bed for the first time in months. The agent in charge informed the immigrants that the wagon train would resume its travels in two days. It was, he said, about 90 miles to Fredericksburg and that trip should take them an additional four days. At the small village, the Adelsverein had arranged for the newcomers to stay in the homes of local citizens, all of whom received compensation from the Verein. A few of its clients were put up at local inns that had been recently established. The military escort, however, set up camp just outside of the colony, near Comal Creek and the legendary Comal Springs.

As he surveyed the scene, Conrad was very impressed with the visual beauty that surrounded New Braunfels. Even in the dimming daylight, it was very easy to understand why Prince Carl Solms-Braunfels had chosen to acquire this property back in 1845. It was positioned at the confluence of the Comal Creek and the Guadalupe River. The Comal, a much smaller stream, was fed by a cluster of majestic springs that produced an abundance of clear water that erupted from the surface like a fountain. The hillsides around the Comal were densely covered with a variety of trees that included oak, cypress, and pecan. In late January, the leafless trees within the forest were silhouetted against a very red western sky at sundown. It was quite a sight and the spirits of those on the wagon train were buoyed by the visual treat of a beautiful Texas sunset.

At New Braunfels, the military escort received orders from Meusebach to move on towards Fredericksburg immediately. Since time was short and there were few horses available in New Braunfels, the men were forced to march on foot. At the new colony, they were ordered to join with Meusebach's party and accompany his surveyors beyond the Llano River. It was rumored that Meusebach was planning to leave Fredericksburg around the 20th of January.

After a good night's rest, the men rose early, hurriedly packed their gear into rucksacks, and assembled themselves near the road in semi-darkness. In a few moments, they were treated to a beautiful majestic sunrise that rivaled the sunset from the previous day. On Emil Kriewitz's order, they formed into two parallel files and began the arduous march towards Fredericksburg. In the cool morning weather, the former First Sergeant set a fast pace. His goal was to cover the 90 miles in six days or less. For Conrad who had been on horseback for much of the previous three weeks, marching rapidly was difficult and he struggled to maintain the pace that first day. After that, all of them, including Conrad Pluenneke, regained their "marching legs" and the group began to move more like a military unit.

The first leg of their journey took them in a southwesterly direction, although Fredericksburg was northwest of New Braunfels. The initial part of their route followed the primitive road that connected New Braunfels with San Antonio but where that road intersected the Cibolo Creek, the unit turned upstream and followed a crude road along its drainage in a more westerly direction. Their first camp was on the south bank of Cibolo Creek, some five miles upstream from the so-called San Antonio Road. Early the next day, they rose, repacked, and continued to march along the path besides Cibolo Creek until it intersected the well-worn Pinta Trail. It was an ancient route that had been initially established by Indians and then improved by colonizing Spaniards several centuries later as a way to connect and supply their mission at Menard with San Antonio de Bexar, the largest city in Texas at the time. Since its establishment, the Pinta Trail had been used by many soldiers, missionaries, and Indians over the course of those centuries and now it was being used by German immigrants as they settled in colonies in central Texas. From the intersection, Kriewitz's men turned right and headed north towards Fredericksburg.

For four very long days, Kriewitz's band of former soldiers marched along the rugged Pinta Trail, averaging about 15 miles per day. As they pressed northward, the men began to see changes in the landscape and in the climate. Tropical plants of the coastal region gave way to desert foliage such as mesquite trees, prickly pear cacti, and yuccas. They also noticed a definite change in climate. The air grew much drier and a bit warmer, even though it was January. As they progressed towards Fredericksburg, the terrain became more diverse as hills and limestone-capped mesas began to dominate the terrain. As the band ascended into the hills, they left behind the coastal plain of Texas for what has become known as the Edwards Plateau, a flat higher plain in the western parts of the state. Dividing the domed hills and mesas were deep dry arroyos that were often difficult to traverse. The Adelsverein had made improvements to the Pinta Trail but it was still very rough in places. Even though it was January, the group of men kicked up dust as they marched quickly through the arid country. There were other signs that the area lacked moisture. Potable water was scarce and so Kriewitz stopped the procession near every available water source and allowed his men to drink and fill their canteens. The drought conditions brought home to the men just how important water was in this area. Along the way to Fredericksburg, Conrad saw such places as Comanche Springs, the Guadalupe River, and the Pedernales River which were all permanent water sources and they gave him hope that not all of Texas was desert. Among the group, those who had farming experience noticed that the soil in that locale was also very dry and not nearly as fertile as what they had observed at the beginning of the trip.

At long last, Kriewitz's small band carefully descended a slope, crossed what was then named Meusebach Creek (today, Baron's Creek), and entered the colony of Fredericksburg from the Southeast late on the morning of January 17, 1847. The roadbed of the Pinta Trail ran through the middle of the fledgling town and had been widened at its center. The main street still had many stumps in it, remnants of the clearing process that had occurred only months before. At times, the men had to sidestep those stumps and avoid large rocks in the trail. Along the street that led into the heart of the colony, there were a few widely spaced buildings that varied widely in quality. According to Roemer (1848), [37] who saw Fredericksburg at about the same time that Kriewitz's men saw it, the fledgling community did not rise to the standards of a town. Some of the buildings were sturdy, well-built log cabins while many of them were either crudely built huts or canvas tents. He noted that perhaps only 50 buildings lined the road into the heart of the emerging colony. In 1847, Fredericksburg was on the very forefront of the Texas frontier and the crude state of its development reflected that condition. Oh, Lord, show me the way!

As the unit entered the colony, Conrad noted that it was situated on a rising plane between two small streams, both of which joined and then flowed into the larger Pedernales River east of the village. By the time Kriewitz's unit arrived in Fredericksburg, most of the colony land had been surveyed and platted into what were termed town lots and outlying lots, an arrangement that mirrored how the Germans had organized their towns and farms back in rural Germany. When Kriewitz's men arrived, most of the town lots that bordered the two streams had already been claimed by the earliest settlers and they were hard at work building shelters for their families. At the center of the town, a large heavily forested square plot of land had been left undeveloped and was designated as the Marktplatz, the center of the new town. It, at the present, had the appearance of a fortress, a fact that was

---

[37] Ferdinand Roemer, a German naturalist and friend of Meusebach, passed through Fredericksburg in January of 1847 and made many observations of what he saw in the new colony in his diary and subsequently in his book..

implied by the name Fredericksburg.[38] The Marktplatz had high palisade walls that were constructed from timber hewn from the site and a
heavy wooden gate. Near the gate was a large brass cannon. Inside the
fortress was the local headquarters of the Adelsverein, which was becoming more generally known as the German Emigration Company.

As Kriewitz's troops came to a halt in front of the German Emigration Company building at the Marktplatz, Conrad Pluenneke sighed
heavily, dropped his pack to the ground, swigged some water from his
canteen, and took a moment to survey the new colony and its setting.
Surrounding the Marktplatz where he stood was a dense forest composed mostly of large live oak trees, elm trees, and some large pecan
trees. The colony was being carved out of that forest even as he
watched. Workers were busy in the Marktplatz clearing land for another building, a multipurpose building, someone said. Now, in January of 1847, it was already taking on a peculiar shape, he noted silently. Its rock base was in the shape of an octagon. Shifting from the
strange building, he scanned beyond the forest to the horizon. To the
north of Fredericksburg, there were limestone-capped hills that formed
a semi-circle around the little village. In all, it was a pleasant location
for a town and he was immediately taken with it.

While the men were resting, Lieutenant Ludwig Bene, an employee of the Adelsverein and an important citizen of Fredericksburg, approached them with a petition that urged John O. Meusebach to stay
on in his position as Commissioner-General of the Verein.[39] While the
citizens of New Braunfels had threatened to do him bodily harm in late
December because of Adelsverein mismanagement, the immigrants at
Fredericksburg wholeheartedly supported Meusebach. Conrad had
nothing but admiration for the man so he and 96 others, including
Christoph Feuge and Heinrich Leifeste, willingly signed the petition
on that day, January 17th, 1847.

When Kriewitz inquired about the whereabouts of Meusebach,
agents told him that he was already on the way to the San Saba River
area to conclude a peace treaty with the Comanches. According to his

---

[38] Burg in German is a fortified defensive structure. Meusebach evidently viewed
his town as primarily a fortress in the wilderness rather than a village, and named
the settlement after a friend, thus making it in effect Frederick's Burg.
[39] Petition signers listed in King (1967), pages 106 and 107.

account (written in 1896), Kriewitz then quickly reassembled his weary men and marched them off in that direction. After a little more than two weeks of marching, they met Meusebach's contingent near the headwaters of the Pedernales on February 6th but unfortunately for them, Meusebach's group was already on its way back to Fredericksburg, rejoicing in the fact that Meusebach had met with Comanche chiefs and begun the process of negotiating a lasting peace with their tribes. Kriewitz's tired men fell in with part of Meusebach's company and returned to Fredericksburg.

With a peace treaty in progress, Meusebach was emboldened to begin surveying the Fisher-Miller Grant with the view that he might be able to settle immigrants on it in coming months. Several days after returning, Meusebach issued orders to Kriewitz to accompany and protect one of his surveyors, a man named Richard A. Howard. He had been ordered to begin the survey of northwestern Bexar County, known in those days as Howard's District 1, whose plots alternated with Fisher-Miller Grant land.[40]

The next day, Howard's surveying detail and Kriewitz's escort unit left Fredericksburg headed towards the Llano River. For the next month, Howard surveyed and mapped the land north of the river while Kriewitz's men patrolled nearby. As they moved westward along the north bank of the Llano, Conrad noted the land and its location. It was secluded, less forested, and much drier than the land around Fredericksburg. The terrain beyond the Llano River was flat for the most part, had many mesquite trees, abundant opuntia cacti, and quite a number of large granite outcroppings that were decomposing into a very coarse soil. Along the course of the Llano River, however, there were groves of pecan and oak trees. As he studied the landscape around him, Conrad felt that it would be difficult but not entirely impossible to farm there. From Howard's assistant, he learned that a few Mexicans had begun raised cattle there and had achieved moderate success. The notion of cattle ranching was new to him and it piqued his interest. He vowed to learn more about it. Oh, Lord! Show me the way!

After Howard completed his portion of the survey, his contingent and Kriewitz's support unit returned to Fredericksburg where they

---

[40] Biershwale (1996, page 61)

were officially released from duty and paid for their service. After much difficult marching, Conrad had finally completed the first stage of his new life: he was in good health and in Fredericksburg. In the new colony, he and friends such as Heinrich Leifeste were hoping to start a new chapter in their lives. It was now May of 1847 and much had to be done to get established. He needed land and he needed to establish a new occupation.

Chapter 6

SETTLING IN FREDERICKSBURG

When Conrad, along with the rest of Kriewitz's band of men, returned to Fredericksburg in May of 1847 in the company of the surveyor Richard A. Howard and his crew, they were met at the gate of the Marktplatz fortress by a large group of German settlers. Word had spread throughout the small community that some of the men who had volunteered at Karlshafen to serve in the Texas militia and who had marched beyond the Rio Grande into Mexico, were returning to Fredericksburg that day. The throng that had gathered were there to welcome the men to their new hometown. Among the welcoming group was Friedrich Leifeste and the younger sister of both Friedrich and Heinrich Leifeste, Sophie Christine Henriette Leifeste.

After Kriewitz dismissed his troop, the men mixed among the settlers and began to get acquainted. Immediately, Heinrich Leifeste took Conrad in tow and led him towards Friedrich Leifeste and his sister. Feigning formality, Heinrich introduced his brother and then sister, Sophie, to his friend, Conrad Pluenneke who, bowing slightly, eliciting a faint smile from her. She was young, perhaps 20 years of age, and unmarried. Like the rest of her family, she was from Boistedt, a farming community only a few miles from Klein-Lafferde. She had a plain, no-nonsense presence about her and seemed to be at ease. While Company H had been on duty in Mexico, Heinrich Leifeste had written letters to her describing his new friend Conrad Pluenneke who, he noted, was from Klein-Lafferde. At the same time, Heinrich had often spoken to Conrad about his young sister while they were performing sentry duty in Matamoros. Through Heinrich, the two had some knowledge of each other before becoming formally acquainted at the Marktplatz that day. As he greeted her for the first time, Conrad noted that she seemed to be pleasant, comfortable in his presence, and not at all vain. At once, Sophie attracted Conrad's attention. There was something about her; maybe it was her fair skin or her radiant smile or possibly the way her bright gray-blue eyes were highlighted by her dark brown hair. It seemed to Conrad that she might also have positive feelings about him but he wasn't at all certain of that. For a while, the four of them chatted about trivia and became better acquainted. As Conrad regarded Sophie obliquely, he liked what he saw and vowed to see her again to learn more about her. Oh, Lord! Show me the way!

Since his men had been on the move constantly since leaving Karlshafen on the first day of January, Kriewitz was aware his men were weary and had no place to stay in Fredericksburg. He went into the Verein offices [41] and talked to agents who referred him to Lieutenant Bene. Through him, the former First Sergeant arranged for the men to stay in the military barracks that were part of the fortress at the Marktplatz.

After a few words of praise to his unit, Kriewitz dismissed them from service as a Verein unit and then led them past the large brass cannon, through the gates of the small fortress, and into the interior that housed a number of large, sturdy buildings. Just inside the large gates and on the left was the headquarters of the German Emigration Company in Fredericksburg. As Conrad soon discovered, it was a complex of buildings.[42] Its main office was a massive building of log-construction that had two rooms near the front entrance, arranged around a spacious courtyard. One room of the headquarters building served as an office for four of the Verein managers and financial people, including P. Bickel, Theo Specht, [43] and A. Schildknecht (who managed the warehouse) as well as his assistant, B. Kremer. The other room was the dining area for Verein employees and the colony's militia. Behind those two rooms was a large warehouse in which the Verein stored goods that it either provided or sold to its immigrant clients. The warehouse, Conrad noted, contained various farm implements such as plows and harnesses as well as barrels of grain and other casks. However, to his eye, the storehouse seemed relatively barren for a rapidly growing new colony. As they moved on, Conrad noted a fully stocked kitchen with a large metal wood stove that was located in one corner of the big warehouse, near what seemed to be the cook's quarters. Outside of the main building, and well apart from it, was another log house designated for Dr. Schubert, the Director of the Adelsverein in Fredericksburg. Behind the warehouse and diagonally across from the Director's house was a large barracks building that provided domicile for soldiers who defended the colony against Indian raids. Beyond the barracks, near the rear wall of the fortress, were stables that shel-

---

[41] In 1847, the Adelsverein in Texas was also known as the German Emigration Company.

[42] This description of the Verein complex in Fredericksburg was derived from Wilhelm Herme's diary. Hermes was an early settler in Fredericksburg and an employee of the Verein.

[43] Theo Specht later became the first Postmaster in Fredericksburg

tered both horses and oxen that belonged to the Verein and its employees. In all, the headquarters of the German Emigrations Company located within the rugged palisade-walled fortress was impressive for having been built during the initial settlement phase of the colony.

At his customary quick pace, Kriewitz led his men through the warehouse and out its back door to the barracks. A well-defined stockyard odor arose and greeted the men as they trudged by the stables on their way to the barracks but they were not offended in the least, having become accustomed to such smells while living around animals during their military duty. Upon entering the barracks, the men discovered crudely made bunks lining its four walls. The bunks along the south wall were already occupied by the colony's militia but those along the opposite wall and at the far end of the space were vacant. Kriewitz signaled for the men to take possession of them and they quickly did so by plunking their pack down on a bed, thereby laying claim to it as their space. Conrad claimed a lower bed on the end wall while Heinrich Leifeste took an upper bunk above him.

After all were settled in and organized, Kriewitz led them back to the kitchen for their evening meal. After camping in the open for over a month, the men were pleased to sit at a table and have a tasty meal prepared for them and served on ceramic dishes. During the meal, there was a lot of good-natured patter about what they had experienced since leaving Karlshafen. After eating, the weary men trudged back to the bunkhouse and retired to their bunks where they hoped to get some badly needed sleep. During the night, however, they were frequently disturbed by loud snoring and by the occasional snorting of horses in the nearby stables. The latter elicited fears of an Indian incursion in a few but the men quickly realized where they were and the security of that place allowed them to relax into a deep slumber.

The next day, Conrad and Heinrich Leifeste arose early and went to the office at the front of the Verein Building. In the office, they approached the agent on duty and inquired about claiming land in Fredericksburg. Conrad explained that he had arrived in Galveston in January of 1846 with his father, Johann Heinrich Pluenneke, who had a contract with the Adelsverein for land in the Fisher-Miller Grant. He went on to explain that his father had died in Karlshafen while he was serving in Company H of the Texas Volunteers with Captain Buchel.

As part of Kriewitz's band, he had arrived in Fredericksburg and wished to settle but had no contract with the Verein.

For Heinrich Leifeste, the situation was different. He too had served in the army but he also possessed a contract that he had signed with the Adelsverein back in Germany and it entitled him to land in Fredericksburg. He explained to the Adelsverein agent that his brother Friedrich Leifeste had already claimed town lot 81 for himself as well as outlying land. Since arriving in Fredericksburg, Friedrich had built a log cabin on his town lot and settled there permanently, along with their sister. Heinrich went on to explain that he wished to claim a town lot near Friedrich's lot so the family's homes would be close to one another. Hearing the story, the agent rummaged through his records and found that town lot 82 was vacant. Without thought, Heinrich seized the opportunity and claimed that town lot for himself. With adjacent town lots, the Leifeste family would be reconnected after nearly a year's separation and would be living in the same general vicinity of Fredericksburg.

Fortunately for Conrad Pluenneke, his appeal for land came at an opportune time for both him and for the Adelsverein. The Society, because of mishandling its own funds, was teetering on the edge of bankruptcy and was also well behind schedule in meeting its contractual obligation to the state of Texas to settle 6000 people or more in an 18 month period.[44] Fearing default, the Verein was more than willing to provide land to a new German settler, especially one who had served his new country in the war against Mexico. Given that background, the agent took Conrad to the far wall of the office and showed him a map of the Fredericksburg colony. On the map, there were numbered parcels corresponding to town lots and outlying lots. The agent explained that because the Fisher-Miller Grant was not open yet, all new settlers including him were being offered one of the town lots plus one 10 acre outlying lot to settle on and farm until the grant area opened. That arrangement had also been employed at New Braunfels and had worked quite well there. He remarked that because Meusebach had just concluded a peace treaty with local Comanche tribes, the grant area might be opening shortly and that he might get an entitlement to a tract of 320 acres in it as well. With little thought, Conrad Pluenneke accepted the proposed arrangement and signed a contract with theGerman Emigration Company.

---

[44] Morgenthaler, *The German Settlement of the Texas Hill Country*, 2007.

The agent redirected Conrad's attention to the map and asked him to select a town lot and then an outlying lot from the map. Conrad had seen enough dry land since he had been in Texas to realize that land near a permanent water source was very important. By the spring of 1847, most of the choice lots along both creeks in Fredericksburg had already been claimed but Conrad managed to spot one lot that was west of the Marktplatz and across Meusebach's Creek but was removed from the creek by only one town lot (609) in a northeasterly direction and by two town lots (261 and 267) in a northerly direction. Wilhelm Reuter owned Town lot 261 and Georg Hetzel owned the other one, 267. It was not clear who owned 609. The location of his town lot, near the center of the colony but across the creek, was the best one available in Conrad's opinion and he seized the opportunity, pointed to lot 248, and said, "I choose that lot, number 248." The agent noted Conrad's selection in his ledger and attached Conrad Pluenneke's name to it. For an outlying lot, Conrad chose the parcel numbered 408, which was adjacent to Friedrich's outlying lot, 407. The first step of Conrad's plan had now come to fruition: he now owned land in Fredericksburg. Oh Lord, Show me the Way!

After making their selections, he and Heinrich determined to inspect their new property. Before leaving, however, they took a moment to make a crude copy of the colony map, which showed the flow of Meusebach Creek, the location of the Marktplatz, and the location of Conrad's town lot as well as those of the two Leifeste brothers. The agent offered to lend them a compass that would be very useful in locating the boundary stakes that identified their lots and they accepted his offer. With map and compass in hand, the pair struck out on foot to see what they had just claimed.

Since the Leifestes' lots were nearer, they decided to view them first. From the center of the colony, the men oriented their map to north, established a bearing line of about 190 degrees to lot 81, and headed off in a southwesterly direction. Shortly they crossed Meusebach's Creek and followed the compass bearing until they found Friedrich's cabin on lot 81. It was a small shack and evidently one that had been erected in a short amount of time because its walls, rather than being constructed with notched horizontal logs, were composed of vertical logs (pickets) that had been jammed into the ground and bound together at the top by either wire or rope. Spaces between the vertical logs had been filled with a sort of adobe, undoubtedly mined from the banks of Meusebach's Creek. At its crudely made door, Conrad and Heinrich were warmly greeted by Friedrich and ushered inside. The room was stacked with possessions in no particular arrangement. Two straw mattresses served as beds for he and Sophie. As they exchanged news, Heinrich told his brother that he had just claimed town lot 82, directly west of his lot, and that Conrad had claimed a town lot perhaps a half mile away, near the creek. As they talked, Conrad peeked out of the open door to the west and noted that Heinrich's lot had several large oak trees on it and that its terrain was practically flat but sloped slightly in the direction of the creek. To get to the creek, Friedrich or Sophie would have to cross four town lots but they had already discovered that their new neighbors were friendly and cooperative in that regard. For a while, the men rambled on about lives in the colony but Conrad became impatient to see his own lot and began moving towards the open door. The Leifestes, being curious themselves, offered to go with him so the three men set off to find Conrad Pluenneke's town lot, leaving Sophie behind.

From Heinrich's lot, the trio used the compass to establish a rough heading of 350 degrees to get to Conrad's town lot. In the process of getting there, they crossed six other lots, some which were being built upon by other German immigrants. As they passed the busy settlers, they waved and bid them well in German. After about half of a mile, they saw stakes and with a little investigation, quickly identified the boundaries of lot 248. Conrad's lot also was mainly level with several large pecan and oak trees on it. Unlike the Leifeste's lots, Conrad's town lot offered a view of the creek bank but was high enough above it to be safe from floodwaters. Conrad was very pleased with his "blind" selection and turned to face the brothers with a broad smile.

"Now," he said to Heinrich, "we now have the business of building sturdy log cabins." Gravely, they had come to realize that the Adelsverein was not going to honor its obligation to build cabins for its clients. It was up to the settlers to learn how to build a log cabin with the few tools they had brought to Fredericksburg. Conrad was now very thankful for the carpentry experience he had gained from Fritz Stein at Indian Point.

After walking around the lot for an hour or so, the Leifeste brothers decided to return to the center of town and meet their sister at the Marktplatz where she had gone to get their share of provisions from the Verein. Entranced by the first land that he owned, Conrad decided to stay behind and study the terrain of his new lot. Quickly, he wanted to identify a spot where he could erect a cabin on the lot and get on with the process of building on it. For an hour or so, he paced back and forth on the lot, orienting himself to the nearby terrain. He tried to determine what part of it might be affected by drainage and what part of it might offer shade in the summer. As he had done on the farm in Germany, he knelt down and grasped a sample of the soil, letting it trickle through his fingers. He found that it contained loam mixed with much sand that had undoubtedly been washed down the creek for many millennia. He finally settled on a slightly elevated place to situate his cabin. That area was blanketed by a dense grove of tall live oak trees on the west that he knew would offer shade in the summer. Alternatively turning right and left, he decided to orient the house towards the Southwest to capture cool breezes coming from that direction in the summer. A solid wall to the Northwest would protect him from Texas Northers in the winter. As he sized up the situation, he saw that he could fell some of the trees in the center of the grove and create a clearing for his hut. Those downed trees could also be used to construct his cabin and thus not require him to move the logs very far. After a few more considerations from different perspectives, he stopped, paused to look over the lot one more time, and then began his walk back to the Marktplatz where he hoped to see Sophie Leifeste and his two friends.

When he arrived at the Marktplatz, there was no sign of the Leifeste family so he ate with members of his former unit and retired early. As he lay awake listening to the loud snoring around him, he tried to focus on what had to be done the next day. He wanted to get started on his cabin but then remembered that the next day was the Sabbath, not a day of work. Earlier that day, he had heard that outdoor services were often held under the large oak trees near the German Emigration Company building, if weather permitted. Since they were currently experiencing a spell that was both warm and dry, it was highly likely that services would be held as planned and therefore he made plans to attend. From an agent, he learned that the services would start about 10 am. He wound his pocket watch and then fell fast asleep.

The next morning, Conrad arose, donned his best and cleanest clothes that mainly consisted of remnants of his former military clothing, and spruced up a bit. He left the barracks and went directly to the dining room where he leisurely ate a meager breakfast that included a mug of strong coffee. Afterwards, he opened the back door of the Verein building and walked out into a warm and bright morning atmosphere. Skirting the main building, he came to a place near the gates of the fortress where people were already gathering under stately oak trees. Nearby, several men were busy moving a heavy oak table into place. Later that morning, Conrad would discover that the sturdy table would serve as the altar for the service. After getting the table positioned and steadied, one of the men draped a white cloth across it that had a large red cross embroidered on it. Another man came to the table and placed a ceramic mug on the makeshift altar along with a platter. Presently, a woman bearing a basket came and filled the mug with what appeared to be red wine. Shortly, she returned and placed pieces of bread on the platter and arranged them in a circular pattern. When the altar was properly set, several men dragged sections of tree trunks to the area and arranged them to form a semicircular arc about the altar. Those stumps were to serve as reserved seating for the dignitaries of the Verein who were likely to be present that day. All other attendees were required to stand in an arc that paralleled the stumps. Conrad pressed forward through the throng and found a standing place almost directly behind Dr. Friedrich Armand Schubert (aka Strubberg), the Mayor of the colony. He had just walked over from his home in the compound and had been ceremoniously seated by a Verein agent, acting as an usher. It seemed to Conrad that Schubert had the airs of someone who regarded himself as royalty but rumors abounded in the colony that Schubert was in reality a scoundrel who used Verein assets to indulge his own pleasures. Among his many offenses, he was alleged to use Verein assets to buy expensive wine and drink it with his closest cohorts.

The service that Sunday was conducted by Reverend Ervendberg who had travelled up from New Braunfels at the behest of the German Emigration Company. As Conrad soon discovered, the liturgy that day generally followed familiar German Evangelical Lutheran theology. It contained a few old hymns, and was quite ritualistic. The reverend's sermon was very mellow and focused on getting people "to love their neighbor." Conrad followed the service with rapt attention, prayed ardently, but felt no closer to God than when he had sat on the wharf at Indian Point in despair, some six months earlier. As always, he came away from the service feeling disappointed.

Oh, Lord, please show me the way, any way at all, just please show me the way! Nothing but silence and darkness ensued.

After the service, Conrad and everyone who attended the service were cordially invited to stay and attend a shared meal supplied by several devout settler families. While they stood around and ate, they also listened to music played by several settlers who had brought musical instruments from Germany. One of the men offered Conrad a mug filled with home-brewed beer that he accepted with great appreciation and promptly swigged down. Noticing his thirst, the man quickly refilled Conrad's mug. A few in the audience began to dance to some of the more secular tunes, particularly waltzes and polkas. For someone that had been on the move for over a year, the simple home-cooked food and the music was a real treat to Conrad. The music, while mostly hymns from the old country, also brought back memories of Germany and the life he had left behind. His mind flashed to images of his deceased wife–how she would have loved milling about with all these people and dancing to the music. Suddenly and unexpectedly, he thought of his dear father and a lump came to his throat. Conrad swallowed hard! Oh, what could have been! Had he let his father down by volunteering and going off to Mexico? A powerful wave of guilt swept over him and his eyes watered up.

He turned away from the musicians briefly and was pleased to see the three Leifestes standing near the large gates. During the religious service, they had stood on the outer arc of the congregation but had retreated to the gate area afterwards. Picking his way through the crowd, he approached them and extended warm greetings. As he looked at Sophie, he noted that her eyes were particularly dazzling in the bright spring sunshine and they made the morbid thoughts in his head evaporate into the crisp morning air. In a matter of seconds, he was transported back among the living, at least for the moment. When the band played a polka, he invited Sophie to dance.

While she enjoyed wheeling about the dance floor with Conrad Pluenneke, she was mildly bothered by the smell of alcohol on his breath. While she was German through and through, she had begun to live a more pious life and thus wanted no part of drinking, smoking, cursing, or spitting. Her vision of a good home was free of such sinful behavior so she wasn't quite sure how Conrad Pluenneke might fit into her future.

After the dance, the four talked about the service, the food, and the music but then the men's conversation turned to the need to build their shelters. Since the Leifestes, collectively, already had a cabin, Conrad was the one most in need of shelter but he could not build one alone. The Leifeste brothers volunteered to help Conrad in return for his help at building another cabin for Heinrich on his town lot. In the process of building Conrad's abode, they would all learn how to build better ones and that would later benefit Heinrich and Friedrich. The men also agreed that they should start soon.

While the men talked about construction, Sophie bided her time by listening to the musicians and talking to people in the audience. After the conversation concluded, Conrad asked the brothers whether they might object if he asked their sister to accompany him on a walk around town that afternoon. They said they were happy that he seemed to like her and quickly nodded their assent. Since it was a sunny but brisk winter day, Conrad turned and approached Sophie who had been patiently standing nearby. He suggested that they might walk around the colony that afternoon and see how the city was developing. A stroll around Fredericksburg would allow him to become better acquainted with the fledgling town and with her. She was a bit coy but finally agreed to the idea of a walk. She turned and looked questioningly towards her brothers who nodded their assent. Diplomatically, Conrad offered to include them but the brothers found a way to demure graciously.

Since Sophie Liefeste had arrived in Fredericksburg, she had been staying at her brother's cabin, performing domestic chores to help in their household, but little else. She longed to socialize, even if Conrad Pluenneke drank now and then.

That afternoon, Conrad appeared at Friedrich's cabin and proceeded to escort Sophie around the small colony, mostly on San Saba Street, Creek Street, and within the Marktplatz. Just north of the Verein complex, they noticed the new oddly shaped building that was beginning to take form. It was said that the octagon-shaped building was of a Carolingian design and would be an all-purpose building which would be named the Verein's Kirche (See Figure 6-1). It was intended to serve as a church, a meeting place, a school, and as a defensive structure.

Figure 6-1 The Octagonal Verein's Kirche
in Colonial Fredericksburg (sketch by Seth Easton, 1849).

As they walked side by side, they talked of Germany, about her family back in Boistedt, and about his own badly depleted family. From letters she had received from her brother, she was aware of the fate of Conrad's wife, three sisters, brother and father. He told her about his time in the army, his stint in Mexico, and about his time of deep despair at Indian Point. It was part of getting to know each other.

As people began to drift out of the Marktplatz, the pair started towards Friedrich's cabin. At the creek, Conrad held Sophie's hand as she tiptoed over five large rocks that formed a bridge. At the house, he said goodbye and excused himself to return to the barracks. Somehow, he felt better about the world.

As he prepared to crawl in bed back at the barracks that night, Conrad realized that most of his tools were still stored in the warehouse down at Indian Point. While Friedrich had a few primitive tools, they were likely to be insufficient for building the type of cabin that Conrad had in mind. He made a mental note to approach the Adelsverein the next day about bringing his belongings up to Fredericksburg, a service for which he would surely have to pay.

After arising the next morning, Conrad stepped into the warehouse on his way to the kitchen and asked an agent about retrieving and transporting his tools to Fredericksburg. The agent checked some papers and informed him that a wagon train was scheduled to leave next week and that Conrad's belongings might be put on it, provided the message got down to the warehouse in time. The agent had Conrad sign a German emigration Company form and pay a fee of $1 to retrieve those belongings from Indian Point. He now had less than $10 in his pocket. With the paperwork done, the agent said he would see to it. If all went well, the agent projected that it might take two weeks for those belongings to reach Fredericksburg. Such a delay concerned Conrad but there was little else he could do but wait for his tools.

Extending the conversation a little, Conrad explained to the agent that he needed to start on his shelter very soon because his welcome in the barracks might expire any day. Did the agent know of someone who could help get him started, someone with tools and with know-how about building good cabins? The agent paused, rubbed his chin in thought, and finally said, "Yes, Heinrich Stiehl, who just happens to be here today." With that, he led Conrad Pluenneke out to the courtyard and introduced him to Heinrich Stiehl. After exchanging a few pleasantries with Stiehl, the agent retreated to the Verein office.

Heinrich Stiehl was a kind man, approximately four years older than Conrad, and someone who believed in sharing his knowledge with others. Conrad immediately liked him because he had an air of confidence and believability about him when he spoke. Stiehl patiently listened to the plight of Conrad Pluenneke, a veteran of the Mexican-American War (which was still raging), and then willingly volunteered to help him. Heinrich was a religious man who strongly believed that it was his duty to God to help people in need. Since it was early spring, Stiehl's farming chores were light at the moment and therefore, he had some spare time. Drawing images in the dirt, he explained to Conrad roughly how to go about building a log cabin and which tools might be needed. After coming to understand that Conrad's tools were still in Karlshafen, Stiehl offered to loan tools to him until his implements arrived from the south. But the first step, he cautioned, was to create logs from trees and gather large rocks for a foundation. When Conrad Pluenneke had created enough building material, Heinrich would teach him how to build a durable log cabin. He promised to meet Conrad at his town lot the next morning and bring all the necessary tools.

Early the next morning, Heinrich Leifeste and Conrad Pluenneke rose early, ate in the compound kitchen, and then walked to Conrad's town lot where they were joined by Friedrich Leifeste. Shortly, Heinrich Stiehl arrived with an oxen-drawn wagon loaded with construction tools. Before they started, Stiehl explained that most settlers were building cabins that measured about 16 feet on a side because that was about the greatest length that could be achieved from local oak trees. He said they would need about 36 such logs for the 4 walls, each one measuring between 9 and 12 inches in diameter. Each would have to be trimmed of both branches and bark. He also said they would need 16 additional logs of a similar diameter to construct a style of roof that did not employ a ridgepole.[45] Those, he said, might be made from some of the larger limbs. When the three men had produced those logs, Stiehl promised to return and demonstrate how to notch the logs for construction. Shortly thereafter, Stiehl said goodbye and departed, leaving the men with his tools to begin their work.

Over the next two weeks, the trio of men toiled away at felling, trimming, and cutting large oak trees to size. As the trees were cut to size and stripped, they were stacked near the clearing in the grove. While the construction was ongoing, Conrad occasionally stayed on the lot, sleeping in a canvas tent provided by the Adelsverein. When they had 52 building logs stacked, Conrad borrowed a horse from a Verein guard and rode out to contact Heinrich Stiehl, who lived northwest of Fredericksburg in a community known locally as Klein Frankreich (which means "Little France" in German). The area was so named because the land reminded the earliest settlers (e.g., the Stiehls, Metzgers, Feuges, and the Stehlings) of land they had seen in France. Upon finding Heinrich out in his fields, Conrad walked into the field, greeted Heinrich, and outlined what they had accomplished. Stiehl agreed to meet them the next day to start the building process. As promised, Stiehl arrived in his wagon early the next day ready to begin the process of stacking and interlocking logs into walls.

Stiehl began by explaining that there were several ways of notching the corners of log to keep them together. The simplest means was called saddle notching but that form of notch had often become rotten because water had no way of draining from the saddles in the logs.

---

[45] The ridgepole spanned the length of the roof and often weighed upwards of 200 pounds. It would have been extremely difficult for the men to lift a 16 foot ridgepole to a height of 12 feet and put it in place. The ridgepole style also required gabled ends that were enclosed by heavy log walls. Stiehl's method offered a more efficient alternative to a ridgepole roof.

Other forms of notching, such as mortise and tenon, were elaborate and very time consuming to carve but were very solid and reliable joints. Stiehl recommended the "V" notch style as the best compromise between the alternatives. Using a saw, hammer, and a wood chisel, he demonstrated by carving an inverted "V" onto the end of one log. The water, he explained, would strike the top of the "V" and would drain off to either the right or left but would not stay in the joint. Rolling the log over, Stiehl went on to carve an inverse "V" on the underside of the log, but one that was perpendicular to the top "V." Stiehl explained that all 36 logs that were meant to be used for walls had to be notched that way on their tops and their undersides. He went on to say that while the logs were being fitted together, minor adjustments in the "Vs" would have to be made with chisels to make them fit tightly. With that short tutorial, the men were prepared to carve notches in the logs. Preparing to return to Klein Frankreich, Stiehl promised that when all the logs had been notched, he would return and help them stack the logs on the walls. He reminded them, however, they still needed about a dozen large, flat rocks to form a foundation on which the lowest logs would rest. With that last bit of advice, he turned his wagon around in preparation to leave. They helped him load some of his tools into the wagon, thanked him for his instruction, and waved as he departed.

During the week, the Verein delivered the trunks of belongings to Conrad and to the Leifeste brothers. With that delivery complete, the men now had their own tools and thus were able to return the rest of Stiehl's tools when they saw him again.

After three long days of hard work, the men had all 36 logs "V" notched and ready to stack into walls. With that task done, they turned to finding suitable stones for a foundation. Scouring the banks of Meusebach's Creek, they located a dozen or so large limestone rocks that were roughly two feet square. With much effort, they dragged, rolled, flipped, and pushed the stones back to Conrad's town lot. With cold chisels and hammers, they formed the rocks into cubes.

While notching the logs, Conrad had thought about how to orient his cabin and had driven small stakes where its corners were to be located. At each stake, the trio dug shallow holes to accommodate a foundation rock and then positioned one of the rock cubes at each corner, taking care to level it and keep about eight inches of each cube exposed above ground. Between each of the corners, they dug two holes that were equally spaced, about two feet square, and about a foot and half deep. In each of them, the trio positioned the remaining eight rocks so that about six inches of their height was exposed above ground. Using a rope to span the corners, they leveled them by eyesight and tamped dirt around them to hold the blocks in place. When all 12 rocks were firmly in position and level, Conrad stood back and surveyed the layout. Here and there, minor adjustments were made until a stable and square foundation was established.

After the following Sunday service, they met Heinrich Stiehl by chance near the Marktplatz and told him they had the logs notched and the foundation established. He agreed to meet them the next day and begin building the walls of the cabin.

During construction of his log house, Conrad tried to see Sophie Leifeste whenever he could find time. She had agreed to see him but she made it quite clear that she did not approve of drinking alcohol, smoking, or cursing. Intrigued by her directness, he agreed to rein in some of this behavior if she would see him socially. In 1847, there was little social activity in Fredericksburg as most settlers were busy building houses or clearing land for farms. Most socializing was on the weekends in the Marktplatz. Occasionally, men brought musical instruments on Saturday afternoon and played for the public. At other times, men and women sang in accompaniment to the music. Many colonists came just to hear the music and meet other people just to chat. A few of the couples danced to the music, including Conrad and Sophie. While she disapproved of many normally accepted behaviors, she did enjoy dancing the polka. Other than such impromptu songfests, the social calendar revolved around church activities.

With little else to do, Sophie and Conrad's courtship often amounted to strolling about the colony and talking, sometimes alone and sometimes in the company of her brothers. The place to which they seemed to gravitate was an old crooked pecan tree on the banks of Meusebach Creek. They would sit on the horizontal part of that tree and talk for hours. Those long chats led to a deepening of their relationship and they came to respect each other's views. Conrad found that he could trust Sophie and confided to her about his worrisome lack of faith in God and other things. She had faith from her Evangelical Lutheran background and had never questioned the existence of

God but she had enough understanding and maturity to cope with someone who didn't believe the way she did.

On Monday, the four men began building the walls of the log cabin. Two large logs were selected to serve as sill logs on which the other logs would ultimately rest. The four men hoisted those two large logs, carried them to the cabin site, and placed them on the foundation with the "V" notches inverted to face upwards. Another pair of sturdy logs were selected to span the sill logs. Those logs, which crossed the gabled sides of the hut, were placed perpendicular to the sill logs and laid on top of them so the "V" notches at their ends fit snuggly together. Other logs were subsequently placed so their "V" notches corresponded and fit tightly. Occasionally, the "V" notches of logs had to be adjusted slightly to create a better fit, as Stiehl had said. Heinrich Stiehl refined the "Vs" with some delicate chiseling. To stack the top logs, Stiehl helped them build a ramp that angled upward at a 45 degree angle. One by one, the men rolled the heavy logs up the ramp and onto the next log and then rotated slightly so that the notches fit firmly together. While the walls were being constructed, Heinrich Stiehl made partial cuts in certain logs for the door, a fireplace, and a window. The window faced east, towards the creek. After he made those cuts, he hammered rocks into the gaps to keep the logs spaced apart and the wall secure. When the walls were finished, Stiehl explained, they would finish off the cut faces by building jambs around them. Finally, they would make a hinged door out of planks hewn from tree limbs. Stiehl explained that the fireplace would actually be a firebox composed of flat limestone rocks with a horizontal vent to the exterior. Outside, a crude chimney would be constructed with additional limestone rocks that would serve to carry the smoke up and away from the house.

While they worked, the men often talked about many things and several times their conversations with Heinrich Stiehl turned to religion. Conrad mentioned that he rarely saw Stiehl at the outdoor services in the Marktplatz, yet he knew Heinrich to be a religious man. Stiehl answered that he preferred to attend Methodist services, rather than the more ecumenical outdoor services that were held in the Marktplatz under the large oak trees. Since conversion to the religion of John Wesley, Stiehl went on to say that he felt more in touch with God at those services than any he had ever attended, including those at the Verein's Kirche. That statement caught Conrad's attention. Maybe this was The Way? Intrigued, Conrad asked questions about Methodism and how it differed from the Evangelical Lutheran faith they all knew and practiced back in Germany.

"It differs mainly in the intensity of the experience," Stiehl answered. In the Methodist faith, each person is responsible for his own salvation" and after pausing for a few seconds, added "we do not believe in Calvinistic Predestination" as a postscript to his previous comment. "We feel that Man has free will and each of us exercises that freedom daily, for both good and bad. Under our doctrine, those who sin in this life on Earth will be exiled to everlasting torment in hell unless they admit their sins publicly, repent, and change their behavior permanently," Stiehl said firmly.

"Why is your faith called "Methodism?", Friedrich wanted to know.

Stiehl answered, "Because we try to apply what some have called *The Method* to our lives. We follow a doctrinal book called *The Discipline*, inspired by the sermons of John Wesley but written in the U.S. by members of the Christmas Conference in 1784. It lays down general rules [46] that will lead one to live a good and pious life. Alcohol is just one of those things specified in *The Discipline* to be avoided." Stiehl quickly added, "Salvation is an entirely different matter. It is gained through Grace, not overt acts."

Conrad asked, "What is else is involved in following *The Discipline*?" Would it difficult for me to follow it in ordinary life here in Texas?"

In a matter-of-fact tone, Stiehl answered Conrad Pluenneke. "We preach that it is not acceptable to smoke or chew tobacco, to dance, to curse, to spit, to consort with shady women, to speak profanely, or to use violence, except as a last resort in the defense of self or family. As I have said, we pray regularly to ask God to guide us towards the good in life and avoid those evils that cause us to sin in the eyes of God. Our pleas are for Divine assistance in the pursuit of moral strength and pious conduct. By following *The Discipline*, we do set ourselves apart

---

[46] Coke, T. and Asbury, F. The Doctrines and Discipline of the Methodist Episcopal Church in America, 1798.

from other settlers in Fredericksburg and that difference might be difficult for some to accept. Not everyone is cut out to be a Methodist."

That discussion gave Conrad a lot to think about in the days that followed construction of his log cabin walls. Would he be willing to depart from the norms of Fredericksburg behavior and live according to *The Discipline* in his new hometown? Would he be ostracized for that? Yes, almost certainly he would. Would Methodism interfere with his ability to get work as a carpenter? Maybe, but Stiehl seemed to get plenty of work.

After the walls were erected, Stiehl showed the trio how to roof a log structure without using a ridgepole. To illustrate his point, he drew a sketch of his proposed roof in the sand. The technique amounted to cutting and juxtaposing pairs of stripped logs at a slant so they met over the center of the house. At the top, opposing logs pairs were secured at a lap joint by pinning them together with a wooden dowel driven through a hole in the joint. The rafters were then cross-decked with flat planks to add strength to the roof. Shingles, split from cedar logs, were then secured to the decking with square nails made of iron. Conrad saw the wisdom of not using a ridgepole. Without much brawn, the three men would never get one into place atop the cabin. Stiehl's method was the most efficient means to build a solid roof with the resources he had at his command and Conrad adopted Stiehl's plan.

"With four of us working," Stiehl said, "we can get the framework of the roof done today. You three men can finish it tomorrow or whenever you have time."

It took the foursome most of another day to cut, erect, and pin the eight sets of roof rafters into place above the walls. To hold them in place, long slats were cut and nailed lengthwise across the rafters. With that chore completed, Stiehl hitched up his team again and departed, leaving Conrad and the Leifeste brothers to finish the roof decking and shingling. That job took them another week.

When the roof was complete, Conrad turned to the job of filling in the gaps between logs in the walls, a process called chinking. First, he forced small rocks into the gaps with his hammer and then covered them with clay mud that he mined from the banks of the nearby creek. When the mud dried, it became very hard and nearly impervious to weather. He had heard that other settlers were beginning to use lime-stone cement, which they created on the premises by building a lime kiln. That approach subjected limestone rocks to intense heat that broke down the rocks and resulted in lime residue. After harvesting the lime residue, they slaked it in water, added sand, and made a putty-like substance which, when applied to the cracks, dried to an almost brick-like texture. Lime worked much better than adobe but it took much time and effort to construct a lime kiln and use it. With limited time, Conrad opted to use adobe mud but after the first hard rains, he came to realize that he would have to repair his chinked walls covered with adobe mud more frequently.

After a month of hard work, the trio stood and gazed at the com-pleted structure with its shingled roof. Its exterior measured roughly 16 feet by 16 feet, providing an interior space of about 256 square feet. At the crown of the roof, the little shack stood about 11 feet high. It had a door made of oak, hinged with buckskin strips. Opposite the door, the hut had a single window opening that was covered during inclement weather with a thin sheet of buckskin. On the west side, it had a crude smokestack made of flat limestone rocks. Conrad was pleased at the sight of it, although this cabin was very inferior to the rock house that the Pluennekes had inhabited back in Klein-Lafferde. Conrad's gaze slowly wandered around the vicinity of the cabin. It was now late spring and around his town lot, the deciduous trees were full and verdant. Wildflowers grew in shadier places and bees buzzed them in search for nectar. He could hear a slight roar that was created by Meusebach's Creek rippling along nearby, now full with spring runoff waters. In all, it was a very pleasant setting.

The next day, Conrad went to the Verein Building to give the Ver-ein notice that he was vacating his bunk in the barracks and to also re-trieve what was left of his stored belongings. His meager stash consist-ed of a few pieces of furniture, some farm implements, a trunk of kitchenware, a trunk of clothing (mostly that of his deceased wife), and another small box of carpentry tools. Borrowing a team and wagon from the military detachment at the Marktplatz, he moved his belong-ings across the creek and into his new log home. After lugging the fur-niture into the cabin and storing the plow nearby, he returned the rig to the Marktplatz. As he walked back to the cabin, he realized that he was going to need transportation. In coming days, he had to find a way to buy a yoke of oxen and perhaps a wagon. At the moment, however, he had very little money. What money he did have he had earned during his time in the Army and it now amounted to $7.

With his new home complete, he began to think about his future again. While he had an outlying lot on which to farm, he could not clear it of trees, cultivate it, plant it, or harvest it alone. In Germany, farming was viewed as a labor-intensive occupation but on the frontier in Texas, it was much more than that. Farming was just too much work for one man to accomplish year in and year out. As he pondered his life and surveyed his new cabin with pride, it came to him that in the past month, he had acquired very good carpentry skills from Heinrich Stiehl, skills that had built on what Fritz Stein had taught him at the warehouse. Other settlers, like himself, might need assistance to build their cabins and he could apply his carpentry skills to help them and get paid for his efforts.

In the coming month, he would help Heinrich Leifeste build his shelter and that would further hone his skills as a carpenter. The notion of becoming a carpenter had merit and it removed any idea that he would revert to farming to make a living. He would still have to farm just enough to support his needs and those of his animals but he did not want to depend on whimsical "rain gods" to deliver their specialty regularly and make his crops grow. In Texas, they were especially capricious. Since there was a scarcity of skilled carpenters and laborers in Fredericksburg, Conrad was able to find work rather quickly at a rate of $1 per day.[47]

The next day, Conrad Pluenneke returned to the Marktplatz to get his first allotment of provisions provided to settlers by the Verein. It was mostly corn, heavily salted pork, and potatoes. Some of the pork was rancid and not edible. Another settler mentioned to him that those provisions came from The Plantation, a large Verein-owned farm near Houston. Even for him as a single man, those meager provisions were not enough to survive on. He would have to supplement his food supply by planting a vegetable garden and by scavenging food from the countryside. Time in his schedule would have to be reserved for hunting, fishing, and gathering of nuts or fruit. His health, and his future livelihood, depended on staying healthy and for a settler, health was paramount.

---

[47] Rate of pay was taken from the Diary of Wilhelm Hermes (page 40), cited in Haas, Oscar *History of New Braunfels and Comal County, 1844-1946.*

In following months, the trio of men finished Heinrich Leifeste's cabin and got him moved in. The three Leifeste siblings were then situated on town lots and had a frequent visitor in Conrad Pluenneke.

The relationship between Conrad and Sophie Liefeste slowly developed into a strong bond but to even consider marriage, he had to establish an occupation that would allow him to support a wife and perhaps a family. In addition, he felt lost in gloomy darkness mentally and in desperate need of light. He did not feel connected to God, or at least, not in a way that he wanted to and not at all in the way that Sophie was. After he and Sophie met, they often talked about religion and their differing religious experiences. Like Conrad, Sophie had been an Evangelic Lutheran in Germany but her experiences had been quite different. She and her family had been affected by the piety movement back then and were deeply religious. Conrad confided that he envied her connection to God and that he had no such connection. It wasn't that he automatically rejected the idea of a God as some free thinkers did but he felt no sense of connection to a tangible God and that concerned him greatly. Some people in Fredericksburg professed to hear the voice of God but he heard only a deafening silence. It was as though his prayers still went off into a deep black hole and became lost. Enthusiastically, he also told her of his discussions about Methodism with Heinrich Stiehl and how they had truly piqued his interest. She saw no reason why they shouldn't attend a Methodist service together and learn more about that branch of the Protestant faith, if it suited his needs. She openly stated that she would be willing to convert to Methodism or any other denomination of Christianity if one of them gave him comfort. Conrad thought about her suggestion, smiled at her willingness, and then agreed to attend a Methodist service with her in the future.

Beginning in June of 1847, Conrad began to spread the word around the small colony that he was available to do carpentry work in Fredericksburg. Within weeks, he began to get small jobs. Some of his work was at Fort Martin Scott on behalf of the U.S. Army. In some cases, he helped settlers build log cabins. In other cases, he helped merchants build shops along San Saba Street. In the beginning, his pay was minimal, usually about $1 per day. As his reputation grew, he began to get a steadier flow of jobs and some of the larger jobs lasted for a month or two. He also took on jobs that demanded more skill. As he successfully completed larger jobs and honed his skills, Conrad's reputation grew and he began to command a higher wage. By the end of

1849, he was getting $1.50 per day. Between 1847 and 1853, Conrad's annual income from freelance carpentry fluctuated between $160 and $240 per year. When he finished jobs, he was generally paid in gold coins. Some of that income was needed for his own subsistence but wisely, he began saving about a fourth of it.

In 1847, Fredericksburg did not have a bank so Conrad had to keep his savings at home where it could be protected. While there was little crime in the new colony, openly leaving gold coins in a home exposed them to theft. It was known that Indians occasionally entered vacant cabins looking for food and they certainly knew the value of gold. Outlaws also sought gold. How could he protect his growing savings from an intruder? After some thought, he concocted the idea of concealing it in the walls of his log cabin. Using his carpenter's tools, Conrad carefully carved out a niche in a log high above the door and then disguised it with a well-fitted wooden plug that matched the log's grain. Over that area, he hung his only memento from Germany: a small brass plaque from Klein-Lafferde. Each time he was paid, he opened the cache carefully, counted his savings, added the new coins, and then resealed it.

With income flowing in and saving some of it, he still practiced thrift but could now afford to buy a little more food and a few items of new clothing. He particularly needed a new shirt and new pants. When Julius B. Ransleben opened the first store on San Saba Street in 1848, Conrad began buying his food and clothing there. He found Julius to be fair when it came to pricing his goods and always enjoyed talking to him even though he was Catholic. Because of high prices, Conrad could only afford to buy small quantities of food to supplement his regular diet of cornbread and venison. In 1847, food sold at the following prices: meat at 4 cents per pound, butter at about 37 cents per pound, flour at $15 to $20 per barrel, eggs at 25 to 37 cents per dozen, coffee at 15 cents per pound, chickens at 37 to 50 cents each, sugar at 16 cents per pound, salt at 6 cents per pound, and corn at somewhere between $1.25 and $1.75 per bushel (Bracht, 1848).[48]

With some of his savings, he bought a pair of oxen with a yoke for $30 and several head of Longhorn cattle at $6 each from the German

---

[48] When one considers that wages were generally $1 per day, those food prices were very high.

Emigration Company in the fall of 1847. He also bought a plow and a harness for $10. To shelter the cattle and house the new equipment, he built a barn and corral on his outlying property which was about a mile and a half west of Fredericksburg. Over a two and a half year span, he steadily increased his herd of cattle. Oddly, he did not choose to buy a horse until 1853.

With some money saved and a promising carpenter career under way, he felt emboldened enough to think of marriage again. Because of the death of his first wife and the pain that her loss inflicted on him, he was in no hurry to remarry but he often thought of Sophie. He continued to work whenever he had the opportunity and courted Sophie in his spare time. This pattern continued throughout 1847 and 1848. By the end of 1848, he had managed to accumulate around $50 in gold coins. In addition, he had a cabin, a small herd of cattle, oxen, and a wagon. Financially, he felt able to take a wife.

In 1848, settlers in and around Fredericksburg petitioned the state of Texas to form a new county, which they proposed to name Germania. That year, the new county was approved and carved from land held by both Bexar and Travis counties but was named for a hero of the Mexican-American War, Captain Robert Gillespie. The new county ranged north into the Llano River watershed and encompassed land that is now part of both Mason and Llano counties.

On Easter Sunday (April 24th, 1849), Conrad took Sophie Liefeste to the Marktplatz and proposed to her in front of the Vereins Kirche. With no hesitation, she happily accepted his proposal. On Wednesday, May 4th of that year, they were married by J. P. Mosel, Justice of the Peace, in Fredericksburg.[49] The next day, she moved out of her brother's cabin and into the rest of Conrad Pluenneke's life.

For three years, Conrad continued to work as a carpenter while Sophie tended to domestic chores at home. In many ways, Sophie was the

---

[49] According to DeVos (1986), they were married on August 23, 1847. That date could not be verified by the author. Their marriage was not recorded in Der Kirchen Buch, the official record of rites performed in the Verein's Kirche, nor does that document contain any record of a religious rite involving a Pluenneke, including births, baptisms, confirmations, or deaths. Record of their marriage does not exist in the Gillespie County Clerk's office or in early Methodist Church records.

ideal wife for Conrad Pluenneke because she was thrifty and willing to work hard for what they wanted as a couple. She planted a garden and began to raise a variety of vegetables to supplement their diet. Whenever word spread that the Verein was doling out provisions, she went to the Marktplatz and collected their share.

Although Sophie was a practicing Lutheran, she and Conrad chose not to attend church services at the Vereins Kirche or elsewhere on a regular basis, although they talked of Methodism.

In July of 1849, Sophie greeted Conrad with news that he was going to be a father. Their first baby would most likely arrive by the end of February or early in March of 1850.[50]

During 1849, Conrad occasionally ran into Heinrich Stiehl at various job sites and at the Marktplatz. Invariably their conversations would turn to the topic of Methodism. He listened attentively and with an open mind as Stiehl expounded further on *The Discipline* and the Methodist way of life. Still, Conrad Pluenneke had nagging doubts about the existence of God and organized religion but he was also determined to learn more from Stiehl.

At just such a chance meeting early in 1849, Heinrich Stiehl informed Conrad that a Methodist church was being formally established in Fredericksburg and that he and Catharina (nee Arnold) were going to be among its 15 charter members. Would he be willing to attend a service? With some ambivalence, Conrad accepted Stiehl's invitation to attend a Methodist service and learn more about the faith. On some days, Conrad felt a growing feeling that Methodism might be *The Way* for him and for Sophie but on other days, he dismissed the idea out of hand. Was Heinrich Stiehl some sort of prophet sent to deliver him to a state of grace and faith in God? Coming days would tell. Oh, God, please show me the Way!

---

[50] Given Conrad and Sophie's fertility and lack of birth control, it is the author's belief that they were married in the summer of 1849 because their first child arrived in March of 1850. Over the decade between 1849 and 1859, Sophie would spend over 50% of that time pregnant.

Chapter 7

CONVERSION AND GROWTH
IN METHODISM

At Heinrich Stiehl's invitation, Conrad and Sophie attended their first Methodist service on Sunday, June 19th, 1849. It was staged under a large oak tree on the south side of San Antonio Street, with Reverend Eduard Schneider [51] officiating. At the time, the Methodist Church in Texas was primarily an Anglo-American institution and the idea of German Methodists was somewhat of an anomaly because they were predominantly either Lutheran or Catholic (Jordan, 1979). Because of what Stiehl had told them, Sophie and Conrad attended with the notion that it would be a novel experience for them, completely unlike any religious service either had ever attended in Germany.

After they arrived and seated themselves on log stumps, they glanced around and recognized several of the people in attendance. In addition to Heinrich and Catharina Stiehl, there was Friedrich and Sophie Ellebracht, Ernest and Dorothea Houy, Ferdinand and Maria Kneese, Ludwig Kneese, Jacob and Catherine Treibs, Melchior and Roseanne Bauer as well as Fritz and Fredericka Winkel. Of the charter members, only the Dursts, Johann and Margaretha, were absent. Most of them were seated on the front row, directly in front what could be construed as the altar.

At the front, near the trunk of the tree, was a simple altar that was most likely the kitchen table of Reverend Schneider. Resting atop it was an open *Bible*, *The Discipline*, and a Methodist hymnal. Stiehl had told the Pluennekes that Methodists were great believers in religious music and that many of the songs that Methodists sang during their services had been written by Charles Wesley, brother of the founder. To the left of the altar was a simple wooden bench. Stiehl had told Conrad about the existence of a *Sinner's Bench* [52] and its purpose in the Methodist service. As they sat and anxiously awaited the start of

---

[51] Reverend Schneider had been induced to come to Fredericksburg by Herr Schumacher, the local tailor, to pray for relief from a cholera epidemic that was plaguing the town. It was reported that Schneider prayed day and night. From Splittgerber, J. "*The Second Train to Fredericksburg and the Growth of the Colony.*" In Penniger, Robert. (1896), page 34.

[52] The *Sinner's Bench* was also sometimes referred to as the "*Mourner's Bench.*"

the liturgy, Conrad's thoughts drifted and he began to ponder what Heinrich Stiehl had taught him thus far about Methodism.

It had been started in the 18th century by John Wesley, an Oxford professor turned pietist. In 1729, he and his brother, Charles, ardently read the *Bible* and came to believe that they could not gain salvation without holiness and pursued it vigorously. Their pious behavior incited others to emulate and follow them. [53] As a pietist, John Wesley simply sought to live a pure and chaste life in a complex secular society. To help himself put that desire into effect, he penned a list acts which was to his way of thinking, a series of acts (e.g., regular prayer) that he thought every pious person needed perform regularly to achieve and maintain a good moral life. Critics derisively dubbed Wesley's approach *The Method* because of the rigidity and discipline with which he applied religion to his own life. The name stuck. Instead of being offended by the sobriquet, Wesley adopted the name for his new sect and his followers became known as Methodists. In short order, John Wesley gained many converts at Oxford who followed his method to a pious life. Wesley, however, was not a typical Anglican because he opposed Obscurantism, the practice of preventing important facts from being widely known.[54] Conversely, he was forever ready to spread the Word to commoners in England in a language they could readily comprehend. To the established gentry in the Anglican Church of that era, John Wesley was a radical and they didn't know how to regard him. He was performing good works for Christianity but in a way of which they did not approve. A detractor, Bishop Warburton, conceded that Wesley was, "Formed of the best stuff of nature that was ever put into a fanatic to make him the head and leader of a sect" (Outler 1964).

In 1735, Wesley went to the American colony of Georgia to do missionary work with Indians. Enroute, he was heavily influenced by a group of German pietists (Moravians) who taught him a deep appreciation of joyful faith to match his exacting, industrious Methodism. When their ship was caught in a violent storm and in danger of sinking, most passengers were terrified but the Moravians calmly sang hymns of faith, certain that they were in God's hands and therefore

---

[53] *The Discipline*, 1798, page 14.
[54] An example of obscurantism in Texas history was the Catholic Church's attempt to forbid Protestants from distributing the Bible in Texas in 1830.

safe. Their faith made a lasting impression on John Wesley. After his mission to Georgia failed, he returned to England where he met Peter Bohler, a Moravian missionary, who convinced him that he lacked supernatural faith in God and that he would need that to go forward in religion. After months of ardent prayer, he found that faith at a meeting on Aldersgate Street where his "heart was suddenly and mysteriously warmed." In that instant, he became a new man. After that meeting, he sought to share his new-found faith with everyone. Eschewing Anglican practices, which mainly served the wealthy and influential in polite society, Wesley sought to communicate the Gospel to "the lowly and disowned as well as to men of reason and religion" (Outler, 1964). It was because of his appeal to the former that his ideas gained traction and spread around Europe and eventually came to America.[55]

Methodism, as an American denomination apart from Anglican religion, began at Baltimore in December of 1784 at what was became known as the Christmas Conference (Hardt and Hardt, 2008). At that meeting, the Wesleyan Movement split away from the Anglican Church in America and formed the Methodist Episcopal Church (MEC) which quickly spread to other states in the union. At that conference, *The Discipline*, an all-important Methodist document, was written primarily by Bishops Coke and Asbury.

Methodism was well suited to America in the 18th century, a country that was populated by common people who cherished freedom and equality but who were hard working and poor. When the new form of Protestantism was organized on the American shore in 1784, the nation was still a new creation, mostly rural, and its far-flung regions were only loosely connected by horse trails, wagon roads, and waterways. Its population was mainly clustered in large cities strung along the Atlantic seacoast but some of it was also widely scattered in the heavily forested and mountainous region beyond the Appalachian Mountains. Those areas were too sparsely populated to form churches and often difficult to reach but the people who lived there "hungered for preaching."

---

[55] The revivalism of early Methodists, compared to that of Lyman Beecher, focused on rapidly building membership a particular denomination. The Methodist circuit riders had unparalleled success in achieving that mission.

To reach and serve those people, the leaders of the Methodist denomination in America (e.g., Bishop Thomas Coke and Bishop Francis Asbury) adopted Wesley's notion of circuits and appropriated the Camp Meeting revival of the Presbyterians as their own. To reach into the most remote areas, they created circuits that looped through the backcountry, each circuit having multiple stops and covering hundreds of miles of rugged territory. To work the circuit, the church hierarchy selected and trained circuit-riding ministers, mostly single men, who traveled those loops regularly and preached the Gospel nearly every day, often at Camp Meetings. The circuit riders, often dressed in priestly black and on horseback, carried a *Holy Bible*, a copy of *The Discipline*, and a gun in their saddlebags. In later years, the circuit riders also carried medicine and books with them as they were often the only contact that rural folks had with the organized, civilized world.

Stops on the circuit were held at brush arbors, groves of trees along a stream, homes of local citizens, taverns, schools, or public buildings–wherever people could come together for a few hours to hear preaching. Those circuits often went through territory occupied by hostile Indians, outlaws, people of other religious sects (i.e., Baptists), and rowdies. Many of the latter, but not all, intended to disrupt Methodist services and were apt to use violence to accomplish their ends. Therefore, circuit riders often had to defend themselves against such acts, although they shunned violence. Therefore, some circuit riders, such as Peter Gravis of Blanco County, [56] became known as *Pistol-packin Preachers* (Barton, 2005).

Once assigned to a circuit, the rider was obligated to repeat it several times each year, regardless of the hardships he endured while riding and serving it. The Methodist Church paid its circuit-riders a paltry sum (usually about $100 per year) to preach so local citizens had to help support the traveling minister by feeding him and housing him as he rode the circuit. As a result, a few circuit-riding ministers were not at all reluctant about intruding into a family's life and asking for a hot meal or a warm bed. It was said that a Methodist minister often came with his hand out but it was also said that those circuit riders wrought civility out of chaos in the backwoods.

---

[56] Peter Gravis' circuit originated from Blanco and served 1,500 people in a 900 square mile area, including Mason, in the 1860s. (Barton, 2005).

A few circuit-riders rose to great fame. Perhaps the most famous and most successful of the early circuit riders was Peter Cartwright who plied circuits in Kentucky, Ohio, Indiana, and Illinois over a 50 year period. In the introduction to the *Autobiography of Peter Cartwright*, Charles Wallis wrote that "He (Cartwright) was the most colorful and the most successful of the pioneer preachers that followed the scalped timber trails and bent the prairie grasses." Peter was raised in Logan County (Kentucky) near the Tennessee border that, at the time, was a very dangerous area occupied by outlaws and Indians. Coincidentally, it was there that the remarkable religious awakening, known to historians as the *Great Western Revival* or the *Great Awakening*, began near the turn of the 18th century. Cartwright was in the midst of that awakening, riding circuits and organizing congregations as well as conducting Camp Meetings on the edge of civilization (Cartwright, 1956). More than once he was confronted and threatened by drunken hooligans who were determined to disrupt and put an end to Camp Meetings. Riding alone, he survived on his ample determination, wit, ingenuity, intelligence, and force, on rare occasions.

In parallel with, but perhaps a little ahead of the *Great Western Revival* was a national temperance movement that was largely initiated by women such as Harriet Beecher Stowe (Howe, 2007). In the 18th century, men in the lawless backwoods regions of America had devolved to a state of tawdry behavior marked by gambling, profanity, spitting, bigotry, and violence, but particularly by heavy consumption of alcohol. It is difficult to understate just how much alcohol that an average American frontiersman drank every day in that era but it was excessive. Alcohol was inexpensive and in good supply so a dependence on it was easily created. The women of that era sought to curb that rowdy behavior and civilize American society west of the Appalachians by organizing temperance leagues that attempted to rein in their husband's alcohol usage and later by getting them to adopt religion.[57] Methodism was a perfect antidote in that era as it looked upon such behavior, particularly drinking and violence, as sinful and amoral in the eyes of God. Women were usually the ones who organized the family for Camp Meetings and other religious sessions, which they

---

[57] Because of the Temperance Movement (and perhaps Methodism), the annual alcohol consumption per capita plunged from 7.1 gallons in 1830 to 1.8 gallons in 1850. "Order exists because of a system of beliefs and sentiments held by members of society which set limits to what those members can do." Wilson, James Q. *The Moral Sense*, 1993.

more or less coerced their husbands to attend, although some went willingly.

A Methodist Camp Meeting generally embraced several local families and might have, all considered, reached 100 or so men, women, and children but sometimes they involved thousands. They were normally held at times that did not conflict with the agricultural cycle. In Texas, that meant late summer or early fall. When they were held, families packed up their food and children in wagons, left their farms with neighbors watching over them, and drove to the site where the meeting was to be held. Once there, they camped as close to the makeshift stages or arbors as they could get and then lived out of their wagons for days, all to get "preaching." The stage (see Figure 7-1) was usually a raised wooden platform from which the preacher spoke. In front of the stage, in full sight of the assembled throng, was the in *Sinner's Bench*. During the Camp Meeting, the attendees were subjected to a series of emotional, fiery "hellfire and brimstone" sermons. During each day and night of the meeting, each of several preachers gave sermons that lasted for hours, some for an entire day. Those meetings went on day and night for several days or even as long as a week.

At a session, people who felt the presence of God during a sermon and who desperately wanted eternal salvation to escape the fires of hell, were urged to move from their place in the crowd to a place in front of the stage. Once there, they were directed to occupy the *Sinner's Bench* where they were verbally harangued by someone known as the Exhorter whose job it was to put pressure on the sinner by shouting intense expressions at them; phrases such as "Your soul is doomed to live in the fires of hell for eternity unless you repent your sins" and "Pray harder, sinner, pray harder!" Such exhortations produced a state of extreme anxiety and guilt in the poor sinner until he or she finally repented their sins and converted to Methodism. When that moment of conversion came, their anxiety and guilt were released in such a rush that it was not uncommon for the convert to either faint or go into convulsions, which became known as the *Methodist Shakes*. Conversion was an extremely intense experience, with a release somewhat like the concept of catharsis in Freudian psychoanalysis. When the crowd saw someone going into the "shakes", they often applauded and prayed aloud for the person's soul. After that deeply moving experience, the new convert was led away, baptized in the healing waters of the Lamb, and welcomed into the congregational fold of Methodists on a conditional basis. From that point onward, they had the certain knowledge of salvation and everlasting life, even if they backslid momentarily.[58]

Figure 7-1 A Typical Setting for a Methodist Camp Meeting

After Camp Meetings, new converts were adopted into Methodist classes with well established church members. Such classes were intended to provide mutual support in the process of growth in faith but they were also used to educate new converts in the ways of Methodism by a member of the congregation designated as the Class Leader. After a successful six month probationary period, the convert was admitted to the church as a full member. When a number of classes had been created in an area, a society was formed and multiple societies led to the formation of conferences. Thus, Methodism built a solid organization from the ground up.

The Methodist Church required that its preachers keep record of how many people were converted at Camp Meetings as well as at regular meetings. The number of conversions was tallied by circuit, district, and conference. The number of souls saved became a metric by which ministries and districts were evaluated. Peter Cartwright, for example, was credited with bringing tens of thousands of people to Methodism in his long and storied career.

---

[58] It has been widely debated in the church whether salvation is absolute or is incrementally earned and therefore subject to loss.

From its inception, the Methodist Church was a highly organized society of believers, a trait imposed on it by its founder, John Wesley. The church was managed by men who rose through the ranks to become Deacons, Elders or even higher, Presiding Elders or Bishops. They were people who had served initially at its lowest rungs as exhorters and class leaders before rising to a higher office. The church itself was organized into districts and conferences that held regular meetings to review the progress of the faith. Annual Conferences were the highlight of the year and attendance was expected, however participation in conferences often meant travel and lengthy times away from home. At such conferences, preachers received their appointments to specific circuits or stations. Often, those annual assignments required the preacher to move to another town or sometimes even another state to best serve the Methodist church. That system required flexibility on the part of the preacher and sometimes, family issues trumped assignments. For that reason, the Methodists hierarchy preferred preachers who were single and willing to be sent to any underserved area.

In its earliest days, the territory known as Texas was largely populated by Hispanics who were predominantly Catholic so there was little or no Protestant presence in the region. In 1835, when Texas was still a state of Mexico, Colonel William B Travis wrote to the New York Christian Advocate, a Methodist publication, and called for a Methodist missionary to be sent there. His words were "I regret that the Methodist Church, which, with its excellent itinerant system, has hitherto sent pioneers of the Gospel into almost every destitute portion of the globe, should have neglected so long this interesting country."

In 1837, three Methodist missionaries came to Texas. In 1842, they were followed by six Methodist ministers from Ohio, including John Wesley Devilbiss, who established a mission in San Antonio.

At the General Conference of the MEC in 1844, the Methodist church formally split over the issue of slavery. Delegates from Texas, siding with the minority, began making plans to form and join a new entity, the Methodist Episcopal Church-South (MEC-S). In 1846, the MEC-S was officially established and the MEC, which opposed slavery, virtually disappeared in Texas (Hardt and Hardt, 2008). What remnants of the MEC that remained in Texas were assigned to the Arkansas-Missouri Conference until 1860 when they were assigned to the Kansas Conference, along with the eastern part of New Mexico.

The small faction of the MEC in Texas during that era became focused mainly on minority and rural poor populations located in coastal regions of Texas. For Methodist people who had abolitionist leanings and who lived inland, they had no choice but to affiliate with an MEC-S conference. In a few instances, the MEC created lengthy circuits into Texas and carried a different brand of Methodism.

In contrast, the MEC-S flourished. It quickly evolved into two conferences: the Eastern Texas Conference and the Western Texas Conference and in the decade prior to the Civil War, it expanded into five conferences.

In 1845, Heinrich P. Jung [59] brought a denomination of the Methodist religion to Texas that took the novel form of German Methodism. He founded a Methodist church at Galveston for German immigrants which was adopted by the MEC-S. He quickly gained converts and was soon joined in that effort by other missionaries. From Galveston, MEC-S circuits were created that reached deep into the interior of Texas and missionaries began to ride those circuits, seeking converts among the German settlers. The new German communities of Karlshafen, Victoria, New Braunfels, and Fredericksburg [60] were a particularly rich mission field for the Methodist missionaries because other religions lacked the personnel to serve the common people in such remote spots of the state. Over the next decade, German Methodism spread in those colonies and established MEC-S congregations. Even though many Germans opposed slavery, there were virtually no MEC churches in Texas to support them so they joined MEC-S churches but many in those congregations continued to hold views more compatible with the MEC. From an MEC-S mission in Fredericksburg, Methodism spread to neighboring counties, e.g., Mason County and Llano County. They vied directly with Catholics, Lutherans, and Baptists for souls and there ensued a fierce competition for converts.

Conrad's awareness slowly returned to the present. He shook his head and scanned the outdoor venue where the Methodist service was

---

[59] Reverend Heinrich P. Jung later changed his surname to Henry P. Young and attended meetings in Fredericksburg in the 1850s.

[60] On May 5th of 1851, C. A Grote gave his first report on the German Mission at Fredericksburg that had been in existence for two years. It had 45 active members and a building for worship.

about to start. He was seated under a huge oak tree and in front of a makeshift altar. He sensed that he was a little apprehensive about what was about to unfold and that made him shift uncomfortably on his log seat. Focusing again on the scene in front of him, Conrad noticed that Reverend Schneider was approaching the altar, signaling the beginning of the service. Silently he asked himself "What is this Methodist service going to be like?" He looked over at Sophie and squeezed her hand. Would he be led to convert today or would it be just another futile attempt to find God and get the Almighty One to speak directly to him?" Unconsciously, he shrugged and settled on the stump, trying to get comfortable.

Reverend Schneider rose and asked everyone present to rise and join him in reciting *The Lord's Prayer* aloud.

"Our Father, who art in heaven, hallowed be thy name,
Thy Kingdom come, thy will be done on earth and in heaven--." Amen!

The prayer was very familiar to Conrad and he mindlessly repeated the words without any real comprehension of what they meant. That prayer had been used regularly in rites of the German Evangelistic Lutheran church that he had attended in Klein-Lafferde. He had heard it so often that he had unconsciously memorized it, although it had been many years since he had last recited it.

Following the prayer, the congregation was asked to sing, *Christ, From whom all Blessings Flow*, a hymn composed by Charles Wesley in 1740. Since there were no musicians in the group, the congregation sang *a capella*. The congregation contained a few good male voices and their loud voices drowned out the others who were not quite so adept at singing.

When the hymn was finished, Reverend Schneider strode to the altar, took out his prepared notes that were neatly tucked in an inside pocket of his black suit, and cleared his throat in preparation to speak. His sermon that day was about the evils of alcohol. For a moment, he stared at the assembled group and then launched into his sermon. For several hours, he berated the congregation about excessive drinking, cursing, smoking, and other disgusting sins, emphasizing the effect that such bad behavior had on families and on the community. In his words, those who allowed even a drop of alcohol to touch their lips were certain to be cast into the depths of Hell and live there in fiery agony for the rest of eternity. Hell, in the mind of the Reverend, was a place like *Dante's Inferno*; aflame like *Vulcan's Forge* - painful and unending. Once the sinner descended to Hell, he felt, there was no chance of escape forever. Reverend Schneider repeated the word "forever" to add emphasis. That is a very long time to be in eternal torment. The preacher's words did not paint a pretty picture for Conrad nor did they offer him any wiggle room. They, as intended, made him squirm on his seat.

As Conrad heard the preacher continue on about the wages of sin, he squirmed even more and became quite uncomfortable. He certainly didn't want that fate for himself or for Sophie. The words, though very harsh by design, forced him to think about his life and what sins he might have committed in the past. Yes, he drank too much tequila while in Mexico. Yes, he had eyed the naked senoritas bathing in Mexican streams. Yes, he had gambled. Yes, he had cursed on occasion but what Private in the Army had not used profanity during wartime? And he still spit now and then. But the worst sin that he could dredge up was failing to believe in the existence of the one true God. He was certain that was a major sin but in his own self-defense, he had tried to communicate with God but had failed! Was that his fault or God's? Why had God chosen not to communicate to him?

At that point, he was certain that he heard a distant rumble in the sky above him and that unnerved him a bit.

He came out of his reverie of self-analysis just in time to hear Reverend Schneider invite sinners to come forward, take a place on the *Sinner's Bench* and publicly admit their sins. Would they be cleansed in the blood of the Lamb today? Conrad looked at Sophie, who was staring back at him with wide-eyed amazement. She too had been affected by the forcefulness of the sermon, which had now lasted well over two hours. His return gaze suggested a lot of uncertainty. "Not today," he seemed to be saying, and she nodded ever so slightly.

Before he acted, Conrad felt that he needed to step back and consider this religion rationally. Later, he and Sophie would talk about all of this together and then meet with the minister, but in private. Conrad was not ready to profess his profound doubts, at least not at this time and in front of so many people that knew him. He wasn't at all certain how the group would respond to his plight. He didn't want to become an outcast in Fredericksburg, especially just as he was beginning to get established as a carpenter but, at the same time, he also felt moved to consider taking action.

After another Charles Wesley hymn, *"O Come and Dwell in Me,"* the preacher passed the hat, said a benedictory prayer, and concluded the service. For a few minutes, those in the congregation milled about and talked to each other. During that time, Conrad and Sophie mingled, met several members of the congregation, and were heartily welcomed to return the following Sunday but a few of them openly admonished Conrad about drinking alcohol. The last person they met was Heinrich Stiehl, whom Conrad heartily thanked for inviting them to the service. Heinrich asked about how they felt about it and Conrad had to admit that the fiery Methodist meeting was a huge departure from the calmer, more sedate Lutheran services that he and Sophie were accustomed to but, Conrad went on to note, they were not daunted. Their Methodist experience would not be forgotten - but they were not ready to commit to Methodism just yet.

After leaving the outdoor Methodist service, Conrad and Sophie went to Friedrich Leifeste's cabin and told the brothers about what they had witnessed at the Methodist meeting. The pair listened with rapt attention as Conrad and Sophie related their experiences during Reverend Schneider's sermon. The brothers seemed intrigued by this new religion and offered to accompany them to a Methodist meeting should they choose to attend another one. There might be more comfort in numbers.

The following Sabbath, Conrad and Sophie went to the Methodist meeting place, this time accompanied by the two Leifeste brothers. As they entered the vacant area, they met the now familiar families that had attended the previous week plus a few other visitors. They introduced the Leifeste brothers to the Methodist families and chatted informally with Reverend Schneider. Shortly, they took places on the stumps and prepared themselves for a religious event.

The Methodist service that day followed the same liturgy as before except that a visiting missionary served as Exhorter. He was positioned near the infamous *Sinner's Bench* and seemed quite intent on doing his job. Under Reverend Schneider's fiery preaching, both Conrad and Sophie were induced to weep and inwardly acknowledge their sins. Her brothers were similarly affected. Silently, they all promised to seek ways to live a better and more religious life but they refrained from moving to the *Sinner's Bench* and openly admitting their sins. As a result, the foursome left the Methodist service with strong and unsettling feelings of guilt that lasted throughout much of the week. In his heart, Conrad felt like a sinner on the path to Hell. While his intentions were good, he knew he had reneged on his pledge to God to lead a better life and that piled even more guilt on him.

During the week, Conrad found that guilt invaded his thought and affected his work habits, making it difficult to concentrate and do craftsman-like work. In those times of weakness, he tried to pray but his feelings of guilt persisted, welled up, and overwhelmed him. In his heart, he knew he was just play-acting. He wasn't really trying to find God but simply trying to eliminate those awful feelings of guilt and shame. He had to admit to himself that he was both a hypocrite, one merely mouthing the words without meaning them, and a Pharisee. He was in misery.

In July, Conrad and Sophie attended the wedding of close friends at the Vereins Kirche, an event where heavy drinking and dancing was quite common in the German community. After the ceremony, Conrad had more than his share of Schnapps as round after round of toasts were offered to the newly married couple. In a celebratory mood, the couple danced until the musicians ended their stint late that night. Barely able to walk, a wobbly Conrad escorted Sophie to their home and then passed out on the floor of the cabin. He was aware that Sophie disapproved of his behavior but she had kept quiet. The next day, Conrad felt even more miserable. In his heart, he knew he should have avoided the alcohol but he recognized that he was admittedly weak. When he was inebriated, his anguish disappeared, his spirits were elevated, and he could briefly enjoy life again but when he sobered up, the shame and guilt returned with a vengeance. Again, he was very distraught. Oh Lord, show me the way!

Over the course of the next two months, Conrad and Sophie sporadically attended Methodist services. During that time, Conrad tried to lead a better life but he fell well short as old habits surfaced again. At other social functions in Fredericksburg, he had tended to drink too much, despite Sophie's admonishments. Meanwhile, Conrad continued to vacillate between believing in God and not believing. One day he believed and the next day he didn't. Like Doubting Thomas, he required tangible proof to have faith in God and while preaching made him feel guilty, that guilt did not provide the proof he required to believe. He needed an overt sign from God.

Later in 1849, 17 members officially left the Vereins Kirche and were joined by other Methodist converts to create a formal Methodist congregation in Fredericksburg. Designated as a mission by the church, several of its members built a log structure on two town lots located on San Antonio Street, lots that were owned and donated to the church by the Kneese family. Its location was just west of the new St. Mary's Catholic church and across from the large oak tree where outdoor Methodist services had been held for several years. The building was a simple log cabin that was subsequently "occupied for divine worship," according to Reverend Charles A. Grote.[61] Affiliated with the MEC-S, the new church was recognized in 1849 as part of the Texas Conference but the Pluennekes were not among its charter members

In March of 1850, the Pluennekes had their first child, a daughter that they named Sophie to honor the baby's mother as well as Conrad's mother, his sister, and his grandmother. The arrival of a daughter dramatically changed the couple's view of the world. Community and family became more important than social events in town and the Pluennekes worked to create a good home for little Sophie. Shortly after her birth, Conrad crafted a bassinet from hickory wood for little Sophie and he also bought a cow from a neighbor so that his young daughter would have milk to drink. For them, the world began to change for the better in many ways.

On his outlying land, Conrad began to raise corn and other grains to feed their cow. Over the course of the year, Conrad managed to buy 11 more Longhorns, including one bull, and built pens to enclose them. With a small herd of cattle, the Pluennekes could count on beef to supplement their diet.

On September 18th of 1850, Henry K. Judd came to the Pluenneke's cabin to take census data for Gillespie County. In response

---

[61] Reverend Grote's report on the German Mission in Fredericksburg, 1851

to Judd's questions, Conrad stated that he was married and had one child (Sophie) whose age was reported as six months. Conrad gave his occupation as a carpenter and reported $50 in assets. Judd issued them a census number of 220.

On December 28th of that year, Conrad and Sophie arranged to sell their town lot and cabin to John Schmidtzinsky, another carpenter in town. The sale was a two-step process. On the date of the sale, Schmidtzinsky put down $50 and paid the remainder ($50) on September 5th in 1851. That $100 went into their savings. During the eight month span of the sales contract, Conrad built another log home on his outlying land, with the help of his two brothers-in-law. Around the 1st of September, they removed their belongings from the cabin on town lot 248 and moved them to their new, slightly larger, and very remote log home. Now living on the outlying lot, Conrad was better able to oversee his herd and fields while carpentering. The outlying property, however, was a mile and a half outside of Fredericksburg and that made commuting into Fredericksburg difficult for him. Through a client, Conrad heard that the sheriff, Louis Martin, had a wagon and a yoke of oxen for sale. He approached Martin, looked it over, and bought the entire rig for $30. After concluding the purchase, Conrad drove it to his home and put the oxen in the pen with his cattle.

In 1850 and 1851, Conrad continued to work in Gillespie County as a free-lance carpenter but occasionally, he still dreamed of owning a large tract of land. Toward that dream, he and Sophie continued their thrifty ways and saved all they could out of his earnings while maintaining a good home for little Sophie. Over that span, they managed to add $100 to their savings. When the volume of the gold coins exceeded his secret storage place, Conrad bought a galvanized box at J.B. Ransleben's store, put most of the coins in it, and quietly buried it near their log house.

During the fall term of the District Court in 1851, Conrad went to the Gillespie County Courthouse on the 12th of November, paid a fee, and filed his application papers to become a citizen of the United States.[62] The papers were recorded that day. During the spring term of the District Court in 1852, Conrad went back to the courthouse and

---

[62] District Court Minutes, Volume A, Page 53 and also Naturalization File, Box 2, Number 124.

took an oath of allegiance to the United State, thus making him a citizen with voting privileges. From that time onward, he paid his Poll Tax and voted in major elections.

Over that two year span, the family also began to attend Methodist services on a more regular basis but continued to refrain from taking steps to join the church. The Methodist meetings, now held indoors in what had became known as the Kneese House [63] on the south side of San Antonio Street, emphasized music and that made the services more enjoyable. As a result, more and more people attended and the congregation grew.

At the Methodist Annual Conference in 1851, Charles A. Grote was appointed to replace Reverend Eduard Schneider as the pastor of the Fredericksburg German Mission. On May 5, 1851, Reverend Grote filed his first report that stated that when he began his ministry there, he found 45 members, "all active and untiring in their effort to diffuse the light of the Gospel." Within weeks, 15 more were added as provisional members. The Methodist faith was catching on in Fredericksburg.

On January 14th, Heinrich Leifeste married Margaretha Rheinhard in a Justice of the Peace ceremony performed by Frank Koenig. Almost three months later, the Pluennekes had their second child, a son whom they named Heinrich Conrad to honor both Heinrich Leifeste and Conrad's late father. Little Heinrich's birthday was March 17th, 1852.

In the summer of 1852, Heinrich Stiehl informed Conrad that a large Methodist Camp Meeting was going to be held on his farm in Klein Frankreich. It was scheduled to begin on Monday and conclude five days later on Saturday, July 24th. Such meetings gave isolated farm people in rural Gillespie County an opportunity to socialize and grow spiritually amidst close fellowship. Stiehl said that Reverend Grote and several other Methodist missionaries from other cities were going to conduct a lengthy and intense session of preaching and praying for the community. He went on to say that word of the Camp Meeting was already spreading throughout the county and that many would likely attend.

---

[63] In 2014, the Kneese rock house on San Antonio Street still exists, although modernized.

As host of the Camp Meeting, Stiehl needed a skilled carpenter to help him build a large platform on the edge of his corn field near the banks of Baron's Creek. From it, various orators would offer their prayers and deliver their sermons. Conrad, recollecting how Heinrich Stiehl had helped him over the years, eagerly volunteered to help him as a way to repay him for his many kindnesses.

After Stiehl's corn crop had been mostly harvested and stored in his barn, Heinrich and Conrad met at Stiehl's log cabin on July 5th to begin building the stage. Just the day before, they had both celebrated America's Independence Day at the Marktplatz in Fredericksburg. From Stiehl's home, they crossed Baron's Creek and walked eastward along its bank to a large field that was situated between the Pinta Trail on the north and the creek on the south. The field still had the stubble of dry and withered corn stalks strewn around it but it was an inspired site for a Camp Meeting that would be open to the general public. It was mostly level, near the Pinta Trail which would provide access from Fredericksburg, and it was near Baron's Creek, which would provide a reliable water source. Along the creek were many tall pecan trees that would provide shade from the relentless heat of a Texas summer.

With two days of steady work, the pair cut down oak trees, notched them, and built a sturdy stage under the canopy of large overhanging pecan trees. As Stiehl had designed it, the platform of the stage was to be 12 feet wide, six feet deep, and elevated above the ground by four feet. The raised platform stage guaranteed that most attendees would be able to see and hear the speakers as they delivered their sermons. They oriented the stage in the field so that the tall pecan trees that lined Baron's Creek would serve as its backdrop while providing afternoon shade. After construction, residual logs and stumps were cut in sections and arrayed in front of the stage to provide seating. In front of the stage and slightly right of it, they also constructed what was known as the infamous *Sinner's Bench*. When construction was finished, the two men stood back and admired the setting with pride. It promised to be a great venue for a Methodist Camp Meeting. Shortly, Conrad said goodbye and departed for home.

When the morning of July 19th arrived, Conrad yoked the oxen to his cart that Sophie had already packed with food, clothing, and other necessities for attending a Camp Meeting. Little Sophie, now just over two years old, was quite perplexed by all the commotion. She wasn't certain why it was necessary to leave their cabin and live in a cornfield for several days but she was assured it was important. The baby, Heinrich, was but four months old and spent most of his time in his mother's arms. For such a short drive, it would be an event that would affect all their lives.

At Stiehl's farm, Conrad maneuvered their oxen-drawn wagon to a shaded area to the right of the stage and halted. After unpacking and setting up their campsite, Conrad mingled with the crowd while Sophie cared for their infant and talked to other wives. Among the early arrivals were families they had come to know as the pillars of the Methodist church, people such as the Kneeses, the Treibs, and the Ellebrachts. In the gathering crowd was Reverend Charles A. Grote and his family. He was particularly prominent because of his black garb and white clerical collar. Several missionaries, up from the Gulf coast area, were also dressed in black and they all had a serious demeanor about them. Each had their own *Bible* as well as their own dog-eared copy of *The Disciple* under their left arm. Some of the men from the Fredericksburg congregation brought musical instruments with them and were busy tuning them and playing ditties to warm up. Outside of the stage area, a flock of children ran and frolicked in the sun. In all, there was a happy, almost carnival-like prospect about the whole scene.

Around noon, Reverend Grote took the stage and the crowd quickly assembled in an arc in front of him and quieted down. He bid them warm greetings and then introduced the visiting missionaries one by one. He also introduced the people who presently served as class leaders in Fredericksburg, others who would provide music, and yet others who would serve as admonishers or exhorters during the Camp Meeting. With the preliminaries out of the way, he launched into "preaching over the crowd."

For the next four hours, Reverend Grote harangued the crowd about every imaginable sort of evil, especially alcohol. Those who drank it consumed the Devil's Brew and were on the road to eternal damnation. They would spend eternity in fire and anguishing torment. To those words, women in the crowd issued a hearty "Amen!" A few people came forward, knelt before the stage, and reconsecrated their faith in God. Late in the afternoon of that first day, a man came forward and took a seat on the *Sinner's Bench*. While the minister continued with his sermon, the penitent man was loudly exhorted to admit his sins openly and turn his back on wayward behavior caused by Satan. The admonishers were relentless on the poor soul. In response to their tirade, he wept, squirmed wildly, moaned, and prayed feverishly but they exhorted him to pray even harder. They assured him he was at the very gates of Hell and this was his last chance for redemption. While this was going on, Reverend Grote turned up the volume. He was now shouting at the assembled mass and some were moved to speak in tongues. Many were on their feet, waving their outstretched arms to Heaven and shouting "Amen, Brother!" or "Hallelujah!" At long last, the sinner repented and proclaimed faith in God.

For Conrad, the sermon brought back those uncomfortable feelings that he had experienced at his first Methodist meeting several years before. He was more certain than ever that he was teetering on the rim of a fiery abyss and was doomed to an awful fate. As the reverend intoned on about deadly sins and their consequences for family and community, Conrad fidgeted and writhed about uncomfortably on his log seat. Troubling memories kept bubbling into his conscious mind. Sophie, seated next to him, was equally uncomfortable but she kept busy tending to little Sophie. After a while, Conrad felt slightly nauseous and his stomach was in knots. He knew that he was a sinner but he was afraid to acknowledge that fact in front of the assembled crowd. What would they think of a man who had led his family to Texas only to have many of them die? It had been his selfish desire for a better life that had spurred the Pluenneke family to emigrate and now six of them, including his first wife and his father, were dead. He felt like their blood was on his hands. More, what would these people think of a man who often drank alcohol to escape his feelings of guilt and avoid those awful depressing thoughts? Worse, what would they think of a man who did not believe in God? With those thoughts racing wildly in his head, his guilt whelmed up and he felt trapped. He wished he could sneak out or vanish and leave it all behind but Conrad knew that would be avoiding the issue. He was at the Camp Meeting for a purpose: he had to face his wayward behavior and find a way to get past it. Somehow, he had to rid himself of the awful nagging guilt and find peace in his soul. Somehow!

By late afternoon, the Camp Meeting was adjourned for the afternoon and families repaired to their camps for the evening meal. As Conrad and Sophie walked back to their wagon with little Sophie in tow, they happened to meet Brother Heinrich Young, a visiting missionary from Seguin.

After formal introductions, Brother Young said, "Peace be with you, Herr Pluenneke and your family as well." It was said in such a sincere manner that Conrad immediately sensed this was a man who lived the Gospel.

Weakly, Conrad replied, "Peace be with you too, Reverend."

After that initial awkward exchange, Conrad struck up a conversation with the missionary and then, much to his own surprise, invited him to share dinner at their camp, an offer which Young quickly accepted. Over the meal, Conrad hinted at his quest to know God and find relief from his unrelenting pain. In response, the young minister recounted to the Pluennekes how he too had suffered mentally and physically before he had finally relented and accepted the call to serve Christ. His soul had been awakened. After his conversion, he had established a Methodist mission in Galveston and was subsequently sent by the church to Seguin where he presently served.

Brother Henry Young fully understood what Conrad was going through and urged him to persevere. "Make peace with God," he urged. If he did that, the missionary pledged, he would experience a rebirth, a metamorphosis like nothing he had ever experienced before. The missionary had a gentle way about him that led both of the Pluennekes to trust him and confide in him so their discussion continued. Conrad and Sophie both had confidence that Reverend Young would treat their admitted transgressions with respect and keep them confidentially. To Conrad, that trust was a blessing and he began to open up. During their lengthy talk, he told Brother Young about his woes, his depression, and his guilt. Those small concessions created a crack in Conrad's psychological armor and he began to talk more freely. He told the missionary more about his sins, particularly his alcohol use, and more about his feelings of guilt, which were accepted without criticism or remonstration, much to Conrad's relief.

Brother Young said, "Men are human and therefore they make mistakes but those are forgiven by our loving God." That comment encouraged Conrad to open up even more and he began to talk about his deepest secrets, thing only known by Sophie.

After the meal, Conrad, Sophie, and their daughter joined Brother Young in a prayer meeting with a few other couples and their children from an adjacent wagon. One by one, the missionary sat with the couple and prayed over them. He especially prayed for Conrad who gradually began to sense that something was stirring in his soul. He still felt the angst and the knot in his stomach but he also had hope for the first time in years. Maybe he would find God, the one who would exist for him.

From the prayer meeting at the Pluenneke's camp, they accompanied Brother Young back to the stage area. After getting seated, they listened while another minister preached for several more hours. At the end, they sang another one of Charles Wesley's hymns and were given a benediction. Wearily, they made their way in the darkness to their camp and retired for the evening. For the first time in quite a while, Conrad went to sleep happy and slept soundly. He had made progress.

The next day, they awoke to a beautiful day along Baron's Creek. The rising sun streamed into the back of their wagon and that roused little Sophie. After getting dressed and eating, the Pluennekes wandered to the stage area where they ran across Brother Young again. Just as his presence had brought comfort to Conrad the night before, it did again. After they chatted for a while, the missionary invited Conrad to walk with him along the banks of Baron's Creek and talk about life. They walked north and began to talk in earnest. In time, they came to a place within view of Christoph Feuge's log cabin where the water flowed beneath a limestone ledge that was surrounded by stately pecan trees. They clamored up onto the ledge and sat down beneath the limbs of an old crooked pecan tree. There, Conrad began to pour out his soul to a man who was but a stranger to him the day before. On that day, that stranger was the most important man in his life. Conrad told Young about his longing for a life of wealth and prestige, about his enormous pride, and his vanity. He talked about how he had pressured the rest of his family to emigrate and how that had led to the premature death of six of them. And how memories of them haunted him. With those revelations, his chest began to heave and hot, bitter tears rolled down his cheeks into his short beard. He yearned to relive that part of his life but he couldn't. Had it not been for him, the Pluenneke family would still be in Germany, maybe not entirely happy, but all of them would be alive. He confided that he had enormous guilt about his role in their deaths.

He asked lamely, "How do I cope with the memory of such a tragic loss?"

The young minister eyed him directly and said, "You must have faith that God understands that you meant no wrong by your actions. You were trying to make their lives and your own life better."

To that, Conrad replied, "That is my problem! I don't have faith that there is even a God out there in the universe much less one that will absolve me of my guilt. I have done many good things trying to demonstrate that I can lead a better life but I am no closer to God than when I started. My prayers go out into a dark void and there is no response."

"You must have faith, Conrad. I believe you are a Lutheran by virtue of your birth to a Lutheran family? Am I correct?" Brother Young studied Conrad's face for an answer but detected very little emotional reaction.

Conrad nodded ever so slightly and replied weakly, "Yes, I was baptized in the German Evangelical Church in Klein-Lafferde many years ago, when I was but a young boy."

The young missionary considered that for a moment and said, "From your religious experience in the Lutheran church, do you remember how Martin Luther, a Catholic priest at the time, found faith in God?"

Without pausing for an answer, the missionary continued on. "Luther engaged in many behaviors that many of his fellow Priests thought were very strange, including lying naked in deep snow. He was trying to prove to God that he was a moral being and worthy of his love. Luther expected a tangible sign from God in return for his odd exhibitions but, like you, received none. After many such unusual attempts, he finally came to the realization that it wasn't what he did overtly but what he believed that mattered to God. You MUST accept it on faith that God exists. Faith is the crucial element, not overt acts that you might perform to get God's attention."

Conrad mulled that over in his head and said flatly, "I don't have that faith. I don't know how to start to find that faith."

Undaunted, Young went on to say, "If the pretension of doing good works got men into heaven, then the Pharisees and all the rich ostentatious people of the world would dominate Heaven. They would occupy the front row pews up there in Heaven and sit beside God, but they don't. Take my word for that. They don't!"

"From that epiphany," the missionary said softly, "Martin Luther went on to protest against prevalent Catholic dogma that allowed humans to buy their way into Heaven or work their way into everlasting life through showy, pretentious behavior. That was the way of Pharisees. After his insight, Luther nailed his 99 theses on the door of the Catholic Church and went his own way. To Catholics, Luther's protest was radical and heretical at the time but over centuries, their view has become more in line with Luther's views. When he broke with the mother church, he became the first Protestant. Today, we Protestants and particularly Methodists, firmly believe that faith, and faith alone, will earn you God's grace and eternal salvation."

That statement caused the rapid succession of thoughts in Conrad's head to freeze for a moment and forced him to consider how he had been behaving. He, like Luther, had been trying to connect with God by promising to lead a better life and performing good works. By occasionally attending church and praying publicly, he had been attempting to prove that he was a good man, a man worthy of God's love and attention. It was as though he had been saying, "See me, God, see what I'm doing." That was infantile behavior, something that little Sophie might do to get her father's attention. But all the while, Conrad simply lacked faith. That realization was another epiphany to him and it caused a major shift in his thinking. Now, he had to stop and look at religion and theology in a completely different manner. Faith was the answer–he had to find a way to develop faith! He was like John Wesley before Aldersgate. For a moment, he felt as though the tectonic plates under his very feet had shifted and he wobbled a bit, perhaps only psychologically. Steadying himself mentally, he realized that he had been on the wrong path spiritually. He had to find a way to develop faith in God's existence. He had to shed those old doubts and simply believe that God was real and relevant to his life. His world view and his theological outlook was changing by the moment. However, knowing the problem and solving it were two very separate issues.

He gave voice to a rhetorical question that was directed to no one person in particular, "How do I actually go about finding faith?" He sought a mechanical answer to that question but there wasn't one.

The young missionary said quietly "Make peace with God. It is time for you to confront your fears and your guilt openly. Accept God into your life and have faith in him. All will be forgiven."

With that, the two men arose and walked silently back to the camp, both deep in thought. Conrad trusted this missionary more than anyone he had ever known and trusted that he would direct him to real faith. The man of religion walking beside him had become Conrad's friend, confidant, and moral example [64]. If this man of God was not offended by Conrad's doubts and sins, then others would surely come to understand. Maybe he could rid himself of the awful guilt by publicly finding faith in God and admitting his sins. Oh Lord, show me the way!

Back at the Camp Meeting, the morning sessions were already underway. Conrad moved through the crowd and found his place near Sophie and their daughter. There he wearily plopped down on a stump. The preacher for the current session was another fiery missionary, this one from New Orleans. He spoke with a clipped French accent and he talked directly to his audience. The theme of his message was that each person's time on Earth was limited and that no one knew what was going to happen in the future. Thus, there is no reason to delay. Accept God today and be assured of eternal life while there is time. Satan is not the answer.

As he was earnestly listening to the sermon, he became aware of a hand on his shoulder. It was Brother Young, beckoning to him to go to the *Sinner's Bench*. His heart raced and he hesitated briefly but suddenly he had clarity. This was the time and the place to attain faith in God. It was as though the young missionary had been sent especially to win him over to the side of Good. His heart warmed, just as Wesley's had at Aldersgate. Without more thought, he stood up, hugged Sophie, and walked toward the *Sinner's Bench*. To his surprise, he suddenly found he had been joined by his wife. He smiled and looked down at her face. The look in her eyes said "I am with you" and he became choked up with emotion. He squeezed her hand and they both moved quietly towards that once dreaded bench. As he moved forward, he noticed Heinrich Stiehl among the crowd. As their eyes met, Heinrich smiled and nodded his head in approval. It was heart warm-

---

[64] The missionary's manner set a moral example for how to accept human behavior as it is.

ing to see friends who simply wanted what was good for him and that made what seemed like an eternally long walk much, much easier. At the *Sinner's Bench*, Conrad and Sophie were joined by their new missionary friend and an exhorter, both of whom began to pray earnestly for the souls of the two Pluennekes.

Without warning, Conrad and Sophie were suddenly overcome with a powerful spirit that left them feeling as though their bodies had been invaded by something that was both Holy and good. It was as though an inner light had been turned on in the deepest recesses of their minds and they now saw their surroundings through a strange and entirely different lens. As a result, they felt light headed and wobbled a bit. They began to pray in earnest, pray as they had never prayed before. Intensely pleading for Mercy and Salvation. At about the same time, their bodies began to convulse. They were experiencing the *Methodist Shakes*. Their bodies seized and moved with convulsive spasms. Their eyes rolled back into their skulls and they both danced and flailed their arms about wildly. They began to loudly and publicly profess their sins.

In misery and yet in ecstasy, they attempted to stop the spasms but nothing seemed to work and they continued their spasmodic dances for several minutes. In her wonderful madness, Sophie's bonnet flew off. Conrad fell to the ground, lay inert for a few minutes, and then began writhing while babbling incoherently. People in the congregation witnessed their state of being and shouted, "Praise the Lord" and loudly urged them to accept God. Their behavior was seen by the crowd not as strange or comic but as a message from God that he was working in those souls. It encouraged more in the audience to repent their sins publicly and many came forward as well. Shortly, Conrad began to blurt out confessions about his long hidden guilt over the deaths in his family. As he aired out that guilt, the angst that had caused Conrad's stomach to ache so severely and which had caused him so much misery now began to flow away and the twitching ceased. It was replaced by a feeling of euphoria! Despite the relief, Conrad continued to repent aloud, more fervidly and more urgently. Yes, he had denied the existence of God. Yes, he had consumed alcohol. Yes, he had let his family down and contributed to their early deaths. But now he had faith in the healing power of God. It felt so good to finally release all that guilt and shame that he had dammed up for six years. He spoke rapidly and fervently, at times not making much sense. Some said he spoke in languages but he was unaware of that. He repented not only his sins but also recognized and accepted Jesus Christ as his Lord and Savior.

"I believe, I do believe!" he shouted over and over. Sophie acted in much the same manner and they hugged joyously.[65]

In time, they felt moved to rise from the Sinner's Bench and go the foot of the stage where they knelt and publicly asked for forgiveness for their many sins. Shortly, they were again joined by their missionary friend, Brother Henry P. Young, and an exhorter who both knelt down with them and prayed. In the crowd, there were many shouts of "Praise the Lord," "Amen," and "Hallelujah!" Their young missionary friend, kneeling beside them, prayed so earnestly that one could have imagined that he was praying for his own soul. After many prayers, Brother Young gestured to them to rise and led them around the stage to a place that served as a makeshift altar, where he asked them again to kneel. He prayed over them at length. On a small table nearby was a ceramic ewer filled with water that had been blessed.

He helped Conrad to his feet and asked, "Do you now believe in the Trinity of God, our one true Holy Being, his Son Jesus Christ, and the Holy Spirit?"

Conrad answered firmly "I do believe! Hallelujah, I do believe!"

The missionary then helped Sophie to her feet and asked her the same question to which she also responded loudly and unequivocally, "I do believe in the one true God."

The young preacher made a summoning gesture to several others dressed in clerical garb seated nearby and bade them to come and encircle them. They did and served as witnesses. When the trio was completely ringed by witnesses, the young missionary took the pitcher of water from the table and asked, "Are you both willing to go forth and serve God?"

They replied firmly and emphatically "Yes, we are!"

---

[65] The act of religious conversion is similar to the Freudian concept of *catharsis* where guilt feelings are suddenly released, behavioral psychosomatic symptoms disappear as a result of that release, and elation is experienced.

"Do you wish to be reconsecrated in the name of the Savior, Jesus Christ, and receive everlasting salvation from your sins?"

They both emphatically shouted, "Yes!"

Do you wish to join our church and serve Him?"

Again the question was met with an emphatic, "Yes, we are!"

With that affirmative response, Reverend Young dipped his hand in the pitcher and sprinkled their heads one after the other while reciting *The Lord's Prayer*. The Pluennekes joined his recitation and at it's conclusion, shouted a hearty "Amen!"

When he finished with the rite of reconsecration, he shook hands with each of them and said joyously "Welcome to our church. As a new Methodist, it is now your duty to follow *The Discipline* and live a good and pious life. Go from here and spread the Word to those who have not heard the Gospel before. Serve God in whichever way He leads you."

Oh God, I see the Way now and I will follow you!

After the Holy rite of reconsecration, they emerged from behind the stage and took their seats in the audience beside little Sophie just as the meeting was adjourning for the morning. The eyes of their daughter were wide open as she tried to understand what was going on around her. Many, including Reverend Grote and Heinrich Stiehl, came by and patted them on the shoulder, congratulated them for choosing to become members of the Methodist faith and shook their hands. Reverend Grote extended a cordial invitation to the Pluennekes to attend church at the Methodist Church in Fredericksburg on the following Sunday and help spread the Word in Fredericksburg. They nodded and affirmed that they would be there.

After the session, Conrad sought out the young missionary, thanked him profusely, and asked him to have lunch with them at their camp, an offer that he readily accepted. While eating, Conrad thanked Brother Young repeatedly for leading both of them to salvation.

The missionary smiled, eyed Conrad very directly, and then said firmly "You must work very hard not to regress from this point and fall back into sinful ways. Study the *Bible* every day and follow the words of *The Discipline*. When you have doubts, pray very hard for guidance. Remember these words from the Gospel: 'This I have done for you, what will you do for me?' You must find a way to share your new faith with others and serve God to the best of your ability."

Having said that, Brother Young arose and walked back towards the stage. Conrad watched him until the young missionary disappeared into the large crowd. He would not see him again but he would always remember Brother Henry P. Young and try very, very hard to emulate him.

After that first day, the rest of the Camp Meeting was a blur to the Pluennekes. Over the next four days, they met many people and exchanged stories about their conversion.

After the final service on Saturday, the assembled group formed a friendship circle around the stage. In the circle, Reverend Grote turned to the person on his right and shook hands and then moved to the next person, again shaking hands until he had bid farewell to everyone in the circle. Others followed suit until everyone had said farewell to all of the others. At that point, Reverend Grote stepped to the center of the circle and pronounced the Benediction after which the group sang another hymn. As the group slowly began to disperse, the Pluennekes repacked their wagon and began the short drive home. Their lives had been changed.

The next Sunday morning, July 30th, they attended another Methodist service at the small church on San Antonio Street. Before the service began, the Reverend Charles A. Grote welcomed Conrad and Sophie Pluenneke in front of the congregation as their newest members. In attendance was the Reverend John W. Devilbiss, the Presiding Elder of the German District of the Texas Conference. By church law, the Pluennekes could not be fully accepted into the church until the end of the end of their probationary period but they were well received and allowed to experience Methodist fellowship from that Sunday onward. As the Presiding Elder passed Conrad on his way out of the service, he patted him on the shoulder and whispered, "God has great things in store for you."

Oh Lord, show me the Way!

From that week forward, the lives of Conrad and Sophie Pluenneke began to change in new and better ways. They had an inkling of an idea about the direction they were heading and, while the Way was still vague, they knew their mission in life was going to be helping others find their way to God. Immediately, they became members of a Methodist class and were taught John Wesley's Method for living a life of piety and faith. In the class, they were asked many probing questions about their personal lives, their souls, their circumstances, and their spiritual lives. The probing was a way for the rest of the congregation to get to know them and learn to trust them. At first, the responses of the Pluennekes were a little guarded but as they came to know the congregation better, they became more comfortable with their scrutiny and openly shared the details of their lives.

On November 2nd, 1852, Conrad Pluenneke's application for citizenship in the United States was approved by the District Court in Fredericksburg. He was at long last an American! Freedoms provided by citizenship in the United States had been part of his dream and he had finally attained it. In addition, he had found God. All he needed was a large tract of good land to fulfill the rest of his dream.

In December of that year, Conrad and Sophie Pluenneke met the requirements of their probation and were accepted into the church with full connection. Conrad was so elated over their conversion to Methodism and membership in the church that he wrote to his mother in Buckhorn about his salvation and she promptly wrote back. In Conrad's own words, his mother's response was of "The kindest manner possible." He quickly wrote back to her with letters of "Consolation and exhortation to care for God's word, to make peace with God with the help of Lord Jesus Christ to live and die as a Christian." As Conrad later recalled in his letter to the cousin in Germany, he felt his letters had "some success."

In early 1853, Conrad also reestablished direct contact with his sister, Conradina. As Fritz Stein had told him back in Karlshafen, she had married Balthazar Hoffmann in December of 1846. After marriage, they had settled in Austin County, some 200 miles east of Fredericksburg. After they reestablished contact, Balthazar, a teamster, took Conradina and his mother-in-law, Sophie Pluenneke, to Fredericksburg in his wagon for a social visit and a long overdue reunion. After their arrival, Conrad wasted no time in attempting to convert his Buckhorn relatives to Methodism. To him, a new convert, Methodism represented the only avenue to eternal life and he desperately wanted them to share that glorious future with them. He had the purest of intentions but his zeal and ardor quickly overcame them. Off-put, the Hoffmanns and Sophie Pluenneke cut the meeting short and returned home to Buckhorn. Despite the soured reunion, they continued to communicate sporadically with Conrad through the postal system.

At the time of their visit to the Pluennekes in Mason County, the tiny town of Buckhorn did not have a church let alone a German-speaking pastor so its local citizens, mainly the Hoffmanns, prevailed upon the Lutheran Synod of Texas to provide one. The Synod sent a young minister, Reverend Votsch, who was fresh from seminary in Switzerland and very idealistic. Shortly after arriving in Buckhorn, as he became familiar with his new congregation, Reverend Votsch happened to read one of Conrad's letters to his mother that undoubtedly exhorted her to find God in a Methodist way. Offended, Votsch interceded in their relationship on the belief that Conrad was trying to poach on his Lutheran flock and convert them to Methodism. An angry exchange of letters occurred between the Lutheran minister and Conrad Pluenneke, after which the minister attempted to get Conrad excommunicated from Christianity. The young pastor also attempted to bar Conrad from communicating with his mother, except through him. The furor created a rift between Conrad and his relatives in Buckhorn that lasted over nine years.

After his conversion in 1852, it was obvious that Conrad Pluenneke was literally "On fire for the Lord." Throughout the rest of 1852 and 1853, he and Sophie faithfully attended the German Mission,[66] met with a Methodist class each week, and did God's work by spreading the word throughout Gillespie County. They bore witness to anyone and everyone who would stop and listen to them. Not many German settlers in Fredericksburg, however, were willing to receive the Gospel in the forceful way that Conrad and Sophie, or other Methodists, delivered it. Conrad's direct, blunt, "Take no prisoners" approach to theology offended Lutherans on more than one occasion. Those offended were mainly German Lutherans who were quite content with their more mellow form of Protestantism that allowed them

---

[66] Later, the German mission in Fredericksburg became the Methodist Church.

to have fun and occasionally partake of wine or other forms of alcohol. To Conrad after his conversion, drinking the "Devil's Brew" was now very nearly a mortal sin.

In several instances, he had angry confrontations with atheists who taunted and ridiculed him about his narrow, rigid Christian beliefs. He was also drawn into heated debates with Baptists about the proper amount of water needed to baptize a new convert. The overriding question became, "To dunk or not to dunk?"

In that era, the Methodists were literally and figuratively at war with the Baptists, Lutherans, and Catholics for souls in Gillespie County. Unlike the other sects, the Methodists were driven to increase the size of their congregations and build the denomination in Texas. For Conrad, the war for souls had dire consequences. In his zealous view, those who did not subscribe to Methodism, "The one true path to righteousness," and who were content with their "wrong" view of Christianity, were doomed to Hell. To the new convert, Conrad's job was to turn them around and lead them to everlasting salvation. In that pursuit, he let nothing get in his way or stop him.

Early in 1853, he began to carry a *Bible* and a copy of *The Discipline* with him to job sites. When given an opportunity, he preached to anyone and everyone who would listen, including fellow carpenters.

In that same year, Conrad Pluenneke was designated Class Leader by the Reverend Charles A. Grote, who had replaced Eduard Schneider back in 1851. The appointment was a sign that his Methodism was maturing. As its leader, Conrad's duty was to convene a class of 12 or so members, support their moral growth by asking probing questions about the state of their soul, and teach them about the Methodist *Discipline*. As he had other things in his life, he took being a class leader very seriously and worked hard to become good at it. *The Discipline* required Methodists to do no harm and to avoid all evils, including blasphemy, drunkenness, slavery, brawling, usury, uncharitable conversation, self-indulgence, softness, wearing gold (or any costly apparel), singing non-religious songs, laying up treasure upon earth, and borrowing money or goods with no intent to repay the debt. Conrad and his class were expected to meet those high standards overtly in their everyday life if they wished to continue on as members of the Methodist Society. Since all were admitted with "a desire to flee from the Wrath to come," he saw to it that his class adhered to *The Discipline*.

The Discipline required him to see each member of his class regularly [67] and inquire about their souls; advise, reprove, comfort, or exhort them; and to receive what they were willing to contribute to the support of church, ministers, and poor. He also had to meet regularly with higher members of the Methodist Society hierarchy to inform them about the progress of his class and forward any monetary proceeds to them. Over the next two years, he set a very high standard for Methodism in Fredericksburg and the size of its congregation grew steadily.

Commuting to carpentry jobs in an oxen-pulled wagon was slow and time consuming for someone who worked full days for pay. To enable him to move faster and get more work done each day, Conrad began to search for a good riding horse in 1853. Through Methodist friends, he learned that Ernst Jordan had a horse that he was willing to part ways with so he went to see Jordan about it. "Yes," Ernst Jordan had said, "I have a very good horse and I will take $70 for it and that includes a good saddle, a saddle blanket, and a bridle." Seventy dollars was a lot of money to a carpenter but after riding the horse for a few minutes and putting it through its paces, Conrad agreed to the price and bought the dark brown mare with seven gold coins.

After performing carpentry jobs for six years, Conrad began to sense that he was growing disenchanted with the profession. As a hired hand during that span, he had been forced to accept virtually every job offered to him because carpentry jobs in a small community like Fredericksburg were sporadic but most importantly, it was because his family needed a regular source of income. The uncertain nature of the carpentry trade did not suit his personality. Worse, many of his customers were poor and either unable or unwilling to pay for well-constructed buildings. Other customers had the means but declined to pay for quality work. He could not fathom why they would opt for anything less than the best when it came to housing. In those situations, he was often forced to decide whether to accept the job and build what

---

[67] Excerpted from *The Discipline*, cited in Coke, T. and Asbury, F. "The Doctrines and Discipline of the Methodist Episcopal Church in America", 1798.

he considered to be an inferior shack, or refuse the job. Sometimes his family's need for income trumped his desire to be selective about his work and he accepted jobs that did not meet his high standards for quality work. In slack times, he fretted that such poor buildings might affect his developing reputation. At bottom, what he disliked most about carpentry was that he had to yield to his client's desires. Once he accepted a job, he had little or no control over the work, either in schedule or quality. In those times, he often wished that he had an alternative way to earn a steady income.

While he performed carpentry jobs, Conrad Pluenneke had also begun to build a small herd of cattle. To feed them, he had begun to farm again but on a small scale. On his outlying lot, Conrad cultivated part of it and grew crops of corn and hay. Although he disliked farming as an occupation, he tolerated it because it fed his family and his cattle. By the end of 1852, he was contemplating a new occupation: full time cattle ranching.

In 1853, the growing Methodist community in Fredericksburg began to build its first permanent sanctuary on San Antonio Street to replace the log cabin that had been built on Ludwig Kneese's land. [68] He and Sophie generally liked the Methodist community in Fredericksburg but they did not enjoy the ostracism that Methodists suffered around town. Conrad, ever the evangelical, wanted to share the promise of eternal life with everyone but most residents were put off by his preachy tone. And they certainly did not want to forego their Schnapps or their tobacco.

In that era, Methodists continued to be lured into heated public and private debates with Catholics, Baptists, and Presbyterians as well as atheists over dogmatic topics where they differed. The debates were over such topics as baptism by immersion versus baptism by sprinkling; free will versus Calvinistic predetermination; the role of Mary, Jesus's mother, in the Christian faith; salvation by works versus salvation by faith; and the existence versus the nonexistence of God in the universe. Each side felt that it and it alone knew the "only truth" and the stakes were deemed to be very high. To be wrong about such a

---

[68] According to Jordan (1978), the new church was constructed of stone quarried from nearby mountains north of town and was situated on town lots owned by the church. In 1855, the white building was completed. Its congregation continued to grow steadily until the middle of the decade.

theological matter, it was said, doomed the errant party to the fires of eternal Hell. Because of their intensity, religious debates sometimes led to major rifts within communities and sometimes within families. Not infrequently, the debates led to violent confrontations and sometimes major rifts in families that took generations to heal.

Other Methodists in Fredericksburg suffered the same fate as Conrad did when it came to saving souls on San Saba Street. They too found that members of the small community were offended by the aggressive "straight-laced" hard line that Methodists often took to convert souls. It was not only Lutherans who were offended but Baptists, Catholics, and atheists as well. All received the same intense message. Being German and seeking gemütlichkeit, many of the colonists simply wanted the freedom to sip Schnapps or wine occasionally, dress well, and enjoy life but, at the same time, try to remain moral. Those pleasures offended the Methodists who were intensely evangelistic and every bit as dogmatic as their Catholic opponents. In a short time, they were shunned on San Saba Street for their zealousness and eventually avoided altogether.

At the same time, rowdy men who were often angry, vengeful, and under the influence of alcohol occasionally attempted to disrupt Methodist meetings because they hated the so-called "Piety Movement," the wave on which the early Methodists rode. It threatened to eliminate the rowdy's way of life and they knew no other form of behavior. The same was true of outlaws. Men on the frontier were rugged and coarse by nature, almost by necessity, because they lived in a Darwinian environment where only the fittest survived. Stealing and killing allowed them to survive. Their outcast behavior was as much defensive as it was offensive. As they saw the movement, pietists were attempting to eliminate their means of existence in the West. When confronted by such men, Methodists, including their ministers, often had to resort to using their wits, their brawn, and in some cases, their guns to escape alive and unscathed.

Being shunned in one's hometown was difficult for the Methodists to accept and more than a few of them began to think about finding a remote place where they could create a Utopian Methodist society and live together, isolated from the slings and arrows of a secular society which they felt was filled with evil. In such a utopia, they could practice their religion among only the faithful. It was a dream that was not that different from one held by Mormons in that era.

Between 1851 and 1855, some Methodist families in Fredericksburg began to consider the largely unpopulated Llano River Valley. As part of the Texas frontier, it met many of their criteria. It was extremely isolated, undeveloped, and with little other Anglo population but still within the most northern reaches of Gillespie County. Among those from Fredericksburg who began to consider land along the north bank of the Llano River included families such as the Pluennekes, Leifestes, Jordans, Kothmanns, Lehmbergs, Hoersters, Dannheims, Martins, and Hasses. At social Methodist gatherings, those families talked openly about establishing a purely Methodist community deeper into unsettled lands. It was known that to survive in such a locale, almost certainly in Comanche country, many of them would have to uproot and move together, thereby creating a critical mass of German settlers that would provide protection because of its sheer numbers. Further, they would all have to find a way to make a living deeper in the frontier. One thing for certain, they knew the people in Fredericksburg would not be overtly saddened to see them all depart.

Sometime late in 1853, several factors in the life of Conrad Pluenneke began to come together. For nearly two years, he had become increasingly involved in the Methodist faith, taking on duties such as Class Leader and Exhorter. At the same time, he came to dislike the carpentry trade and that nagged at him to the point where he began to actively pursue an alternative profession. Over the past five years, he had developed a keen interest in cattle ranching but he was astute enough to realize that he would need much more land and more cattle to make that happen.

All the while, he and Sophie grew even more disenchanted with life in Fredericksburg. They didn't want their children ostracized for their Methodism and they longed to find a remote place where he and Sophie could rear their children in a purely Methodist atmosphere and yet earn a good living. As he pondered options, it seemed his ideal solution was to find affordable land deeper into the frontier where he could raise cattle and also live among fellow Methodists. His friend, brother-in-law, and fellow Methodist, Heinrich Leifeste, felt the same way and was fairly certain that his brothers had similar attitudes. Perhaps they and the Pluennekes could find a good parcel of land and move onto to it en masse? It was an idea worth pursuing but they would need to identify that place before concrete plans could be established. If found, they would lead the exodus from Fredericksburg.

At a Methodist class meeting, Conrad casually mentioned that desire to several members and was pleased to find that many other Methodists were thinking along similar lines. But, where could they locate?

Someone in the group mentioned the northern bank of the Llano River, west of Castell. Immediately, that idea struck a chord in Conrad's mind. He and Heinrich had been there in 1847 with Howard's survey party and both had been impressed by the large river and its scenic rocky setting. Although more arid than Fredericksburg, it was very remote and its terrain would likely support cattle ranching. Thus, it had two key features that were highly important to Conrad Pluenneke in 1853. In coming days, he would ask people he knew about land in the Llano River Valley and vowed to pursue that idea. At the end of 1853, several diverse aspects of Conrad Pluenneke's career were coming together to form the basis for a very different life for their family. Oh Lord, continue to show me the way!

Chapter 8

SETTLING AT LOWER WILLOW

In the fall of 1853, Conrad Pluenneke was alerted to an upcoming tax auction that was to be held in Fredericksburg in November. The man who informed him was a friend and fellow Methodist who worked in Gillespie County government. Among the properties to be auctioned, the friend said there was one very large parcel of land on the north side of the Llano River about seven miles west of Castell. According to him, the property not only had a very broad frontage on the Llano River but also straddled the lower part of Willow Creek. From the Llano River, the property was said to extend several miles back into the wilderness. In all, it amounted to about a third of league of land. The friend also mentioned there was already interest in the property among other men in Fredericksburg and the bidding for it, therefore, might become very competitive. He went on to say that the property was being auctioned off to settle the estate of a deceased resident of Travis County, Lamar Moore.

The news about good land piqued Conrad's interest immediately. Shortly after hearing about the auction, Conrad told Heinrich Leifeste about it and the pair decided to ride out to the Llano River Valley and look around. Back in the spring of 1847, they had been in that general vicinity when they served with Emil Kriewitz's unit that protected Meusebach's surveyors in Richard Howard's District #1. Back then, Conrad had noted that the land was extremely arid, almost desert like, and very isolated from civilization but visually pleasant. To get there, they decided to go through Castell and follow the Llano River westward to its juncture with Willow Creek. Alternately, they could have taken the Pinta Trail toward the recently created Fort Mason[69] and, after crossing the Llano River, traveled eastward along its banks to Willow Creek but they decided to go through Castell to see Heinrich's brother, August. At Castell, they crossed the Llano and went to August's place but they were not home. From there, they followed a narrow trail westward that paralleled the big river's north bank to the

---

[69] Fort Mason was established in 1851. Shortly afterward, the Army improved the Pinta Trail to accommodate mounted troops and wagons that were used to move materiel between it and Fort Martin Scott. In time, it was extended to Fort Bliss near El Paso and named the Upper Road on Army maps.

point where it was met by the largest tributary in that area, Willow Creek. Where the two streams came together, Conrad looked about and instantly realized that the site before them was where he wanted to settle and live out his life. It had water, it had abundant trees along the two streams, it had grass, it had plentiful stone, and it was available. Heinrich was equally impressed with the area. That day, Conrad and Heinrich Leifeste jointly determined that they would find a way to buy that land and move there. For them, the main question was how to afford such a large piece of prime real estate. There had to be a way!

On the first day of November in 1853, the tax auction was held at the county courthouse in Fredericksburg and both Heinrich Leifeste and Conrad Pluenneke attended. Before bidding, Conrad studied the Lamar Moore Survey on a county map that had been tacked to a wall in the courtroom. It confirmed what his friend had said. The land, as shown on the county map, was indeed one-third of a league in size, roughly 1,476 acres,[70] on the Llano River and straddling its confluence with Willow Creek. The land, known locally as Survey 229, was part of the estate of the late Lamar Moore.[71] To pay debts owed by Moore's estate, the County Court of Travis County had ordered that the land be sold.

When the auction began, Conrad waited until the Lamar Moore parcel came up and then bid aggressively, raising his offer several times. After some spirited bidding, he emerged as the successful bidder with a winning bid of $600.[72] It was a momentous occasion in his life.

To finance the land, Conrad deposited $400 in gold coins with the Travis County Court. Of that amount, $300 came from savings that he

---

[70] A league is both a measure of distance and area. In area, it corresponds to 4428 acres.

[71] Lamar Moore was a volunteer soldier in the army of the Republic of Texas who fought in its War of Independence in 1836. For his service, the Republic awarded him a bounty grant for a Second Headright of land in 1838. The state later raised his entitlement to First Headright status and thus allowed him to claim one third of a league of land for his service. In 1838, he selected land on the Llano River and had it surveyed in 1845. It thus became known as the Lamar Moore Survey, #229.

[72] Paying $600 for raw land in 1853 would be equivalent to paying roughly $240,000 for it in 2014.

and Sophie had accumulated from his carpentry work over the previous six years. Another $100 came from the sale of his town lot and log home in Fredericksburg. To cover the remainder, he tendered a mortgage to the court for $200, debt that was to come due in 12 months. Conrad's mortgage was backed by his brother-in-law, Heinrich Leifeste, and by David Bayer, both of whom served as his sureties. Conrad's proposed means of financing the purchase was satisfactory to the court and on November 30, 1853, the sale was approved by Chief Justice John B. Costa in Travis County. That day, a new Deed of Trust was issued in the name of Conrad Pluenneke.

To help pay for the new property, Conrad also sold his house and the outlying lot on the perimeter of Fredericksburg to Ludolph Meyer on November 29th, 1853 for $30. As a condition of sale, he asked and was allowed to use the property until he could move his family, livestock, and other belongings to his new property. He pledged to Meyer that they would vacate the property by March. Since Ludolph had gotten to know the Pluennekes on the *brig Apollo*, he had no trouble trusting them.

According to DeVos (1986), Conrad Pluenneke verbally promised some of the land to his friend Heinrich Leifeste at the time of the auction, a pledge he officially honored in 1866 by issuing a deed to not only him but to his three brothers and to Julius Lehmberg. [73]Because all of them received deeds on the same day, it is highly likely that Conrad agreed to share the Lamar Moore Survey with all the Leifeste brothers and Julius Lehmberg at the time of the auction, in return for money needed to pay off the large mortgage.

Survey 229 was ideally positioned. It laid on the north side of the Llano River, gently sloped towards the Llano, thereby giving it abundant access to water. At the time, the land was situated in what was then Gillespie County but today is part of Mason County. Conrad's new property was rectangular in shape, with the longest extent running north and south, (see Figure 8-1). Its longest boundary line was over 5, 530 varas long (almost three miles) and its width was over 1,444 varas (roughly three quarters of a mile). It was a huge parcel of land and exactly what Conrad had dreamed of owning ever since he had first read Ernst's letter about Texas back in 1844

---

[73] Gillespie County records, September 27, 1866. Volume A, pages 215-222.

The Lamar Moore Survey shared boundaries with the Isaac Hamilton Survey on the east and the Thomas Osburn Survey on the west (see Figure 8-1).

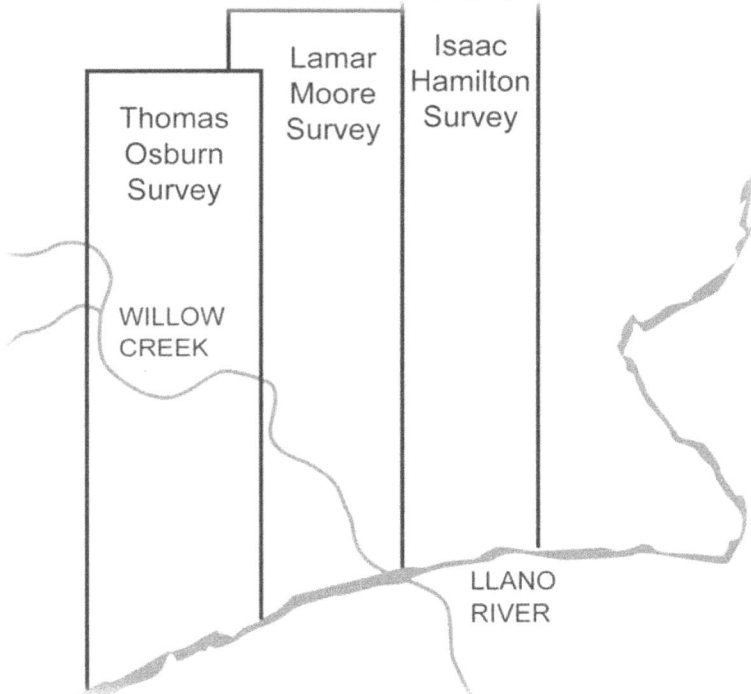

Figure 8-1 The Isaac Hamilton, Lamar Moore, and
Thomas Osburn Surveys Along the LLano River

To move from the protection of a developed colony such as Fredericksburg to such an isolated place with a pregnant wife and two young children in 1854 presented a severe challenge to Conrad Pluenneke. At what would come to be known as Lower Willow, not only would he have to hew civilization out of raw land but he and his family would have to live in relative isolation and with little protection (See Figure 8.2). The remote location of his land brought great risk because the Pluenneke family's homestead would be completely enveloped by several overlapping Indian nations, some of which violently opposed settlement by white people. Yes, Meusebach had negotiated a treaty with some Comanches in 1847 but that did little to prevent other tribes such as the Lipan-Apaches from raiding secluded settler's homes, stealing horses, killing white men, and taking women and children as captives. If alone against such forces, the Pluennekes would have little chance against the marauders because help was too far away. At Lower Willow, their cabin would be roughly 12 miles away from Fort Mason, 7 miles away from Castell, about 4 miles away from Hedwig's Hill, about 12 miles from Loyal Valley, and about 36 to 40 miles from Fort Martin Scott at Fredericksburg. In 1854, the upper reaches of Willow Creek was roughly 6 miles away but that area was still largely uninhabited. In that era, Lower Willow defined the very edge of frontier Texas and the Pluennekes would move there shortly.

The concept of frontier has drawn much interest from historians, beginning with the eminent Frederick Jackson Turner who in 1893, defined it as "the existence of an area of free (unoccupied) land, it's continuous recession, the advance of the American settlement westward ."

When people push into a frontier area, such as crossing the Appalachians or moving to the interior of Texas, they leave behind part of their civilization as personal survival becomes paramount in their lives. Strict adherence to social mores and the rule of law are often abandoned in such wilder places, replaced by a coarser social order and *frontier justice* (Klose, 1964). In 1854, the Llano River Valley was frontier and people behaved predictably.

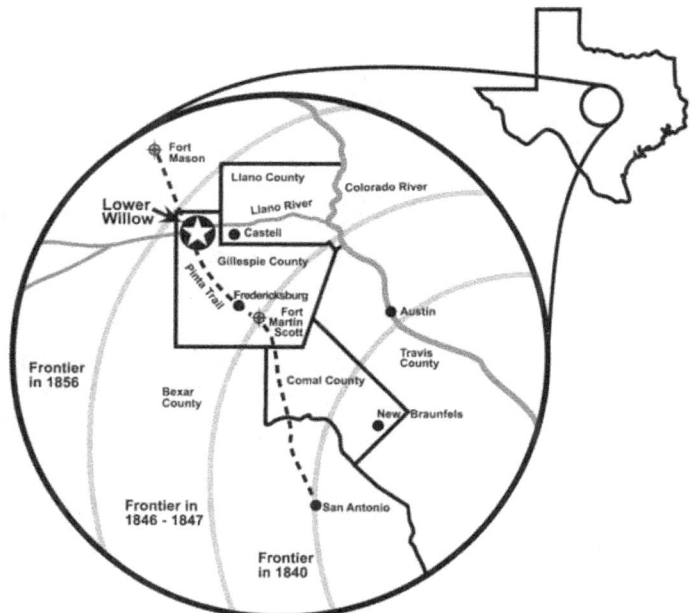

Figure 8-2 Three Arcs of the Shifting Texas Frontier,
Relative to Lower Willow in Mason County.

In the 19th century, civilization in Texas was continuously evolving and expanding in a northwesterly direction (see Figure 8-2). [74] In 1840, the frontier might have been defined by an imaginary arc that roughly connected San Antonio and Austin. In 1845, with the colonization of New Braunfels, that arc of civilization was solidified and when Fredericksburg was founded in 1846, the arc was moved about 80 miles further into wilderness. In just eight years, that arc of frontier expanded again and assumed a position some 40 or so miles northwest of Fredericksburg, to a point beyond the Llano River. And, quite obviously, deeper into Indian country.

In what would shortly become Mason County, that arc of Texas frontier can also be thought of as a hypothetical line separating two opposing cultures: Anglos and Native Americans. On one hand, the arc was a line that marked the forward expansion of the Anglo-American population and in 1854, that frontier region had a very sparse population of Anglo-Americans. To exemplify this point, the 1850 Census showed only about 100 people with Anglo-American names lived on or near the Llano River and most of them lived at Castell or one of three other short-lived German colonies. Beyond that expanding arc, however, lay a vast wild and untamed land that was only slightly known to light skinned people. It was mainly occupied by thousands of Indians from several tribes but also by a few indigenous Mexicans plus bands of desperadoes who were dodging the Texas Rangers. Conversely, the frontier, when viewed from the Indian's perspective, represented the boundary of advancing white people who were encroaching on their land, trying to take it from them, and disrupting their culture. Predictably, the Native Americans pushed back fiercely against that frontier, using an effective form of guerilla warfare. In a few decades, however, that unknown and unruly land would be tamed and occupied by Anglos as the frontier of Texas marched westward again. America was in the throes of Manifest Destiny.

When Texas Commissioner James Bartlett crossed the Llano in 1850, he had two distinctly different opinions of the area. On one hand, he was very impressed with the water quality of the Llano River but upon finding two deserted houses that had been attacked and torched by Indians, he recorded that he "could conceive of no reason why settlers would come so far into Indian territory when land near a

---

[74] See Pool (1975), page 65.

settlement could be found at a reasonable price" (Bierschwale, 1996). Courageously, Conrad Pluenneke would do just that four years later.

Historically, the Llano watershed was an interesting place and had a long and colorful past. For a millennium or more, lands in the Llano River valley had belonged to a succession of aboriginal tribes, including the Jumano, Lipan-Apache, Comanche, and a few others. The Jumanos had existed there at least since the 16th century when Spanish explorers made initial contact with them and noted their presence in their diaries. For centuries before and after contact by Europeans, various native tribes alternately dominated the land, often making war with one another to gain dominance in key hunting lands that sported herds of buffalo. In historical times, according to Bierschwale (1996), the area that is now Mason County was visited by several Spanish explorers, including men such as Juan Domingo de Mendoza, who entered descriptions of pecan and oak groves that lined the clear streams in their diaries. In the 18th century, Spanish priests attempted to colonize the area by establishing a mission in the San Saba River area and mining for silver. They subjugated natives and forced them to adopt Christianity while working in the mines. The Apaches rebelled, drove the Catholic Priests away, and destroyed the mission. The mines, if there were any, have been lost to history and never relocated.

In 1831, legendary James Bowie and his party searched unsuccessfully for the silver mines in the San Saba area and were met with staunch opposition from Apaches. They were forced to flee. In 1847, Meusebach and his group explored the ruins of the old mission and the general vicinity during his negotiations with the Comanches but they too failed to find any evidence of silver mines. Beginning in 1846, Texas divided the land north of the Llano into head-rights of different classes and awarded them primarily to men who served the state in its War of Independence with Mexico. Those plots of land were meant to attract more Anglos into the area but few chose to settle there at the time. In August of 1848, Colonel Jack Hays, of Texas Ranger fame, set out with 35 men to define a practical road from San Antonio to Chihuahua (Mexico) by way of El Paso. They followed the Llano River to a point on it where Camp Llano would be established later and crossed there. They also crossed the James and Comanche Creeks. Hay's expedition did not establish a road but it did arouse interest in the land north of the Llano River for future settlement. Much of that land was part of the Fisher-Miller Grant that was eventually settled, mostly by German immigrants between 1847 and 1856.

At the frontier, there were fierce clashes between the settlers and the various Indian tribes. To deal with the Indians and defend the settlers, the U.S. Army established Fort Martin Scott at Fredericksburg and Fort Croghan at Burnet. Those two forts, however, proved to be insufficient to quell Indian raids on settler's homes along the Upper Road at places like Cherry Spring, Loyal Valley, Hedwig's Hill and Beaver Creek. More protection was needed. In early 1851, citizens of Gillespie County who lived in those areas issued an appeal to the Governor of Texas (Peter Hansborough Bell) for more protection. In May, the Army issued an order to "Establish a post on the Llano River in the vicinity of the German settlements" and name it Fort Mason in honor of Lt. George T. Mason who had been killed near Fort Brown during the so called Thornton Affair in 1846."

Regarding the Fort Mason area, Billy Cox was very likely Mason's first white pioneer. He settled on Comanche Creek in 1846, very close to the present day town of Mason. In a few years, he was joined by a group of relatives who settled nearby and shortly thereafter, Billy Cox established a blacksmith shop. After Fort Mason was fully established and functioning, other families moved in near the fort, mostly because of the security it offered. In time, the small village of Mason came into being near the fort. Despite settlement around the fort, the northern reaches of Gillespie County were still very sparsely populated in 1853.

When Conrad Pluenneke first contemplated acquiring the Lamar Moore Survey in late 1853 and moving there, he quickly came to the realization that his family could not survive alone at what they termed *Lower Willow* for any length of time. Even with the U.S. Army garrisoned at Fort Mason, their homestead was too far away from it for the Dragoons to arrive with timely assistance. They would need the protection of other Anglo neighbors who would come together and organize to defend their homes and ranches.

To gain that protection, Conrad looked to his wife's family for support. From the very beginning, Heinrich Leifeste had embraced the idea of buying land and moving to a remote place, such as the Lamar Moore Survey. He too was a devout Methodist and he too wanted to live at a secluded place surrounded by other Methodists who believed as he did. Before Conrad bought the Lamar Moore Survey, Heinrich talked to his two brothers, Friedrich and Christopher Leifeste, about joining the Pluennekes and they supported the idea.

After Conrad acquired the Lamar Moore Survey, the Pluennekes and the Leifestes began to plan in earnest about how they would all move to what would be called Lower Willow. August Leifeste let it be known that he would eventually sell out at Castell and join the Leifeste clan at Lower Willow. Within a year of their settlement on the Survey, Christopher's brother-in-law, Julius Lehmberg and family arrived from Germany and expressed a similar desire to settle at Lower Willow to be close to family. By sometime early in 1854, six staunchly Methodist families, all interrelated by some degree of kinship, were prepared to settle on the Lamar Moore Survey and became firmly entrenched around Willow Creek. Before they could move, however, they had to come to understand the countryside and that would require a systematic reconnoiter.

On a cold Saturday, the 10th of December in 1853, Conrad Pluenneke rose early, saddled his new brown mare and joined Heinrich Leifeste on the outskirts of Fredericksburg to ride out and scout the Willow Creek area. Their intention was to ride around their new property and thoroughly analyze its topography and its agricultural potential in some detail. Such information would allow the men to make wise decisions about where each of the six families would build and where to farm on it.

As they departed from Fredericksburg, the morning air was quite brisk but as they rode on, sunshine began to prevail and the day warmed. After riding about 30 miles on the Pinta Trail towards Fort Mason, they came to the Llano River and crossed it on a low wooden bridge. From there, they veered east onto a narrow horse trail that paralleled the Llano to its junction with Willow Creek, a distance of roughly seven miles. As they rode towards the rising sun, Willow Creek was identifiable because it was the first major tributary that emptied into the Llano from the north. At the confluence, Conrad and Heinrich nudged their horses up a small ridge that rose about 30 feet above the two rivers. There, they dismounted and tethered their horses, all the while looking about for the presence of Indians. As they scanned the countryside, every acre north and east of them was part of the Lamar Moore Survey.

The area where they stood atop the small ridge was practically flat but to the north, the terrain sloped upward very gradually toward another area that was forested by sporadic groves of post oak, live oak, and cedar trees. Outside of those groves, a thicket of mesquite trees and opuntia cactus surrounded the ground, interrupted periodically by large granite boulders. Along the Llano and up the Willow were a number of large pecan trees. Walking up the slope a short distance, Conrad knelt down, scooped up a handful of dirt with his hands, and rubbed it between his fingers. It was red sandy loam, mixed with decomposed granite, which he deemed adequate for growing grain on a small scale but it was not as good as the soil at Fredericksburg. In his opinion, it would only support limited farming.

He and Heinrich turned and fixed their gaze on the Llano River and noted how floodwaters had reached quite high on its banks. Obviously, the river had a very large watershed and flooded dramatically at times. Such floods might wash away the wooden bridge on the Upper Road and leave them stranded for a few days but that was a concern they would deal with on another day.

In the dry, semi-desert environment, Conrad recognized that droughts might present a problem to agriculture and was thankful that they had two dependable water sources nearby on which to draw. On that day, the Llano was full and flowing steadily with very clear water while Willow Creek, an intermittent stream, was a trickle of muddy water flowing into the Llano because of recent winter storms north of the area. Along both streams, particularly the Llano, there was an abundance of grama, buffalo, and other grasses that would support cattle ranching. All else was covered in dense sagebrush, mesquite, and cactus. In March, when the climate warmed, they knew from experience that there would be many rattlesnakes and copperheads in the dense mixture of sagebrush, agarita, and broom-weed.

After checking the tether of their horses, the two men walked down to the Llano River and hopped from boulder to boulder until they were out on a very large boulder in the middle of the stream. In deeper pools of very clear water around the massive boulder, they could see schools of catfish, bass, and perch swimming around in search of food.

After hopping their way back to shore, Conrad noticed a stand of large pecan trees and oak trees on the west bank of Willow Creek, perhaps 50 yards up the slope.[75] He immediately recognized that the grove would make an ideal site for his new home. Those trees would provide shade during brutal Texas summers. From the grove westward, the land was flat and devoid of boulders. In all, the level area encompassed 20 to 40 acres and contained only a few sparsely located mesquite trees and cactus plants that would have to be removed. He felt he could easily clear them with an axe and use his oxen to drag the stumps away. In that opening, he felt he would be able to create a field where he could grow corn and wheat for his family and perhaps oats for his livestock but that was the extent to which he intended to farm.

After surveying the area where the two streams met on foot, he and Heinrich walked back to their horses, removed the tethers, remounted, and rode east, crossing Willow Creek. At a park-like opening near the middle of the Survey, Heinrich decided to stake his claim. His part of the property, like Conrad's, would extend north for several miles. On that amount of land, Heinrich felt he could run hundreds of cattle.

While they scouted the area, they kept a wary eye out for Indians. The Lamar Moore Survey was well within the Comancheria, the hunting grounds of the Comanches. As far as they could tell, nothing moved nor did anything make unusual noises. They both knew that Comanches often made animal sounds to communicate with one another while watching their enemies but that day, silence prevailed. They rode north to locate the end of the property and as they neared the boundary, they came upon a small herd of white-tailed deer that gracefully bounded off into the brush. The deer were a good omen. In that semi-arid land, they would have to rely on venison and fish to supplement their supply of food at times and this land had both. At the northeast boundary of his property with that of his neighbor (Isaac Hamilton), Conrad found a corner stake, near a small gully.

From there, they wheeled their horses around and slowly rode back down to the Llano River. As he rode along and viewed the land around him, Conrad could not help but feel proud of it. He was certain that Heinrich felt the same way. After crossing Willow Creek again, the pair brought their horses to a halt and twisted their bodies around in

---

[75] Although there are no large trees along Willow Creek today, their presence was noted in Jordan (1979, page 13) and in Bierschwale (1996, pages 20, 36)

the saddle to take one last glance at the landscape. As the sun slowly began to descend in the western sky, they headed for home.

As they rode back to Fredericksburg, Heinrich and Conrad talked about how to go about settling on the Lamar Moore Survey. In Fredericksburg, Conrad left Heinrich and rode south towards his house where Sophie and the children would be waiting anxiously. As he rode in semi-darkness, Conrad began to plan his course of action. He needed to divide the Survey fairly between himself and his relatives but the question was how to accomplish that. He knew the others would want access to the Llano River as did he but he also knew that several of his brothers-in-law would want differing amounts of land. To accommodate all of those differing interests, he would propose to divide the Lamar Moore Survey longitudinally, giving everyone access to the river. He would keep the western portion for himself and let the others sort out land ownership amongst themselves. Since the individual parcels could not be easily walled off from one another, their herds would roam and graze together. Viewed that way, the amount of land each man owned was not important except for rendering it to Gillespie County for taxation or for sale. In 1854, none of them would be thinking about selling. Besides, such remote land had little value and was not appreciating like more developed land near a settlement. By their prior agreement, each of Conrad's relatives would pay him $100 for a share of the Survey, regardless of size. The proceeds from those "sales" would allow him to pay off his substantial mortgage by the end of 1854, as required by his deed.

As he neared the cabin, his thoughts turned to what lay ahead. Before he and Sophie could move to Lower Willow, however, he would need to build a substantial house there, clear land for a small field, plow it, and then build other things such as a corral and a cellar. It would take a lot of effort and he wished that his son was older. At the beginning of the new year (1854), he would begin the long process of settling on the Lamar Moore Survey and in the process, tame his wild new land. He smiled as he thought about telling his wife of all the beauty he had just witnessed and he gently spurred his horse to a full gallop as he neared Fredericksburg.

When he arrived at the cabin just outside of Fredericksburg, Conrad dismounted, dusted himself off, put his horse in the corral, fed it, and then went inside where he immediately began to tell Sophie and their young daughter about what he had seen and heard on their new land. She could tell by his voice and by the look in his eyes that he was excited about the property and very, very proud of it. That pleased her immensely. Almost immediately, they began to formulate plans about how and when to move there. Since Sophie was six months pregnant at the time, their relocation would not be easy for her.

Following church on Sunday, Conrad and Sophie shared the news about the Lamar Moore Survey with her brothers, Christopher and Friedrich. Heinrich, who had also seen it, had already shared his views with them but they were interested in learning what Conrad thought about the land and how he thought it might be developed. For an hour or so, he told them about his impressions of the lay of the land, the soil, the trees, and the rock outcroppings. In his view, the property had everything necessary to settle there, ranch, and prosper.

While they were gathered, Conrad also shared his idea of how to divide the land so all could live together on it and equally prosper. Using a crude drawing of the rectangular property, he showed them the 200 acre portion (part I) that he had chosen for his family. It was on the far west side of the property and straddled Willow Creek, perhaps a mile upstream. Regarding division of the remaining land, Conrad proposed that the others should divide the rest of the parcel up as they saw fit. He had no opinion about who should claim what part of the Survey. Since the land could not be fenced off easily, its division was more symbolic than real. After some discussion, they unanimously concurred with Conrad's plan and began to lay claim to different parts of the Survey (see Figure 8-3). Christopher Leifeste claimed 350 acres (part VI) on its eastern edge. For his brother-in-law, Julius Lehmberg (who was still in Germany), Christopher Leifeste chose 350 acres just west of his land (part V) that encompassed much of the confluence of streams. Heinrich chose 205 acres near the middle of the Survey for his own (part III) and Friedrich took 205 acres (part IV) between Heinrich and the Lehmbergs. Later, August Leifeste laid claim to 178 acres (part II) next to the Pluenneke's land. [76]

"When we have time and are all comfortably settled on the land," he said, "Sophie and I will have the division of the Lamar Moore Survey legally established and we will issue deeds to all of you."

---

[76] There appears to be no rational basis for the men's choices.

As both their friend and as their relative, the five men trusted Conrad Pluenneke and were comfortable with the arrangement. The "sale" of five parts of the Lamar Moore Survey to the other families reduced Conrad's share to less than 200 acres but he was more than delighted to have the Leifestes and the Lehmbergs nearby. With the money they paid him for their shares, he was able to pay off his mortgage on the Lamar Moore Survey in December of 1854. Beginning at the outset of 1855, the Lamar Moore Survey was now their land, free and clear of debt. Another important step had been accomplished in Conrad's plan.

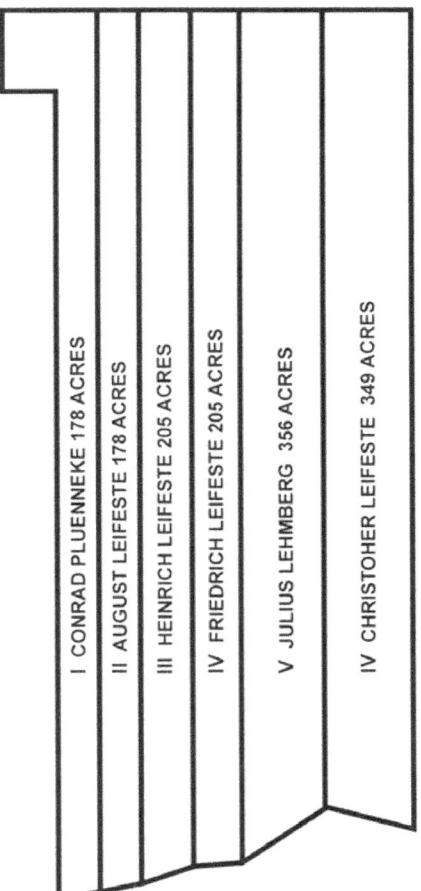

Figure 8-3 Division of the Lamar Moore Survey

As before in Fredericksburg, Conrad Pluenneke and the Leifeste brothers agreed to help each other build new homes on the Llano Valley property. When his brother-in-law Julius Lehmberg arrived from

Germany, Christoph Leifeste was certain he would help as well. With at least four men working, building cabins would be much easier on them than when they had less help. With her brothers and their families plus the Lehmbergs firmly ensconced nearby, Sophie felt more comfortable and secure about moving to such an isolated location. The presence of family would not only provide extra protection but it would also allow for socialization and for Methodist devotionals that would be held regularly in their homes.

Several weeks later, they celebrated the birth of Jesus which happened to fall on a Sunday that year. The Pluennekes attended the Christmas Eve service at the Fredericksburg Methodist Church where they heard Reverend Grote retell the story of Christ's birth in a Bethlehem manger. The front of the church was decorated with a cedar tree and many candles. The aroma and the candles reminded Conrad and Sophie of the Yule Season in Germany. For little Sophie, it was her fourth Christmas but the first one that made a big impression on her because her mother had made a stocking doll for her that year.

The Christmas season of 1853 was marked by a severe Texas Blue Norther that dropped temperatures more than 50 degrees [77] in a matter of hours. The strong winds howled day and night for several days in a row. Between Christmas and the start of the New Year, the Pluennekes huddled in their tiny cabin and tried to stay warm. To pass time, they talked about the upcoming move and how they might use the new land. As the New Year approached, the Norther passed by and warmer conditions moved into central Texas.

On the last day of the year, Conrad went out into the pasture and sat on a low hanging limb of an old live oak tree. He needed to think. In the quiet of wilderness, he thought about key issues that would confront him in the coming year. He had firmly decided that he was going to ranch on the Lamar Moore Survey but what type of livestock would he raise there? He presently owned Longhorns but he wasn't certain how they would adapt to the drier climate of the Llano River Valley. Were there other types of cattle that might be more suitable? To answer those questions, he would have to consult with county agriculture

---

[77] Olmstead (1860) noted that a Norther dropped temperatures from 79° one afternoon to 21° the next morning. His description of one: "First a chilly whiff then a puff -- grass bends flat and then bang! It is upon us."

specialists in Fredericksburg in coming days. He also thought about what type of crops he would need to grow there to support his family and his herds. Certainly corn would be one of the crops. With more land available to cultivate, they might need more draft animals and more equipment, such as plows and wagons. With much of the money they had saved now invested in land, how could he afford to buy such things? He needed more income. In January, he decided, he would have to take on more carpentry jobs before relocating.

Another issue that he thought about was what role he would play in the local Methodist church. Earlier, he had been licensed as an Exhorter by the MEC-S. That assignment had required him to attend services at the Methodist mission in Fredericksburg and loudly urge sinners to repent their sins. He took the job of Exhorter very seriously and worked very hard to become good at it. Only a year earlier, he had been in their position and fully empathized with their plight. Because he had converted in the face of agonizing guilt, he was able to serve as a role model for the small flock that was developing their faith in God. When they moved to the Llano area, which had no Methodist churches in 1854, how would he and Sophie serve God? In coming days, he would have to speak with Reverend Grote about his move and determine how to go forward in Methodism. In the recesses of his mind, he sensed that he was called to do even more for Methodism and that the Exhorter job was just a steppingstone to greater responsibility.

It was into that frontier context that the pioneering families of Pluennekes, Leifestes, and Lehmbergs moved in 1854. The land at Lower Willow was raw and rugged at the time of their move, full of challenges. Their immediate task was to tame the land and make it productive. Two years later, in 1856, the families at Lower Willow would be joined by other Methodist families from Fredericksburg who would settle on the upper reaches of Willow Creek, families such as the Jordans, the Dannheims, and the von Donops. They would settle upstream, near the headwaters of Willow Creek, and that community would come to be known as Upper Willow.

During the first week of January of 1854, three Leifeste men and Conrad Pluenneke rode out to Lower Willow to begin work on Conrad's house. While the men worked, Sophie and the other wives stayed in Fredericksburg and took care of their children while tending to livestock and performing other chores. For wives, life on the frontier was a full-time job and they worked just as hard as their counterparts did. During construction, the men commuted between Fredericksburg and Lower Willow, but one of the men always stayed behind to protect their new buildings.

Late in January, Johanna (Lehmberg) Leifeste chose to accompany her husband Christopher to Lower Willow to see what their new home site would look like. It was a fateful decision because she abruptly died there on the 23rd of January in 1854. The men were stunned. In haste, Christopher Leifeste chose to bury her body on his brother-in-law's land, overlooking the Llano River. Her gravesite was the first at what would eventually become known as the Lower Willow Cemetery.

By 1854, building log cabins was a familiar task for the men and they had become quite proficient at it. By that time, Conrad had over six years of experience at carpentry and the other four had built homes on their town lots in Fredericksburg. They began with Conrad's log house. With saws and axes in hand, they went down to the forested areas along the two streams and felled many tall oak and pecan trees, which left the watershed in the immediate vicinity almost devoid of trees. To move the trees, the men brought their oxen from Fredericksburg and used them to drag the logs to the building site where they cut them to length, stripped off their bark, and notched the ends with the now familiar "V" pattern. With logs fully prepared, they created a raised foundation from limestone rocks found on the property and leveled it. On the level rock foundation, they placed the sill logs and then stacked the other logs on them and interlocked them at the corners, forming the exterior walls. To get the highest logs into place, they built another skid ramp just as Heinrich Stiehl had taught them seven years earlier and rolled the logs up it. While building the walls, they made provisions for two windows, a door, and a fireplace. When the walls were up and notched firmly together, they built a shingled roof on the structure, following Heinrich Stiehl's plan. With the exterior in place, they chinked the gaps between logs with rocks.

To cover the chinking, they took time to build a lime kiln and from limestone, they made a lime-based mortar which they slathered into the gaps to fill gaps. They finished the house by installing a raised wooden floor and added a loft. To reach the loft, where Sophie and little Conrad would sleep, their father crafted a solid ladder from hickory wood and installed it along the west wall. By the end of February in 1854, the Pluenneke's house was ready for occupation. It, like the one in Fredericksburg, contained a single room that provided about 256 square feet of living space.

In subsequent months, the men built log houses for Friedrich, Heinrich, and Christopher Leifeste.[78] When all four houses were fully complete, they built barns and pens. When all had been erected, the four families began to plan how they would move from Fredericksburg and relocate on the Lamar Moore Survey. They decided that Heinrich and Friedrich Leifeste would move at the same time as the Pluennekes. Christopher Leifeste, still reeling from his wife's death, decided to move later when his circumstances allowed.

Moving entire households into the Texas frontier, especially ones with young children and pregnant women, was exceedingly difficult and dangerous. Coincident with the move, family members, horses, cattle, belongings, and houses had to be cared for and protected from Indians and depredations by outlaws. For the most part, it was felt that the three families would be relatively safe traveling together on the Upper Road between Fredericksburg, Cherry Spring, Loyal Valley, and Hedwig's Hill because that route was heavily travelled by the military, local ranchers, and commercial wagons. When they departed the Upper Road at the Llano River and headed towards Willow Creek, however, they would be alone and therefore vulnerable to an Indian attack or a robbery.

At the time they were preparing for the move to Lower Willow, Sophie was pregnant with the Pluenneke's third child. Just two months before, little Sophie had celebrated her fourth birthday. Her brother, whom the family referred to as Conrad Jr. was nearly two and would celebrate his birthday before they departed. During the move, their wellbeing had to be considered as well.

Because Conrad and Heinrich Leifeste had sold cattle to the Army at Fort Mason from its earliest days of existence,[79] they were known at the fort and had a connection with the commanding officer, Colonel

---

[78] Sometime around this time, Christopher Leifeste returned to Germany and August Leifeste continued to live at Castell. The Lehmbergs would arrive a year later.

[79] Bierschwale (1996), page 73

May. In April, Conrad went to the Fort and asked the Colonel for military protection for their families as they moved north. Because part of Fort Mason's charter was to support settlers, Colonel May approved their request and agreed to send a small detail of uniformed men to meet what would likely be a caravan of wagons and cattle herds on the Upper Road at Hedwig's Hill. After the Colonel checked his duty roster and calendar for April, he and Conrad agreed that the move would take place on April 15th. The Army detail would meet the settlers on the Upper Road where it crossed the Llano River early in the morning and proceed from there to Willow Creek.

As the day of departure neared, the men's major chore was to get the three herds together in one place. On his land, Friedrich Leifeste's cattle herd numbered 40, Heinrich had 35, and Conrad Pluenneke's herd had 60 plus several oxen.[80] The three herds collectively numbered over 140 animals. [81] It was not easy to round them up because the cattle were spread across several unbounded properties and mixed with several other herds. Therefore, each man had to enlist the aid of his neighbors to sort them out. One by one, the three men rounded up the cattle herds on horseback and separated them according to cattle brands. After each roundup, they drove their cattle to Conrad's outlying land where they planned to pen them together in a makeshift corral, composed of loosely palisaded mesquite branches and brush. After a week of work, they managed to gather all the cattle and herd them into the pen on Conrad's land. Thereafter, the men fed the cattle and watered them daily until they departed.

To move the aggregate herd out of the county, their cattle had to have a trail brand that could only be issued by the Gillespie County Brands Inspector. To get that official trail brand, the Brand Inspector had to come to the corral and verify the brand of each animal to ensure that they were all consistent with each owner's registered brand. When he was satisfied about the cattle's ownership, the Brand Inspector issued a new road brand to the group. After getting his approval, the men applied the new brand to all members of their herd and that took most of a day.

---

[80] Conrad always carried a stubby pencil and paper on which he accurately kept track of his herd size.

[81] Based on Gillespie County tax records for 1854 and 1855. The term *Cows* is used herein to refer to bovines of all genders.

Because they knew their caravan of wagons and herds would move very slowly, the men determined that the trip to Hedwig's Hill would take two days. On horseback, the trip would normally take part of one day but the caravan would move much, much slower. Accordingly, they planned for a single encampment near Cherry Spring on the way to their new homestead. To meet the Army detail on the morning of April 15th, they would have to awake early on April 14th, get organized, and depart before sunrise.

In the days before leaving Fredericksburg, Conrad sold his small herd of sheep to a neighbor but kept his Longhorn cattle, riding horse, and two oxen. In preparation for the move, he and Sophie also began to clear the cabin and loaded many of their possessions in the wagon.

Before the crack of dawn on April 14th, Conrad rose from bed and went to the barn where yoked the oxen to the wagon. Shortly thereafter, Heinrich and Friedrich arrived with their wagons. By then, Sophie and the children were ready to travel. Conrad loaded the rest of their belongings in the wagon and then helped his pregnant wife and their daughter get into the back of the wagon where he had placed the mattress from their bed. After that, he put young Conrad Jr. up on the wagon seat where he could sit beside his father during the trip.

Conrad, Heinrich, and Friedrich tethered their Longhorn herds and horses to the rear of their respective wagons with ropes. With all in order, they set out for Fredericksburg. As they departed, they made quite a procession: three oxen-pulled wagons, each followed by herds of plodding Longhorns and horses, and by several barking dogs. The caravan made an interesting sight for anyone in Fredericksburg who was up early in the morning and out on San Saba Street that morning.

Conrad and Heinrich drove their respective wagons but Sabina Leifeste drove their wagon, thus freeing Friedrich to ride behind the caravan and keep an eye on the herds. As they moved along, the cows bellowed in protest and their collective complaints caused quite a commotion.

In Fredericksburg, they turned onto San Saba Street and began the daylong trip toward Cherry Spring. Outside of Fredericksburg, they paralleled Baron's Creek and stopped briefly near Heinrich Stiehl's place to allow their livestock to graze and drink from the creek. After conversing briefly with Heinrich and Catharina Stiehl, who wished them well, the caravan moved north. Early in the afternoon, they topped several hills and gradually began to transcend into the Llano River watershed. By late afternoon, the caravan arrived at Cherry Spring and the men set up camp. Dinner was simple: dried sausage, cooked cheese, and crusty bread plus some coffee. That night, the men took turns alternating between watching the camp and trying to sleep. Early the next morning, the men rose before sunrise and began to break camp while the women produced a simple breakfast of hard biscuits and coffee. After an hour or so, they hit the road again but made better progress because the road sloped towards the Llano River. At the junction of the Upper Road and the Llano River, they stopped and met their mounted military detail as planned. The two soldiers were armed and decked out smartly in their dark blue uniforms.

After greetings were exchanged, the military detail escorted the caravan across the Llano and then turned eastward. As the large river was crossed, the settlers noticed that the Llano was running full, a result of recent spring rains in its upper watershed. Since there was no road from the Upper Road directly to Willow Creek at the time, the going was exceedingly slow. At several places, the heavily loaded wagons got stuck in small sandy washes and had to be pulled out with the help of oxen teams from other wagons. While the settlers were getting wagons out of the sand, the military detail rode about and looked for signs of Indian activity but found none. It took all morning for the lumbering wagons to get to the vicinity of the new houses. Shortly after they arrived, the settlers began to unload their belongings and move some of their belongings into the houses. The military detail bivouacked nearby and stayed through the night to ensure the safety of the settlers. When it was apparent they were secure on their land, the pair of soldiers returned to Fort Mason the next morning.

Late the next day, Conrad suddenly felt alarm for no particular reason. As he looked around, he noticed a band of approximately 20 Indians on horseback, intently watching him from a distance of about 200 yards. His first instinct was to make a run for his rifle that was in the wagon but he stifled that impulse because the band showed no sign of hostility, only curiosity. Slowly he raised his right arm as a gesture of peace but they made no counter gesture. In a few minutes, Sophie came up besides him and they stared intently at the band of motionless Indians. From their dress, Conrad guessed that they were Pinetka Comanches and probably friendly but he wasn't certain. Slowly, they turned their ponies around and rode west along the Llano River. As they left, Conrad and Sophie fully exhaled for the first time in what seemed like an eternity.

That first night in the new house was also a bit harrowing for the Pluennekes. While they were used to living on the outskirts of Fredericksburg where they had perhaps a dozen neighboring houses scattered about them, their new property had only three other houses nearby and they were several hundred yards away. They were not accustomed to living in such isolation. To be prepared for trouble, Conrad loaded his rifle and his pistol that he always kept nearby. That night, he placed the loaded weapons near bed but he knew he would be no match for a band of Indians, should they choose to return and attack them. In coming days, he would have to find some way for them to stay more alert to the presence of Indians.

Before they went to bed, Sophie and Conrad walked out to the barn to ensure that their animals were fed and closed in for the night. In the growing darkness, they noticed an incredible array of stars overhead. That was Heaven, Conrad thought. As they walked back to the house, they could hear the roar of the rain-swollen Llano River as it washed over the many granite boulders that lay in its stream bed and moved a few of them. It was a pleasing, soothing sound and far surpassed what they had heard when they lived on the town lot in Fredericksburg. For a while, they sat on stumps and just listened. But then, among the pleasing sounds, they also heard strange sounds in the darkness. In the distance, they could hear the eerie howl of a wolf or a coyote and what sounded like the hooting of an owl in a nearby tree. They had heard the stories about how Indians made such sounds to communicate with one another in the darkness just before they attacked and that made them very, very uneasy. Aware that Sophie was on edge, Conrad whispered softly to her, "Apaches only attack on full moon nights and that won't occur for another two weeks." He hoped that would reassure her but it didn't. Instead, she worried all night about full moon nights that would be coming month after month.

Praying that the sounds natural, they went into the house and tried to sleep but every new sound brought them to full attention. That first night, they became acutely aware of how isolated they were. Over the following weeks, they adjusted to sounds in the night and slept a little better but always dreaded the nights when the moon was full.

That first year on the Llano River, 1854, was very difficult for the Pluennekes and security was not their sole issue. Although Conrad and his brothers-in-law had worked very hard to weatherproof their houses, the tiny log cabin still had many cracks that allowed cold wind and driving rain to penetrate to the interior. During Northers,[82] the Pluennekes sat on the floor with their backs against the wall, shivered, and huddled between blankets in an attempt to stay warm. There was no privacy. When clothes or bedding had to be washed, Sophie bundled it up and walked to the Llano River to do it and trudged back to the house. When water was needed at the house, either Sophie or her daughter had to go to the river and fetch it. To get enough water, they used a board that spanned their shoulders that enabled each of them to carry two pails at one time. To pass time during bad weather, they read the *Bible* and sang Methodist hymns such as Blow Ye the Trumpets, Blow. After the Northers passed, Conrad plugged gaps in the walls and roof with whatever material was available at the time. Later, in drier times, he made more limestone and sealed the cracks permanently. Eventually, the new log cabin became home.

Not only was their house tiny and rustic, their furniture was too. It consisted of a table and several chairs plus a chest that Conrad had crafted from cedar wood. They used straw mattresses for bedding and covered them with quilts and blankets brought from Germany. For food, Conrad hunted for deer and fished while Sophie scavenged for nuts and berries from the nearby countryside when they were in season. When his first small crop of corn came to fruition that first summer, they existed almost entirely on corn bread that Sophie baked in the hearth and venison or beef. With the meager amount of money they had left after buying the land, Sophie carefully supplemented their food supply by purchasing potatoes and pinto beans at markets in Fredericksburg. Life was so hard that at times, they wondered whether they would survive but they had faith that God would get them through their difficult travails and they prayed for His help. They also sang Charles Wesley hymns to help get them through those difficult times: *A Charge I have to Keep.*

After they were fully settled in their new house, Conrad turned to the task of clearing land for a field. His desire was to put a late-

---

[82] A *Norther* was described this way by Olmstead (1860): A black cloud rose in the north and with incredible swiftness, a frightful roar spread over the Heavens. The cattle (went) running headlong for cover --."

harvesting corn crop into the ground by early May which was only weeks away. For nearly a week, he chopped down mesquite trees and scrub brush with his axe to clear the level area west of the log cabin. As he had noted from the first time that he saw the area, their field would be well above the river's highest flood level. In all, his first field was roughly 10 acres. A field that size was known to see a family through a year and its small size would allow Conrad to plow it and plant it, with only a little extra help from Sophie. As Conrad chopped down mesquite, she dragged it into a clearing, piled it up, and burned it carefully so as not to start a wildfire. Even in early April, clearing land was hot, dusty work. Before the field could be planted, however, the crusty virgin soil needed to be broken up and completely turned over. To do that, Conrad Pluenneke went to the barn, yoked up his pair of oxen, attached the heavy iron plow to the yoke, and headed for the field. As he started to plow, he was reminded of a time some 20 years before when he plowed his father's field in Klein-Lafferde and dreamed of owning an estate. While the Lamar Moore Survey did not rise to the level of an estate yet, he and his extended family owned a third of a league of good land and he was far from finished.

The surface of the field was quite hard and that made plowing very difficult. Plowing it for the first time, Conrad had to exert a lot of force to drive the plow head deep into the virgin soil while keeping the oxen moving in a straight line. Winds kicked up and often blew dust from the plow directly into his face and occasionally blew his hat off. Unseasonable warm temperatures added to his misery and quickly dehydrated him. During his seven years in Texas, he had learned to keep a canteen of water handy. As he trudged through the field, he regularly paused to drink and give water to his oxen. After three weeks of hard work, the soil was completely turned over and furrowed now all they needed was timely rain before planting.

While Conrad plowed, Sophie watched for signs of Indians and cared for their two children. Sophie, now four years old, helped care for Conrad Jr. who had just celebrated his second birthday on the 17th of that month. The children contented themselves to play with the dogs and throw rocks.

After settling in the Llano River Valley, Conrad and Sophie became acutely aware of just how quiet the frontier could be. At times, they could hear sounds from Heinrich's house or Friedrich's house.

Those sounds were reassuring to them but on other nights, particularly on nights lit by a full moon, they could hear what they thought were either lobos and coyotes baying in the distance but were never completely certain about that. Removed from the protection of a larger settlement and the Army, they had to stay vigilant for any sign of Indians who might be seeking to steal their horse or create mayhem. They also had to be prepared to take action. Although Meusebach had negotiated a peace treaty with the Penateka band of the Comanches, other hostile Indian tribes such as the Lipan-Apaches roamed the valley at night and occasionally attacked settlers in their cabins. After a period of relative safety, they would relax a little but then news would reach them about an atrocity that had occurred at Beaver Creek or somewhere near Mason and their fears would return. After some raids in those areas, Indians often retreated through the Willow Creek area and caused even more fear.[83]

In May, a good steady rain came and that made it possible to plant the corn kernels. Conrad again hitched up the oxen and plowed the field, making straight, even rows in it. Planting corn was a two person job. The first person, usually Sophie, walked each row and used a stick to make a hole that was about four inches deep. The second person, Conrad, dropped a corn kernel into each hole and kicked dirt over it. To offset the tedium of planting, the two switched roles occasionally, even though Sophie was eight months pregnant. When she made the holes, they stopped to rest as well as eat and drink more often. While they were planting, young Sophie sat on the edge of the field and played in the dirt while keeping an eye on the two boys who sat on an old blanket in the shade of an oak tree. In a week, the planting was finished. In early June, another timely rain came and the Pluennekes became confident that they would have a good harvest of corn in August.

While Conrad plowed and planted, he continued to assess the soil in his field and confirmed his earlier opinion. The soil, a sandy loam mixed with decomposed granite, would only support limited farming. Whereas Conrad had been a carpenter in Fredericksburg, he had farmed a little and had also raised livestock in his spare time to help support his family. Those endeavors gave him experience at dealing with the Texas environment. His intent in the Llano River Valley,

---

[83] Bierschwale (1996), page 117.

however, was to raise cattle on a large scale. He knew that the earliest settlers, particularly Mexican rancheros, had successfully raised cattle in the area and Conrad intended to follow in that tradition.

On June 9th of that year, Sophie gave birth to their second son at their home in Lower Willow, with Conrad's assistance. They named the boy Heinrich to honor her brother and Conrad's steadfast friend. In the family, he would be known as Henry.

After the division of the Lamar Moore Survey, Conrad claimed a little less than 200 acres of it on which he and his family now lived and ranched. Having that amount of land wasn't like owning the entire survey but it far exceeded the 11 acres he had owned in Fredericksburg. According to prevailing Texas lore, 200 or so acres of land would only support a herd of about 15 to 20 cows, with normal rainfall. In drought conditions, however, it might only support four or five cows. In that open-range era, the land was not fenced so Conrad's cows as well as those of the Leifestes and the Lehmbergs roamed and grazed freely on large expanses of unoccupied land adjacent to the Lamar Moore Survey. That wider range allowed all of the men to run more cattle on the land but Conrad had implicit assurances from the Leifestes and Lehmbergs that they would manage their herds according to grass conditions. In that sense, they all behaved more like partners than relatives when it came to managing the survey.

Conrad's ranch not only enabled his family to survive but it allowed them to rise above subsistence living through regular sales of cattle to the U.S. Army at Fort Mason and at other markets in Fredericksburg. To improve beyond that status, however, he would need to sell more cattle and that meant acquiring more land, more breeding stock, and finding new markets for his animals. With that in mind, he began to eye neighboring land on the Isaac Hamilton Survey and the Thomas Osburn Survey, both of which abutted the Lamar Moore Survey. If all or part of either property was ever put up for sale in future, he determined to buy it. With more land and more cattle, he now felt there was almost no limit to what he could achieve in Texas.

While Lower Willow was developing, the upper reaches of Willow Creek were also being settled. In 1856, an extraordinarily dry year, the Ernst Jordan family moved to Upper Willow as did a number of other families. In that very remote locale around Willow Creek, Methodists surrounded themselves with people who believed as they did and who yearned to lead pious lives. According to Jordan (1979), "It (the Llano River Valley community) was an isolated religious enclave, not at all different from what the Mormons created in Utah."

Living in that remote area on large tracts of land took some adjustment by the settlers because they were generally separated from their neighbors by miles of open space. In Germany, they had lived in tightly clustered communities and farmed outside of them. In Texas, they lived on their farms outside of villages and that was very difficult for them because they could not separate work from everyday life and because they lacked opportunities to socialize. The Methodist enclaves were ultraconservative (in a religious sense) and all the people who lived in them were expected to conduct their lives by strict rules of morality. Thus, there were no dances or festive occasions where alcohol was consumed. Their lives were about Methodism and raising families.

Moving to the sparsely populated Llano River Valley came with more risks than just being attacked by nomadic Indian tribes that roamed the area. The early settlers were also affected by Mexican bandits and coarse backwoods Americans who had drifted to that part of Texas from states such as Kentucky, Tennessee, and Arkansas. The latter came to resent the presence of the German immigrants, the *damned Dutch* as they called them. They resented that the settlers of Germanic heritage spoke a different language, held to their European culture, practiced a different religion, and had managed to accumulate enough money to buy choice land on Willow, Beaver, and Comanche Creeks. Those early Texians were also offended because the German element seemed clannish, aloof, and unwilling to change. The newcomers were proving that people could succeed working hard and without resorting to slave labor and that rankled the Texians even more. Almost to a fault, the German immigrants were industrious, thrifty, and highly successful at many things. From their earliest days in America, the German settlers saved their money and used it to buy more land, more livestock, and later, to build sturdy rock homes. The Texians, by contrast, were constantly on the move, always willing to uproot and look for more and better land. As a consequence, they were less willing to build permanent homes and settle down. Those cultural differences led to bigotry and its presence would erupt into the Mason County Hoo Doo Wars two decades later.

Most of the early German families who settled in Mason County (such as the Jordans, the Kothmanns, the Leifestes, von Donops, and the Pluennekes) followed that script to success. In a matter of years, they collectively owned thousands of acres of the best land in the Llano River watershed. All being of the same Methodist faith, they supported one another and interacted frequently. According to DeVos (2003), it was customary for the people of Upper Willow and Lower Willow to attend the other's church services and social gatherings. After the Methodist church and school was established at Upper Willow, the children from Lower Willow, including the Pluenneke children, attended it and they became fast friends with the children of Upper Willow families. The children grew up learning to ride horses, fish, shoot guns, and swimming in the Llano River together. In time, a cohesiveness developed among the Methodists, regardless of their location.

Back in 1851, the Army had established Fort Mason on Post Oak Hill, near Comanche and Centennial creeks, to provide settlers with protection from the Indians. After three years, the Army closed the fort but in a stunning reversal of policy, it reoccupied the fort in 1856 and garrisoned it with Companies B, C, D, H, and I of the Second Cavalry, all of which were under the command of Colonel Albert Sidney Johnston. Colonel Johnston was well known to Conrad Pluenneke and Heinrich Leifeste as well as some of the other German settlers who had served under him in Company H at Matamoros and Camargo. Whether he harbored any resentment about the German volunteers of Company H who had voted to disband his regiment is unknown, but his presence at the fort may have given Mason County ranchers an entree to sell more of their beef to the Army. With five companies rather than two, as happened in 1851, the fort would be a major procurer of not only cattle but other goods. Reoccupation of Fort Mason [84] provided a huge economic boost to the emerging community of Mason and gave it a sense of security to the Llano River area, just as it had for Fredericksburg when Fort Martin Scott was established near there in 1848.

That sense of security also aided the growth of Methodism in the area. With the protection of cavalry troops, circuit riding Methodist ministers ranged further and wider into the wilderness and served truly

---

[84] Fort Mason was the last Union command of Robert E. Lee

isolated people on the ever-expanding frontier of Texas. The newly formed Llano Circuit had 63 charter members, including Conrad and Sophie Pluenneke; Heinrich and Margarete Leifeste; and Friedrich and Sabine Leifeste as well as other families. The circuit was lengthy, covering about 60 to 100 miles of rugged terrain that crisscrossed the Llano River. In 1986, Julius E. DeVos calculated that the circuit encompassed over 450 square miles. Over several decades, the region's population grew and it became the most purely Methodist area in Texas (Jordan, 1978). Conrad and Sophie Pluenneke were instrumental in that growth. Although the Methodist community along Willow Creek sprouted and grew in membership, it was still isolated and with poor connections to the outside world.

On the 17th of September in 1855, Conrad Pluenneke, Friedrich (Fritz) Leifeste, and two other settlers (Kneese and Hasse) at Willow Creek petitioned Gillespie County to establish a road between Willow Creek and the road that connected Fredericksburg and Mason (the Pinta Trail, also known as the Upper Road by the army). According to an article in the February 1856 edition of the Mason Centennial newspaper, Conrad Pluenneke was designated as one of four citizens to serve on a panel that determined the route of the road and, after its approval, was appointed Overseer for County Precinct VI. To establish the road, Gillespie County appointed 17 men to work on it, including all four of the Leifeste brothers and Julius Lehmberg. In addition, the Negro slaves of Stephen Peters and G.W. Todd were ordered to work on the road as well. [85]

As Overseer, Conrad directed two road construction jobs. One went from Upper Willow to the emerging town of Mason and the new route from Lower Willow Creek to the Upper Road or the "trading home route", in Gillespie County parlance. According to county records, both roads were completed by early 1857.

During that time, Conrad Pluenneke also served in varying capacities for Reverend Grote's Methodist ministry in the Llano River Valley, both at Castell and elsewhere on the Llano Circuit. At times he served as an Exhorter and at other times as a Class Leader. In those roles, his zealous nature led him to press sinful people to repent their

---

[85] Few families in Mason County owned slaves. This may have been one of the first times that Conrad Pluenneke witnessed slave labor.

sins, become baptized, and join the church, which many did. His zeal was duly noted and he was urged by Reverend Grote to consider going into the ministry. After much prayer, Conrad felt ready to accept a ministerial role, should one be offered. At other times, he wavered and had nagging doubts about his ability to preach. Finally, in his own words, "He accepted the duty to proclaim Christ's Gospel to immortal souls" and serve the Methodist cause.

After moving onto the Lamar Moore survey in 1854, Conrad Pluenneke was content to graze his growing herds of cattle and oxen on his portion of it and master the art of raising cattle. His herd had steadily grown from 40 to 120 cows in three years. Even before they left Fredericksburg, Conrad and his friend Heinrich Leifeste had begun to sell cattle to Fort Mason and they continued to do that in subsequent years. The income from those sales, albeit small but steady, gave Conrad a humble measure of financial security that he had not known in years and it allowed him to think about taking a larger role in Methodism. Should he consider the ministry, he knew the salary that the MEC-S could afford to pay him would be quite small. Therefore, his ranch would have to sustain the family and it began to appear that it could, especially if he could acquire more land.

In July of 1857, part of one of his most coveted pieces of property was put up for sale by its owner, David M. Lyle of Fayette County. Conrad Pluenneke had walked that land frequently and therefore was very familiar with it. He wasted no time expressing an interest in it and set up a face-to-face meeting with David Lyle. After some negotiating, he bought 320 acres of the Isaac C. Hamilton Survey (See Figure 8-1, number 228) for $160 in gold coins and thereby increased his land holdings in Lower Willow to roughly 500 acres. His new property comprised the western quarter of that Survey, including over 1,000 feet of frontage on the Llano River and adjoined Christopher Leifeste's portion of the Lamar Moore Survey on the east. To pay for it, he used money that he and Sophie had saved from the sales of beef to Fort Mason. Interestingly, his two parcels now flanked both sides of the Lamar Moore Survey.

In August, after acquiring the new land in July, Conrad attended a livestock auction in Fredericksburg and bought 10 Longhorn cow-calf pairs and a bull to stock the new property. After herding them from the seller's ranch at Cherry Spring to the Lower Willow area, he marked their ears, branded them with his CP branding iron, and then released them onto his part of the Isaac Hamilton Survey. As he watched them spread out into unfamiliar territory, he begin to think ahead to the next roundup which was only two months away. With more cattle, his ranch would take more work but he had discovered that he truly enjoyed ranching. Seeing his herd grow was highly rewarding.

With the addition of part of the Isaac Hamilton Survey, Conrad Pluenneke's ranching effort expanded. He now had to tend to about 170 cows spread over nearly 500 acres and in perhaps a year or two, his herd would increase to about 200 Longhorns. He loved that the herd multiplied on its own each year and with even more land, he could contemplate buying more cattle to make it grow even faster. With that idea in mind, he began to eye the land west of the Lamar Moore Survey as a means to expand his ranch. He imagined that if the Thomas Osburn Survey became available someday, he had to be financially prepared for that possibility so he and Sophie continued their frugal ways, and saved money from cattle sales.

But before he could do more about building his ranch, Conrad would have to take an equally large step in his Methodist spiritual life. For some time, he had entertained the idea of going into the Methodist ministry. His prayers seemed to lead him in that direction and if God had that work in store for him, he was willing. However, that role in the Llano River Valley could only achieved by riding the Llano Circuit.

Oh Lord, show me the way!

Chapter 9

RIDING THE LLANO CIRCUIT

As a result of his radical view of salvation and highly charged, zealous preaching style, leaders of the Anglican Church blocked John Wesley from a church pastorate in England and ordered him to preach in only one parish. Instead, he elected to become an itinerate preacher and issued the statement that he was "taking upon all the World as my parish." Crowds came, his ministry soared, and soon he had thousands of converts. Word spread and many more expressed a wish to hear him preach but he recognized that he alone could not meet the huge demand. To solve the problem, he conceived the idea of itinerate preachers going to the ends of the earth to spread *The Word* and converting people to his form of Christianity, Methodism.

At each place touched by an itinerate preacher, people who converted to Methodism were formed into a class which might be characterized as a Christian Brotherhood Society. As Garber (1928) noted, "There was a binding solidarity between (those) early Methodists. They watched over each other, they advised each other, and they became common burden bearers." What affected one Methodist, affected all of them. As such societies were formed, they were joined with other societies and organized into larger units such as Districts or Conferences. To serve a string of such societies, circuits were formed and preachers were assigned to ride them, spreading the Gospel.

Methodist circuits were not static. If a need arose in a community near one of the stops on the loop, the minister who had charge of that circuit was expected to meet that need and bring the new community into the fold. As circuits grew too large for one circuit rider, they were split and new charges were created, producing yet another demand for an itinerate preacher. Circuit riding preachers were frequently rotated among the charges of their Conference as church leaders, Presiding Elders or Bishops, saw the need. As noted earlier, Wesley's intent was to project his Methodism deep into rural areas and continually expand until all had been reached. With that approach, Methodism could thus reach the poorer and disenfranchised members of society and serve them spiritually.

When John Wesley conceived of his system of preaching at multiple meeting places (circuits) in less urban areas, he was made aware that it would require an itinerate force of preachers with special capabilities. In his terms, preachers would serve circuits composed of two or more local communities (societies) that were to be served at least once per year and more often, if circumstances warranted. In 1769, he sent 14 circuit riders to America and they flourished there.

The preachers who manned Wesley's system became known as *circuit riding preachers*, or sometimes as *saddlebag preachers*. As representatives of the faith, circuit riding ministers had to be thoroughly vetted and selected very carefully. Not everyone had the stuff to be a circuit riding Methodist minister. Most of those chosen were zealous and dogged to a fault.

In America, the first prominent circuit rider was Bishop Francis Asbury who was reputed to have traveled tens of thousands of miles and delivered something like 16,000 sermons in his illustrious preaching career which spanned more than 50 years. As a result of his work, Methodism spread over the Appalachian Mountains and down into what would become new frontier states, Ohio, Indiana, Kentucky, and Tennessee.

In that very remote and rural setting, a young man named Peter Cartwright would convert to Methodism and spread the Word as a circuit rider well into the 19th century. In his autobiography, he said of the job:

"A Methodist preacher, when he felt that God had called him to preach, instead of hunting up a college or biblical institute, hunted up a hardy pony and some traveling apparatus, and with his library always at hand, namely, a Bible, Hymn book, and Discipline, he started, and with a text that never wore out nor grew stale, he cried 'Behold, the Lamb of God, that taketh away the sins of the world.' In this way, he went through storms of wind, hail, snow, and rain, climbed hills and mountains, traversed valleys, plunged through swamps, swollen streams, lay out all night, wet, weary, and hungry, held his horse by the bridle all night or tied him to a limb, slept with his saddle blanket for a bed, his saddle bags for a pillow. Often, he slept in dirty cabins, ate roasting ears for bread, drank buttermilk for coffee, took deer meat or bear meat or wild turkey for breakfast, dinner, and supper. This was old-fashioned Methodist preacher fare and fortune."

Methodist circuit riding ministers went everywhere, literally to the ends of the Earth. Methodist historian Paul Garber (1928) related a story about a new circuit rider that was sent by his conference to a place deep in the backwoods of northern Mississippi that had neither a church or a known settlement. Dutifully, the preacher rode into the wilderness for 11 days without seeing any sign of civilization. At last, he came upon wagon tracks and followed them to a place where settlers were just beginning to unload their wagon. The would-be settler, after greeting the stranger, groaned upon learning that the rider was a Methodist minister. He had fled from Virginia to Georgia and finally to Mississippi, trying to evade Methodist preachers. Now he was confronted by one even before he could unload his wagon. He was distraught, to say the least. Paraphrased, the young preacher's response to that settler was, "You will find Methodist preachers everywhere, even in Hell. You better make peace with us now and enjoy the rest of your life." They were omnipresent and dogged, to say the least.

The position of circuit rider had prerequisites. When the Methodist hierarchy selected men to be circuit riders, they generally preferred celibate single men because they were believed to be better suited to meet the hardships, isolation, and endless travel required of the job. Unlike the situation with married men, a Methodist Conference could easily assign single ministers to a remote station or to a circuit in another state without any regard for how that move might affect the minister's family. On the other hand, married men tended to be more stable but they had obligations to their wife and to their children that had to be met. Those familial obligations sometimes conflicted with their ability to serve the circuit. Married or not, if a man was admitted to a Conference and received an assignment (in Methodist terms, a *charge*), he was duly obligated to serve there. For that reason, some married men chose not to register with their Conference every year and stayed home.

To be an effective circuit rider, one had to have a certain amount of grit or toughness about them. In the backcountry, they often had to endure severe hardships that were created by adverse weather, floods, and rugged terrain. The job was made even more dangerous by hostile Indians, ferocious animals, poisonous snakes, and food deprivation as well as by "rowdies" and outlaws. Weak-hearted, unfit, or less than fully committed ministers often quit the circuit and found a way to serve Methodism in more civilized areas. Along with innate toughness, circuit riders also had to possess a real zest for missionary work. They had to have a tremendous desire to save souls and a willingness to suffer hardship to win those souls. Those who lacked that zeal and who lacked the willpower and energy that was demanded by the job, quit and took up another line of work.

In the 19th century, the Methodist hierarchy was in a fierce competition with other denominations and therefore, could not afford to waste its precious time and its limited resources on someone who was apt to quit or do poorly at the job. Candidates for circuit riding ministerial jobs, therefore, had to undergo rigorous examinations in front of the Presiding Elder and members of the Conference before they were issued licenses to preach. Even though selected and fully licensed, all of them were required to report on their activities before every Quarterly Conference and were kept under constant scrutiny. Those who managed to pass muster and who were willing to take charges for remote circuits had to be exceptionally qualified, and they were.

Methodist missionaries brought the circuit riding system to Texas in the middle of the 19th century and extended it from Galveston to German immigrant communities in the interior of the state. When Reverend Charles A Grote established the Llano Circuit in 1856, he was carrying on a longstanding tradition in the Methodist faith.

The Reverend Charles A. Grote was a stocky man with a full dark beard that encircled much of his face, emphasizing his high forehead and his piercing eyes (see Appendix 4). A dedicated Methodist, he began his pastoral career at Victoria in 1848. In 1851, Grote was moved by the MEC-S to Fredericksburg where he replaced Eduard Schneider, whose appearance was more fragile (again, see Appendix 4). After a few years under his stewardship, the congregation grew to the point where it needed a larger and more permanent church building. In 1855, they managed to build a rock sanctuary on San Antonio Street but at about the same time, some of his congregation began to move north, beyond the Llano River.[86]

Caring for them and not wanting them to backslide into sin, Grote went to Castell and preached there in 1855. Beginning that year and continuing for several years, the Reverend Charles A. Grote made horseback trips to the Llano River Valley, preached to settlers in vari-

---

[86] Pioneers in God's HIlls, pages 47 and 48.

ous German communities north of the Llano River, and eventually moved there. Some of the people in those communities had been in his congregation at Fredericksburg and he intended to see that their souls were cared for, regardless of where they lived. In that way, he was the very epitome of a Methodist circuit rider.

His first visits were to Castell where the services were held under a large oak tree on August Leifeste's [87] land. After that, he began to preach at other areas in the western part of the Llano River Valley, places such as Lower Willow (in 1854), Upper Willow (in 1856), and Beaver Creek (also in 1856). In addition to those three communities, Grote visited other sites such as Squaw Creek, Canaan, Simonsville, and Saline Creek on a semi-regular basis. Those communities were all located in the Llano River Valley and were places where German immigrants had firmly put down roots and began to establish Methodism.

In 1855, Reverend Grote moved from Fredericksburg to Castell and on March 8th of that year, the stops where he preached became organized as the Llano River Valley Circuit, or simply the Llano Circuit. The circuit was officially recognized at a Quarterly Conference of the German District of the Texas Conference of the MEC-S. Reverend Devilbiss, Presiding Elder of the German District, conducted the meeting and Reverend Charles A. Grote was designated as its first circuit rider. [88] For more than a year afterward, Reverend Grote rode the Llano Circuit and fearlessly preached the Word to all, including Indians.

When the Llano Circuit was established in 1856, there were few roads in what would soon become Mason County and the existing roads did not conveniently connect all the stops on the Llano Circuit. The most developed road in the area was one that the Army had superimposed on the ancient Pinta Trail. It went by several other names. The Army referred to it as the Upper Road [89] that connected military facilities in San Antonio with a string of forts that led to its most western outpost, Fort Bliss, near El Paso. To Americans in the area, that same road was known as the Emigrant's Trail. In Mason, it was known as the Fredericksburg Road and as the Trading Road. Regardless of

---

[87] August Leifeste was Sophie Pluenneke's oldest brother

[88] In *What Hath God Wrought*, Daniel Walker Howe described a circuit rider as a "Christian Lone Ranger."

[89] The so-called Lower Road took a more southerly route and passed through the Big Bend area of Texas before reaching El Paso.

name, the U.S. Army improved the Upper Road after Fort Mason was established in 1851, so that its heavy, mule-drawn supply wagons as well as its cavalry units could readily navigate the rugged terrain between the far-flung forts. An improved Upper Road was also beneficial to settlers but more roads were needed.

Back in 1854, residents north of the Llano River had successfully petitioned Gillespie County to establish roads between the Willow Creek area and the Upper Road as well as between the Upper Willow area (then called Plehweville) and Fort Mason. Serendipitously, those new roads also benefitted the Methodist Church.

Evidently, Charles Grote's circuit started at his home in Castell and used the newly established roads (see Figure 9-1) to access the Pinta Trail. In addition, he used informal roads and trails that had been developed by early settlers to provide access to their remote communities. Those informal roads likely included the Threadgill Creek Road, which reached from the Upper Road to communities at Squaw Creek and Threadgill Creek. He also likely used the Simonsville Road, which connected the namesake community to the Fort Mason area and to the Upper Road, crossing the Llano River at a low water point.[90]

Conrad and Sophie were charter members of the Llano Circuit, as were her brothers and their families. Collectively, they and other settler families formed what became known as the Lower Willow point or station on the circuit. From the very beginning, Reverend Grote's services at Lower Willow were held in either the Pluenneke's home or at a brush arbor erected on the property of Heinrich Leifeste. Reverend Grote had played a major role in the religious life of those families at Fredericksburg and by creating the Llano Circuit, he extended and augmented his effect on their Christianity which far outlived his presence there.

Beginning after their conversion to Methodism in 1852, Conrad Pluenneke, along with his wife Sophie, had served the church in varying capacities. At each position, he had shown the willingness to study, work hard, and excel just as he had with every other aspect of his life. That work ethic was duly noted by Reverend Grote and other Conference officials.

---

[90] The Simonsville and Threadgill Creek roads are graded county roads today.

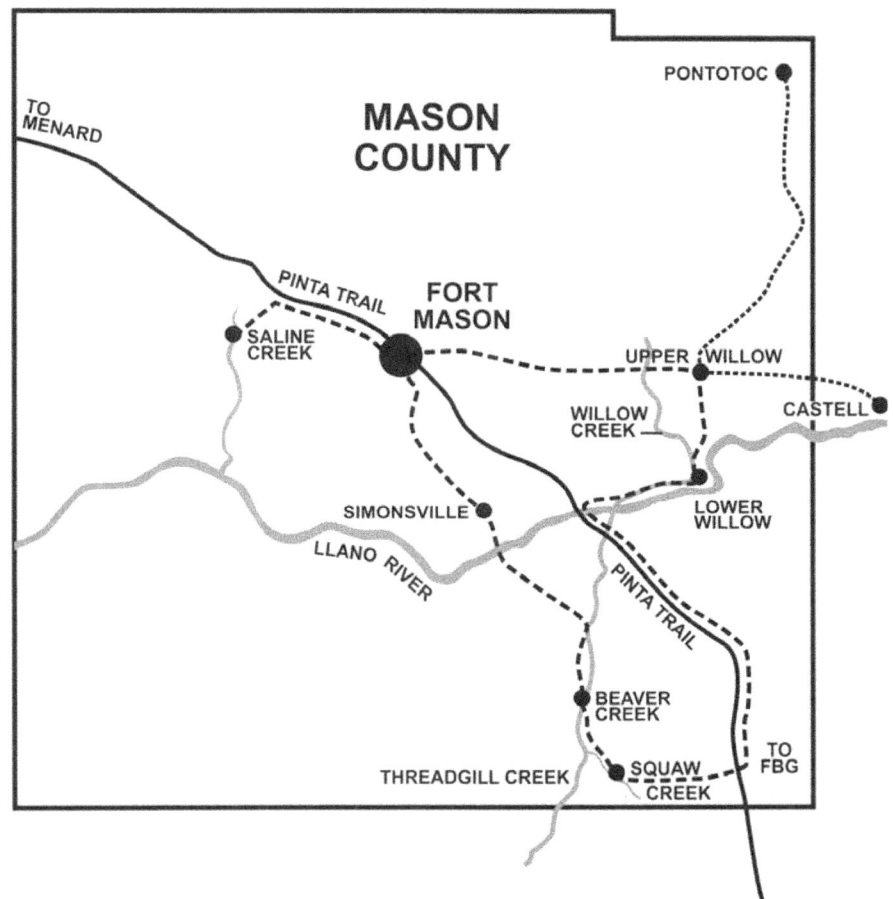

Figure 9-1 Mason County and the Llano Circuit Circa 1858

At the first Quarterly meeting of the Llano Circuit in 1857 that was held at Castell, Conrad was approached by the Presiding Elder, John W. Devilbiss, and the two men engaged in a brief conversation. Their talk mostly centered around Conrad's life in the Llano River Valley and his participation in the Methodist mission as well as its status in the New Braunfels District. Devilbiss, as leader of the German District within the Texas Conference, expressed an impatience for growth in the area. He wanted the denomination to expand in the Llano District."

Elder Devilbiss was a large, handsome man with dark eyes, heavy eyebrows, and a very thick dark beard (see Appendix 4). He also had a booming voice that matched an imposing personality. He had what one might call stature in every sense of the word and it was difficult not to be awestruck by his looming presence.

"As a mission," he said, "the Llano Circuit is dependent on the MEC-S for financial support. It needs more members and more contributions if it is to become self-sustaining." To that, the Presiding Elder quickly added "That means the circuit needs to be expanded deeper into the backwoods and reach outlying places like Pontotoc and Fly Gap, whose people hunger for preaching. We need people to reach them."

Conrad thought about that for a second and then asked, "I understand the need to extend the circuit but could it not be also grown by enlarging the membership at several of its present stations?"

Devilbiss studied Conrad's face for a moment, smiled at the earnestness of the comment, and then said bluntly "I like that idea. Would you be willing to become a minister in the Llano Circuit and help develop it? We need people like you in our ministry." As Devilbiss saw him, Conrad Pluenneke fit perfectly into the mold of a Methodist circuit rider: he was one of them. He was of German heritage, courageous, willing to speak up, physically fit, and clearly zealous.

Offering the opportunity to be a circuit rider to Conrad Pluenneke must have been an easy chore for the Presiding Elder, John W. Devilbiss. It was, however, not a novel idea to Conrad Pluenneke. He had watched Charles Grote perform for several years and had thought about doing ministerial work ever since, partly at Grote's urging. He had some concerns about his family situation and how it might affect his potential ministry but now that he was being given the opportunity, he inwardly felt obliged to "answer the call."

Before Conrad could answer, the Elder went further, "For several years, the conference has been trying to move Charles Grote to another post where we feel we can better use his talents but we have not found an adequate replacement for him in Llano. He has accomplished great things for God in the Llano River Valley and we simply can't allow his work here to lapse. We need someone like you to take this charge and grow it into a self-sustaining station."

With little hesitation, Conrad Pluenneke nodded affirmatively and said, "If it is God's will, and if Reverend Grote is approving of this, I am willing to accept the charge. What do I need to do?"

The Presiding Elder explained to him that he would be required to face a stern oral examination before the Conference at its next Quarterly meeting in June and that he would have to expose his life and that of his family to intense scrutiny during the test.

Conrad Pluennecke did not flinch. He said with determination, "I want to become a minister and serve God in whatever role he has in store for me. I will gladly take the test and prove that I am worthy of this honor."

The next day, Devilbiss met Conrad Pluenneke in Castell and handed him several books, among which were collected and bound sermons of John Wesley plus some key *Bible* commentaries that the Presiding Elder had thoughtfully added. He told Conrad to go home and study them diligently in preparation for a difficult oral exam at the next Quarterly Conference. He did. For three months, he read everything that he could find about the Methodist faith.

In June, Conrad Pluenneke stood before Elder John Devilbiss, Reverend Charles A. Grote, and other Quarterly Conference attendees in Castell to have his life examined. For more than two hours, he answered their pointed questions about his life, his faith, and Wesley's teachings. At the end of the grueling questioning session, Devilbiss thanked him and then dismissed him from the building. He opened the meeting to discussion about Pluenneke's answers and then held a vote. Shortly, the Presiding Elder summoned Conrad back to the room and told him with great pleasure that he had been affirmed by a wide margin. He had passed the test. Humbly, Conrad Pluenneke bowed his head to a loud chorus of Amens. He was now on the path to becoming a minister. Oh Lord, show me the Way!

In response to the positive Conference vote, the Presiding Elder Devilbiss issued Conrad Pluenneke a probationary local minister's license and assigned him to be Reverend Grote's assistant pastor for the remainder of 1857. In that span of time, he still had to prove that he could handle the Llano Circuit charge and preach.

It had been well known for some time that the Rio Grande Conference wanted to move Charles Grote to a more fertile mission field. If Conrad Pluenneke passed the probationary period, he would be named as Grote's replacement at the final Llano German Mission Quarterly Conference in December and the Conference could confidently reassign Charles A. Grote to another post for the following year.

Devilbiss was certain Conrad Pluennecke was up to the job and for that matter, so was Conrad. Always confident in his abilities, he knew he would do whatever it took for him to succeed as a preacher.

For the next six months, Conrad studied diligently. He reread Wesley's sermons, *The Discipline*, and studied the *Bible* relentlessly in preparation for assuming charge of the German Llano mission. At every opportunity, he grilled Grote on the inner workings of Methodist Conferences and circuit politics. During that time, Reverend Grote acted as his mentor and instructed him in the ways of Methodist management. He also mentored Conrad on preaching the Word.

Near the end of the year, it was deemed by Reverend Devilbiss that Conrad Pluenneke had met the requirements of his probation, and it was lifted. At a meeting of the Texas Conference in San Antonio, he was recognized as a licensed Methodist minister with full connection. With that credential, he could now perform baptisms, weddings, and funerals but was not allowed to conduct communion. That job was reserved for Elders. With full connection, the Texas Conference assigned him to the Llano Circuit for 1857. At the same time, C. A. Grote was reassigned to a station in New Orleans. In time, he would return to Texas and to the Llano area.

At a small Christmas gathering in Castell, Conrad met Charles Grote and they talked about Methodism at length. Afterwards, they parted ways and for Conrad, their parting was bittersweet. He was losing a dear friend and mentor but gaining a post in the Methodist faith. As he watched Grote depart that day, Conrad suffered an uncharacteristic momentary lapse in confidence. He was suddenly confronted the fact that he now was solely in charge of the Llano Circuit. Was he up to the task? He shuddered and then stiffened his back as if to say, "Of course I am and I will succeed!"

Now assured of the Llano Mission charge, Conrad began to think ahead about what the job might entail. The job of circuit rider had requirements but it also offered the preacher much flexibility in meeting them. At minimum, Conrad was required to preach regularly.at each of the stops on the circuit. Regularity could be interpreted to be as infrequent as twice a year or it could be construed to require more meetings. It was up to the minister to determine the needs of his congregations and meet them. He also had the option of making the circuit on one trip or he could visit points one at a time. Again, it was his choice. Conrad, being a new minister, felt strongly he should make the entire loop (six stops) once per month, at least for the first year. That way, he would get to know the different communities and congregations very well.

That approach, however, meant he would be obligated to be away from home one full week every month. While he was out on the circuit preaching, Sophie and the children would have to take up the slack at home and keep the cattle ranch operating. In 1857, his daughter was seven and able to help her mother with their youngest son, Henry, but their oldest son (Conrad Jr.) was just five years old and barely able to help around the ranch. That put a heavy burden on Sophie. His regular absences would make circuit riding almost as difficult for her and the family as it would for be for Conrad himself. Since the church provided little if any money for circuit riding, the Pluenneke family would have to pay for ministry expenses - items such as appropriate clothing, horses, and books - out of their own pocket. That meant more frugal living.

In December, before assuming his official circuit duties in January, Conrad Pluenneke rode back to Fredericksburg to do some shopping in order to outfit himself for his new role. He needed another sturdier and faster horse plus he needed ministerial clothing. In the town, his first act was to buy a young but saddle-broken black stallion from a man that he met at the Marktplatz. After some haggling, Conrad paid the man $150 for the mount, a new saddle, and reins. After the sale, he saddled the new horse, tied the reins of his brown mare to the saddle horn, and set out for San Saba Street to shop for clothing that would befit a man of the cloth. At Saenger's Haberdashery, he bought a pair of durable black trousers, a long sleeved black shirt, and a black broad-brimmed hat. To that ensemble, he added a full-length black woolen coat to round out his ministerial appearance. In all, he paid $27 for the clothing. For both the horse and the clothing, he used money that he and Sophie had saved from the sale of cattle. The amount he spent for clothing, $27, was equivalent to three months of his anticipated annual salary but, as a proud man, he felt he needed to look the part of a preacher. His last stop in Fredericksburg was at the Methodist Church on San Antonio Street. At the front of the stone church, Conrad was greeted by its present pastor, Henry Bauer. The reverend gave Conrad a new *Bible*, a new copy of *The Discipline*, and a new Methodist hymnal for his ministry. After praying with the reverend, Conrad stuffed the books into his saddlebags and began the journey back to his homestead on the Llano River.

Although they could scarcely afford it, Conrad subscribed to Wilhelm Nast's publication *Der Christliche Apologete* in 1858 and paid $1 per year for it. The publication was delivered monthly to the new post office at Hedwig's Hill. He hoped that the Apologete would provide him material for new sermons and keep him informed about what was happening in Methodism.

In 1861, Conrad Pluenneke wrote a letter to a cousin back in Germany that in part described his role as a "traveling minister" or "missionary" in the Llano River Valley in the years 1858 and 1859. In that letter, he wrote that during his two year stint, he rode a circuit which was over 60 English miles in length[91] and had 6 stops. Since there were few roads that would accommodate a wagon between some of the stops, he rode the route on horseback, occasionally following primitive trails through sparsely populated wilderness areas. In some areas, he moved along on newly constructed but infrequently used roads. Riding the Llano Circuit, therefore, was often a solitary job but Conrad Pluenneke, like many circuit riders before him, rode the countryside and "preached the Word urgently in season and out, (always) reproving, rebuking, exhorting long suffering (sinners), and was unfailingly patient in his teaching," to paraphrase the Apostle Paul's directive to Christians.

When Conrad's tenure as a circuit rider began, he decided to start on familiar terrain. He would start by preaching at Lower Willow where services were generally held on his own property or on property owned by one of the Leifestes.[92] From there, he decided to visit Castell

---

[91] The exact route of the Llano River Circuit is unknown today. Therefore, its length can only be estimated. By connecting the six stops directly ("as the crow flies") on a scaled map, the author has estimated that the circuit was about 45 miles in length. Adding another of 33% for zigzagging through rough terrain lengthens the estimate to roughly 60 miles, which agrees with Conrad's estimate of it.

[92] In 1854, Methodist services were held in a brush arbor near the home of Heinrich Leifeste. Such services were the norm until 1868 when a rock church was erected at Lower Willow. The thatched roof of the arbor protected the settlers from the elements.

and then backtrack to Lower Willow. From home, he planned to travel clockwise, beginning with Squaw Creek (Canaan) and Beaver Creek. From there, he would head north and connect with a primitive road that crossed the Llano and continued northward to the small community of Simonsville. From there, his intention was to travel northwest on the Upper Road through Mason and then turn west to the Saline area before returning through Mason to Upper Willow. After preaching there, he would return home (see Figure 9-1) by way of the Lower Willow Road.

At each stop, he hoped to stay at the home of a Methodist family where he would pray with them, take food with them, spend the night with them, and preach somewhere in the general vicinity at least once before moving on to the next station. On the small stipend that the MEC-S gave him, which was supposed to be $9 per month, he had no choice but to stay with a host family. It was the only way he could afford to serve the MEC-S and keep his own homestead financially stable. When host families were not available or not forthcoming (which was rare), he planned to camp near a stream in the area and survive on food provided by members of the congregation. As he planned the route, he kept in mind that Elder Devilbiss had said that the job was not going to be easy.

On the first day of his tenure in the Llano River Circuit, Conrad Pluenneke preached to his own congregation at Lower Willow on Sunday, the 3rd day of January in 1858. In attendance were all four Leifeste families, the Lehmbergs, the Martins, the Steinmanns, and the Eckerts as well as a few others. Although he had preached there under the supervision of Reverend Grote, that third day of January marked the first service that the new minister in charge of the Llano River Circuit would conduct entirely on his own. For Conrad, it was both an exhilarating and a daunting experience. Since his appointment at the Conference, he had thought a great deal about his first sermon as a fully ordained Methodist minister and what it might address. He was extremely proud of being a new Methodist minister, one who was now solely responsible for six congregations, but at the same time, he worried. He desperately wanted to begin his ministry with a smashing success so he was conflicted about the tenor of his first sermon: should he confront the sins of his neighbors or ease into his new role on a more upbeat theme, something heartwarming such as "love thy neighbor"? After much prayer and soul searching, he chose the former path, true to his nature. His sermon would confront his neighbors about the awful consequences of sin on the mortal soul. On his first Sunday, wearing his new black clerical garb, he delivered a fiery sermon that caused many to weep, some to twitch Methodist style, and all to cry out loudly, begging for mercy from the one and only true God. His debut was successful. With that first service behind him, Conrad took his ministry on the road the very next day.

As the sun dawned bright on a clear, cold January Monday, the fourth day of the new year 1858, the new minister of the Llano Circuit rose from bed and donned his black clerical garb again. Sophie and the children watched as he pulled on his black riding boots, groomed his hair, and then combed his beard. Sensing the coldness of the day, he removed his heavy black overcoat from a nail on the wall and pulled it on over his shoulders. As a final step, he put his black hat on before going outside in the freezing weather. He strode purposefully to the corral where he quickly saddled up his new black stallion, tossed the saddle bags containing his three books over the back of the saddle, and led the horse back to the house, where he tied it to a nearby tree. As he walked towards the house, Sophie emerged from it with his rifle, a canteen of water, and a bag filled with food, mostly bread, jerked venison, and Kuch Kase. [93] He stored the food in the two saddlebags, slung his canteen over the saddle horn, and, after checking that it was loaded, put his rifle into its leather holster that was strapped to the saddle. After checking that everything was secure, he turned towards his family. One by one, he said goodbye to the children, hugging them and admonishing them to pray in his absence, and then gave Sophie a long, affectionate hug. Disengaging, he turned, said a brief prayer, and mounted the black stallion. As he rode off in a southeasterly direction towards the Llano River and Castell, he waved back at his family who were standing at the door of the log cabin. Against the cold of the January morning, he buttoned his coat to its top and tugged his hat down to ward off the cold wind that was now blowing directly at him. He reached down and patted the neck of his horse in a reassuring manner as they rode on together. In a short time, he had become quite fond of his black stallion that he had named Storm.

The narrow but well defined horse trail from the Lower Willow enclave to the Llano River generally paralleled Willow Creek and

---

[93] German cooked cheese.

sloped gently as it meandered southward. The crude trail was lined with many cedar and mesquite trees as it wound down the slope, frequently veering around large outcroppings of granite boulders. Far to his right and somewhat behind him, Conrad could see what was coming to be called Jordan Mountain in the distance. To his right, he could make out the outline of hills that were just beyond Loyal Valley and Meusebach's home. As Conrad descended, he kept a wary lookout for the presence of Indians, often looking over his shoulder in both directions. He knew well that the area around Upper and Lower Willow was part of the Comancheria, the Comanche tribe's hunting grounds. Although Meusebach had negotiated a treaty with the Paneteka tribe of the Comanches, other tribes such as the Lipan Apaches, Kiowas, and other tribes of the Comanches roamed the area. They often attacked Anglos when there was an opportunity to take horses, cattle, or other property. To them, taking livestock or property was not wrong–it was simply part of their culture that contained no concept of ownership. Even within the tribe, members freely took from one another and there was no issue over possession. The Anglos, who adamantly recognized and valued property ownership as a form of status, saw the matter very differently and were greatly offended where their property was taken. To them, taking property was stealing, which was wrong legally and sinful in the eyes of their God. The God of the Comanches had a different opinion.

Conrad was well aware that a Methodist minister, such as himself, dressed in black and alone on horseback, was highly visible and not at all exempt from such predations. While his black clerical grab might create a small amount of respect among the Indians as one sign of a religious person, it was no guarantee for his safety. More than himself, he worried about the safety of his wife and children back at home who would be alone for the next week but he also had confidence in his wife. Sophie was a strong, resourceful person who, given a chance, could handle matters herself. He knew it was her strength and her self-reliance that allowed him to travel the circuit and preach.

After about two miles on the horse path, Conrad Pluenneke came to the Llano River that had a very wide streambed but the river itself was quite small and shallow in places. In the heart of the streambed, the water burbled around many large white boulders that had been exposed by many floods over the centuries. It was evident that the Llano River at flood stage was a formidable thing. Fed by the Comanche,

Centennial, Beaver, and Willow creeks, it drained much of Mason County into the much larger Colorado River some 30 miles downstream. The stream banks of the Llano River were lined with graceful willow and pecan trees that leaned well out over deep pools of slowly moving water. It was a picturesque sight and while Conrad viewed it, he said a silent prayer of thanks to his God for such beauty. As he approached the river, he guided his horse in a more easterly direction, heading for a trail that paralleled it. The trail was one that he had used many times when he had gone to see August Leifeste and other Methodist friends in Castell.

Where the stream made a large bend to the north, he veered left and nudged his black horse up a small rise that looked down on the river and dismounted to give both he and Storm a rest. He hobbled his horse in a grassy area near the water and went to the saddlebags where he retrieved some bread and Kuch Kase. As he ate and looked out over the wide stream bed with its large white boulders that floods had smoothed for eons, he thought about the Llano River at flood stage and recalled a story about Reverend Grote, his mentor, who had crossed it on horseback while the river was engulfed in a flood. That had been more than six years ago, by his reckoning. That day, the Reverend had nearly drowned in the process of trying to cross the swollen stream and had been saved only by the heroism of several Indians who managed to get him across on a horse and then by rope. He made that dangerous crossing to preach to the Methodist faithful at August Leifeste's place in Castell and he was not to be turned back from his mission that day. Memory of the story brought the briefest of smiles to Reverend Pluenneke's face–that Charles Grote was one dedicated preacher! Inwardly, he hoped that he too could show such dedication when the time arose. Shortly, he remounted and rode onward.

For about seven miles, Conrad slowly paralleled the Llano River until he gained sight of Castell that was situated on the north side of the stream[94]. In the tiny community, he caught sight of August Leifeste's cabin by the river and rode slowly towards it. August Leifeste was his brother-in-law, the oldest brother of his wife, and his good friend. Back in 1853, August had bought 12 acres of land on the

---

[94] Later, the village of Castell would be moved to the south side of the Llano River where it is today.

Llano just upstream from Castell for $100, moved his family there, and had established a successful farm. Now he was planning to sell and move to Lower Willow.

It was now near noon and the day had warmed a bit so he unbuttoned his coat as he rode. As he approached, he noticed that a number of the Castell congregation had already assembled under the large old live oak tree and that pleased him. Squinting in the bright sunshine, he could make out Heinrich Leifeste leaning against the big tree talking to another man. For weeks, word had spread around Castell that Conrad Pluenneke would be preaching on January 4th so Methodists from a wide area were coming to hear the new minister. At the cabin, a shout went out "He's here!" and people crowded around him as he rode up. He dismounted from Storm, stretched his legs, and then began to greet members of the congregation. His host emerged from the cabin and gave him a warm greeting. August Liefeste was followed by his wife, Sophie, who also welcomed him. In moments, he was swarmed by well-wishers and family. Not losing sight of his mission, he got everyone's attention and said a long prayer for safe deliverance.

The women of the congregation had prepared food for the occasion, each bringing her own special dish. As the midday meal was set out, Conrad led the group in reciting *The Lord's Prayer*. At it's conclusion, the group ate heartily and exchanged news. After the meal, the Reverend Pluenneke got down to business. He was not there to socialize, he had God's work to do. For four long hours, he preached "hellfire and damnation," concentrating on the sins of alcohol abuse, stealing, and adultery. He singled out one member of the congregation who was allegedly having an adulterous affair with a widow in the area. That unfortunate soul was banished from the meeting until he repented and atoned for his sin. The tone of his ministry had been set. The reverend, although he was one of them, was not going to allow his flock to backslide into sin. Methodists had strict rules of conduct that were set down in *The Discipline* and everyone in the congregation was expected to follow those rules. When the adulterous man did repent, Conrad welcomed him back into the fold with open arms, but he was admonished to pray hard for salvation. Conrad saw himself as a strict but fair and forgiving man.

Conrad spent that night at August's house. After dinner, a small prayer session was held and everyone retired for the evening. At daybreak the next morning, he again donned his clerical garb, saddled his horse, and said goodbye to his Leifeste relatives. Turning Storm to the west, he started back to Lower Willow. The day was cold and clear but the rising sun was on his back and it warmed him a bit as he retraced the path he had taken just ridden the day before. The Norther that had brought freezing temperatures to central Texas had passed through the area and that promised a much warmer day. In a few hours, he arrived at his home. He hurriedly ate with his family and then headed for Squaw Creek where he knew Fritz Ellebracht and his wife would be waiting. Tomorrow's service would be held in their house. As a crow flew, it was only about 10 miles from Lower Willow Creek to Squaw Creek but he decided to take improved roads much of the way. Although it was 17 miles, that route would reduce the travel time it took to get there. As he left home, he took the new Lower Willow road to where it intersected with the Fredericksburg Road, turned left, and crossed the wooden bridge over the Llano River. From there, he traveled another 7 miles on the improved road before turning on a primitive path that led to Threadgill and Squaw Creek. It would be late afternoon before he reached their house on Squaw Creek so he put Storm into a smooth gallop most of the way.

On the east side of Squaw Creek and above the settlement was a peculiarly shaped mountain called *Platt Kopf* by local German folk (Flat Head in English). It provided a readily identifiable landmark for anyone searching for the community. After an hour on the trail, Reverend Pluenneke spotted the *Platt Kopf* and rode towards it, following blazes on trees that were made by the earliest settlers.

In the community of Squaw Creek, he rode straight to the Ellebracht's house, which backed onto the creek. When he arrived in the late afternoon, he spotted Fritz Ellebracht as well as Dan and Sophie Bickenbach who were conversing near the front of the house, most likely awaiting his arrival. He waved as he rode up to the group, dismounted, and shook the trail dust off his long coat. After warmly greeting one another, Fritz took the reins of Storm and led the stallion down to the barn where he fed him a bucket of oats and shut him in for the night. While Ellebracht was so occupied, Conrad talked to the Bickenbachs, some of the earliest settlers in the area. He learned how their family had suffered through some very difficult confrontations with local Indians. The natives, mostly the Lipan Apaches, resented white settlers in the community of Beaver Creek because they settled on land in the heart of the Apache's hunting ground and reduced the amount of game in the area. The way the Apaches saw it, a deer killed by the settlers was one less deer for them. The Lipans and Kiowas often marauded isolated settlers in an attempt to drive them away from their territory, but the settlers were resolute. For the present, they were going to stay and attempt to live peacefully amongst the tribes.

As darkness began to envelop the valley, the group moved into the house where Sophie Ellebracht was busy putting a sumptuous meal on the table. Conrad greeted her warmly and then sat down at the table. When the five of them were seated, they were joined by Carl, the 12 year old son of the Ellebrachts. Reverend Pluenneke asked everyone to bow their heads while he offered a lengthy prayer of thanks to God for their many blessings. After the meal, Conrad prayed with them. In darkness, the Bickenbachs departed for their homestead which was only a mile or so away and the others retired for the night.

The next morning, Conrad rose early and donned his clerical garb. As he dressed, he began to think about the services that were to be held that day and prayed that he would be effective. After eating with Ellebrachts, he walked down to Squaw Creek and was surprised to find a small throng of worshipers who had already gathered on rocks near the creek in anticipation of his preaching. Among them were the Willachs, the Bickenbachs, and the Welges. Near that group was another one composed of Conrad Mund, John Dietz as well as Charles Kensing [95] and his wife. All of them were from the Flat Head settlement. Another cluster contained a few people from Canaan, which was located further down Squaw Creek. Phillip Buchmeyer and Fritz Winkel were among them. As he approached, the groups gathered around him. Conrad waded in among them, embracing those that he knew while meeting some for the first time. All the while, he was catching up on local news. They all hungered for preaching. Shortly, the assembled throng was joined by the Ellebrachts, the host family,

Now mid morning, Conrad Pluenneke wasted no time getting to his task at hand. As the small crowd sat on boulders, he delivered a fiery sermon on the evils of sin. For four hours, he harangued them about drinking "the Devil's Brew" and exhorted them to live better lives. Many Amens arose from the settlers as they hung on his every

---

[95] Membership of Squaw Creek cited in Passmore (1924)

word. At the conclusion, he asked for a small donation to the Conference and received a few coins that he noted on a scrap of paper that he
kept in a pocket of his black suit. Afterward, they came up to him one
by one and thanked him for taking on the local ministry and for coming to their community after which they departed for their homes. For
Conrad, the experience was heart warming. He was one of them and he
was enriching their lives.

As Conrad saddled up Storm in preparation for leaving, Sophie Ellebracht emerged from the house with a bag of food and stuffed it in
his saddlebags. Fritz hurried from the barn with a small bag of oats for
Storm and stuffed it in the saddlebags beside the food provided by his
wife. They all embraced and said a short prayer before the minister
resumed the circuit towards Beaver Creek.

In 1858, there was no cleared roadway between Squaw Creek and
the Beaver creek community. Back in 1856, when Reverend Grote had
established the route, he had marked his zigzag trail through five miles
of wilderness by hacking blazes onto trees and by stacking rocks into
visible cairns along the way. When Conrad had ridden the circuit with
Grote during his probation, he had tried to memorize all the key twists
and turns in the trail. Now, in 1858, he had to find his way alone and
finding those trail markers took all of his attention. Occasionally, he
missed a marker and went off course. Sensing that the countryside
looked unfamiliar, he backtracked to a known spot, searched around to
find an emblazoned tree or a stack of rocks before proceeding onward.
To minimize errors and stay on the route, he slowed his horse to a
walk, moved cautiously forward, and scoured the landscape for markers. Oh, Lord, show me the Way!

In his effort to stay on course, Conrad scrutinized every tree along
the path and in doing so, lost track of almost everything else in the surroundings. At one point, he realized to his total amazement that he was
almost completely encircled by a small band of Indians who were intently watching the strangely dressed white man plod through the rugged countryside. When he realized his folly, he brought his horse to a
complete halt and raised his right hand as a gesture of peace. Otherwise, he remained motionless atop his black horse that nickered and
fidgeted about, sensing other horses. Conrad slowly lowered his right
hand and calmed his stallion by gently patting its neck with his left
hand while keeping a steady gaze at the natives ahead of him.

Since arriving in Texas 12 years ago, Conrad had briefly encountered many Indians in a variety of settings. He had chased them from his corral and he had conversed with a few of them on San Saba Street in Fredericksburg. His first meeting with natives, however, had occurred well south of New Braunfels when the wagon train he was escorting met a band of Karankawas. When the cornerstone of the Vereins Kirche was laid in 1847, many Comanches had filed into Fredericksburg to take part in the ceremony and claim their goods from Meusebach. He, in the company of many other white settlers that day, had greeted them warmly. In subsequent years, he had traded with Indians, obtaining bear fat and honey in return for corn and beef. He and Sophie even had an Indian or two visit their town lot in Fredericksburg, pleading for food. In those earliest meetings, he had been made aware of cultural differences but over the years, had to come to respect most of the natives. He even found a way to relax a bit in their presence but he was well aware that some of them were still hostile to his presence in their land.

In his present situation, he looked carefully at their dress and their markings. From what he knew, they appeared to be members of the Paneteka tribe of the Comanche nation and therefore, were probably friendly. Most likely, they wanted something and were probably most interested in his horse. In his nervous state, Conrad Pluenneke thought rapidly but with great clarity. He knew that the local Indians had been exposed to Christianity in Fredericksburg and were somewhat in awe of the white man's God. If they were hostile, his only hope was for escape but he knew they would chase him down and kill him. Then inspiration came to him.

Slowly, he raised both hands towards heaven, looked upwards, and began to pray loudly and fervently for their souls. His prayers reached such a pitch and were so animated that the Indians began to edge their horses back into the forest, fearing that the white man had gone mad or that he was invoking his God's wrath on them. When he was certain they had fully retreated, he ceased praying and began to move along the trail again, carefully watching for both markers and Comanches. It would not be the last time that he would have to use his wits to get out of a difficult situation. In the back of his mind, he also realized that future scrapes might not end so peacefully. Slowly, he wound his way along drainages and over ridges to Beaver Creek[96] and followed its

---

[96] Beaver Creek is formed by the joining of Threadgill Creek and Squaw Creek

course southward to a large outcropping of granite along the stream bed which was on Gottlieb Brandenberger's property. It had been pre-arranged to meet at the outcropping on Tuesday afternoon and word had spread that preaching would occur that day.

As he approached, he saw a few people already sitting atop the large boulders and waved to them as he drew near. Amongst them, he recognized families such as the Dannheims, the Eckerts, the Koth-manns, William Geistweidt, the Heinrich Kensings, and the Branden-bergers, his hosts. He noted that their horses were hitched to a tree so he urged Storm towards a nearby tree where he dismounted, hitched him to a tree with other horses, and began to shake hands with many in the crowd. Here, for the first time, he was greeted as Reverend Pluenneke and regarded as a minister, not just a relative or an old friend. He had been to Beaver Creek several times in the past year as Reverend Grote's assistant but had remained in the background so as to observe and allow the reverend to do his work. He had gotten to know quite a few members of the community over the past four years and more recently in the capacity of assistant pastor but did not know them well. Now, as their new minister, he waded into the group with enthu-siasm and began to make new friends in the congregation, even though he was very weary. As he mingled in the group, more people showed up and took their places on the boulders.

As at Castell and at Squaw Creek, he wasted no time in turning to religion. After all, these people had come to pray together and hear good preaching. Standing below the outcropping, the Reverend Pluenneke looked up at his flock and asked for quiet. In the hush that followed, he began to recite *The Lord's Prayer* aloud. On cue, the congregation joined him. After a loud concluding Amen, he asked them to sing "O Come and Dwell in Me" along with him, a Charles Wesley hymn. He began the hymn but was soon drowned out by sev-eral large men who sang quite loudly but off key. Reverend Conrad, not offended, admired their enthusiasm. As the hymn concluded, he launched into his sermon with gusto.

The basis for his sermon that day was *The Discipline*, which he slowly took from his coat pocket and then held high over his head with his left hand. Pointing up at it with his right hand, he said, "This is John Wesley's Method and we are charged to follow it, not just at church but everyday. It is the way to a pious life, a good life, and a heavenly reward after life." From there, he preached about the guide-lines that *The Discipline* established for Methodists. Following it would not be easy, he admonished. It would mark them as Methodists and set them apart from worldly people. For that, they might be casti-gated and reviled as zealots but they would be rewarded with eternal life. For three more hours, he railed specifically against drinking and admonished them not to allow the "Demon Alcohol" to touch their lips. To that, the women in the audience shouted a hardy "Amen!" Nor were they to spit, chew tobacco, or use profanity. He concluded with another Charles Wesley hymn and then a prayer of benediction. By the time he finished, the sun was fading in the western sky. After the ser-vice, they crowded around him and thanked him for coming to Beaver Creek. Slowly, the congregation dispersed, hurrying to get back to their farms before complete darkness set in.

The Brandenberger's invited him to their house for the evening meal, but were unable to accommodate him for the night because they had visitors from Fredericksburg. At their house, he ate and prayed ardently with them for an hour and then rode back to the creek.

Now alone, Conrad decided to camp next to Beaver Creek for the night. Finding a secluded spot, he dismounted from Storm, removed the saddle and the saddlebags from his back, and then hobbled him. From the saddlebags, Conrad removed the bag of oats that had been provided by Fritz Ellebracht and fed his horse. He took the saddle and saddle blanket and spread them on a flat sandy area under a large live oak tree. Before retiring, he went to his saddlebags and took out the food that Sophie Ellebracht had so caringly stuffed in them that morn-ing. With a tin cup, he dipped water from Beaver Creek and sat down to have dinner. As he ate leisurely, he thought back to the meetings in Castell, at Squaw Creek, and at Beaver Creek. They had gone well, he thought. Those attending had seemed pleased with his ministry and responded well to his preaching. Shortly, his eyes began to droop so he put his head on the saddle, covered himself with the saddle blanket and went to sleep.

He was awakened the next morning by the sound of movement near the creek. Fearing Indians might be on the prowl again, he sat up abruptly and reached for his rifle. Across the creek, a large Black Bear was rummaging through the underbrush in search of Blackberries but, upon sensing Conrad's presence, it became alarmed, crashed through the brush, and disappeared into the forest. He watched it until it vanished and then he arose to dress for the day. To quell his hunger, Conrad nibbled on the last crumbs of bread in his saddlebag. After repacking, he saddled Storm and began the long ride to Simonsville.

Before he departed, he was approached by Wilhelm and Margrete Bierschwale who asked whether he would be willing to preach in their home before departing. Always willing to oblige a good request, Conrad assented. He hurriedly saddled up Storm and followed the Bierschwales to their house further down Beaver Creek. When he arrived, he was astounded to see people gathered. After getting to know some of them, Conrad turned to business and asked the group to assemble in front of the cabin. To be visible to all, he stepped up onto the porch of the house in front of them and then asked them to recite *The Lord's Prayer* with him. At the Prayer's conclusion, he asked the group to sing one of Charles Wesley's hymns, *Come, Holy Ghost, Inspire Us* and then launched into his impromptu sermon. As he had done at the previous stops, he did not pull any punches that day. In fiery terms, he challenged the assembled group to turn away from sin, to repent past sins, and to ask God for forgiveness. For an hour, the Reverend Pluenneke preached, prayed hard, and offered a Benediction. Knowing that he had to be in Simonsville later that day, he quickly released the flock to go home after bidding them farewell. Shortly, he remounted Storm and departed.

He rode south, following Beaver Creek until it crossed the narrow road that led to the Llano River and the community of Simonsville that lay just beyond it. Along the way, he noted blazes on trees that Charles Grote had made back in 1856. At the road, he forked left and headed northwest. He followed the primitive road for several miles and came to the low water crossing of the Llano. There, Conrad decided to rest Storm and allow him to have access to both water and grass beside the big river while he rested.

As he thought about the four meetings that he had just held and of the new people he had become acquainted with, Conrad came to realize that some of those German settlers had come from a wide area of southern Mason County and northern Gillespie County. Some came from Hedwig's Hill, a few came from Loyal Valley, and others from the Doss area. Although the meeting at Beaver Creek had been scheduled to be a single day "preaching" event on the regular circuit and not a week long Camp Meeting, the faithful Methodists came from far and wide to attend. They thirsted for religion -- they wanted preaching and that pleased him.

The community of Simonsville lay just south of the developing community of Mason that abutted Fort Mason. As he rode north, he recalled what he knew about Simonsville. A few German families had settled there in the past five years, notably Paul Bast and his wife. For the most part, they moved there to be under the protection of nearby Fort Mason but now more Americans lived there than German speaking people. In the past year, a few of those Anglos, mostly military men from the fort, had attended services held by Reverend Grote. They were not Methodists nor were they interested in hearing preaching, especially in German. They spoke English. They had gone to Methodist meetings to witness the spectacle of Dutch Methodism and had been openly unruly and disruptive. They had shouted and jeered during his sermon, causing some in the congregation to leave. Charles Grote had been tested to his limit by similar "rowdies" but had managed to preach well enough to add two souls to the Methodist rolls. He, however, had no antidote for those hooligans and departed immediately after the service.

Conrad Pluenneke thought about how he might handle such rowdies, should they attend while he preached in Simonsville. Unlike Reverend Grote, he had military training, was fit, and could stand his ground with them if required but that seemed unbecoming to a man of the cloth. He decided he would appeal to something they might have in common with the soldiers: they had all served in the Mexican-American War. In the 12 years since his service in Mexico, he had learned a little English and so he planned to use his limited language skills to appeal to their *espirit de corps* in their language.

At Simonsville, Conrad was once again met by a small crowd of German settlers at the designated meeting place, this time at a roadside tavern. Normally, they would hold the meetings at the home of Paul Bast but Conrad had learned that they were away so the tavern became the only available indoor place for a service. When he dismounted from his black stallion, he was quickly surrounded by well wishers. It was heart warming for him to be so well received, considering that he was new to the job. Slowly, he led Storm to a hitching post, tied him to a rail at a watering trough, and fed him the last of the oats from his saddlebag. It was now Thursday afternoon and the tavern grounds were mostly vacant. From members of the congregation, he learned that the military was on patrol near Junction so most of the remaining soldiers would be at their duty stations within the fort. That news gave him some comfort. On his first official visit to Simonsville, he did not want to confront rowdy soldiers during the service, although he was prepared to do that if required.

As he walked into the tavern with his small throng of followers, he noticed the barkeeper behind the bar busily cleaning glasses and arranging them on shelves. Although the Reverend Pluenneke was dead-set against the use of alcohol, he recognized that the bartender was his de facto host for the day. Conrad was not there to make trouble so he slowly and deliberately walked over to the man and calmly extended his hand in a gesture of friendliness.

In broken English, he muttered to the bartender, "I am Reverend Conrad Pluenneke but before I became a Methodist minister, I served in the Texas Volunteer Army at Matamoros under Colonel Albert Sidney Johnston." Surprised by the Reverend's preemptive move, the bartender eyed him warily but then shook his hand firmly. "Ah!" he said and then added, "Matamoros! I also served there in Colonel Johnston's regiment and at Camargo. Wasn't the Rio Grande area a huge mess? A real Hell hole, if I ever saw one." Having said that, he went about his business behind the bar and left the Reverend to his work.

Reverend Pluenneke tipped his hat and quietly removed himself to the far end of the tavern. As on the previous stops, the reverend got down to business quickly. He urged the faithful to gather around him in the large room and seat themselves at tables. When they were all seated, Conrad went through his now familiar routine. He asked them to join him in reciting *The Lord's Prayer* and then in singing a Charles Wesley hymn. At its conclusion, he launched into his sermon that was again about the evils of alcohol use. For more than three hours, he recounted his own battle with the Demon Tequila and how, after hours and hours of ardent prayer, he had come to see the light. He saw how alcohol had affected both his life and that of his wife. At a Camp Meeting, he told them how he had repented his sins and vowed to avoid tequila for the rest of his life. He urged them to pray hard, to ask God for forgiveness of their sins, and to beg for mercy. As the flock heard his Gospel, his sermon was loudly interrupted by many amens.

Their response spurred Conrad on, causing his voice to take on an even more urgent and strident tone.

A married couple, moved by the Holy Spirit, began to exhibit the *Methodist Shakes*. They rose from their chairs, danced about wildly, spoke in tongues, and eventually came forward to sit on the *Sinner's Bench*. From behind the bench, they were loudly admonished by an Exhorter to admit their sins and pray hard. Unfazed by the couple, Conrad continued to harangue the others about their sins.

While this was happening, a pair of cowboys came into the tavern and went directly to the bar, where they leaned against it and slyly observed the German Methodist service at the other end of the room, all the while drinking shots of rye whiskey. After a few shots, they became obnoxious and began harassing the assembled group of German Methodists, calling them "*foreigners*," and "those *damned Dutch*." The pair pointedly laughed at the repentant couple, who were still ecstatic and twitching. Before Conrad could react, the bartender got the attention of the cowboys. He leaned across the bar and whispered to them very pointedly that the minister they were ridiculing had served under Colonel Albert Sidney Johnston in the Mexican-American War and was now a respected member of Mason County. Abruptly, the pair of cowboys stood up, faced the Reverend Pluenneke, and after a moment of staring, tipped their hats to him. Conrad returned the salute by nodding ever so slightly. With that gesture, the two cowboys departed though the swinging doors and rode away. Oh Lord, show me the Way.

After the service, Conrad approached the bartender to thank him for his role in averting what might have become an ugly scene. To his surprise, the bartender said, "No, it is I who wish to thank you." The man had listened to Conrad's sermon and while not entirely fluent in German, had understood enough of the sermon to see the Light, and now expressed a desire to repent his sins and join the congregation. There, on the floor of the tavern, Conrad knelt with the bartender and for over an hour, prayed earnestly for the man's soul. On his knees on the floor of a bar, the man found faith in God. With water from the bar, the Reverend Pluenneke baptized him and welcomed him to the Methodist church. Since the congregation had long since dispersed, he promised he would present him publicly as a new member of the church on his next visit to Simonsville. The man vowed to stop drinking and quit working as a bartender. He fully intended to become an ardent Methodist, and he did.

As Conrad was preparing to leave, the bartender asked where he was planning to stay that night. Conrad replied that he had no plans but likely would camp somewhere near the community. The man asked the minister whether he might be interested in going home with him and meeting his wife. He was certain she would want to meet the preacher, pray with him, and hear some preaching, that is, if the Reverend was willing. And he was. The man extended a warm invitation to Conrad to eat with them and to spend the night at their house.

Conrad quickly accepted the offer and rode with the man to his home that was about a mile away. In his mind, Conrad Pluenneke recalled how God often acted in mysterious ways and what was unfolding now was one of those mysteries. It had just been that morning that he had worried about how he might be received in Simonsville and now he was about to stay there in the home of a stranger, his newest convert, and pray with the man and his wife. Clearly, God was at work in Simonsville.

When the pair arrived at the house, they were greeted by the fellow's wife who immediately sensed that something had changed in her husband. Instead of coming home alone and inebriated, he was accompanied by a man dressed like a minister, a man of the cloth. As they entered the simple log cabin, the man introduced his wife to Conrad Pluenneke, circuit riding Methodist minister, and eagerly began to tell her of his conversion on the tavern floor. True to form, she became quite excited, fell on her knees, and loudly thanked God and Conrad Pluenneke for saving her husband. For many months, she had tried to get her husband away from alcohol and away from that tavern but had been unsuccessful. As a result of drinking, he had often come home and inflicted violence on her. She knew he was a good man at heart but alcohol changed him into something different and very bad when he drank. Now there was hope in their marriage.

The three of them knelt on the cabin floor and Conrad prayed hard for their souls. In an hour or so, the wife renewed her faith in God and accepted Christ as her personal savior. With water from a handy pitcher, Conrad baptized her and welcomed her into the Methodist church.

Afterwards, he went outside briefly to where Storm was tied to a rail, unsaddled him, and then gave him a carrot that his new converts had supplied. From the saddlebags, he removed his copy of *The Discipline* and took it into the house. He read it aloud with the couple, line by line, and then made a present of it to them, encouraging them to study and follow it. He told them about John Wesley's life and promised that on his next visit, he would pray with them and help them grow as Methodists. Meanwhile, he suggested that they get to know Paul Bast and worship with he and his wife in the Simonsville society. After eating, they retired for the night. Conrad spread his saddle blanket on the floor and crawled under it but had a difficult time falling asleep. He was so pleased that he had been instrumental in saving two souls that day that he was already looking forward to the coming day when more souls might be saved.

Early the next morning, he ate breakfast with the couple and then saddled up his black stallion to move on to his next stop, Saline. As he rode away, he waved back at his newest converts. Yes, he was going to enjoy this job! Oh Lord, show me the Way!

As he rode northwest towards Mason, the rising winter sun was behind him and its rays striking his black coat added warmth. In the cold January weather, his breath and that of his horse were visible in the cold air. As cold as he was, he could not help but think of the young couple he had just left and the memory of their dramatic conversion warmed him.

In an hour, he came to the small town of Mason that abutted Fort Mason on the north. Conrad was very familiar with Mason and Fort Mason, having sold cattle there for several years. As he approached the center of town, he stopped at the general store owned by W. C. Lewis. Inside, he greeted the owner and asked to buy a small quantity of oats for his horse plus some jerked beef, cheese, bread, and a cup of hot coffee for himself. Lewis had heard that Conrad Pluenneke had been assigned to the Llano Circuit and inquired about his job. Conrad told him about the four meetings that had been held in recent days. While Lewis was not a Methodist, he appreciated the business that the denomination had brought to his store.

Casually, Conrad inquired about the location of a community known as "The Saline" or possibly just "Saline". As Lewis filled Conrad's orders, he provided him with cursory directions. "It is going to be difficult to find," he said, "because it's a place, not a community."

He directed Conrad to ride about six miles north on the so-called Upper Road and turn left onto a rough unmarked road that generally led southwest toward the junction of two branches of the Llano River. "At the turnoff," Lewis said, "there's a big stack of limestone rocks on the left side of the road." To that he added, "In about four or five miles, the road will cross the Saline Creek. I don't know exactly where the Fiedler place is located. You'll have to ask someone out there."

Conrad thanked him for the directions, paid him, and took his purchases outside. He fed Storm and then sat on the steps of the general store and began to eat. It was not like being at home with Sophie, eating in a dignified manner. As he ate, his thoughts ranged to his wife and he wondered how she was faring. If things around the ranch became difficult, he knew he could count on her brothers, Heinrich and Friedrich Leifeste, to help her. If all went well, he would be home by Sunday and everything would return to normal. Devilbiss's words came back to him again, "It isn't going to be easy."

Then his thoughts turned back to religion. From what John Devilbiss had told him, he was assigned to hold services on Thursday near Ernst Fiedler's house on the Big Saline Creek, a very remote part of what would be very shortly called Mason County. From what the Bickenbach's had said at Squaw Creek, recognition of the new county should take place in coming weeks.[97] As he munched on his crusty bread, he wondered what kind of reception he would receive in Saline. All he knew was that they desired preaching and he was determined to deliver.

After eating, he remounted and rode north on the well-worn Upper Road at a brisk clip. About 30 minutes later, he spotted the pile of rocks and turned Storm onto the crudely constructed narrow road. Moving at a slower pace, he scanned the landscape ahead of him for signs of a stream. In an hour, the road crossed a stream. As he looked upstream, he saw no evidence of human activity but to the south, he saw wagon tracks. He urged Storm down a path by the stream and followed the tracks. Shortly, he came to a house where a woman wearing a bonnet was working in a garden. He stopped and inquired about

---

[97] Mason County was established on January 22, 1858.

where the Fiedlers lived. She pointed down stream and muttered "one mile" in English. He tipped his hat and departed in that direction.

In a short time, the area around the creek opened into a large park-like grassy expanse. On the other side of the park, he spotted a cabin at its edge and rode towards it. Near the house, he met a man who was waving at him and gesturing for him to come forward. It was Ernst Fiedler. Behind Ernst was his wife, Mathilda, and their two children as well as a dozen other people. He hastily alit from Storm and began to greet people who were obviously overjoyed at seeing a preacher in their remote locale.

The Fiedlers invited him into their home and fed all of them a hearty meal. As they ate, the Fiedlers and their neighbors told Conrad of their thirst for preaching. It had been over a year since a preacher had wandered into their remote area and delivered the Word of God. That preacher had been a Baptist, sent from Brownwood. They wanted Methodist preaching.

As had become his way, Conrad Pluenneke began his service by preaching from *The Discipline*. Since he had given his only copy to the couple back in Simonsville, he had to recite from *The Discipline* by heart and having recently passed his ministerial test, he knew it very well. He told them about John Wesley and how he developed his Method. He told them of Wesley's desire for piety, about his preachings against alcoholism and tobacco use, and about his quest for faith. He exhorted them to repent of their sins and accept Jesus Christ as the only one who could save them from the terror that existed beyond the grave. Several were moved by his sermon, went into convulsions, and publicly admitted their sins. Those he baptized with waters from The Saline. As he brought the service to its benediction, he asked for donations and told them he would return to the Saline later in the year to conduct a Methodist Camp Meeting on the banks of the stream. Before leaving, he organized a class and appointed Ernst Fiedler to lead it. After that, he repaired to the Fiedler's house where he ate and prayed at length for their souls before retiring for the evening.

The next morning, he dressed and departed early for Upper Willow. He retraced his path up Saline Creek to the rugged road and followed it back to the Upper Road or Emigrant's Road, as some Americans called it. There he turned southeast towards Mason. After arriving In Mason, Conrad veered east onto the road that connected Mason with Plehweville, or Upper Willow, as local residents referred to it. The road was one that Conrad Pluenneke had been instrumental in establishing. In its earliest days, it had been a very crude road, barely capable of accommodating loaded wagons, but since 1857, it had been steadily improved and was now quite a serviceable road.

On that wintry Friday, Reverend Pluenneke turned his horse eastward into a stiff wind. He bowed his head and pulled his hat down over his face trying to protect it against the icy brisk wind. As he tried to stay warm, his thoughts turned to Upper Willow where he would see familiar faces again and where he would be invited into a sturdy home with a roaring fire. While warming himself, he would catch up on news of both Methodism and community. He reached down and patted Storm on the neck. That thought pleased him and so as the road widened out and became smoother, Conrad allowed his black horse to canter for a few miles. It felt good for both he and the horse to stretch out and move fast again. For nearly a week, they had been poking along, slowly following Charles Grote's trail markers, but now they were on familiar ground again and they could make good time.

After about three miles, horse and rider turned a sharp bend and were surprised to see a pair of men on horses in the middle of the road about 100 yards ahead of them. They had bandanas across their faces and pistols in their hands. It was clear they meant to rob the next rider coming their way and that was Conrad Pluenneke.

Never a man to flinch in a tight situation, Conrad wheeled his horse around and set off westward in a full gallop. This was territory he knew well and he hoped that the outlaws didn't know it quite as well as he did. A short ways back down the road, he knew there was a side trail that went over the ridge to his right and then turned back to the east, eventually leading to the upper reaches of Willow Creek. In that basin, he knew German settlers would come to his aid. The faint trail was known locally as the Stanke Trail. As he reined Storm off the road and onto the trail, he quickly looked over his shoulder and saw that the outlaws, perhaps surprised by his quick move, were just now giving pursuit but were several hundred yards behind him.

As he rode furiously up the narrow trail through a forest of post oak trees, he thought about his options and developed a plan. Just over the high ridge ahead of him lay a deep sandy wash that contained a maze of large granite boulders that could easily hide a horse and rider. Its sandy floor would obscure his tracks and force the outlaws to slow down to track him, thus buying him more time to escape. Near its source, the wash forked and only those who truly knew this territory would know that the right fork led to the Stanke Trail that crossed the ridge and descended into the basin of Willow Creek. In that area were the ranches of the Stankes and the Dannheims.

At the wash, he put his plan into action by slowing his horse to a walk and then turning abruptly into it. Gently, he dismounted and led his black stallion around boulder after boulder until he reached the fork. There, he paused to listen for his pursuers but heard nothing but wind in the trees above him. Leading Storming into the right fork of the wash, he remounted and rode up the ridge some distance and then stopped again to listen. He heard nothing but silence. Again, he dismounted, and using a dead mesquite branch, covered his tracks by walking back to the fork while dragging the branch behind him. After walking Storm to the top of the ridge, he remounted and rode slowly over the ridge and down into the Willow Creek drainage.

The deviation in his route needed to elude the "would be robbers" had added nearly an hour to his trip from Mason and put him behind schedule. Now certain that he was safe, Conrad urged his horse into a trot and began to follow the trail that paralleled Willow Creek down to the community of Upper Willow. As he descended, he began to think about his job again. Preaching that day was to be held at the Jordans and so he rode directly towards their house. As happened at all of his previous stops, there was a crowd anxiously waiting his arrival but unlike the other stops, he was overdue for his appointment and his flock was worried. When they spotted him coming from the north, and not from the west, a murmur went up among the crowd. Why would Reverend Pluenneke choose to come from that direction? He knows this area, why didn't he take the Mason Road?

After dismounting, he shook off the trail dust and began to answer their many questions by telling how he had been nearly waylaid by robbers and how he had barely managed to escape by taking the seldom-used Stanke Trail through Dry Creek Wash. As he had hoped, he was quickly ushered out of the cold wind and into the Jordan's home where there was a roaring fire in the fireplace. Ernst Jordan saw to it that his horse was fed and sheltered for the night. The congregation followed him into the house and soon they were all crowded around the fireplace, trading bits of news.

Several of the wives at Upper Willow had put together a large spread of food and were now directing everyone to fill their plates. Before the meal, Reverend Pluenneke asked everyone to bow their heads and then asked Ernst Jordan to offer a prayer of thanks for safe delivery and for the fellowship of friends. After another loud Amen, everyone sat down and ate heartily.

After the meal, Conrad got everyone's attention before starting through his familiar liturgy. He started by reciting *The Lord's Prayer*, asking all to join him, and then leading the group in singing a hymn before preaching the Gospel. His sermon for that day was again about the evils of alcohol. He told his congregation the story of the bartender at Simonsville and how he had been saved at their meeting, although he was not part of the congregation and not there to attend a Methodist service. To that there was a chorus of Hallelujahs. He went on to tell about going to the man's house and how his wife had also joyously joined the ranks of Methodists. His primary message that day was that God works in mysterious ways and humans don't always understand those ways. Sometimes good things happen to bad people and sometimes, bad things happen to good people. Who are we to try to understand Him?

After another hymn, *"Blest be the Tie That Binds,"* [98] Conrad said the Benediction and dismissed the service. Afterward, he milled among the crowd, shaking hands with friends, and chatting with various families, including the Stankes, the Vaters, the Dannheims, the Donops, the Hasses, and the Kothmanns. He had no problem being both friend and Reverend Pluenneke at the same time among these people. As daylight began to wane, the families departed for their farms or ranches, leaving him alone with his hosts, the Jordans. As it was getting late, he knelt on the floor and said prayers with the Jordans and then retired for the night. He was elated to think that tomorrow, Saturday, he would return and be at home with his own family.

---

[98] The hymn *Blest be the Ties That Bind* was written by John Fawcett in England in 1772.

As Saturday dawned, he put on his clerical outfit again, washed his face, and ate breakfast with the Jordans. Later, he saddled up and bid the Jordans goodbye. He started slowly down the trail towards the confluence of Willow Creek and the Llano River where his cabin was located but the thought of being home with his family gladdened him so he put the big black horse into a full gallop. In a little less than an hour, he caught sight of their cabin. He knew Sophie and their children would be watching for him and that as he came into sight, they would all come running towards him. When they did, he shouted and waved to them. As they reached him, he hopped down from the horse and embraced all of them. His first circuit was complete and he felt greatly relieved. In the cabin, he sat down and told his family about all of his adventures. After that first circuit, Conrad Pluenneke rode the loop regularly for the next two years.

In March of 1858, a post office was opened at Mason and at Hedwig's Hill. George W. Todd served as the Postmaster for Mason.[99] Later that year, another post office opened in Fredericksburg, with Theo Specht serving as Postmaster, and other communities opened post offices soon thereafter. Mail became an important asset to Reverend Pluenneke because it provided him with a means to communicate with the Methodist hierarchy and his far-flung congregation regarding scheduled visits or Camp Meetings. In time, riding the loop became routine for him and his congregation at the six locations were more ably served. However, the circuit could not reach potential Methodists of German heritage who lived well outside of the loop and who hungered for preaching.

That lack of Methodist presence was brought to attention of the New Braunfels District of the MEC-S. Outlying communities, particularly those east of Menard and those north of Mason, were in desperate need of preaching, so stated a letter to Reverend Devilbiss, the Presiding Elder of the German Methodist Conference. Those areas, including Pontotoc, Fly Gap, and areas beyond The Saline, were too remote and too sparsely populated to warrant their inclusion in the regular circuit so Devilbiss decided to extend Methodism to them via Camp Meetings. How that would be accomplished was left up to Reverend Conrad Pluenneke, minister of the Llano Circuit.

---

[99] Mason County was established in 1858 and the state of Texas required that all counties had to have a county seat. By public election, the town of Mason was picked and in the same year, it was awarded a Post Office.

In early June of 1858, Conrad began to consider holding a Camp Meeting for the community known as The Saline, or possibly just Saline. Back in January, he had promised the community that he would conduct such a meeting for them and he intended to honor that promise. To set it up, he needed to work out a schedule that would accommodate most people nearby Saline. To do that, Conrad saddled up Storm one day and rode to The Saline to visit Ernst Fiedler, the man who had written to the Elder and whom he had stayed with earlier in the year. When he got to the Fiedler ranch house, he met Fiedler's wife who pointed him to the field where her husband was working. Conrad walked out to the man and reintroduced himself as the Methodist minister sent by Elder Devilbiss. After becoming reacquainted, he explained what needed to be done to prepare for a Camp Meeting and described the requirements for a brush arbor or a stage, a *Sinner's Bench*, and seating. Ernst Fiedler suggested that the meeting be held under the trees along Saline Creek at what locals called the "Big Park." Conrad commented that he had ridden by the place and thought it would be a perfect setting. They agreed on Monday, July 12th as the day on which the meeting would begin and that it would last for six days. Fiedler said he would see to it that word was spread around the community "far and wide." He further stated that he would send Conrad a letter at the Hedwig's Hill post office when all had been arranged in The Saline.

Back home, Reverend Pluenneke posted a letter to Elder Devilbiss which informed him that a Camp Meeting was going to be held at the Big Park in The Saline, beginning on July 12th and continuing for six days. He wrote that several additional preachers would be needed to cover the week. In two weeks, a reply came to the Mason Post Office stating that he, Presiding elder Devilbiss, would attend the meeting and would bring three other ministers with him. The presence of the Presiding Elder at such a Camp Meeting signaled that the German Methodist Conference had strong intentions about extending its range to The Saline and thus enlarge its domain in Mason County. Such a strong showing would preempt incursions by Baptists or Catholics in the area. After the Camp Meeting, The Saline would be served more regularly by the Llano Circuit and by Reverend Pluenneke.

After services at Lower Willow on July 11th, Conrad and Sophie hitched a yoke of oxen to their wagon and packed it with camp equipment and provisions. When all was arranged, they placed their children in the wagon. Shortly, they set out for Saline Creek with their children. As they departed, they waved to Heinrich Leifeste who had volunteered to feed their animals and watch over their ranch in their absence.

After a long dusty and bumpy ride, the Pluennekes arrived at the meeting place just before sundown and began to set up their camp near the brush arbor that Fiedler had erected. Presiding Elder Devilbiss and the other ministers were already camped nearby. That night, the ministers ate together at the Pluennekeof camp and prayed at length for a successful meeting. As a last step before retiring for the night, Conrad checked the arbor area and found everything ready for the next day. Shortly after dark, he doused the lantern and bid Sophie and the children good night. It was not easy for two adults to sleep with several children in a wagon but they managed somehow.

The next morning, wagons began to pour into the park and their occupants began to set up camp while their children romped and played along the stream. In July, the Texas climate was hot and humid. Large thunderheads loomed overhead. The four ministers dressed in black made the rounds, introducing themselves to the people of Saline as they arrived. The local citizenry seemed highly pleased that the Methodist ministers, particularly the Presiding Elder of the Conference, were there to preach to them.

After noon, a horn was blown that signaled the start of the Camp Meeting and everyone hustled to get to the main staging area. The service began with Elder Devilbiss welcoming the people of The Saline and then offering a lengthy prayer of invocation. He introduced Conrad Pluenneke as the first speaker, stepped aside and took his seat on the stage to Conrad's left. Wasting no time, Conrad dove into preaching with intensity. For nearly four hours, Reverend Pluenneke preached loudly about the sins of alcohol use, adultery, violence, and blasphemy. At the end of his sermon, he gave a powerful "invitation." As a result of his forceful delivery, a number of people came forward and took their place on the *Sinner's Bench*. One of the ministers, acting as Exhorter, admonished them to pray hard for forgiveness. As a result, three people joined the ranks of Methodism that afternoon. After the evening meal, another minister took the stage and preached mightily for two more hours. As a result, two more joined the church.

The next morning, Presiding Elder Devilbiss preached and ten more souls were saved. After the sermon, Mr. Fiedler nervously approached the Presiding Elder and informed him that he had been told that some local rowdies were planning to create mayhem that night because they feared that the Methodists and their "dry agenda" were trying to curtail their liquor business in the area. After the evening service, Conrad and the other ministers patrolled the area around the arbor and where the ministers were encamped. About 10 o'clock, they found two young men trying to push the Elder's carriage down into Saline Creek. The ministers confronted them and a scuffle ensued. During the melee, one of the young men was shoved into a deep pool of the stream. He thrashed about, went under, came up, and yelled for his cohort for help because he couldn't swim. Rather than save his friend, the other man turned and fled the scene. One of the preachers jumped into the water and dragged the drowning man to shore. After he recovered, he vowed to never harass Methodists again and was released to go home.

The ministers continued their relentless preaching all week, sermonizing at length and with vigor three times a day. The meeting concluded on Saturday morning. In all, more than 40 people became Methodists and Devilbiss rated the Saline Camp Meeting a tremendous success. The next month, another meeting was held in Pontotoc with similar results, followed shortly thereafter by one at Fly Gap. Methodism was on the march, spreading like wildfire across Mason County and into other adjacent counties.

For two years, Conrad Pluenneke served as minister to the Llano River Circuit, often helping his congregation in many unusual ways. For his efforts, the community made certain that his family was always fed and cared for. At butchering time, neighbors in Upper Willow brought meat to the Pluenneke's home and after harvests, grain was also brought to them. All of that helped supplement the *circuit rider's* meager salary.

As his two year term came to a conclusion, August Engel, a missionary from California, replaced Conrad Pluenneke as the circuit-riding minister for the Llano Mission. In 1859, Conrad happily stepped aside and worked by the side of the missionary as a local minister. Now home more often, he began to develop his ranch and herd of Texas Longhorns.

In August, the third son was born to the Pluennekes on the 5th and was aptly named Heinrich August Pluenneke. In the family, he was known as August.

During that year, Conrad became aware that the West Texas Conference of the MEC-S had created an English-speaking circuit that extended into Mason County and that Peter Gravis had been designated as the Llano Circuit's minister. Having learned some English over the past decade, he sought to discover when Gravis would stop in Mason and made plans to attend. Upon getting the date, Conrad made an effort to attend the meeting in Mason, mainly to make the acquaintance of Gravis. For Conrad Pluenneke, attending the English-speaking service was not only a means for him to meet another Methodist preacher, one who was already becoming legendary, it was also a means to witness how MEC-S ministers conducted their English-speaking services. It also offered him an opportunity to practice his use of English. When the day arrived, Conrad loaded his family in their wagon and drove to the small town of Mason. The meeting was to be held in a brush arbor on the property of Thomas Myers, who served the Llano Circuit as a Lay Pastor at the Mason mission. Shortly after locating the Myers place and arriving there, he walked about in search of Gravis who had just arrived from Blanco County and who was busy setting up his camp. Gravis, a small sandy haired man with a receding hairline and a trimmed reddish beard, was a force of nature. Known to be resolute, comfortable in the wild, [100] and unwilling to back away from danger, he was also someone who was affable and easily met.

Upon meeting, Conrad instantly liked Peter Gravis, a preacher who had been admitted on trial to the Texas Conference that year at La Grange. Gravis was fond of telling people that because he was "light for running and small to shoot at," the Methodist church gave him rugged assignments on the frontier, which he dubbed "the outside row." [101]. In 1859, Mason was on that outer row of civilization in Texas.

In a short while, Conrad Pluenneke and Peter Gravis were busy talking Methodism and exchanging stories about circuit riding on the

---

[100] In 1892, Gravis wrote these words in his original autobiography "There is in the frontier of Texas, a peculiar spirit or sensation in harmony with the wild, romantic and picturesque: the love of adventure ---."
[101] Gravis (1966)

frontier. While they talked, English-speaking and German-speaking people milled about in the vicinity of the brush arbor and communicated as best they could. A few of the Mason Methodists thought that the German-speaking Methodists should learn to speak English fluently but as Jordan (1979) has pointed out, learning to pray and preach in another language is very difficult. To those of German descent, God spoke to them in German.

Although uneducated, Gravis spoke with great eloquence that day and several souls were won over for God and Methodism, despite protests by rowdy Campbellites. After the meeting, Gravis was fed and sheltered by his hosts, the Myers family. Rarely paid, the ministry of the chronically destitute Gravis was largely sustained by such kindnesses on the Llano Circuit.

As Methodism gained in popularity, a demand for preaching arose in distant parts of Mason County (Hoerster, 2008). The German-speaking circuit rider went to places such as Leninger, Fredonia, Mason, Fly Gap, Eaton School, Prairie Mountain, Loyal Valley, and even London at times.

In the early sixties, the men at Lower Willow began to construct a rock church in their neighborhood that was completed in 1868. With their large families and their ranching businesses burgeoning, it became difficult and time consuming to drive to other locations regularly. A local Methodist church was the solution, with Conrad Pluenneke as its pastor. It, however, was overcome by events. When Beaver Creek switched to the MEC and Reverend Pluenneke became its first minister, the people of Lower Willow went there. For a time, the rock church at Lower Willow was used as a school but eventually it was abandoned and fell into ruin.

In the fall of 1860, the Methodist hierarchy recommended Conrad Pluenneke for a Deaconship in the church. After passing an exam, he was ordained on December 2nd at the Annual German Methodist Conference held in San Antonio and chaired by Bishop James Osgood Andrew. During the conference, Conrad and all attendees were called by name, asked to stand as their character was examined and evaluated. They were also asked, "Are you blameless in your life and in official administration?" Those evaluations posed a daunting prospect for anyone not fully pious but Conrad was leading an exemplary life. The trip took a month and Conrad arrived back in Lower Willow just in time for the birth of his fourth son, Carl Friedrich, on December 28th.

In deference to his family and his ranching interests, he opted out of the normal rotation of MEC-S preachers in 1860 and chose to lead the life of a local minister. For him, it would have been very difficult to uproot and move his growing family every two years and it would have been equally difficult to leave them alone and unprotected on a still largely untamed frontier to take a pastor's job elsewhere. For that year, Conrad Pluenneke was content to run his ranch and help the church in whatever capacity it needed.

The 1860s would bring many changes to the lives of German settlers in Mason County and to Methodism. Some of the small communities in the county would begin to build permanent churches. Despite the looming prospect of Texas' secession and a civil war, a permanent Methodist Church was built at Plehweville in 1858. Later, a Methodist church would be built at Beaver Creek and another one at Lower Willow. Those three churches began a trend that spread to other areas of Mason and Llano Counties. In 1871, Castell would follow suit and build a permanent church along the banks of the Llano River. Those Methodist churches, all part of the MEC-S, would meet with difficulties and changes when the issue of slavery came to the forefront in America.

From its very inception, the United States of America had been divided over the issue of slavery, a glaring contradiction for a country that was supposedly based on democracy, freedom, and equality. That was also true of the Methodist Church in America. In 1844, it had divided over the issue of slavery. In that split, Texas Methodists had largely sided with the South. So much so that many Methodists did not realize that the MEC still existed. If it came to a civil war, Texas and its German-speaking residents would not be spared from the ugliness of a civil war that might last for years or even decades. In that looming conflict, Conrad Pluenneke and his frontier family would be faced with not only personal danger but deep moral decisions as well. Oh, Lord Show me the way!

Chapter 10

THE CIVIL WAR ERA IN CENTRAL TEXAS

At the end of 1860, Conrad Pluenneke felt very good about his life and for very good reason. Back in 1853, he had boldly bought the large Lamar Moore Survey, partly on credit. It proved to be the pivotal act of his life. After he moved his family onto it, he took up cattle ranching which was a new and very different profession for him, and one that suited him well. In the ensuing seven years, his ranching endeavor had gradually flourished and after a disappointing start, he was at long last beginning to experience success in Texas.

At about the same time that he acquired the Lamar Moore Survey, Conrad also took up another and very different occupation: religion. After his conversion to Methodism in 1852, he had moved up through the ranks of the Protestant denomination with apparent determination. He had risen from being a probationary convert without connection in 1852 to an ordained Methodist Minister with full connection by 1857. In 1860, he became a Deacon of the church. Perhaps weary from two years of riding the Llano Circuit, or perhaps needing to spend more time with his family, or perhaps needing to spend more time tending to his cattle, Conrad decided to become a local pastor in 1859 and 1860.

From as far back as 1855, the Pluennekes had been able to accumulate some money through sporadic sales of beef to Fort Mason and through thrift. Those savings had allowed the family to live better and feel more secure about living on their remote ranch. Late in December of 1860, he and his wife Sophie welcomed their seventh healthy child into the world and were not wanting for anything, physically or spiritually. It was a good place to be in life and Conrad thanked God for his good fortune. Looking forward, he was very optimistic about their future in America.

Firmly ensconced on a ranch in Mason County on the cutting edge of civilization in Texas, Conrad and Sophie Pluenneke were only scarcely aware of what was happening on the other side of the American continent. Through scant news passed to them at church and from neighbors, they were barely aware that there was discontentment in America. In Texas, citizens throughout the state were upset for several reasons but mainly because the federal government had failed to deal with hostile Indian tribes in Texas as they had in other states. In other southern states, the Army had forcibly removed Indians from their land and marched them west of the Mississippi River to federal reservations, even though some of the bands were among the so-called *Five Civilized Tribes*. In Texas, the Army refused to take that sort of action because dispossessing and moving hostile, armed nomadic tribes onto distant reservations would be dangerous and very difficult, if not impossible. It did try, however, by establishing a small reservation for Comanches on the Brazos River in 1855 but abandoned it a few years later. [102]

The Pluennekes were also largely unaware of growing sectionalism in the country. South was clashing with North, mostly over the issues of slavery and state's rights. As a result, Congress became geographically polarized and increasingly cantankerous. Lincoln had won the election in 1859 by carrying all the populous northern states by overwhelming margins while carrying none of the southern states. Outside of the North, he garnered less than 100,000 votes yet he won the Electoral College. Nationwide, Lincoln won by a plurality, outdrawing all three of his opponents but in Texas, his candidacy received no support and its Electoral College delegates split the state's electoral votes between his three opponents. According to Fehrenbach (1968), Lincoln might have become another inconsequential president like Millard Fillmore had the South taken a "wait and see attitude" after his election, mainly because of the sectional nature of his election. It didn't!

Through informing sources in Mason County, Conrad learned that Abraham Lincoln had indeed been elected on November 8th, 1859 and that he was thought to have abolitionist leanings. To the Pluennekes, the abolition movement was something that was happening a world away from them. Mason County had few slaves in 1860 and they posed few problems for local citizens so the local citizenry was somewhat indifferent to the issue. The general attitude around the county was that Washington DC was more than 1,500 miles away and things that happened there had little direct effect on them. That notion would prove to be false.

---

[102] Only a few Comanches were persuaded to move there and in 1859, they were removed to Oklahoma.

While serving as a lay minister in Fredericksburg, Conrad heard rumblings in town that southern states might secede from the Union if Lincoln was elected but he disregarded them as just rumors, nothing more. As new citizens and great admirers of the United States, he and Sophie hoped that the Union would weather the storm, remain intact, and continue to provide the freedoms that they had come to relish since arriving in 1846. Privately, they harbored some doubts about what freedoms an independent South might offer immigrants such as themselves. Since they did not own slaves and only a handful of people in Mason County did, abolition of slavery was a moral issue to them and they agreed with the concept but abolition of slavery was unlikely to affect their lives so far removed from Washington D.C. Still, they did not want to see armed strife in their adopted nation, even over an important moral issue. They carried on with their daily routines and hoped that the issue would be resolved peacefully.

At the time, it was difficult to get unbiased information about national issues in central Texas because there were no local newspapers. Newspapers from larger cities, i.e., San Antonio, carried articles about abolition but propagandists from both sides wrote distorted news items that fit their viewpoints. It was difficult to get to the truth of the matter.

At a Methodist Conference in San Antonio, Conrad Pluenneke became acquainted with the German Methodist publication Apologete, printed in Galveston by Peter Moelling, and he subscribed to it immediately. As editions arrived in Mason County, he read many of the articles that were contained in each issue. Through the Apologete, he and Sophie gleaned some state news and some Methodist news from coastal Texas but they were less able to learn about local sentiment because there were no locally printed newspapers, much less one published in German. The one exception was the New Braunfelser Zeitung but it had limited circulation in Mason County. It would be another 17 years before another German language newspaper would be published in the Hill Country and it would be published in Fredericksburg.[103]

What news the Pluennekes did receive was either passed on by neighbors or obtained by reading out-of-date newspapers from larger Texas cities. Whenever Conrad attended Methodist Conferences in large cities such as San Antonio, he made a point of reading their

---

[103] The Fredericksburg Wochenblatt began in 1877.

newspapers, much as he had done as a young man in Germany. When matters such as secession came up for a vote in Texas, he wanted to be fully informed and as a duly registered citizen, vote intelligently. If it came to a vote, he intended to vote against secession.

In contrast to frontier folks like the Pluennekes in Texas, people who lived in older, more developed states along the Atlantic seacoast and along the Gulf of Mexico were in a dither. What had them aroused was an emerging movement to abolish slavery throughout America, an institution upon which southern people heavily depended. In 1860, after centuries of evading it, the issue of human slavery was coming to a reckoning point in the life of the young nation. Dating back to the Declaration of Independence, the nation had been plagued by the issue of slavery for 94 years. Compromises in the Constitution of the United States had failed to address the core problem of inequality among its residents. Instead, framers of the Constitution sidestepped the issue with the so-called "3/5's rule" [104] and shuffled the problem along to future generations, thereby allowing slavery to become even more entrenched in the South and more contentious in American life.

Through his readings, Conrad knew that not all democracies had acted so indifferently to slavery. For example, John Wesley and his Methodists had railed against slavery in England thereby helping to establish a British Abolitionist movement that eventually led Parliament to ban it throughout the British Empire in the 19th century. Earlier, France had abolished slavery in 1792. Paradoxically, America, known worldwide as the land of equality and freedom for all, repeatedly failed to address the issue in its early history. Because of Europe's history with the Feudal System, Conrad knew that slavery was not invented in America. In the history of the world, human slavery had a long and sordid past that went back many millennia. The so-called slave trade had existed in the Old World long before Columbus sailed west and discovered the New World. For eons, African rulers had been trading their captured enemies as well as some of their own people to European leaders for goods made on the continent, including Germany. Similarly, African leaders also traded slaves to Muslim leaders in the Middle East for gold and goods from the *Fertile Crescent*. The *Bible*, as a historical document, is replete with Old Testament accounts

---

[104] Each slave counted as 3/5s of a human in population census taking and thus affected district representation in the House of Representatives.

of people being delivered into and out of bondage. When the Portuguese brought African slaves to the New World in the 16th century, they were merely extending and improving the slave trade business by adding a transatlantic dimension to it. In the new scheme of slave trade, European countries sent goods to Africa, Africa sent slaves to the American colonies, and the Americans sent produce from the New World across the Atlantic to Europe. Everyone benefitted except the slaves who were horribly subjugated and made to endure almost unbearable misery at the hands of some colonial plantation owners in America.

Over time, Americans, mostly plantation owners in the southern colonies and territories, co-opted the slave trade and it became ingrained in southern society. Not only were their state economies based on slave labor, their personal economies and lives were as well. Plantation owners, freed from the rigors of farm labor while also freed from having to pay for field help, became wealthy and politically powerful. With political power and influence, they saw to it that state laws were enacted to protect and prolong the institution of slavery. In two centuries, American slavery became so ingrained in the psyches of Southern slave owners that they could not comprehend how morally wrong their behavior seemed to the rest of the world. The world noted that hypocrisy.

Beginning with the *Great Awakening* in the 18th century, many people in the United States, particularly those who lived north of the Mason-Dixon Line, became aware that the institution of slavery was morally wrong. [105] Harriet Beecher Stowe's novel *Uncle Tom's Cabin* had a major impact on public sentiment and helped elevate abolition to the forefront of public debate. As a result, many citizens came to hold the view that it had no place in a civilized modern country, especially one that proudly touted freedom for everyone. In Northern churches, slavery became equated with sinfulness. It, therefore, had to be stopped. Educated, powerful, and influential people, mostly in the North, began to press for abolition. In the Presidential campaign of 1859, Abraham Lincoln had stated that the "nation could not continue forever as a house divided" but he had also pledged to adhere to con-

---

[105] John Wesley (1791) had called American slavery "execrable villainy," "a scandal of religion", and "the vilest sin that ever saw the sun." Cited in Outler (1964), pages 85-86.

stitutional limits placed on the Presidency. The latter sentiment was lost on southerners. Newspapers in the deep South began a frantic drumbeat for secession and the idea gained traction. Mysterious fires in the South were attributed to abolitionists and that exacerbated the situation.

The South feared that the North, much larger, richer, and more populous, would try to impose its moral will on states below the Ohio River Valley and abolish slavery. Their only defense was to insist on a "strict constructionist" view of the U.S. Constitution that guaranteed that states had certain rights. The question became, "Do states have the right to practice slavery?" A corollary question was, "Under the equal protection clause of the Constitution, can the Federal government free slaves and abolish the practice of slavery in its states?" Sectional conflict came to a head over those key issues.

A deep economic recession in 1857 and 1858 briefly quelled the fervor of that debate but when abolitionist John Brown and his men attacked the Federal arsenal at Harper's Ferry in West Virginia on October 16th of 1859, that act touched a raw nerve in Southerners who had long harbored a fear that their slaves would rise up and slaughter them. Brown's aim had been to do exactly that: arm the slaves, incite them to revolt against their owners, and end the practice of slavery in America. He had backing from six northern industrialists as well as men of letters. When Brown was captured and hanged, many in the South cheered but most of them continued to harbor strong fears of a slave revolution. To southern slave owners, John Brown's raid had demonstrated that their worst fear was grounded in reality. Most southern plantation owners also sensed that northern states, heavily abolitionist in nature, might not support them should a slave revolution occur. In their view, abolition would free the slaves who would organize and then turn on them to exact revenge for the hellish treatment they had received on the plantations.

Concerned about the possibility of an abolitionist President being elected in 1860, many southerners began to openly talk about seceding from the United States should that happen. As an entity apart from the Union, a unified set of southern states would have the authority to enact laws favorable to the South and the means to build up and command a military that would defend them, protect their interests, and keep their slaves in their subservient places.

When Abraham Lincoln was elected in November of 1860, another of southerner slave owner's worst nightmares became reality. Throughout the South, it was thought that Lincoln's election and his upcoming inauguration would doom the Southern way of life. Abolition was now on their doorstep and the hot-brands in the South were going to act to prevent it, perhaps rashly.

In December, news reached Mason County that South Carolina's legislature had hastily called a convention and had voted to secede from the United States of America. The state's leadership hoped that other southern states would quickly follow its lead and also secede, which they did. In rapid succession, six other southern states voted to secede from the Union. In February of 1861, delegates from six of the seven seceding states met in Montgomery, Alabama where the Confederate States of America (CSA) was formally established. It gave legal recognition to the institution of slavery and vowed to defend it as a right of southerners. Texas, however, did not attend that meeting because its Ordinance of Secession that had been adopted by the state legislature by a 167 to 7 margin on February 1st, had not been ratified by state voters.

On February 18th, more bad news for Union supporters arrived. Conrad learned that General John Twiggs, commander of the Union Army's Department of Texas, had arranged to meet privately with three state commissioners in San Antonio, all of whom who were Confederate sympathizers. At that meeting, he had surrendered his Army command without authorization and without a fight. It included the Federal Arsenal at the Alamo and other military installations, armaments, and men throughout the state. It was stated that he acted on the belief that secession was *fait accompli*. John Twiggs was subsequently fired from the Union Army for "treachery to the flag of his country." His solitary act dealt a huge blow to the slim chance that the Union might have had for keeping Texas in the Union.

Later in February of 1861, the Ordinance of Secession was put to the voters of Texas and they approved it by a wide margin (44,317 to 13,020). Conrad did go to the polls and voted against secession. In that vote, Mason County voted to side with the Union by a 75 to 2 margin while [106] its neighbor, Gillespie County, also voted heavily to stay with

---

[106] Bierschwale (1996)

the Union (400 to 17). Clearly, those two counties differed from the sentiments of the state as a whole. [107] According to Bierschwale (1996), "The German settlers (of Mason and Gillespie counties) had emigrated from a military country partly to avoid wars; they disliked being troubled in the new land where they were building homes, establishing themselves, growing crops and raising cattle." [108] Those lopsided votes in Mason and Gillespie counties, which were heavily populated with German immigrants, would long be remembered by Confederate sympathizers, some of whom had more than a little Xenophobia.

By March of 1861, all seven of the original secessionist southern states had held conventions wherein delegates had voted to withdraw from the Union and form the Confederate States of America (CSA). To that fold, six more states and one territory would secede from the Union and join the CSA. Oddly, "lame duck" President, James Buchanan, did nothing to quell the growing unrest in the nation.

Once organized, the CSA issued a formal Declaration of Secession but the federal government of the U.S, led by newly elected and now inaugurated President Abraham Lincoln, opposed their secession and, in effect, ignored their declaration. That rebuff caused the CSA to take more drastic action. On the 12th of April in 1861, civil war erupted in America when CSA forces attacked Fort Sumter in South Carolina. At President Lincoln's order, Union forces fought back vigorously in an attempt to maintain control of the Fort and on a larger scale, also try to hold the Union together. In time, the conflagration spread into most of the states of the Confederacy east of the Mississippi River.

Compared to other southern states, Texas had fewer slaves and had used them for a relatively short length of time. The first black slaves had been introduced to Texas around 1821 at Moses Austin's colony, which then was still part of Mexico. With only 39 years of experience with it, slavery was not as deeply rooted in Texas as it was in other southern states. In contrast to other southern states that had large black populations that exceeded 50% of the state's total, Texas only had about 183,000 slaves in 1860 or about 30% of its population. Most of

---

[107] Kearney (2010) has pointed out that some Germans did own slaves. The residents of those counties also benefitted from the protection of U.S. Army forts.
[108] Comal County, also heavily populated with German immigrants, voted 239 to 89 for secession.

the slaves in Texas were concentrated in large plantations along the Gulf Coast and along major rivers that drained into the Gulf, most of them brought there by migrants from the South. The Texas slaves therefore, had little contact with people who lived in other areas of the vast state and they caused them little concern. When viewed that way, Texans probably did not harbor the same degree of fear about a slave revolt that other people in the Confederacy did but they had strong fears about two other constituencies that were already free to attack them: Indians and Mexicans.

While the economy of Texas was not as heavily dependent on slavery as states in the deep South, it did rely on taxation of slave plantations to help sustain the state's historically weak and shaky economy. In that way, slavery was important to Texas but perhaps not that much more important than other taxable entrepreneurial endeavors such as raising cattle or shipping. Regardless, the nationwide movement to abolish slavery was seen in Texas as a potential threat to its economy.

However important slavery was to the state economy, Texans were affected more by what many of them saw as the right of the state to defend itself. In their eyes, the Federal government had failed to protect them from Indian raids and cross-border incursions by Mexican bandits. Settlers on the frontier of Texas had filed request after request to the U.S. Army for more protection. In response, the army created a widely spaced chain of forts across the state but they were largely ineffective. Indian raids continued and the citizens of Texas could do little or nothing about it. As a state of the United States of American, Texas was legally barred from establishing its own Army because national defense was the exclusive domain of the Federal government but it did have a militia which participated in the defense of its citizens. As a republic, the state had been able to meet its own defense needs but in the Union, the Texas militia had a lesser role. Thus, the issue of States Rights became more dominant in Texas politics than slavery. By March of that year, Texas, citing that failure to keep its citizens safe from depredations, formally voted to secede from the Union and joined forces with the Confederacy.

Although most of the battles of the Civil War were waged east of the Mississippi River, the Civil War had a divisive and lasting impact on the citizens of Texas, particularly in counties of central Texas where many German-speaking immigrants lived. The first effect of the war on lives in Mason County was felt at Fort Mason but the Civil War would go on to impact almost all aspects of the lives of German settlers living there, including security, patriotism, the local economy, and church matters.

In March of 1861, less than a month after General Twiggs surrendered the Union army in Texas to the Confederacy, Fort Mason was formally ordered closed. To local settlers, the fort's closing seemed abrupt and without planning. Troops at the fort who wished to remain loyal to the Union were allowed to march to the Texas coast where they boarded Union ships and were transported to northern naval bases. The remainder of the garrison at Fort Mason had been expected to stay at the fort and defend the area but that did not happen. The fort became more or less vacant as Confederate soldiers were ordered to address more pressing duties elsewhere. The fort was used sparingly as a jail and as a supply station. As a result of the absence of military troops of any type, local settlers were left without protection from Indians and Mexican outlaws. In the eyes of local settlers, their situation was worse under the Confederacy than it had been under the Union.

Shortly after Fort Mason had been established, the Indians had quickly come to realize that when massive troop deployments left the fort, it was almost defenseless as was much of the surrounding territory. Whenever they detected such troop maneuvers, the Indians swarmed into unprotected parts of the county. They took horses and sometimes massacred farmers and their families before fleeing. Now with Fort Mason effectively vacant, there was nothing to deter the Indians from marauding at any time or at any place. Even the illusion of protection was now gone.

Inactivity at Fort Mason also affected settlers like the Pluennekes economically. In the five years before 1861, Conrad had managed to sell small quantities of cattle to the Army and the proceeds from those sales, in the form of gold coins, represented their only steady income. Without cash, they lacked the means to buy new clothing, shoes, tools, or supplemental food. When the Civil War began, they reverted to subsistence living and grew, raised, or made almost everything the family needed while waiting for the war to end. It was not an easy life and they hoped for an early end to the war. What little money the family had between 1861 and 1865 came from Conrad's salary as a minister in the MEC-S. In 1860, his stipend amounted to about $100 per year but during the war, it often went unpaid.

In December of 1861, the Texas Legislature enacted a law that required all men between the ages of 18 and 50 to enlist for Frontier defense duty. In March of 1862, Herman von Biberstein organized a company of 28 men to defend Mason County. At the same time, Ranger companies were organized in neighboring counties. Known as the Minute Men, they had to assemble on short notice and gallop off to deal with Indian incursions. Conrad Pluenneke did not enlist in any of those organizations but among the volunteers for von Biberstein's group were Ernst Jordan, August Leifeste, Louis Martin, and Dietrich Kothmann. The law required that men furnish their own guns and horses. For a while, those units were successful at suppressing Indian raids and the local citizenry felt a small degree of safety but as the Civil War raged on, more men were needed in the Confederate Army and some local men left to be mustered into CSA forces. Those departures gutted the local defense groups.

Without an organized military defense in the county, the German settlers along Beaver Creek and Willow Creek were forced to defend themselves during the years of the Civil War. Self-defense was an imperfect solution because of the rapidity and forcefulness with which Indians could strike at seemingly random targets but it was their only means of defense. The lack of protection in more remote areas would cost innocent lives in Mason County during the war.

In October of 1861, just six months after hostilities began in the Civil War, the MEC-S appointed Reverend Pluenneke as the seventh minister of the Methodist Church in Fredericksburg, although he lived and ranched 40 miles away in Mason County. According to Hardt (2011),[109] "It was not unusual for a MEC-S conference to make such an assignment. It was based on needs of the church rather than the convenience of its ministers." His new charge at Fredericksburg included a charge to serve at Cherry Spring, a small community located on the Upper Road, some 17 miles from Fredericksburg. One aspect of the new charge that was attractive to Conrad Pluenneke was that the larger congregation in Fredericksburg would be more able to pay him than the Llano Circuit had been.

---

[109] Personal communication from William Hardt.

His new yearlong assignment required Conrad Pluenneke to travel through sparsely populated areas between Lower Willow, Cherry Spring, and Fredericksburg on a regular basis. Along that route, there were a few settlements such Hedwig's Hill and Loyal Valley but mostly, it was open space punctuated here and there by large cattle ranches owned by settlers like him. The relative isolation of that route made him extremely vulnerable and uneasy at times but traveling it was part of his job. Devilbiss had told him the job was not going to be easy.

Paradoxically, the German colony of Fredericksburg was becoming a dangerous place for people of German descent in 1861. Soon after secession, according to Baulch (2011), Confederate sympathizers in Gillespie, Blanco, and Kerr counties began to badger those who voted against secession, challenging their motives and their loyalty. Neighbors wrote letters of complaint to the Governor about neighbors or anyone who openly voiced support for the Union. Often those letters were based on rumors rather than fact and their recipients rarely verified their accuracy. Several Fredericksburg men, including Philip Braubach, William Doebbler (the sheriff of Gillespie County), and J.R. Radcliff were openly critical of the confederacy and were cited in those letters. The military commander for south Texas, General Henry E. McCulloch, thought the dissidents had gone too far by voicing opposition to the CSA, noting that CSA army conscription had failed in the Hill Country and that Confederate money was being depreciated. Blaming German immigrants, he recommended martial law. His successor, General Bee, concurred and sent a partisan detachment of Rangers under Captain Duff to the area to impose and enforce martial law. Duff and his men bullied citizens into spying and informing on one another, arrested the most outspoken, and then used torture to extract confessions from the accused. Duff's campaign of terror caused Hill Country residents, already leery, to distrust state troops and the Confederacy even more. In the swirl of Duff's inquisition, he was led on by blatantly false rumors which suggested that as many as 1,500 "Bushwhackers" [110] were living in the hills and burning down homes of Confederate sympathizers. Anyone of German descent in Gillespie, Mason, Kerr, Blanco, or Kendall County automatically became a suspect. Worse, the trust between friends and between neighbors was

---

[110] *Bushwhacker* was a pejorative term used to describe Union loyalists who hid out in remote areas to avoid serving in the Confederate Army.

stretched by Duff's pressure on citizens to spy on other county residents. Thus, it became difficult in the Civil War years to know whom to trust. If the Confederates hoped to win over the German immigrants to their side with such tactics, they failed miserably.

Even within the Methodist congregation at Fredericksburg, it was difficult to know whom to trust during the Civil War era. Therefore, the prospect of preaching at a MEC-S church during the Civil War presented a severe challenge to Reverend Pluenneke. As a German immigrant with unspoken abolitionist leanings, should he dare to confront the evils of slavery from the pulpit? From his history with the Fredericksburg church, he knew that the congregation was split over the issue. Many believed, as John Wesley did, that slavery was morally wrong and sinful but they found themselves in a Methodist church that took a tolerant and distinctly southern view towards slavery. Others, even though they did not personally own slaves, saw biblical justification for the awful plight of black slaves as the descendants of Ham, whom Noah cursed for having seen him naked. Noah's God saw to it that Ham's people would forever be punished by giving them black skin. Others simply saw no wrong in the ancient practice. It had been around since biblical times and therefore they condoned it but only a few of them actually held slaves.[111] Thus, preaching to an audience with such mixed beliefs had risks.

At first, Conrad Pluenneke's sermons dealt with routine Methodist topics such as the need for piety, evils of alcohol, tobacco use, and other domestic topics that he had honed during his stint on the Llano Circuit. Over the course of his first year at the Fredericksburg Methodist Church, however, he silently weighed the consequences of speaking out about slavery. In his internal deliberations, he had many factors to consider. First, his family. In a southern state filled with increasingly hostile CSA sympathizers looking for reasons to terrorize the German-speaking community, speaking out about slavery might put he and his family at risk, particularly when he was away at a church convention. The clerical collar gave Reverend Conrad Pluenneke a measure of protection but it, in the end, might not be enough to quell an angry mob bent on lynching Loyalists or abolitionists. Second, his job. As an ordained minister of an MEC-S church, he had voluntarily joined the southern denomination of Methodism and therefore felt he had to comply with the church's dogma or risk being dismissed from service.

---

[111] In 1860, there were 33 slaves in Gillespie County.

He was fully aware that he would be able to do less for God's cause if he were defrocked. Third, the plight of the black slaves in Texas. He felt compassion for them and knew something had to be done for their cause. Their lot was terrible and they deserved justice. Finally, there was God. Would it displease God if he chose to sidestep the issue of slavery in order to protect his family and his job? He didn't know how to answer that question and prayed ardently for guidance, often shedding hot tears in the process.

It was a difficult dilemma for a mere mortal. In time, his prayers were answered when he came to realize that it was possible to preach against slavery obliquely and not take it on directly on. The key was in how people treat other people. "Do unto others as you would have them do unto you." Thereafter, his sermons on slavery concentrated on the Golden Rule and his message was simple: Treat All people as you wish to be treated yourself. That subtle message may have gone over the heads of some in the audience but it allowed him a moral space in which to work his ministry in Fredericksburg.

Back in Mason, settlers were increasingly subject to attack by Indians. Sophie, alone at home with seven children to protect, grew fearful when Conrad had to go to Fredericksburg or travel to San Antonio for annual Methodist Conferences. Besides preaching, he conducted baptisms, marriages, and funerals for his congregation and those rites required time away from home as well. It was hard on her to be put in such precarious situations but as long as Conrad was in the Methodist ministry, she knew he had to accept his absences. Her acceptance of it, however, did not lessen her worries.

In 1863, Heinrich Kensing (a local blacksmith) and his wife were brutally killed by Indians near Squaw Creek (Passmore, 1924), some 15 miles from Lower Willow. They had gone to visit Heinrich's brother in what was called the *Platt Kopf* settlement near Squaw Creek, some five miles from their home at Beaver Creek. On their way home, the couple were surprised and attacked by a roving band of Indians while driving in a horse-drawn wagon. Heinrich was killed immediately but his wife was taken from the wagon, raped and scalped before being stabbed to death. The attack was so brutal that it sent shockwaves throughout the German settlements in Mason County, making the residents in Squaw Creek and Beaver Creek feel even more isolated and fearful. Because of the remoteness of Squaw Creek, it took several days to get notification to von Biberstein's unit and alert them to the tragedy. As a result, the offending Indians escaped to maraud again. Such massacres caused even more concern on Sophie's part and with justification.

The calm that Conrad Pluenneke and his family had felt in 1860 was now gone, replaced by fears for their personal safety. During the day, everyone working around the ranch or in the house stayed alert for the presence of Indians. At night, everyone slept uneasily. Occasionally, they were awakened abruptly by animal sounds that they knew Indians often used to communicate with one another. Or, on other occasions, they were awakened by the sounds of their horses or cattle being aroused in the corral. At family meetings, the Pluennekes, the four Leifeste families, and the Lehmbergs talked about how to band together to defend their homes and developed signals to alert all of the families in Lower Willow to danger.

As if the threat of Indian massacres were not enough to fret about, they also became increasingly concerned about reprisals from Confederate sympathizers who were ranging northward from Gillespie County to areas along Threadgill Creek, James Creek, and the Llano River, looking for deserters or German dissidents who sided with the Union.

Meanwhile, the Civil War raged on in the South. Since the war was waged mostly in southern states between the Atlantic seacoast and the Mississippi River, Texas became a "supply state" that furnished men, arms, produce, and horses for the Confederate Army fighting east of the big river. Throughout the war, the Confederate government in Texas put extreme pressure on its male citizens to enlist and support the Confederacy. It fully expected the entire state to rally behind the war effort and help the cause, but many didn't on moral grounds. By law, all citizens, including officials of the state, were required to sign an oath of allegiance to the Confederate States of America (CSA) or face dire consequences. When the Governor of the state, Sam Houston, refused to sign the oath, he was unceremoniously removed from office, even though he was the "Hero of Texas Independence." Other resisters were not treated so gently.

In response to General Bee's campaign to impose martial law, some of the German immigrants formed a secret Union Loyal League (ULL) to protect citizens from effects of martial law and from Indians.

When word of the ULL leaked out, the Confederacy raided the homes of suspected leaders and arrested them. A few were imprisoned but most were shot or hung without a trial. That crushed the spirit of the ULL and it disbanded. The likely source of the leak was identified and shot. News of that retaliation reached General Bee and he pronounced the Hill Country to be "in open revolt" and sent the troops back to rout out the remaining Bushwhackers.

Some of the former ULL members sought to leave Texas. In 1862, about 60 German immigrants who were loyal to the Union attempted to leave Texas for Mexico with the understanding that the Governor of Texas had granted them free passage from the state. In reality, it proved to be a ruse to flush out Union sympathizers. After the group departed, a mounted band of Confederate soldiers chased them down and massacred most of them near the Nueces River, leaving their remains to rot as a warning message to other Loyalists. A few managed to escape and tell the story of the massacre. They became known as the "Nueces Survivors." When that news reached central Texas, the atrocity and other similar ones at the hands of Confederate soldiers left an indelible mark on the minds of the German immigrants that lasted well beyond the Civil War. Inwardly, the fear that German immigrants might have had towards the CSA turned to contempt and festered within but much of the overt resistance to the Confederacy waned after that event. In the minds of German families who lost fathers, husbands, and brothers, a strong desire for revenge developed.

First at the docks in Galveston, then on the road to the colonies, and finally on the streets of the Adelsverein colonies, which were largely populated by Germans, the German settlers had been reviled as *foreigners*. Despite the fact that they had fought for Texas against Mexico, had helped build three Texas communities, had paid taxes, and had helped move the frontier of Texas westward, they had not been welcomed or appreciated in their newly-adopted home and they were offended. Enough was enough!

When the Confederate Army began to experience acute manpower shortages in 1863, it stepped up its enforcement of martial law and especially its conscription laws. Men between the ages of 18 and 60 had to serve in the Confederate Army. The cavalry was sent into central Texas to find the Bushwhackers and force them to enlist or kill them. Under pressure, a few did enlist and served as teamsters but most went deeper underground. When the Confederacy did find Bushwhackers, it lynched them, burned their ranch houses, destroyed their crops, and either beat or imprisoned their families. Those atrocities did little to improve the recruitment program of the CSA and they left a deep bitterness in the minds of the German immigrants that lasted well beyond the cessation of hostilities (Baulch, 2010).

Near the end of the war, part of the Confederate Cavalry known as William Quantrill's raiders, came down from Kansas to get horses and supplies in Texas. James Waltrip, a Gillespie County farmer, and other Confederate sympathizers in northeastern Gillespie County, met and joined forces with Quantrill's band to create what became known as the "Hangerbande." Its purpose was to terrorize Union supporters in the Hill Country. At night, they roamed a four county area in central Texas, terrorizing citizens and lynching suspected Union sympathizers with little or no evidence. Their brutality caused great fear in the German settlers and further angered them. It is difficult to understand how the German settlers endured that treatment for nearly two years.

One of those Hangerbande raids occurred at Cherry Spring, along the Upper Road. They sought Karl Itz, one of the Nueces River massacre survivors. Failing to find him, the Hangerbande took his two brothers and murdered them. Another Hangerbande raid occurred on the James River where they sought John Joy, an alleged deserter. Not finding him, they terrorized his brothers by dangling a noose and threatening to hang them in nearby oak trees. The next night, the Hangerbande attacked in Blanco County. They seemed to be everywhere and everyone in Gillespie, Kerr, Blanco, and Mason counties were terrified of them. Shortly thereafter, the Hangerbande captured Warren Cass at Cherry Spring. They struck again in the South Grape Creek area where they shot Peter Berg in the back and seized four of his neighbors and hung them. Such scattered and unpredictable acts of violence further struck terror in the hearts of the German immigrants (Baulch, 2010) and lasted until the war was over.

Between 1863 and early 1865, a person of German descent could expect to be routinely stopped and questioned about his or her loyalty to the CSA. Those who were stopped were required to show proof that they had signed the Loyalty Oath. The specter of meeting a CSA cavalry patrol and having to deal with the loyalty issue made Conrad Pluenneke's frequent drives through northern Gillespie County to

Fredericksburg anything but routine. Confederate forces, particularly the cavalry, roamed county roads, looking for Bushwhackers. If stopped, one had to prove their loyalty or face dire consequences.

As one might expect, Conrad Pluenneke was fairly typical of the German settlers along Willow Creek and of most members of the German Methodist Conference. He abhorred the very idea of human slavery [112] and spoke out against harsh treatment of fellow human beings from the pulpit at every opportunity but remained silent in public for fear that his family would suffer reprisals because of his abolitionist views. His age (41), his position as a Methodist minister in Fredericksburg, his family status (married with seven children), and his cattle ranch gave him a small measure of immunity from the CSA but in that nearly anarchistic era, one could never be certain. To the CSA, all German immigrants were under suspicion and vulnerable to attack without cause.

When the war began, Conrad quietly chose not to go into Fredericksburg and sign the loyalty oath nor did he use Confederate money but he also remained silent about his noncompliance with martial law requirements, except to Sophie and his friend, Heinrich Leifeste. To provide an extra margin of safety, he began wearing his clerical garb everywhere he went, especially when he left his ranch for Fredericksburg or Cherry Spring. He hoped God was watching out for him.

On a beautiful Saturday morning in the spring of 1864, he saddled up his black horse, Storm, and started to ride to Fredericksburg to preach the next day. Always wary, Conrad was hardly surprised when he rounded a curve in the road well past Cherry Spring and found that his path was blocked by a small troop of mounted Confederate soldiers. As he eyed the Confederate men dressed in their gray uniforms, he recalled the atrocities that such rebels were purported to have inflicted on his fellow German immigrants. Brief emotions of fear and then anger flashed through his mind. For a brief instant, he was inwardly intimidated but managed to mask those emotions as he neared the Rebel force.

---

[112] Tax rolls for both Gillespie and Mason counties verify that Conrad Pluenneke never reported owning slaves.

Eyeing his clerical collar, the leader of the group asked for evidence that he was loyal to the Confederate States of America. Conrad could scarcely fail to notice that a rope with a hanging noose at one end was dangling from the back of the leader's saddle.

He straightened himself up and formally addressed the leader. "I am Reverend Conrad Pluenneke, minister of the Methodist Church in Fredericksburg but I live on the Llano River, west of Castell. As you may already know, our Methodist denomination split in 1844 over slavery and the church in Fredericksburg is now a Methodist Episcopal Church-South. Beyond that distinction in Methodism, I am forced to remain neutral in the eyes of God. My faith in the one true God demands that I serve all men equally."

Before the Confederate soldier could reply, Conrad seized the offensive and asked forcefully, "Captain, where do you plan to spend eternity? Have you been saved in the Blood of the Lamb, Jesus Christ?"

While maintaining steadfast eye contact with the leader, he slowly reached back into his saddlebag and produced a leather-covered *Bible*. Patting it, he added, "When you pass into eternity, will your soul ascend into Heaven to live with God or will you spend eternity in the fiery depths of Hell, serving Satan in excruciating agony? What you believe in now and how you behave here on Earth will determine your future in the hereafter. He, the Almighty, has said to each of us, "What you have done for the least of my children, I will do for you. What have you done with your life, Captain? How have you served your fellow man?"

The Captain blinked and then blanched! The man was clearly caught off guard and affected by what Conrad said. He stammered, tried to talk, but his utterances came out as gibberish. He was not prepared to defend his eternal soul on the road to Fredericksburg that spring morning and he certainly did not want to risk the wrath of God by challenging the loyalty of a Methodist preacher, although he was an agnostic. For a moment, the Captain writhed and twisted in an agonizing state of indecision, caught between his perceived duty and what the man in front of him represented.

Eyeing his obvious discomfort, the Reverend Conrad Pluenneke quickly continued his offensive. "God looks after his own and will inflict immense pain and suffering on those who harass his people, especially one chosen to proclaim the Gospel from a pulpit. But, He will freely offer eternal salvation to you and your men, provided you will publicly express faith in Him. If all of you (gesturing to the mounted troops) will climb down from your horses, kneel with me here on the road, and join hands with me, I will pray for your eternal Souls and those of your families. I urge you not to tarry. In wartime, your future and the future of your families is very uncertain, at best. You might pass through the Valley of Death tomorrow, or maybe even later today. You must not put this off!"

The Captain finally gained enough composure to speak and blurted out "Reverend, I can't deal with this now nor can my men. We have jobs to do and we need to return to Fredericksburg."

He went on to add, "As a Man of the Cloth and as a vital stockman in the county, you are entitled to receive an exemption from military service in the Confederacy. When you reach Fredericksburg, go to the CSA office at the courthouse and explain that you are a minister of the Southern Methodist church. They will grant you an exemption card. From now on, carry that card with you at all times," he cautioned. "Always!"

Having said that, he and his detachment of cavalry abruptly wheeled their horses about and galloped south at high speed, leaving Conrad Pluenneke alone in the middle of the Upper Road. For a while, Conrad sat atop Storm and watched the dust of the retreating band of cavalry, trying to comprehend what has just occurred. After a few moments, he looked up into the heavens, bowed his head, and offered thanks to his God for once again delivering him from danger. Quickly, his mind harkened back to times when he had been almost waylaid by outlaws on the Mason Road and when he had been surrounded by Comanches near Squaw Creek during the first week of his circuit-riding career. On those days, God had protected him then and Reverend Conrad Pluenneke was certain God would protect him in the future.

He urged his black stallion forward and then set off towards Fredericksburg at a steady pace. When he arrived in town, Conrad went straight to the courthouse on the Marktplatz and applied for a formal exemption at the CSA office, which was issued immediately. He carried the card on his body for the duration of the war and never forgot the momentary fear that he felt when confronting the Confederate soldiers. From that day to the end of the war, Conrad was occasionally asked about his loyalty and without uttering a word, he just smiled and presented his Exemption Card to Confederate officers.

While his exemption card protected him and his family when he was present, it did not protect Sophie and the children when they were left isolated at Lower Willow Creek while Conrad preached in Fredericksburg. Nor did it protect them when he attended conferences in distant places like Helena, Bastrop, Industry, or San Antonio. He didn't want to leave them but he had to attend those meetings because Texas Methodism was rapidly changing and he had to stay abreast of those trends to serve the faith.

In late 1863, Secretary of War Stanton issued an order, at the urging of Bishop Ames of the MEC, to confiscate all MEC-S church buildings where a loyal pastor was not installed. Although Stanton's order only led to confiscation of one church in Texas, that in Galveston, it caused the rift between MEC and MEC-S congregations to widen even further during the Civil War. By 1864, the tide of war was changing to favor the Union and it was clear that the MEC-S was suffering. Its constituents, now poorer, became increasingly unable to support their churches and some of them teetered on the edge of bankruptcy.

In October of 1864, Conrad was required to attend the annual Rio Grande Conference at Helena, a small town located about 40 miles south of San Antonio. On horseback, Helena was a hard two-day ride from Mason County and the conference required him to be away from the ranch for at least two weeks. Amidst the terror created by the Hangerbande, he was reluctant to leave his family but the meeting was mandatory and it promised to be of great importance to his career. At Helena, he was admitted as an Elder with "full connection." [113] As a respected member of the Conference, he was certain he would be reassigned to the Methodist Church in Fredericksburg for the 1865 term but he had to attend to assure that assignment.

In that pivotal year of the Civil War, the Hangerbande killed as many as 20 German settlers, people who had been accused of either

---

[113] The Rio Grande Conference is now the Southwest Texas Conference

being a Bushwhacker or consorting with known deserters. It was a desperate attempt to force them to support the sinking Confederacy. Word of those atrocities had spread throughout Gillespie, Mason, and Blanco counties like wildfire. Although the nearest lynching to the Pluenneke's home had been at Cherry Spring, some 12 miles away, Sophie was understandably alarmed. Shortly after those atrocities, another murder occurred on the James River, in Mason County. She pleaded with Conrad to stay home but Conrad patiently explained that he was required to attend the meeting to represent the Llano River Valley Conference and the Methodist Church in Fredericksburg as well as his own interests. He suggested that should they hear the hoof beats of a large group of horses on Lower Willow Road at night, they should hide in the cellar and wait until dawn before emerging. To offer them some protection, he gave young Heinrich his Colt revolver and ammunition but cautioned him to be careful and keep it away from the younger children. For years, perhaps since Heinrich was about 8 years old, Conrad had been teaching him how to handle guns and for a young boy, he was fairly proficient with the pistol. The boy had grit.

After Conrad departed for Helena, a week passed at the ranch without incident and the family relaxed into their normal routine of chores and prayers. But in the afternoon of the eighth day, near sundown, they were surprised when a large group of galloping horsemen pulled up in front of their house. They had been completely caught off guard. The leader shouted for Conrad Pluenneke to emerge from the house. It was too late for the family to make a dash for the cellar so Sophie picked up Conrad's shotgun, loaded it, and walked out onto the porch. Beside her was young Heinrich with the loaded pistol tucked under his belt.

"Who is asking for Reverend Pluenneke?", she asked, deliberately keeping the barrel of the shotgun pointed down.

"I am," the uniformed leader answered. "Major William Banta. I am the Commandant at Fort Davis.[114] Me and my men here," gesturing over his shoulder, "are looking for Bushwhackers. We have been told that some of them fled north from Cherry Spring and are hiding on this

---

[114] Fort Davis was located at the junction of White Oak Creek and the Pedernales River, near Kerrville.

side of the Llano River where they are plotting to thwart or overthrow the Confederate States of America."

Guardedly, Sophie asked, "I don't know about any bushwhackers, as you call them, and what does that have to do with my husband, Conrad?"

The Major replied, "An informant in Gillespie County says Conrad Pluenneke is sympathetic to the Union and is likely harboring Bush-whackers."

"That is completely false," Sophie shouted in anger. "He is the minister of the Methodist Episcopal Church-South in Fredericksburg and is away at a Methodist conference south of San Antonio. There are no fugitives or Bushwhackers here."

She paused to gesture towards their buildings where the children were peeking out from windows. Turning to the face the officer again, she said resolutely, "I am alone and you are alarming my children with this wild talk. Please leave now!" She gestured with her shotgun to-wards the Lower Willow Road and repeated, "Please be on your way!"

Seeing the steely look on Sophie's face and her menacing shotgun, the Major glared and replied, "We'll look around first" and guided his horse slowly to a place between the Pluenneke's house and their barn, all the while listening for any sound that might indicate someone run-ning or in hiding. Occasionally, he halted, stared in the direction of the barn, and then quickly turned to look back at Sophie, hoping to catch her signaling someone nearby.

As they bided time, the men whispered insults about the family. "Those *damned Dutch* and their women - just look at her," they said but if she heard them, Sophie ignored their comments. Their remarks were likely aimed at her appearance. She was a stout, plain woman with closely cropped hair and wearing a very plain dress that day. Whereas an American woman of that era might have worn a frilly dress that covered most of her body,[115] the wives of German settlers wore dresses that were plain, cut low at the top, and relatively short at

---

[115] On the frontier, such dresses were quickly found impractical as the long sleeves caught fire while cooking or caught on brush, reducing them to tat-ters. (Jeffrey, 1979) (Roberts (1928).

the bottom. Sophie's skirt barely covered her knees and her shoes were practical, not fashionable. Generally, American men were repulsed by that practical sense of style.

Heinrich, meanwhile, put his hand on the pistol grip but did not move. Instead, he intently stared after the Major as he inspected their corral and thought about how he might respond should something happen. He would defend his mother, no matter what. And he hated to be called "Dutch"–they were from Germany, not Holland.

At last, Major Banta was satisfied that Bushwhackers were not lurking on the Pluenneke property and wheeled his horse around to leave. Slowly, the mounted troop of Confederate soldiers turned their horses and followed the Major down the lane and out to the Lower Willow Road. As their hoof beats faded away, Sophie slumped and the children sighed in relief. It would be a story to tell Conrad when he returned and one Heinrich would recall bitterly a decade later.

For four years, Reverend Conrad Pluenneke attended the Rio Grande Conference and was recognized as an Elder in the church but after his charge at Fredericksburg ended in 1865,[116] he was assigned to the Llano River Valley circuit in 1867 and 1868. During those years, he continued to suffer conflicts between his duties to God, to the Methodist church, to his family, and to his thriving ranch but God always came first.

Having *admitted status* in a Conference, which Conrad Pluenneke had between 1861 and 1865, meant that he had to make himself available to serve in whatever capacity and wherever the Conference desired. To some ministers, that often meant serving the church well away from one's present home. With a large family and a large ranch to tend, Conrad could not accept an assignment to serve in a distant conference (New Orleans, for example) like Charles Grote did. At times, he had to remove himself from assignments when there were no local charges to be filled. By making himself unavailable to serve in remote Methodist churches, however, he limited his stature in the Methodist organization and that conflict with duty did not suit Conrad

---

[116] In one of Conrad Pluenneke's final acts as the preacher at Fredericksburg Methodist church, he performed the marriage service for Christoph Theodore Feuge and Catharina Stiehl, daughter of Heinrich Stiehl.

well. He was bent on succeeding at everything he did and he began to search for a solution that would allow him to stay at Lower Willow and yet serve God and the Methodist church in Mason County.

The Civil War had been felt in Mason County. During the war, Union forces had vacated Fort Mason and Confederate soldiers had done little there but perform garrison duty. The Confederacy had done little to stem raids by Indians or the influx of outlaws and Mexican bandits in the area. In the power vacuum that was created by the Civil War, an era of lawlessness had gradually developed in the region and showed no signs of going away. Mason County had a duly elected sheriff but he was overwhelmed by the vastness of the territory he and his deputy had to cover. The lawlessness had also begun to spill over into the cattle ranching business and it affected many of the German immigrants, like Conrad Pluenneke, who depended on cattle for their livelihood.

The German settlers along the Llano wanted protection from the lawlessness and they longed for the relative isolation that they had enjoyed just a decade before. Their idea of an isolated Methodist Utopia in Mason County had evaporated like so much Virga [117] falling from the Texas skies. By 1867, the frontier of Texas had moved well past them. Other people with different ideas about frontier society were moving into their space. Again, there was a new reality that had to be faced and again, that reality was not a pleasant one for people of German descent in Mason County. It would be shaped by prior ethnic injustices and prejudicial attitudes that festered in the souls of the new settlers.

The reign of terror that German immigrants had experienced while living under the Confederacy in Texas during the Civil War served to compound bad feelings that had initially surfaced in Galveston and later on the trip inland. In their adopted state and even in their own German colonies, some Americans had continued to revile them as *foreigners* because they clung to their language and culture, not realizing that acculturation takes time and opportunity in a new land. In New Braunfels and in Fredericksburg, the collapse of the Adelsverein eliminated any programmatic effort that might have served to teach English and American culture to the new settlers.

---

[117] Virga is rain that falls from clouds but does not reach the ground.

Many of them were hard pressed to understand their harsh treatment because they had come to America through legally accepted means and had to get there. In Texas, they had worked hard, saved their money, bought choice land, and produced. On top of that, they paid taxes to Texas on that production. Some of them, men such as Conrad Pluenneke, had even gone to war for Texas against Mexico but none of that seemed to matter to Texians.

After the long and bitter Civil War ended, the German element in Fredericksburg and the Llano River Valley relaxed but only a little. They looked forward to getting back to their pre-war way of life, perhaps reunifying the Methodist church. None of that was going to happen soon as hard feelings that were created before and during the war would continue to affect the Methodist Church as well as the attitude that some CSA sympathizers had about the German settlers. Differences had grown into contempt and open hatred.

By the late 1860s, the German settlers in Mason County had become fed up with that treatment and they silently vowed to take no more. That pent up contempt, in the lawless times after the Civil War, would lead to violence in coming years.

Chapter 11

THE RECONSTRUCTION ERA IN TEXAS

In 1865, exceedingly good news reached Mason County, Texas. After four long years, the brutal and costly Civil War in America had finally come to an end at the Appomattox County Courthouse in Virginia. There, General Robert E. Lee surrendered his Confederate forces to the Union. Northern sectionalism, which could also be called nationalism, had soundly defeated southern sectionalism and the Union had been preserved. The end of hostilities meant several things to the settlers in Gillespie County and Mason County, both good and bad. Primarily, it meant they would no longer be harassed by Confederate soldiers and CSA sympathizers who had attempted to force them to support the South. It had not been their war and with it now over, they could look forward to resuming their old way of life or, at least, trying to. To those in Mason County, it also meant that Fort Mason might be reopened by the Union Army. It was hoped that reopening the fort would provide a measure of protection from Indians that the settlers so desperately needed and lacked since 1861. In addition, the fort would provide a boost to the local agrarian economy that had suffered during the war. But citizens also worried that victory by the industrial North might also mean that northern sentiments about American society would prevail and dominate the future of southern states, including Texas.

Unlike much of the South, Texas had not been physically affected by the Civil War. Its fields and pastures were intact but the psyches of some of its residents had been traumatized by the Confederacy. During the war years, the state's economy had managed to grow a little, adding businesses here and there. During the war, Texas farmers had generally continued to plant their crops and had tended to their land with little disruption. The ranches of local cattlemen, whose markets had dried up during the Civil War, were now burgeoning with large herds of cattle. Left on their own over for nearly four years, the cattle had multiplied throughout the state. It was said that Texas was awash in cattle. To recover during Reconstruction, Texas ranchers had to resume their prewar search for new markets and northern markets gave them some hope. Optimism, a scarce commodity for a number of years, was making a comeback in parts of the Lone Star State.

The other side of America, however, presented a very different picture. The agricultural south was devastated. Its fields were destroyed and the landscape was littered with the debris of war. Worse, many farmers and their sons had gone off to war and had not returned alive. It has been estimated that as many as 150,000 farmers died in Civil War battles. Consequently, there were few southern men who were present and physically able to pick up the pieces and begin to rebuild the war-torn farms. What industrial capability the South had possessed before the war, now lay in ruins. Railroads and even dirt roads were torn up by artillery fire, rendering them useless for transportation. That was physical damage. On the psychological side, many southern men were in a state of utter despair. They had put everything into the war and had lost. The Plantation Caste system was all but gone forever. The slaves, who had once worked the plantation fields, had been freed and there was no substitute labor force to work the fields. In short, life was extremely harsh in the post-Civil War South.

After the highly destructive war, the U.S. Government was faced with the enormous problem of how to reconstruct the war-torn nation and get the national economy functioning again. During those war years, both sides had suffered more than 500,000 casualties, including roughly a fourth of all able-bodied Southern men. Reeling in shame and humiliation, states in the South were barely able to function. In addition, its economy had been devastated while the North's industrial economy had flourished. However, both sides were tired of war and just wanted to put the Civil War behind them

Many who lived north of the Mason-Dixon Line wanted to see the South humiliated and punished for causing the costly Civil War through its unwarranted secession. Against the wishes of his cabinet and the U.S. Congress, President Lincoln wanted to extend an "olive branch" to the South. He wanted an undivided and functioning nation again. Beginning as early as 1863, he had optimistically begun to put together a Presidential Reconstruction plan that he intended to put into effect when the Union Army won the war. It was a magnanimous gesture and quite simple: to be readmitted to the Union, each southern state had to enact laws that recognized that former slaves were free, that southern states had no right to secede, and that southern states would pay off their own war debts. Those stipulations had to be written into new state Constitutions and approved by voters. When those three criteria were met, states would be required to formally apply to

Congress for readmission to statehood. A favorable vote by both houses of Congress would allow a state such as Texas to be accepted back into the fold.

Unfortunately, Lincoln was assassinated before he could implement his Reconstruction Plan. It fell to Vice-President Andrew Johnson, a compromise Southern Democrat on Lincoln's 1864 ticket, to carry on with the Presidential Reconstruction effort. With little political skill and without Lincoln's forceful personality, President Johnson lost control of the Reconstruction program to the U.S. Congress who had opposed Lincoln's plan from the beginning. The U.S. Congress, now entirely northern and without representation from southern states that had seceded, intended to punish the South and make it suffer for its transgressions.

After Johnson's repeated failures, Reconstruction became the bailiwick of Congress and the Congressional Reconstruction Plan took a completely different tack. With their plan, Congress intended to exact revenge on the South by taking political control of its states. It began by determining who could hold office in the South, a move clearly intended to disenfranchise former confederate executives, soldiers, and sympathizers. It instituted what was called the Iron Clad Oath and required all candidates for public office to take it. The oath pledged loyalty to the U.S. Government and served to oust every man or woman who had ever served in the Confederacy, in any capacity, before or during the civil war. Implementation of that oath severely reduced the number of qualified people for public offices in the South. By using the oath, Congress and its representatives were able to dictate who could hold public office and they appointed Loyalists to virtually every office in the South. Some candidates found acceptable via the Iron Clad Oath proved to be incompetent and generally did poorly in office. In that era, any sign of loyalty to the Confederacy, be it a flag, or a grey uniform, or a CSA symbol, was met with a sharp reprisal.

Men in the South, already bitter from having lost the war, became even more embittered by having so-called "carpetbaggers" run their lives. Needing a scapegoat, the South took out their anger on the former slaves. The thinking of southern people adopted the notion that the slaves were the cause of the Civil War, and by extension, they were responsible for the South's destruction. For the next century and more, that enduring hatred of black people, carpetbaggers, and Yankees became institutionalized in the South and that attitude would prevent the South from truly reintegrating into the Union.

The South's retribution to slaves was disenfranchisement. States, such as Texas, haltingly acknowledged that the former slaves were free but they contended that freedom did not automatically make them citizens with voting privileges. Again Congress vociferously disagreed with the South. They rammed through the 13th and 14th Amendments to the Constitution that specifically prohibited denial of citizenship and voting privileges on the basis of race, creed, or color. As a result of the South's recalcitrance, an additional requirement was added to the Congressional Reconstruction plan: state constitutions now had to include wordage that guaranteed citizenship and enfranchisement rights to newly freed slaves. Southern states gagged on that requirement but eventually complied and were readmitted to the Union.

In Mason County, Reconstruction had little impact, mainly because it had few slaves that were freed by Abraham Lincoln's Emancipation Proclamation and because its local economy was functioning. For those reasons, northern carpetbaggers had little reason to swoop in and meddle in local affairs or swindle property. Some impact of Reconstruction was felt at Fort Mason where Union forces took possession again. In a few cases, local politics were affected by the disenfranchisement of former Confederate supporters. However, the greatest impact may have been on local Methodism.

The war and its aftermath did affect the U.S. Army. While it had refused to subdue the Indians in Texas before the Civil War, the Army had taken token measures to try to protect settlers within the state. Their response had been fundamentally a policing action that featured regular "scouts" from fortresses to locate Indians and subdue them. On such scouts, companies of soldiers would leave their fort in the direction of another fort and patrol the region between, searching for bands of Indians with the intention of engaging them. The natives soon understood how the scouting patrols worked and avoided contact with the soldiers. Instead, they raided unprotected areas and quickly retreated into safe havens in the wilderness. In the end, small unit scouting from the chain of forts proved to be totally inadequate in the face of what amounted to Indian guerilla warfare tactics against a superior force. The U.S. Army in Texas, which likely numbered a few thousand men, were stacked against combined Indian forces from several tribes that outnumbered the Army by a factor of four or five. However one chose to look at the defense of Texas from Indians, the settlers were frequently left unprotected. After the war, the same policy was implemented, with equally poor results, and the settler's hopes for protection went unmet. They wanted the Indians resettled in the Oklahoma Territory. [118]

Back in 1861, Union forces had abruptly vacated Fort Mason. During the war, it had been used very sparingly and, as a result, it had deteriorated badly. After the war, it took the U.S. Army nearly 20 months to repair and reoccupy the fort, finally doing so by stationing 505 troops there on December 4th, 1866. The reopening of Fort Mason came at the behest of James E. Ranck, the state representative from Mason County.

Between February of 1861 and December of 1866, however, a state of lawlessness developed in Mason County. In addition to Indian depredations in that span, there were frequent murders, robberies, fistfights, and bouts of cattle rustling. Soldiers often fought with soldiers, particularly in saloons after getting "liquored up." Outlaws from other states, drawn in by the vacuum created by lack of law enforcement during the war, began holding up supply trains that were moving along the Upper Road towards Fredericksburg or Menard. Similarly, mail wagons and stagecoaches were particularly hit hard by bandits. The U.S. Army had to deal with all of that. If the settlers at Beaver Creek or Willow Creek thought the end of the war would bring relief from the "Hell" created by Indian raids, they were wrong. Now they had to contend with outlaws as well. One factor alone, the rising price of beef, would ensure that cattle rustling would be on the upswing in Mason County.

After the fort was reopened and rehabilitated, it began to procure supplies in 1867. Agents for the army put out the word that the cavalry would require 275 well broken horses state wide and that the general army at Fort Mason would need 2,250 bushels of corn, 175 tons of cured hay, an unspecified amount of oak or mesquite wood, and an

---

[118] When Indians tribes had bothered settlers in the southeastern part of America, Congress had passed the Indian Removal Act of 1830. As a result, tribes were coerced and then forcibly removed to Federal Territory west of the Mississippi River.

unspecified amount of beef. To bid, Texas ranchers and farmers had to provide evidence of loyalty by signing the Iron Clad Oath and send a sealed written proposal to the Depot Quartermaster's Office in San Antonio. The successful bidder had to provide the items within eight days. According to Bierschwale (1996), a number of settlers in Mason County met the requirements and found a solid local market.

In the county, it was well known that most of the German settlers had not supported the Confederacy. That included Conrad Pluenneke, the Liefeste brothers, and others. They, therefore, had no difficulty signing the so-called Iron Clad Oath and after a hiatus of nearly six years, Conrad Pluenneke and Heinrich Leifeste began to sell cattle to Fort Mason again, a market they pursued for the next two years. Subsequently, larger markets for cattle emerged and they turned from local markets and begin to sell into them.

Reconstruction also affected the Methodist world and Conrad Pluenneke's career in it. Since becoming an assistant minister to Reverend Grote in 1857 as well as taking charge of the Llano Circuit in 1858 and 1859, Conrad Pluenneke had been required to travel frequently and that travel had created problems for him at home. He began to comprehend why the Methodist church preferred single circuit riders over married ones.

As his ministry developed, Conrad was required to not only preach in Mason County and Gillespie County but attend more conferences in distant cities, sometimes as far away as Houston. Added to his stints as a circuit rider, his four years of duty in Fredericksburg during the Civil War had been too much for Sophie. Over those four years, she put wifely pressure on Conrad about being away from home for such extended periods of time, especially when so much violence was occurring in central Texas.

Conrad fully understood his wife's concerns but did not know how to placate her while also continuing to preach. He was torn between three masters: Methodism, family, and ranch. Somehow, he had to find a way to be with his family and yet serve God, the Methodist Church while also tending to his ranch in Lower Willow. Throughout the 1850s and well into the 1860s, there were no alternatives to circuit riding in the Methodist world of the Llano River Valley, but that would change shortly.

In 1868, the Llano Circuit deliberately chose not to obligate itself to the Rio Grande Conference of the MEC-S. Instead, it split from it. In the Methodist world, that was "a sure sign that something was afoot." [119] The split in the Llano Circuit came because a majority of its constituency could no longer condone the "Old South" policies of the MEC-S, especially since that organization had been steadily deteriorating since the Civil War. At the same time, the MEC was returning to prominence in Texas. The end of the Civil War brought new opportunities for evangelism in the Lone Star State and the MEC offered an alternative to the MEC-S. It had the means to pay for full time pastors in permanent churches.

With the South torn up and reeling from a lost war, support for MEC-S churches throughout the South, and particularly in Texas, dwindled significantly. Many of its citizens were barely able to survive and most had little to contribute to the Methodist church. As a result, many underfunded MEC-S congregations in Texas ceased to exist or functioned in such a limited fashion that their churches fell into disrepair. In a chain reaction to post-war economic conditions, the salaries for MEC-S preachers at those underfunded churches were either slashed or eliminated completely. Many pastors, particularly those with large families, found they could no longer serve their churches and support their families. As a consequence, they were forced to leave the ministry or convert to another Protestant faith. Some became Baptists.

Seizing on the situation, the MEC grew in Texas. In 1866, it held a meeting in Bastrop County that was open to all German Methodist ministers, regardless of whether their prior allegiance had been to the North or to the South. The purpose of the meeting, presided over by Reverend Frederick Vordenbaumen, was to determine whether MEC-S preachers would be willing to leave their organization and join the growing MEC. Letters from high officials in the MEC, the so-called Mother Church, were read aloud to the attendees. Part of the letter's content was a statement of salaries that the MEC was willing to pay German ministers who would switch from the MEC-S to the MEC and accept German-speaking charges. A representative of the MEC-S at

---

[119] Quote from Tim Brinkley, Archivist at the Bridwell Library, Southern Methodist University, Texas (2012).

the meeting (I. G. John) stated for the record that his organization could not match those salaries. Conrad Pluenneke, from the Llano Circuit, attended that meeting and listened with great interest. After much prayer, a vote was taken and the result was almost unanimous: MEC-S ministers were willing to join the MEC (I. G. John, 1893). Conrad was among the 13 MEC-S preachers who agreed to switch to the MEC. After that positive vote, the only issues left to be resolved were when the switches would occur and what were the mechanics for making the transition. For Conrad, that meeting put into motion what would ultimately be for him the solution to his most pressing problem.

As he thought about the matter on the way home from Bastrop, switching from the MEC-S to the MEC would solve several of his decade old dilemmas. One, he would become a minister in the MEC which matched his inner abolitionist feelings. He had always preferred the MEC but it was never a viable option in Texas until after the Civil War. Now it was an option. Two, the Mother Church had the resources to support him, should he choose to "locate" at a Methodist church in the Llano District. If it became possible for him to pastor a church in the Llano River Valley, then he could live at home, tend to his ranch more frequently, and yet serve the Methodist cause without having to travel very much. He would still have to attend Conferences but that was nothing like riding the circuit. In the future, he decided to consider the MEC offer very seriously. To do that, however, he would need a church that was financially able to support him and one willing to switch to the MEC with him.

Only a year removed from the end of the Civil War, switching allegiance from a southern institution, such as the MEC-S, even though destitute, to a northern organization, such as the MEC, was still very risky. Some southerners were bent on revenge and used every means to strike back at those who defeated the South. To make such a switch shortly after the Civil War, therefore, required much courage on the part of the congregation and its minister. Sometimes, such a switch even required the support of Federal troops, but not in Mason County.

On the way home from the meeting at Bastrop, Conrad pondered the Llano Circuit and debated within himself about which church within it might be willing to switch allegiance and join the MEC. By the time he arrived back at Lower Willow, he had the answer: Beaver Creek. Of all the stops on the circuit, it was the largest congregation and was the most able financially to support a full time minister. In addition, it had the most members who were decidedly for maintaining the Union. At his next visit to Beaver Creek, he decided that he would quietly raise the matter with a few key members of the congregation and use their opinion as a sort of weather vane for general congregation sentiments. He did and found some support.

In 1867, he was reappointed to the Llano Circuit that was part of the German District of the Texas Conference of the MEC-S. Again, it was the only assignment available to him in central Texas so he accepted it but with some reluctance. In January of that year, he began to ride the circuit once again and reacquaint himself with its six congregations. In 1868, he was reappointed to the Llano Circuit and served another year without incident.

At one of Conrad Pluenneke's regular visits to Beaver Creek in the fall of 1868, a committee of seven men approached him privately after Sunday services. They represented the majority of the Beaver Creek congregation who wished to change their Methodist allegiance from the MEC-S to the MEC. Word had traveled around Methodist circles in Texas that Elder Carl Biel (see Appendix 4) at Industry (then the largest church in the German District) and five other preachers had successfully defected from the MEC-S to the MEC in 1866. The committee, having gotten word about Reverend Biel and the others through the *Der Christliche Apologete*, wanted to accomplish the same result at Beaver Creek. They were well aware that the MEC would provide financial assistance but they needed someone to lead the way. They approached Conrad Pluenneke and their question to him was simple and to the point: "Will you lead us into the MEC and become our first permanent pastor?"

While they discussed the potential switch, Conrad thought about the implications of such a move. His first reaction was inward elation because such a position solved his most pressing problems. For some time, he was aware that he was more comfortable with the social views of the MEC so a switch to it would be welcomed. It also meant he could live at Lower Willow and at the same time, serve Beaver Creek which was only 12 or so miles away. He knew such a position would thrill Sophie but it also meant that he would have to "locate," which in Methodist terms, meant he would have to reject the MEC-S and surrender his ministerial credentials to it at the next annual meeting of the Texas Conference. Locating, therefore, was not an easy step to reverse. Should the MEC or the congregation fail to support the switch or his pastoral assignment, he might be forced to ask for re-admittance to the MEC-S and that might prove to be humiliating. As the committee talked, he asked probing questions about the congregation's motivation and their ability to support a pastor. In the end, he accepted their offer with the proviso that the split up of the Beaver Creek church be accomplished civilly.

It was agreed among the group that the entire congregation would have to vote on the issue of separation. Questions were raised about when the vote would be held and who would own the building after such a division. From Conrad's perspective, the vote needed to be held before the end of 1868 so he could surrender his credentials at the 1868 Conference in San Antonio and make himself available to the MEC at the beginning of 1869. The committee, however, felt that they would need at least a year to negotiate a fair settlement with those members who did not wish to leave the MEC-S. Accordingly, they agreed to vote on the issue in April of 1869.

A committee of seven men had already privately conducted what amounted to a straw vote of the congregation and found that about 85 to 90 (or roughly two-thirds) of the 135 members wanted to switch to the MEC. When it came to the actual vote, they were certain that Beaver Creek would opt to switch and become an MEC church. With the switch a virtual certainty, the question became how to deal with the minority. After some discussion, it was agreed that the majority would compensate the minority by buying the church building at a reasonable price. The minority would then be free to remain with the Llano Circuit of the MEC-S, which would likely contract to just two stops: Upper Willow and Castell. Everyone was confident that the MEC-S, though impoverished, would appoint a minister to ride that circuit and thus serve its members from Beaver Creek who had shown their loyalty.

Confident that Beaver Creek would leave the MEC-S, Conrad located at the annual German District Conference in December of 1868. Immediately thereafter, he notified Elder Gustav Elley of the MEC and made him aware that he had located, that the congregation of Beaver Creek intended to join the MEC, and that he would likely be elected its first pastor. Elder Elley offered him advice on how to proceed and the two agreed to communicate frequently over the coming year, mostly at MEC Conferences and by mail.

In April of 1869, the vote was held and predictably, a majority of the congregation voted to join the MEC. The vote was 85 to 50. Afterwards, a fair price was negotiated with those 50 members who voted to stay with the MEC-S and they left amicably. As predicted, they attached to the Castell/Upper Willow group and the Llano Circuit was reformed.

Between April and September of 1869, temporarily freed of ministerial duties, Conrad Pluenneke elected to participate in the Kothmann cattle drive to New Mexico.[120] In his absence, various lay preachers conducted services at Beaver Creek. When he returned to the church in September, regular services were conducted again and planning for joining the MEC began in earnest. Switching from the MEC-S to the MEC posed no problem for the Beaver Creek congregation because they had been using MEC materials from its inception. When word spread around the Llano River about Beaver Creek's impending switch, members from other Methodist communities in the area expressed a desire to join Beaver Creek, which already contained members from Squaw Creek, Canaan, Simonsville, and other nearby places. As a result of the additions, the new church was assured of having a large, viable congregation after it was established.

At the end of 1869, the various facets of Conrad Pluenneke's life began to fall into place. By locating at the Beaver Creek Methodist Episcopal Church, he would be able to stay home with his family and tend to his ranch while serving God. Dreams do come true! The previous two decades had shown that he would continue to advance in the ranks of Methodism and assume a place of prominence, which made him very proud. Since 1852, he had been a dedicated servant of God and now God was reciprocating.

Over the previous two decades, Conrad had also shown that he had a shrewd eye for good property, that he could manage his resources to buy land, and that he had the knack of raising cattle and doing so very profitably. With his ranch now producing cattle for distant markets, he began to accumulate money and therefore did not have to rely entirely on the Beaver Creek congregation for support. The demand for beef had continued to rise throughout the decade and promised to continue

---

[120] The Kothmann cattle drive will covered in Chapter 12.

that trend well into the next decade, making the cattle in Conrad's pasture very valuable.

In the early 1870's, as a result of the cattle boom, agents of the government as well as agents for meat packing companies came into Mason County and Gillespie County to sign contracts with local ranchers for their cattle. The agents amassed large herds and hired cowboys to trail them to distant market. That lessened the need for local ranchers, such as Conrad Pluenneke, and the Kothmanns to trail cattle long distances. All they had to do was get their cattle to trail heads, such as Fredericksburg, Bandera, or San Angelo and relinquish them to agents.

To take full advantage of the booming market, Conrad Pluenneke needed more land to increase his cattle herd. Before he left Mason for New Mexico, he learned that the Thomas Osburn Survey was going to be put up for sale by its present owner in the spring of 1870. It was approximately the same size as the Lamar Moore Survey (roughly a third of a league) and was bounded by the Lamar Moore Survey on the west (see Figure 8-1). Importantly, it also had significant frontage on the Llano River. Because it was next to property that he already owned, Conrad had ridden the property on horseback several times and was therefore well aware of its terrain and its boundaries.

After he returned from New Mexico and maneuvered Beaver Creek into the MEC, he went into Mason to meet with an agent, James Hudson, who represented the seller, Thomas Osburn, who lived in Bastrop at the time. The asking price was $1,000. After some intense negotiating, the two men arrived at a price of $938 for the 1,476 acres of Survey 230. At that price, Conrad paid roughly 64 cents per acre, an increase of 23 cents per acre over what he paid for the Lamar Moore Survey back in 1853. In 17 years. the relative price of the two properties had risen 56%, a clear indication that land along the Llano River was becoming more valuable.

On July 15th of 1870, the purchase was officially recorded. Conrad withdrew $938 in gold coins from his savings and paid Hudson at the County Clerk's office. Those 1,476 acres, added to his present 498 acres, brought his total land holdings to just under 2,000 acres, all with good water access. The coins that he used to buy the Thomas Osburn Survey came from the proceeds of the 1869 cattle drive to New Mexico and he had some of them left over. With the remaining money, he stocked his new land with 200 Longhorns that he bought from another Mason County rancher at auction. His successful bid was $4 per cow. After the auction, with the help of the Leifeste brothers, he herded them to the Osburn Survey, rebranded them, and turned them loose on the banks of the Llano River.

With his cattle spread over part of the Lamar Moore Survey, part of the Isaac Hamilton survey, and now over the entire Thomas Osburn Survey, tending to them became difficult and time consuming. Twice a year, he and his two oldest sons, Conrad Jr. (18 years old) and Henry (16 years old), had to round up the herd and brand new calves. In the process of helping their father, both boys became able ranchers in their own right and both now had their own horses and guns. After each roundup, Conrad counted the size of his herd and recorded that information in a small ledger. When it came time to reckon his taxes at the end of the year, he had an accurate estimate of the number of cattle that he owned. With the value of cattle going up markedly, his herd represented most of his wealth and exceeded the value of his land by a factor of two. In 1871, the value of his land was estimated to be $1,133 while his 520 cattle were worth $2,200.

Clearly, cattle had become a precious commodity by 1870 and Conrad Pluenneke looked forward to the coming decade when he hoped to achieve his dream of wealth through them. His earlier decision to buy land and take up cattle ranching on a large scale was being vindicated.

Chapter 12

RANCHING AND THE TEXAS CATTLE BOOM

In 1870, Conrad Pluenneke looked back on nearly two decades of cattle ranching with much satisfaction. He, like so many other German settlers in that region, had turned to cattle ranching as a new occupation shortly after arriving in Texas, partly to avoid farming and partly because of the opportunities it offered them. Ranching was an occupation that had been practiced for centuries in the American southwest, but for Conrad to engage in it full-time and earn a living by ranching, he had much to learn and the learning curve, by necessity, was quite steep. Little did he or his brothers-in-law realize in 1854 that when they decided to enter ranching on a full-time basis, they would one day master the art of cattle raising and do it on a grand scale like other local families, such as the Kothmanns and the von Donops. Building a successful ranch on the extreme edge of the frontier took courage, determination, energy, resilience, and shrewd investment in land and livestock as well as common sense.

Cattle are very useful animals and that fact was not lost on the new ranchers of German heritage who sought to earn their livelihood by raising and selling them. They quickly learned that cattle, depending on gender, could yield milk, tallow, leather, and meat, all of which could be sold at market. Cattle could also be used to provide brawn for transportation, farming, and construction, all highly useful on a developing ranch. Given these attributes, it is no wonder that cattle have historically been regarded as one of the oldest forms of wealth.

In Texas, a place known for erratic and severe weather, Conrad discovered that cattle ranching could be a very challenging profession. Over the years, he had to contend with droughts, floods, wildfires, high winds, and other calamities. Fortunately for him, cattle proved to be durable and mobile. Their mobility allowed him to offset adverse climatic conditions by moving his herds to places where there was more grass or more water. Contending with not only changes in climate but changes in market prices from year to year sorely tested all ranchers of that era but Conrad Pluenneke prevailed because he discovered that he possessed the necessary traits, innate toughness (grit) and an ever optimistic attitude. Those traits allowed him to endure ranch life. Not everyone is cut out to be a rancher.

From the perspective of history, cattle herds were introduced to Texas by Spaniards whose ancestors brought livestock across the Atlantic ocean on sailing ships as early as the Columbus era. From the West Indies, the Spaniards moved cattle to Florida and then westward to Texas, mainly to support Catholic missions. The Spanish missions were established to lay claim to the territory by occupying it with priests and soldiers. Their intent was to domesticate indigenous natives and convert them to their form of Christianity, thereby increasing their hold on the land. In Texas, the Spanish priests established missions in places such as San Antonio, Goliad, and the San Saba River, near Menard. The soldiers and missionaries who garrisoned those missions needed reliable food sources, transportation, brawn for construction, and leather for clothing. To satisfy those needs, so-called seed cattle, horses, oxen, goats, and sheep were brought to the American mainland in increasingly larger numbers, peaking around 1690. The initial herds were bred and husbanded to increase the herd size for each new Diocese. [121] When the Mission Era ended in the 18th century, the job of raising livestock was turned over to private parties, i.e., men of wealth and influence, who lived like royalty. In fact, the very name ranch derives from the Spanish name for the place where the wealthy cattle raiser (ranchero) lived, the rancho.

The private ranchers were granted land by the Spanish government and or the Catholic Church to support the task of raising livestock for its missions. Men such as Tomas Sanchez de la Barrera y Garza, Antonio Gil Ibarvo, and Martin de Leon were given huge tracts of land and as a result, cattle ranching evolved into a commercial, entrepreneurial venture. At first, Spain regulated the cattle market but around the turn of the 19th century, it loosened its control and Texas cattlemen began to establish wider markets for their beef. As markets improved, more men were lured into the cattle ranching business.

During most of the 19th century, the Texas range was open and unfettered except for natural barriers such as rivers, steep ravines, or mountains. With open ranges, cattle roamed freely. With some regular-

---

[121] Catholic district

ity, some of them strayed off into the wilderness and became separated from the main herd. Occasionally, ranchers searched about for strays and found some of them, but others remained lost. Many of those strays were eventually found by others and claimed. Some of those individuals used them to start their own small herds. Not all the ranching entrepreneurs were legitimate. Outlaws often raided untended herds and rustled cattle that they later sold to entrepreneurial citizens at reasonable prices. Buying stolen cattle became a quick way for the average man to afford to become a rancher or increase the size of his existing herd. As a result of such activities, the occupation of ranching was no longer the unique domain of large landholders. In time, democracy and lawlessness saw to it that almost anyone could become a rancher if they had the willpower, grit, and perseverance to follow through. Not all did. Many "would be" ranchers failed to manage their herds properly and disappeared from the scene.

When the Army sought to provide protection for settlers in the early 1840s, it began building a string of forts diagonally across Texas, roughly approximating civilization in the state. The soldiers who occupied those forts also required reliable sources of food, transportation, brawn, tallow, and leather to support their effort. Local ranchers were more than elated to supply those forts with livestock, including horses, oxen, and cattle as well as with limited amounts of grain. Sale of livestock to the U.S. Army provided a huge boost to the local economy and nearby ranchers quickly benefitted from their presence. As early as 1852, Conrad Pluenneke and Heinrich Leifeste were selling beef to the U.S. Army at Fort Mason, although they lived in Fredericksburg at the time, some 40 miles distant.[122] The Army, however, created only a small demand and so other markets had to be sought.

When gold was discovered in California, tens of thousands of people flocked to the gold mines in the Sierra Nevada, particularly around Sutter's Mill, seeking to strike it rich. Large nuggets found in streambeds and thick veins of gold ore in mountainsides made some miners very wealthy overnight. News of such easy fortune created a national mania and what has come to be termed the Gold Rush of 1849 began. With so very many miners drawn to the rugged and remote Sierras, food became scarce and by the law of supply and demand, very expensive. Cattle that were worth $5 to $10 per head in Texas now fetched

---

[122] Bierschwale (1996), page 73.

3 to 10 times that amount in California. In 1850, cattle drives from Texas were organized by agents who had contacts in California. Drives were launched from Fredericksburg or San Antonio and passed through El Paso before ending in San Diego or Los Angeles. From southern California, the herds were subsequently trailed to San Francisco where they were processed. By 1857, a glut of beef existed in California and only a trickle of cattle was trailed to the gold fields after that time. Another gold discovery in Colorado in 1858 lead to a similar flurry of cattle drives, but that soon fizzled out. Those gold rushes, however, awakened Texas cattlemen to the idea of distant and lucrative markets for cattle.

During the Civil War, the Union Army and the Confederate Army both required food on a vast scale to feed their far-flung soldiers. In 1861 and 1862, ranchers in Texas shipped beef to the Southern troops but when the Union Army established and enforced a naval embargo on the Mississippi River in 1862, that market was effectively eliminated. Up North, it was a different story. To feed the Union Army, enterprising northern butchers such as Gustavus Swift and P. D. Armour established large-scale beef processing plants in Chicago. To supply the plants, the men bought cattle from an immense area encompassing much of the Midwest. To get the meat to soldiers on the battlefronts, they processed the meat and packed it in cans or barrels that they shipped to the widely dispersed Union Army. The meat packing industry was born and the nation learned to eat meat out of a can.

Meanwhile, in Texas, now a state with much beef on the hoof but without ready markets, cattle continued to multiply naturally on the range, thus creating a huge surplus. After the Civil War, demand for beef rose markedly but much of the demand did not come from an army. It came from two sources: Indian agents in western states who had to provide food to Indians on reservations and east coast restaurateurs. To feed the Indians, the Bureau of Indian Affairs contracted for beef at places like Fort Sumner and Fort Union, both in New Mexico. That demand was far less in comparison to demand from the East coast.

Most of that eastern demand came from restaurants in large east coast cities such as New York, Boston, and Philadelphia that catered to wealthy clients who desired beefsteaks. Their clients were willing and more than able to pay dearly for tasty beef. To meet the new larger demand, cattle were raised on a larger scale and trailed to convenient markets such as New Orleans, Santa Fe, or Kansas City. From there, they were shipped by boat or rail to the east coast. All the while, the meat packing industry continued to thrive.

Those initial shipments, however, only whetted the appetite of Easterners for more and more beef. As a result of the increased demand, the price of beef rose sharply and created what might be called a *cattle boom*. The mania over beef caused increasing numbers of people in the West, particularly in Texas, to take up cattle ranching as a way to cash in on the boom. In parallel with the upward trend of cattle ranching, the nation's railroad lines were being extended further and further into the Southwest as a way to gather and harvest cattle. To accommodate large herds, stockyards were built at major railheads and at the ends of cattle trails. Legendary Chisholm Trail and Loving-Goodnight Trail ended at stockyards. Places like Abilene, Kansas City, Chicago, Denver, and later Fort Worth quickly became famous for their stockyards.

From the stockyards, the cattle were herded into rail cars and shipped to slaughterhouses back east. When refrigerated rail cars came on the scene, slaughtering was done at stock pens out west and the meat was frozen. It became routine to ship frozen beef eastward in those special cars.

Trailing cattle from Texas to Kansas or New Mexico was eventually found to toughen meat on the hoof so other enterprising ranchers began to buy land in Colorado and the northern plains in order to raise cattle there. That location not only shortened the distance to market but also increased the supply of cattle.

Before the Civil War, it was estimated that as many as three million cows inhabited the ranges of Texas. In the two decades that followed its conclusion, more than five million head of cattle were shipped from the state, most of them bound for Eastern markets. In a few years, however, the supply of beef from Texas and from the plains states began to far outstrip the Easterner's demand for it and the price of beef plummeted precipitously. That era, known in ranching as the "the Panic of 1873," was disastrous for Texas cattle ranchers. By the mid 1880s, the *cattle boom* was over and many ranchers were forced to revert to simply meeting the local demand for beef. When Conrad Pluenneke took up cattle ranching in 1852, he was unwittingly setting out to participate in one of the largest boom and bust eras of his or any other generation but, true to his nature, his timing in that market was optimal for creating wealth.

At the outset, Conrad Pluenneke began ranching on a very small scale. When he settled in Fredericksburg in 1847, he didn't own a single cow or a horse. Sometime between that year and 1850, he started building his cattle herd by acquiring breeding stock at a slow but steady rate. His first cattle were likely a pair of Texas longhorns that were a good choice for a first-time rancher because they were abundantly available and therefore affordable (see Figure 10-1). The long-legged lean longhorns were an alert, intelligent, independent, and self-sufficient breed and thus, well suited to the Texas frontier and its climate. Even with their characteristic long horns, Longhorns[123] have been found to be surprisingly adept at grazing around mesquite trees with their thorny low hanging branches. In the process of building his herd, he acquired other breeds that had evolved from feral Mexican cattle and mixed them with the rangy Longhorns. By 1850, his herd of cattle had grown to 12. Through natural breeding in the open range and through careful purchases of selected breeding stock at small auctions, the size and the quality of Conrad's herd slowly began to increase. By 1852, the herd had grown to 30 head of cattle and by the end of 1853, it reached 60.[124]

A prevailing metric for planning the size of cattle herds that certain lands will accommodate is "acres per cow." In Mason County, that metric ranged from 15 acres per cow in wet years to as many as 50 acres per cow in drought years. In 1852, with only 10 acres of land to his name, Conrad Pluenneke should have been able to accommodate only a cow or two on that amount of land but according to Gillespie County tax records for that year, he had a herd of 30 cattle. To understand that seeming contradiction, one has to consider that in the open range era, his small herd could range well beyond the legal boundaries of his land. Without fences or other barriers to deter them, it would have been impossible to keep them on his property. Hence, his cattle roamed and intermixed with other herds in the territory surrounding

---

[123] A recent DNA analysis of the Longhorn genome indicates that 15% of their genetic makeup reflects India-African influence. Over many centuries, they were moved westward from India through Africa and then Spain by African Moors (Hillis, D. and McTavish, J. Proceedings of the National Academy of Science, 2013)

[124] Gillespie County Tax rolls for 1852 and 1853

his outlying land. Consequently, the herds of several families inter-mingled and interbred and thus expanded the gene pool. As a result, the cattle became almost indistinguishable, except to owners who knew to look for special markings or other features (e.g., color) of their cattle. Such mixed herds were common in open-range Texas and genetically beneficial to the ranchers but they also created a problem because ownership issues arose over unmarked livestock. Those issues were often heatedly and occasionally violently contested and resolved. Branding was the solution to the problem.

Figure 10-1 Texas Longhorn

Branding cattle was an ancient Spanish institution that was estab-lished in Europe and was brought to the New World by the first vaqueros (Spanish cattlemen). Under both Spanish and Mexican rule, brands were registered in books controlled by the Ayuntamieros (mu-nicipal councils). The Republic of Texas required that brands be regis-tered in each county of the Republic beginning in 1836. After 1848, the state of Texas decreed that the brand and earmark of each Texas rancher was to be registered with the relevant county clerk. A corollary law stated that theft of cattle with unregistered brands would not be prosecuted. It, therefore, behooved ranchers to not only develop and register a unique brand and marking system but to rigorously apply them to all of their livestock.

On September 5th, 1851, Conrad Pluenneke filed for and obtained a unique brand and mark for his livestock in Gillespie County. At about the same time, many of his fellow settlers did likewise. His first mark was a notch in the left ear and a hole in the right ear. His brand was simple: a capital C paralleled by a capital P (i.e., CP). After obtaining his registered brand, Conrad set out to brand and mark all of his cattle. To do that, he needed a branding iron so he went to a local blacksmith, Valentine Hohmann, and had him forge one for his use. To accomplish the branding and marking, he and his neighboring families worked together to round up the herds after which they sorted the cattle out amicably, resolved ownership issues, and then identified them with marks and brands.

However, cows with dependent calves created a separate and thornier problem. Generally, calves were branded after only a few months of life. If the calf was unbranded or unmarked, its ownership was determined by the brand of the mother. However, when an unmarked calf strayed away from the herd and became separated from its mother, its ownership proved to be difficult in herds of mixed ownership. Ranchers who knew their cattle very well could, at times, spot key features of the face or the hide that identified it as one of his herd. He would thereby lay claim to the calf as one of his but that identification was not always reliable and troubles arose. In Texas, special laws had to be enacted about the ownership of stray calves to avoid bloodshed. The same held true for mavericks and other unbranded feral cattle.

In the open range era, it became very easy to poach young unbranded cattle that roamed about in the wild. The practice, called *mavericking*,[125] was technically legal and common but considered wrong by most ranchers. Some unscrupulous stockmen took full advantage of the ambiguous situation and established or augmented their herds by *mavericking*. They deliberately sent ranch hands out to find mavericks and mark them with their unique brand, often paying a bounty for each one added to the herd. Those ranchers grew their herd at the expense of other ranchers and profited handsomely from the practice. When a

---

[125] The name maverick traces back to a rancher, Samuel A. Maverick, who accepted a large herd of cattle to settle a debt. The herd was left with a caretaker who neglected them and failed to brand them. Local ranchers began to refer to unmarked cows as "one of Mavericks." Over time, unmarked cattle came to be called *Mavericks*.

herd was taken to market and strays with another rancher's brand were discovered among the herd, local convention generally dictated that money from the sale of those strays were to go to the rightful owner, based on the honor system. Many *maverickers* were honorable about strays but others weren't so honest. Since ranchers depended on their cattle herd to make a living, anything that subtracted from their herd became a serious matter to them. Years later, those shady practices and bigotry would lead to an all out war on Mason County rangeland.

On the open range with abundant water and grass, Conrad's herd began to multiply on its own. By the end of 1855, Conrad's herd of Longhorn cattle had grown to 70 cattle and were collectively valued at $420.[126] By 1859, Conrad Pluenneke's herd had almost tripled to 175 cattle. Along with them, he had three draft horses. In a letter dated January 14, 1861, he wrote to his German cousin Heinrich Bremer that "in the previous year (1860), he had sold oxen for $400 and owned 108 cows for calving, which had produced 97 calves", a 90% increase in the size of his herd. Each calf was estimated to be worth between $15 and $17. In addition, he had 48 oxen, each worth $15. In all, he estimated that he owned "300 cattle, in round terms." Adding this together, he had over $3,000 worth of livestock in 1861 plus cash from the sale of oxen. In that era, that amount of wealth was rare. In the letter, Conrad described ranching as his "chief task." In addition to his cattle and oxen herds, he owned two riding horses and a pair of young oxen that he reserved for plowing and pulling his oxcart. Clearly, Conrad Pluenneke was mastering the art of ranching in 1860 while also serving in various capacities as a Methodist minister.

The size of one's land holdings and the size of one's cattle herd were just two measures of wealth to a cattle rancher. Buying power was another measure and perhaps an even more useful one. Having more cattle on more rangeland only benefitted the rancher when his cattle were sold and he received the proceeds. Through public auctions or through private sales to other ranchers and perhaps to the military, Conrad's cattle were systematically converted to gold coins or other valuable assets. With gold on hand, he could contemplate buying even more land and more cattle.

---

[126] All figures have been verified by the author, using Gillespie County tax records for the years 1855 through 1861.

While waiting for opportunities to arise, he had to protect his accumulation of gold coins, just as he had done in Fredericksburg. In Mason County, he befriended William Koock who owned a general store and mill just outside of Mason on the road to Menard. As regular customers, the Pluennekes became acquainted with the Koocks and were accepted as people for whom Koock would store assets. His third rendition of a general store was a solid limestone building with a secure safe. When Conrad sold cattle, he stashed the proceeds with William Koock and trusted him to protect them, which he did very well.[127] [128]

From 1853 and throughout the next two decades, several other ranchers in the Llano River Valley ambitiously began to build up large herds of cattle with a view towards selling them for a profit. According to Johnson (2006), those men included Fritz Kothmann, Heinrich Kothmann, John Gamel, Karl Lehmberg, and Heinrich Hoerster, among others.

Beginning when Fort Mason was established in 1851, Pluenneke and those other local ranchers began to sell cattle to the U.S. Army at Fort Mason, Fort Concho, and Fort McKavett but in small numbers. Their only other market was to sell cattle to other ranchers at auctions in Fredericksburg or San Antonio. In that era, the price of beef on the hoof was nominal because there was a surplus of cattle in Texas. Texas ranchers puzzled over how to move Texas cattle to meet east coast markets. Some tried to trail cattle to New Orleans but conditions on the Mississippi River made that avenue problematic. Others tried to trail cattle into Mexico. Yet others branched their trailing efforts to New Mexico and Colorado. At the time, however, the demand in those areas did not warrant lengthy cattle drives but that would all change over time. Without sales to reduce their number, the cattle multiplied on their own.

Since there were no fences, Conrad's cattle intermixed with the herds of the Leifeste brothers, that of Julius Lehmberg, and their neighbors. At regular intervals, the men rode through the countryside, searching for their wide-ranging cattle. Some were found grazing along Willow Creek while others were located as far away as Upper

---

[127] Hunter, J Marvin (1929, pages 153-43)

[128] An official bank would not be established in the area until the Mason County Bank opened in 1886. The next year, the Bank of Fredericksburg opened.

Willow. As they were located, the men rounded up the cattle and drove them into large pens that they had constructed near the center of the Lamar Moore Survey. After getting them penned, the ranchers sorted out the large herds by brands or by marks and counted them, mostly for tax reports or for auctions. During those roundups, the six men amicably agreed on ownership of unidentified calves. At the same time, other unmarked cattle that happened to be included in the aggregate herd were returned to neighbors in the Lower Willow area. Together, the men collected limbs and built fires to heat their branding irons. One by one, they branded and marked all the members of their herd that lacked identifying symbols and then released all of them back onto the Lamar Moore Survey.

In general, the state of Texas and the Llano River drainage were subject to periodic shortages of water. In 1847, Bracht (1848) noted that Gillespie County went nine months without a significant rain. A similar drought hit Mason County in the spring of 1861 and forced Conrad to round up his cattle and move them nearer to the Llano River where there was still moving water and more grass. When Conrad moved his herd to counter drought, he often hired Heinrich Behrens to help him.[129] While he might have relied on one of the Leifestes to help, he knew that they had to move their herds as well.

When no rain fell in the first half of 1861 and as the Llano River and Willow Creek began to dry up, the devout Methodists at Upper Willow and Lower Willow prayed fervently for rain but none came. "Had they unknowingly offended God?", some asked. A few saw the drought as a test of faith: God would spare them if they remained faithful to Him. The summer of 1861 brought intense heat but no appreciable rainfall. Occasionally, small traces of rain fell at random places in the county but they only served as cruel teasers and grim reminders of the drought they were suffering through. Daily, the ranchers looked to the heavens for rain clouds, wrung their hands in angst, but the clouds they spotted dropped rain elsewhere. By late summer, high winds brought choking billows of rolling dust into Mason County that often blocked out sunlight and caused both men and cattle to choke on it. There was no defense against it. The gritty ranchers could only endure and hope for an early end to the ruinous drought. Their families, their livestock, and their land were all taking a ferocious

---

[129] The biography of Henry Julius Behrens, Mason Historical Book, page 10.

beating. Mercifully, it began to rain in the fall and by the start of 1862, the drought had eased. From that year onward, Conrad would always be wary of drought and never again viewed rain as something that was to be taken lightly.

To mitigate periodic water shortages, the men of Lower Willow developed tanks in the bed of Willow Creek to retain water. In bends or other places where water was apt to pool naturally, they excavated dirt and gravel from the stream bed and lined those places with tightly fitting rocks, thereby creating a sort of rock cistern or water tank. When the stream flowed, those cisterns filled up and then overflowed, keeping the flow of Willow Creek intact while storing water on their land. In drier times, those cisterns helped retain water for their thirsty cattle.

In the spring of 1867, shortly after the end of the Civil War, Mason County ranchers Fritz Kothmann, Karl Kothmann, Fritz Lehmberg, Charley Lehmberg, and Christel Winkel drove a large herd of cattle to New Orleans. Along the poorly defined trail in east Texas, the herd stampeded. In the swampy morass, the men had a very difficult time rounding up their cattle and keeping them together. When they finally reached the Mississippi River, they found it was swollen by spring runoff from northwestern states. After some delay, they boldly decided to swim the cattle across the wide and swift moving river. When they finally arrived in New Orleans with the herd, they were chagrined to learn that the market for beef was "off." Unable to sell their herd for meat, the five men sold their cattle to concerns that slaughtered them for their hides and tallow. In that market, the ranchers only received a pittance. For all their efforts, the cattle drive to Louisiana was a huge financial setback for the five ranchers. With little money to show for their ordeal, the men did an about-face and headed back for Mason County. Fritz Kothmann, the de facto leader, had not only lost the money he invested in his herd but also lost his supply wagon on that drive. Nearly penniless, he literally was forced to start anew. It would be two years before he recovered enough physically and financially to mount another cattle drive to an out-of-state market.

Beginning back in 1864, near the end of the Civil War, other ranchers in northern Texas began to look at alternative and more lucrative markets for their cattle. Men with large herds, such as John S. Chisum, Charles Goodnight, and Oliver Loving began to explore the idea of moving cattle from Texas to New Mexico where there was a robust market for beef. The U.S. Army at Fort Sumner needed beef to feed over 10,000 Navajo and Apache Indians who had been forcibly removed to the Redondo Bosque reservation that surrounded the fort. Through government agents, notably James Patterson and his brother, Texas ranchers began to get lucrative contracts to deliver huge herds of Longhorn cattle to Fort Sumner. To avoid contact with Comanches who roamed the Texas plains, Chisum determined to take a more circuitous route across west Texas to the Pecos River and then follow the river north to Fort Sumner. That route, from northern Texas, was nearly twice as long as the direct route across the Comancheria but was thought to be much safer. Soon, word of both the market and the trail spread throughout Texas and other ranchers began to trail cattle herds to New Mexico and Colorado.

That news was not lost on ranchers in Mason County and some of them began to think seriously about trailing cattle to markets in New Mexico, using Chisum's Trail or other routes. Among them were Fritz and Dietrich Kothmann. At the end of December in 1868, the Kothmann brothers invited Conrad Pluenneke and five other ranchers to join them on a cattle drive to Fort Union, New Mexico. They expected to depart from Mason in April and return by sometime in September. After talking to Dietrich and Fritz Kothmann, he realized that his cattle would bring much more in New Mexico than in Texas. He had an impending hiatus in his ministerial life so opted to join them and use the lull to take some of his cattle to a new market in New Mexico.[130]

Fritz Kothmann, working with the Patterson brothers in New Mexico, had secured a contract to deliver about a thousand Longhorn cattle to Fort Sumner in the summer of 1869. As Fritz saw it, the drive would follow what was becoming known as the *Chisum Trail*, and by others as the *Goodnight-Loving Trail*, which they could intersect at the Concho River, near Fort Concho. He along with his brother, Dietrich, volunteered to lead the cattle drive and began to study the route, using Army maps they bought at Fort Mason. They paid particular interest to General Ruger's map of the *Staked Plains*.

---

[130] In that era, it would have cost Pluenneke between $100 and $150 to hire a wrangler to take his cattle herd to New Mexico. That would have reduced his profit and he knew he would need about $1000 to buy the Thomas Osburn Survey. Being a thrifty German, it is the author's opinion that he went.

In the past decade, Conrad had discovered that he could not manage a herd larger than about 500 cattle. With a herd now approaching 500, he needed to move at least 100 of them to create the capacity for his herd to grow in coming years so he readily agreed to add that number of his cattle to the trail herd. Besides the Kothmanns, Conrad would be joined by Karl Keller, Dan Hoerster, Rudolph Eckert, Otto von Lange, and Lace Bridges. [131] Those ranchers were expected to contribute 100 cattle to the herd but Fritz Kothmann intended to add double that number of cows to the trail herd. In all, the trail herd would contain somewhere between 900 and 1,000 cattle. To help him with the larger herd, Fritz hired a drover, Karl Enderlin, to accompany them on the drive. Along with his herd of 200 cattle, Fritz Kothmann took his new camp wagon and two other wagons loaded with bacon which he hoped to sell to the U.S. Army, either at Fort Sumner or at Fort Union in New Mexico. With a contract in hand and the trail herd established, Fritz Kothman set a tentative departure date late in April. Leaving then would increase the likelihood of abundant grass and water filled streams along the trail. Based on what he had learned from other Texas outfits that had used the Chisum Trail, Fritz estimated that it would take approximately 90 days to get the cattle to Ft. Sumner and another 30 days or so to ride back. If they left in late April, they would likely be home by the end of August or early September.

During his absence, Sophie and their oldest son, Henry, would take care of the ranch and tend to the remaining herd of cattle, now over 400 strong. He also had confidence that his old friend Heinrich Leifeste, in whom he had great trust, would be there should his family have trouble. At 18 years of age, young Henry already had experience and had become a highly capable rancher in his own right. Because of his father's itinerate duties and annual Conference obligations, Henry had frequently assumed management of the ranch in his father's absence. At times, those absences lasted for as much as a month and even more when his father attended Methodist Conferences in distant places like Industry, San Antonio, Helena, Houston, or Bastrop.

On April 27th of 1869, the eight ranchers rounded up their cattle and drove them to the Kothmann ranch at Upper Willow. After the individual herds had been assembled, the Trail Boss, Fritz Kothmann,

---

[131] Those were all men that the Kothmann brothers knew, trusted, and respected for their knowledge of cattle operations.

and his brother, Dietrich Kothmann led the large herd of cattle westward from the Kothmann ranch onto the road towards Mason. Behind them, the wagons and *remuda* (herd of spare horses) followed. While the Kothmann brothers led out front, two other cattlemen rode on the sides of the herd and the others rode behind it. Near Fort Mason, they veered onto the military Upper Road and followed it in the direction of Fort Concho (near modern day San Angelo). Near the fort, they intersected the Loving-Goodnight Trail,[132] (See Figure 10-2) which paralleled the Concho River. Where it forked into three separate streams, the trail paralleled the Middle Fork and they followed that branch to its end without incident.

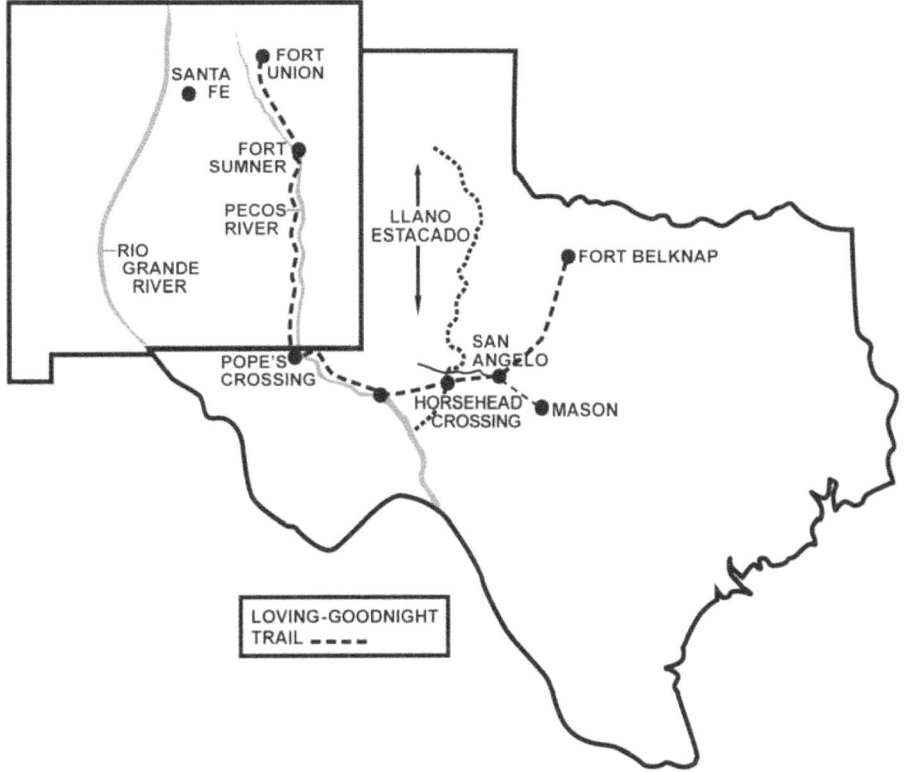

Figure 10-2 The Loving-Goodnight Trail

---

[132] The Goodnight-Loving Trail was established in 1866 by two Texas cattle ranchers who sought to bypass Comanche strongholds in west Texas and drive their cattle to markets in New Mexico. The trail originated at Fort Belknap in Young County (Texas) and ended at Fort Sumner, New Mexico. It was nearly twice as long as other trails but was considered much safer.

Near the head of the Concho River, they rested the herd and prepared to cross the dreaded *Staked Plains*.[133] In that area, the Middle Fork of the Concho dwindled into small, isolated pools of water that had been created by runoff from recent spring rains. Those pools were the last water the men would see until they reached the Pecos River, some 80 miles ahead. The cattlemen filled eight large casks with water, which they stored on the wagons with great effort. Normally, stored water would be reserved and used only for cooking and drinking but in the desert ahead, they knew they might have to use some of it to keep their cattle and horses hydrated when no other source of water could be found. On such a cattle drive, the herd had to be kept healthy if they were to have any chance of selling it to the U.S. Army.

To meet their own needs for water, each man filtered the murky water through a bandana, filled his canteens with it, and slung them over the saddle horn. In the next four days, they would use the water in those canteens to slake their thirsts but only sparingly. Ahead, they faced an ordeal that none of them had ever experienced before: dire thirst.

After the cattle were well-watered, grazed, and rested, the ranchers began to move the herd of nearly a thousand cattle slowly westward towards the *Staked Plains* and what promised to be a gut-wrenching experience for man and beast. On the trail, the cattle strung out for over a mile. After a day of drifting along the Loving-Goodnight Trail, the ranchers caught sight of a sharp line of cliffs that formed the horizon ahead of them. Those cliffs defined the eastern edge of the Llano Estacado, or the *Staked Plains*, and from a distance, it looked like the wall of a dark, foreboding fortress that lay across their path (see Figure 10-3). As far as they could see north and south, the line of cliffs were continuous and had no apparent end. The cliffs presented a formidable barrier and had a daunting effect on the men.

None of the cattlemen, including Fritz Kothmann, had ever driven cattle along this trail so all of them were a little unsure about how they would get their herd and wagons over the formidable palisade that lay

---

[133]The term *Staked Plains* is a corruption of Llano Estacado, the name given to it by Francisco Vasquez de Coronado in 1541. In Spanish, the term Llano Estacado means "palisaded plains" (i.e., a cliff made of vertical stakes). The Llano Estacado is featureless, quite extensive in area, and has no permanent sources of water. In the 19th century, it was a formidable stretch of land to cross on horseback with herds.

ahead. What they knew for certain was that once they were atop those cliffs, the land beyond was arid, flat, and featureless. Worse, it had absolutely no sources of water, except for possibly a few scattered water puddles left after hard rains. From that line of cliffs, it would be another 80 to 100 miles of dry desert before they reached the Pecos River and abundant water. At their present rate, Fritz estimated that it would take the herd four or possibly five days to cross the *Staked Plains*. To shorten the time required to cross the desert, he considered driving the cattle at faster pace and perhaps crossing it in three days, but he chose not to do that because the U.S. Army sought cattle as a source of meat, not hides or tallow. Forcing the cattle to run in hot and arid conditions for two or three consecutive days would likely cause them to lose weight and that would likely reduce what the Army was willing to pay per head. That was contrary to the cattlemen's purpose on the drive. From experience, Fritz Kothmann and his brother, Dietrich, had learned that the art of driving cattle was to allow the herd to move at its own natural pace.

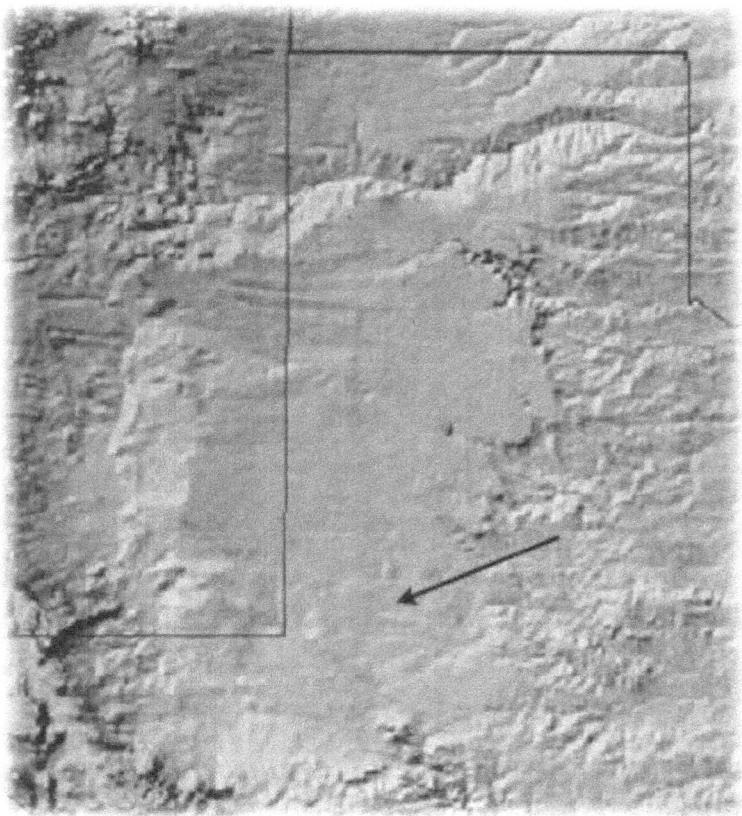

Figure 10-3 The Llano Estacado ("the *Staked Plains*")

As they neared the cliffs, they saw that the caprock escarpment was broken in several places, making the palisade appear less ominous than it had from afar. The cliffs were nearly 300 feet high and precipitously steep in some areas but here and there, natural erosion had created small canyons that offered ways to penetrate the caprock, whose composition was brick-hard caliche. Following an old Indian trail, the military (i.e., General Ruger's command) and the Butterfield company had built a dependable road in one of the shallower canyons, using a series of switch-backs. That route had been mapped by General Ruger's Engineers. In 1857, the canyon route had been improved for the Butterfield Overland Stagecoach route and further improved by both Chisum and the Loving-Goodnight crews in 1866.

As they drove the herd and their wagons up the narrow canyon, Fritz Kothmann realized that the road would become quite steep at the very top where the canyon finally broke through the caprock. At that point, the Kothmann crew would have to change their tactics. When they neared that point, Fritz halted the procession and decided that the drovers should move the herd to the top and then return to help get the wagons up to the rim. To prevent the wagons from rolling backward, the men located a number of large rocks along the edges of the canyon and with much effort, dragged them to the wagons where they served as chocks behind the wagon's wheels. With the wagons securely in place on the steep trail, the men herded the cattle slowly onto the top of the mesa where they were allowed to graze on what little prairie grass they could find. Karl Keller, Lace Bridges, Rudolf Eckert, and Otto von Lange remained on top to tend the herd while the other five men, including Conrad Pluenneke, descended to move the wagons. They unhitched the oxen from the rear wagons and then hitched the four of them together with the yoke of oxen pulling the camp wagon. The six oxen had no difficulty pulling the heavy camp wagon up the slope, through the caprock, and onto the top. That procedure was repeated until all three wagons were on top of the Llano Estacado. From the rim of the palisade, the men stood and looked back to the east, admiring the faraway drainage of the Concho River. Somewhere beyond it was Mason and their ranches.

As he viewed the barren plain ahead of them, Fritz recalled that an experienced drover in Llano had told him that once they topped the palisade wall and crossed the barren *Staked Plains*, they would descend through the caprock to the Pecos River. At the end of a steep chute, the Loving-Goodnight trail would meet the Pecos River at Horse Head Crossing but then, instead of crossing, it would parallel the east side of the river to Popes Crossing. At that point, the trail would cross the Pecos River and parallel it all the way to Fort Sumner on its west side. From there, they would continue to follow the Pecos to its headland, near Santa Fe. Fort Union, the drover had said, was northeast of Santa Fe.

Ahead of the ranchers lay the dreaded *Staked Plains* and they wasted little time taking in the view from its rim. They had work to do and needed to move on, which they did. They hitched the oxen to the three wagons, quickly remounted their horses, rounded up the cattle, and headed westward across the desert. As promised, the land was absolutely barren. As far as they could see ahead, there was only flat land, no trees, and a big sky. Without a reference for scale, the sky seemed enormous. One of them likened it to an ocean. In the vast expanse, there were no landmarks to provide navigation guidance, only the ruts of Loving and Goodnight's dusty trail and they followed them carefully. They moseyed onward, moving at the pace of the herd.

Because the trail had been used by cattlemen for several years, there were signs here and there of where crews had camped. After about eight miles, they came to what appeared to be the first such campsite, named Camp Charlotte on General Ruger's map. There was nothing special about the site except that it was near a small rock outcropping. Small basins in the rocks, called *tinajas* by Spaniards, offered the possibility of holding rain water but on that day, they were only filled with dust.

Since they were still near the Comancheria, they had to be alert for Indians who would be more interested in their horses than their cattle. To form a defensive position, they brought the three wagons together and set up camp within the ring created by them. The *remuda* was kept next to the wagon circle to protect the spare horses, which would be badly needed in coming days. As it was nearing sunset, they took some of the water from the casks and poured a little of it into the dry *tinaja*s from which the oxen and horses could drink. From the camp wagon, the cook prepared the evening meal and served it just as dusk set in. Without wood, there was no campfire so the ranchers ate in the dark and stared at the sky filled with stars. Even though they were many miles from a church, the men bowed their heads while Conrad Pluenneke stood and offered up a prayer for their safe passage though the remainder of the *Staked Plains*. After eating, pairs of men acted as sentries on horseback, rotating in two hour shifts.

The Llano Estacado was the driest place Conrad Pluenneke had ever experienced. After leaving the Concho River, the air had become completely devoid of humidity and smelled like dust. Horizon to horizon, there were no clouds to be seen. Even in temperate May, Conrad's throat was parched and his lips were cracked and sore. His eyes were filled with dust from the trail but through it, he could see the Hand of God in the starry sky above him. As he looked upward, it seemed as though there was an infinite number of points of light in what was surely Heaven. He had never witnessed so many stars before. In the northern sky was Polaris and the seven stars forming the Big Dipper. He silently wished that the dipper had water in it but alas, it did not. With those thoughts, he crawled into his bedroll and went to sleep, awaiting his turn as sentry.

Early the next morning, the eight cattlemen rounded up the cattle, hitched up the oxen to the wagons, and set out for the next camp site. As far as one could see, the land continued to be absolutely flat and the horizon seemed so far away that it was discouraging to even consider it. Beyond it was more flat land. On General Ruger's map, their next destination was an old Butterfield Overland Stagecoach stop that was near the Mulaney Waterholes. Those mud holes or *tinaja*s offered their only hope for potable water on the Llano Estacado. After twelve miles of dry and dusty trailing through a treeless landscape, the outfit came to what appeared to be the deserted mail station on Ruger's map. Nothing remained but crumbled walls and a few rusty metal watering troughs that were bone dry. Although it was unlikely they would come across Indians in such arid conditions, the ranchers again set up camp in a defensive formation near the walls, watered the livestock in the rusty troughs, and tried to rest. The cattle, now somewhat dehydrated, mooed loudly and that made sleeping near the herd very difficult.

The next day dawned with bright sunshine and increased heat but far to the southwest, a huge bank of dark clouds was sighted near the horizon. In place of aridity, there was a slight breeze coming from that direction and a very slight hint of moisture in the air. From those hints, the men knew that by nightfall they might experience thunderstorms. While a storm would bring desperately needed water, it might also bring lightning and thunder which could spook the cattle. On the

Staked Plains, cattlemen feared everything that might produce a stampede because one would markedly add to their workload and almost certainly prolong their stay in that desolate environment.

They hurriedly broke camp and got the herd moving. As they rode, the wind increased and it kicked up dry, powdery dust which seemed to hang over the trail. To cope with it, the men pulled their hats down over their eyes and wrapped dampened bandanas over their mouths and noses in a vain attempt to block out the fine granular dust. Conrad sensed that sand and grit were now going down his shirt and into his pants, making it very uncomfortable to ride. Somehow, the men and their herd pressed forward in limited visibility. The clouds that had been on the horizon early in the morning were now prominent in the southwestern sky and were being chased by the fierce winds. The cattle were also distressed by the blowing sand and mooed loudly in protest as they moseyed forward. After about nine more miles of miserable travel, they came to the Wild Cherry waterholes that were, of course, also dry. With weather looming, Fritz and Dietrich Kothmann decided to camp for the night at the waterholes and prepare for bad weather. Quickly, the cook prepared food for the men who wolfed it down and then got their slickers out of the camp wagon. In the face of the impending storm, Fritz decided that everyone would be needed to tend the herd and keep it calm until the storm passed. That included the cook.

Driven by wind, the clouds were now overhead. In the dimming light of dusk, they were constantly illuminated here and there by electrical flashes deep within the billowing masses. The storm was bearing down on them and the men prepared for it by donning their slickers and then by moving the herd in tight to the camp.

Gazing up, Dietrich Kothmann said, "We're going to really get it tonight."

As the men studied the swiftly moving cloudbank and then their tightly clustered herd, they noticed a strange and wonderful sight. An electrical display covered the prairie in an eerie sea of blue and yellow light. Tiny balls of fire flashed on the horns of the cattle and fiery waves of light seemed to roll down their backs. "It was one of Nature's wonderful displays," Dietrich Kothmann later recalled. [134]

---

[134] The Kothmanns of Texas, 1931

Shortly after dark, the storm arrived and as feared, brought with it vivid lightning and booming thunder. After several claps of loud thunder, the herd began to mill about nervously and their protests intensified. Shortly after some rolling thunder, a single streak of jagged lightning struck the ground close to the camp and the ensuing, deafening crack of thunder sent the herd into a panic. Most of the cattle stampeded back down the trail but a few just scattered about in the desert. Several of the men, already mounted, took off in pursuit of the runaway herd and attempted to get ahead of it to halt its leaders. Meanwhile, the other ranchers began to round up the strays. In the midst of the stampede, torrential rain began to fall. In the deluge, all was pitch black until punctuated by lightning. Only during brilliant flashes of lightning could the men see errant cattle. In darkness, they followed them by the sound of their hoofs on rock. Those who chased the main herd rode as only cowmen ride, dangerously close to the running cattle. As they neared the front of the stampede, the cattlemen fired their guns into the air and managed to stop the herd's forward progress before turning it back towards camp.

For several hours afterwards in the dark of night, several men came back to camp with individual strays and ran them into the herd which was tended by the other ranchers. In a few hours, the storm passed and that helped calm the herd. With less pressure to keep the herd in check, a few of the weary stockmen returned to the camp where the cook had prepared hot coffee for them. As each man came to the camp wagon, he grabbed a tin cup filled with coffee and then remounted his horse to make another round in search of strays. The search went on all night.

Wet and tired, the men counted the herd at sunrise and found that they had managed to capture almost all of them. During the storm, however, they did lose one horse. One last ride in daylight allowed the cattlemen to find the last of the strays, put a rope on them, and force them back into the herd. After a wet and tiring night, the men were pleased to learn that the nearby Wild Cherry waterholes had water in them. They herded the cows, oxen, and horses to the waterholes and allowed them to drink at length while the men took turns resting. By mid morning, canteens were filled and the herd was on the move again.

The passing storm all but ensured that the next stop would also have water and it did. When they arrived at Central Station on the Loving-Goodnight Trail late in the afternoon, there were puddles of water everywhere and the livestock took it in while the men strained some of the dirty, brown water through their bandanas and refilled their canteens. The nighttime sky was filled with dark clouds, which obscured the men's view of stars but they bring small, intermittent sprinkles during early morning hours.

After the damp night, the next day broke bright and sunny. It would be a very hot, dry day to push a herd across the desert so Fritz Kothmann decided to hold the herd and move at night. Even as the men and their herd tarried at Central Station without the benefit of shade, the *tinajas* on the barren *Staked Plains* began to dry up. As the men looked ahead, there were no more dependable waterholes or stopping places on General Ruger's map between Central Station and the Pecos River, a distance estimated to be about 25 miles of nothing but flat, desolate territory. Somewhere in the desolation, they would have to find a suitable place along the trail to camp for the night. After studying the map, Fritz Kothmann concluded they could cover that distance in two difficult days if they pushed the cows a bit more and then allowed the herd to rest along the banks of the Pecos. In the shade of small Salt Willows strung along the banks of the Pecos, the herd would recuperate from the ordeal of crossing the Llano Estacado and be ready in a day or so to move north along the river. After some discussion, that became their plan.

After sunset, they rounded up the cattle and set out for the Pecos. The recent heavy rain had dampened the trail dust a bit and that made it easier to move the cattle at a slightly faster pace. With good conditions, they covered 15 miles and camped near a rock outcropping at the mouth of Castle Gap[135]. As they made camp, they were very pleased to find tiny pockets of water left by the earlier storm. To Conrad and some of the others, the water was a gift from heaven but it wasn't enough to slake the thirst of a thousand head of cattle. With only 12 or so miles remaining before they reached the river, they felt assured that they would make it safely across the *Staked Plains* and for the first time in five days, they relaxed a little. Conrad bowed his head and offered up a silent prayer of thanks for the water. O Lord, show me the way!

---

[135] Castle Gap is a narrow one mile long break in the limestone cap of the Llano Estacado and the chute beyond it leads directly to the Pecos River.

The next morning, the cattlemen rounded up their herd and started the final push towards the Pecos River and Horse Head Crossing (see Figure 10-4). [136] The cattle, tired and thirsty, seemed on edge and mooed loudly as they plodded along. As they descended through Castle Gap and neared the river, the men stayed alert for the presence of Comanches who might be prowling near the crossing. For centuries, the Comanches had crossed at that spot on their way to and from Mexico where they marauded ranches and stole horses. It was one of few fordable places on the river. Castle Gap and Horse Head Crossing worked together to create a natural funnel that forced all creatures to one place where the mighty Pecos could be crossed. Fritz Kothmann's plan, however, was to cross upstream at Pope's Crossing.

Before Fritz Kothmann made the decision to move the herd to Horsehead Crossing, he wanted to be certain that there were no Indians in its vicinity so he again asked Conrad Pluenneke to ride ahead and scout the crossing.

"Should you see any sign of Indians," Conrad was told, "Fire two shots from your pistol in rapid succession to alert the rest of us to danger, but if you find nothing, fire a single shot."

As Conrad rode slowly down the trail towards the Pecos, he intently looked for any sign of movement on the trail ahead as well as on the horizon but saw nothing that would indicate the presence of Indians. In an hour, he came to the east bank of the Pecos and stared down at the narrow stretch of water below him (see Figure 10-4). Nothing was moving and it appeared that nothing, except perhaps a few coyotes, had crossed there in days. He took his pistol from the holster, looked around one last time, and fired a single bullet into the air.

When Fritz heard the single gunshot, he and Dietrich Kothmann began to move the herd forward through Castle Gap and down to water. As the herd descended, the lead cows somehow sensed water ahead and began to trot and then run at full speed, despite the efforts of the men to hold them back. Soon, the entire herd was stampeding to-

---

[136] Horse Head Crossing was named by surveyor John H Bartlett who found it marked by a stack of horse skulls in 1851. The Pecos River was described by early setters as 65 to 100 feet wide, 15 feet deep, fast moving and with few fordable places. Horse Head Crossing was one of those few places.

wards the Pecos River. When they reached it, they plunged into the fast moving water and crossed it. That was not Fritz's plan. The men had no choice but to swim the rest of the herd across to the west bank and hold them there until everyone was safely across the river.

Rather than camp near the crossing and risk an encounter with Indians, Fritz Kothmann urged the group to go another mile up stream on the west side of the river and make camp there. By nightfall, they were encamped on the west bank of the Pecos River, in the cover of taller salt cedar trees and beside a small fire. The cattle, now somewhat less than a thousand strong, was strung out between the ruts and the banks of the Pecos River for nearly a mile north of the crossing.

Figure 10-4 Horse Head Crossing of the Pecos River

For dinner, the cook prepared steak, beans with bacon, and bread. While they ate, the men talked about the storm, the stampede, and crossing the fearsome *Staked Plains*. Weary from the ordeal, some of them retired to their bedrolls for the first good sleep in a week while others tended the herd. As had become their routine, the men took turns watching the herd on horseback at night.

Early the next morning, Fritz Kothmann got out the Ruger Map and studied the Pecos River area in detail. As he had been told, the

Goodnight-Loving Trail crossed the Pecos at Pope's Crossing,[137] which was about 50 miles northwest of their present location at Horsehead Crossing. He recalled that the Llano drover had cautioned him to stay on the east side of the river because Indian depredations were more likely to come from the west side of the river in that area. As Fritz saw it, crossing at a more remote and lesser known spot was also safer so he chose to move the head back to the east side of the Pecos and informed the men of his decision.

The next day, the Mason County stockmen rounded up the cattle and swam the herd back across the Horsehead Crossing. When the herd was completely across, the men began to move it up the east side of the Pecos River on the Loving-Goodnight Trail. Near its junction with the Delaware River, they came to a fork in the trails. While the Loving-Goodnight Trail continued in a northerly direction along the Pecos, the left branch of the trail led to El Paso. They moved the herd north and crossed at Pope's Crossing without incident. For the next two weeks, they moved the cattle slowly and patiently up the river's west bank, traveling at a rate of about 10-12 miles per day. Along its bank, spring grasses grew in abundance and the livestock grazed as they inched along. By moving slowly and allowing the cattle to graze, they remained fat and ready for market at Fort Union.

As they moved up the trail, they came upon another herd of Longhorn cattle being driven by ranchers from Abilene, also on their way to Fort Union. They were resting their herd and obligingly moved it aside for the Kothmann's herd. The men from Mason patiently shepherded their cattle around the stationary herd of Longhorns and moved on up the trail. However, Fritz used the opportunity to hang back and talk to the other ranchers about what they knew of conditions ahead. While they had heard rumors of Indian activity, they had not been met with any hostility.

In late June, they arrived at the Bosque Grande, a large cow camp that was situated about 30 miles south of Fort Sumner on the Pecos. In 1867, just two years earlier, it had become the headquarters for John S. Chisum and his first herd of "jingle-bob" [138] cattle that he brought

---

[137] Today, Pope's Crossing is submerged under Red Bluff Reservoir which was created in 1936.

[138] "Jingle-bob refers to Chisum's practice of marking his cows with slits in both ears, so that one ear flopped up and the other one stood erect, making them easy to identify.

from his ranch in north Texas. As the men prepared to drive the herd into the Bosque, the group met three strangers on horseback who told them that Apaches had been reported on the trail north of the camp. After hearing their story, Fritz Kothmann decided to hold the herd in the Bosque for a day or two to assess the situation ahead of them. They rolled the wagons into a defensive position and brought the herd in close to camp. Once again, Fritz dispatched Conrad Pluenneke to scout the area between the cow camp and Fort Sumner for signs of Indian activity. Conrad rode up the trail at a brisk pace but returned the next morning to report having found no sign of Indians. On that news, Fritz issued orders to break camp and begin moving north again.

A week later, the cattlemen and their herd came to Fort Sumner and upon arriving, found the fort closed. It had been established by the U.S. Army in 1861 to protect settlers from attacks by Mescalero Apaches, Kiowas, and other tribes in the New Mexico territory but had been shut down in 1868. During its operation, more than 8,000 Navajos were interred at nearby Bosque Redondo. It was largely for them that Loving and Goodnight trailed cattle to Fort Sumner in 1867. In mid July, the herd was less than 100 miles south of Fort Union and that position assured the Mason County cattlemen that they would deliver the herd to the U.S. Army by early August, as required by the Army. With time pressures off, the Kothmanns decided that they could afford to rest the herd as well as their horses so they camped near the abandoned fort. For several days, the men repaired equipment, oiled their guns, and did other chores in preparation for the final stage of their trip while the livestock grazed and rested in the shade of large cottonwood trees that lined the banks of the Pecos. The climate in New Mexico was very hot but also very dry, even by the river. Far to the northeast, the men could barely glimpse the tops of rugged mountains, the Sangre de Christos. The Pecos River originated on the east side of those mountains and drained southwesterly. Santa Fe, the territorial capital and largest city of New Mexico, was on the west side of the mountains.

After idling for a few days, Fritz Kothmann grew impatient to get on the trail and issued orders to bring the herd together and to prepare to be on the move again. Within hours, the drive was reinitiated and the cattle were moved north on the trail that connected Fort Sumner with Fort Union. In 1867, Loving and Goodnight had ended their cattle trail at Fort Sumner but when the fort closed in 1868, the trail was extended to markets in northern New Mexico (such as Fort Union) [139] and Colorado.

As the men trailed the herd north, they passed the confluence of Gallinas Creek and the Pecos. The Gallinas, if one followed it towards its source, led to the vicinity of Las Vegas, New Mexico, an old western town. After the streams came together, the trail veered northeastward and continued for about 20 miles to Fort Union. As they neared the Fort, Fritz halted the drive and sent Conrad Pluenneke ahead to notify the Army that their herd was approaching.

On the trip, Rudolf Eckert and Dietrich Kothmann had decided to deliver their cattle to markets in Colorado where they expected to receive better prices for their herd. As the large herd milled about a few miles from Fort Sumner, the two men cut their cows from the herd and moved them away to an area near the Pecos River. After a few days, they gradually began to move their cattle north towards the Kansas-Pacific railhead at Denver.

When Conrad returned, Fritz issued signals to the men to move the rest of the herd towards Fort Sumner. At the fort, they found that its gates were now wide open and soldiers atop the walls were using hand signals to beckon the drovers to move the cows inside the fortress. With some persistent urging, they drove the large herd through the gates and into awaiting pens. When the herd was secure, the Quartermaster appeared and looked over the cows very carefully. After scrutiny, he declared that most of them were fat and healthy and accepted the entire herd. Since the Army paid on by the head, [140] he and his staff had to count the cattle as each one passed through a chute to another holding area. Independently, Fritz Kothmann oversaw the counting process and made his own count. After all critters had been counted, he and the Army Quartermaster agreed on payment. The going rate that day was $17 per head so he offered Fritz Kothmann $16,354 in gold coins for the entire herd of 962 cattle. That was much better than what they would have received in Texas where there was a glut of cattle waiting for market. Not wishing to move further up the trail, six of

---

[139] Fort Union was the territorial headquarters for General Sumner, who commanded military Department # 9 which covered all of New Mexico.
[140] According to email from Gary Kraisinger (2014), cattle were sold by the pound or by the head in 1869. In that era, Fort Union did not have a scale so cattle were sold by the head and had to be counted.

the men, including Conrad Pluenneke, agreed to accept the Quarter-master's offer. In return for his cattle herd, Fritz Kothmann accepted four mules and two wagons from the Army plus some coin. After the sale and after his own personal barter with the Army, Fritz divided the remaining proceeds among the five other cattlemen. For his herd of 97 cattle, Conrad received roughly $1,650 in gold coins, which he care-fully wrapped in a leather pouch and stored deep in his saddle bags.

After concluding the sale, the six men briefly visited the Santa Fe. Conrad, in particular, was impressed with the nearby Sangre de Chris-to Mountains and the adobe architecture of the old town, then more than three centuries old. In a few days, the six ranchers from Mason County began the long trip back to Mason County, returning by way of the Loving-Goodnight trail. Seven days later, they arrived safely, alt-hough along the way they heard many rumors about outlaws looking to rob Texas cattlemen ladened with gold coins on their way back to Texas.

When Conrad and the others arrived back in Mason County in late August, he stopped at Koock's General Store to deposit his gold coins into Koock's vault, get a cold drink, and buy some things for his fami-ly. He hadn't had a cold drink since leaving Santa Fe and the dusty ride home had created quite a thirst in him. Before he left back in April, he had been told that the Thomas Osburn property might be for sale in 1870 and he had wanted to be prepared to buy it should that happen. Now he had well over $3,000 in Koock's vault. After chugging down his drink, he bought a few things for the family, remounted, and head-ed for Willow Creek where his family would be awaiting his return. He had not seen them since April and looked forward to a joyous reun-ion.

By the first week of September in 1869, Conrad Pluenneke was back ranching at Lower Willow and deeply involved in Methodist politics. There is no record of Conrad Pluenneke going on another cat-tle drive but he undoubtedly sent cattle on other drives, possibly with either of his two eldest sons, Conrad Jr. or Henry Pluenneke, tending to his cattle.

The *cattle boom*, with its lengthy cattle drives to distant markets would continue but by the end of the decade, the cattle boom began to end as markets shifted and tastes changed. In the 1880s, introduction of barbed wire fences by farmers in Texas, Oklahoma, and Kansas, whose fields had been trampled by the huge trail herds, brought cattle trailing to a complete halt. In that 15 year span, however, Conrad Pluenneke managed to ride the Texas *cattle boom* to personal prominence and wealth.

Chapter 13

LOCATING AT BEAVER CREEK METHODIST CHURCH

When Conrad Pluenneke flipped his calendar over to the first month of 1870, it marked the beginning of a new era in his life. Behind him was the highly successful Kothmann cattle drive of 1869 that had firmly established him and several other Mason County ranchers in the Texas cattle business. With viable markets established in New Mexico, Colorado, Kansas, and elsewhere, Conrad Pluenneke and other ranchers in the county were no longer constrained by local market economics and began to think on a grander scale. The cattle drive to New Mexico demonstrated that they were capable of trailing cattle to distant markets and earn much more money at those places than selling to local markets. With a large ranch that now included part of the Lamar Moore Survey, part of the Isaac Hamilton Survey, and the entire Thomas Osburn Survey, all well stocked with Longhorns, Conrad was well positioned to take advantage of the nationwide cattle boom and looked forward to a peaceful decade of lucrative cattle sales.

With success in his ranching operations, Conrad Pluenneke became financially able to participate more actively in his other and perhaps more important pursuit, religion. In previous years, he had laid the groundwork for locating at the Beaver Creek church but under the auspices of the MEC, not the MEC-S. He had surrendered his ministerial credentials to the MEC-S at the Annual Conference in December of 1869 and through the guidance of Elder Gustav Elley, he was about to reestablish that license and standing as an Elder, but in the MEC.

On the afternoon of January 9th of 1870, Reverend Pluenneke saddled up Storm and left home to begin a long trek to Houston, more than 200 miles away. In Houston, he planned to attend the Annual meeting of the Texas Conference where his former MEC-S ministerial credentials and his Elder standing would be hopefully approved and transferred to the MEC. In prior meetings, Elder Elley had promised him as much and had invited him to attend the conference as a prospective MEC minister. By way of the postal system, the Elder had notified him that the Conference was set to begin on Friday evening,

January 14th, and conclude on Monday, the 17th. Traveling by horseback, the trip would cause him to be away from home for two weeks and possibly longer. If he intended to stay in the Methodist ministry and locate at the Beaver Creek Methodist church, this was a meeting he had to attend and his family understood that. While he was gone, his two older sons, Conrad Jr. and Henry, would help their mother and shoulder many of the ranching chores.

On the day before he departed, a blue Norther had howled through Mason County and left much of central Texas with temperatures in the low to mid 30s. Although the weather was clear and sunny on the day of his departure, the cold winter air stung his face as he rode along the Lower Willow road, heading towards the Upper Road. To counter the bite of the cold air, Conrad wound a scarf about his head and face but the cold wind still penetrated it, leaving him shivering in the saddle.

Since he had much ground to cover in five days, he kept Storm moving at a steady, measured pace. After intersecting with the Upper Road, he turned south towards Fredericksburg and crossed the Llano River. As he rode, his thoughts drifted to Fredericksburg and the cities beyond where he intended to spend nights with Methodist friends. In Fredericksburg, he planned to stay with the Kneese family where he knew he would be welcomed. It previous years, he had stayed with them on many occasions. On Monday, he would ride through Austin to Bastrop where again he would stay with a German Methodist family, the Eduard Schneiders. At each stop, he would kneel on the floor of their humble cabins and pray with them for their collective souls. From Bastrop, he intended to ride to Brenham where he would spend the night with Ferdinand Mumme and his family, also German Methodists. Like Conrad, Reverend Mumme was joining the MEC at the Conference. From there, he would move on to Cypress and spend the night before finally arriving in Houston. After a lengthy final segment of the trip, he would arrive at Houston late in the afternoon of the 13th, where he would be the guest of the Presiding Elder, Gustav Elley and his wife.

The trip went as planned. Using a map provided by the Elder, he found his way to the Elley's home and was warmly greeted at the door by the Elder's wife. After a warm cup of coffee, he and Gustav Elley led Storm to the barn, fed him, and put him away for the night. Back at the house, they turned to talk of the Conference and what might transpire. In the past, Conrad had similar talks with Elder Devilbiss when he joined the MEC-S so he knew what to expect at the Conference.

The Annual meeting of the Texas Conference was a combination of prayer and business. It opened with convocation followed by many prayers and testimonials, interrupted only by Charles Wesley hymns and followed by several sermons. In the business portion, the names of prospective ministers, Deacons, and Elders were read one by one to the assembled group who were allowed to ask questions about each one's family, personal history, and faith. After a thorough grilling, Conrad's candidacy was put to a vote and he was easily accepted but on probation, which meant he would not be a minister and an Elder with full connection until sometime in July. With positive results, he left the Conference after its conclusion in high spirits and began his long return trip to Mason County.

Well before he left Mason, he had written to his mother and his sister Conradina about his upcoming trip to Houston. Their home in Buckhorn was only about 60 miles from Houston but well out of his way. In return letters, they agreed to meet at Chappell Hill, a small community along his route and not far from their home at Buckhorn. In the village, they came together at the *Stagecoach Inn at Chappell Hill*, a frequent stopping place for travelers. It had been established in 1850 and had operated continuously since then. Over dinner, he, his mother, and the Hoffmanns talked mostly about family. For his part, Conrad kept his Methodism in check, something he had learned to do the hard way, and the four of them had a pleasant time. Near dark, the Hoffmanns and Sophia Pluenneke departed for their farm. Not wishing to ride at night, Conrad registered and spent the night at the Inn. Early the next morning, he mounted up and rode west, arriving back home late on Saturday afternoon, the 22nd of January.

After shaking off the trail dust, he put Storm up for the night and then went into the house to tell his wife and the children the good news that he was bringing from Houston. He would be a full time Methodist minister in the MEC and located at the Beaver Creek Methodist Episcopal Church.

On February 7th of 1870, the first Methodist Episcopal Church in a three county area was organized at Beaver Creek with 90 members attending. Elder Gustav Elley, as promised, travelled from Bastrop and presided over the meeting. As predetermined, Conrad Pluenneke was elected to serve as its first full time preacher. In the postwar Reconstruction era, a new MEC church was a cause to celebrate in Mason County. It meant that another former MEC-S charge had gone over to the expanding MEC in Texas.

For Conrad, the new assignment was a blessing and he thanked God for it every day as did his wife, Sophie. At long last, she became more comfortable and felt settled at Lower Willow. When she looked back over the years between 1854 and 1870, she realized that she had come a long ways from that early time when she had been so fearful about living in such a remote location amongst Indians and outlaws. Gradually, she had become more comfortable living on the frontier and everyday events became more routine and predictable. She still worried about Indian massacres but the presence of her four brothers and the Lehmbergs on the Lamar Moore Survey had gone a long way towards comforting her. She had relied on Heinrich in particular during Conrad's lengthy trips and knew she could ask for help from any of her brothers whenever she felt threatened or overburdened by ranch chores. With her husband located at Beaver Creek, all that was past.

When the new MEC at Beaver Creek formally began, it had 85 members, 73 more than when the congregation had been established back in 1856.[141] Five years after its establishment, men within the congregation built a sturdy wood and rock church that measured 24 feet in length and 22 feet in width. In addition to the church, they built a small rock parsonage near an artesian well and established a cemetery, all on property that was donated by founders Gottlieb Brandenberger and Fritz Kneese. In 1862, Reverend John A. Schaper became the first minister to live there. Even during the Civil War, the Beaver Creek church continued to grow in membership and develop physically. In 1863, the sanctuary was extended to provide a teacherage. In 1867, a wooden floor replaced the earthen floor and wooden pews were added.

In 1870 and 1871, the Texas Conference of the MEC formally charged Conrad Pluenneke to serve the Beaver Creek community and parts of the Llano River valley. Having previously served the Llano

---

[141] There were 12 founding members (150 Years of God's Grace, Hilda United Methodist Church, 2006).

Circuit several times and preached at Beaver Creek regularly since 1857, he was well acquainted with the congregation and the facility. For him, it was his dream assignment. He was able to preach to familiar people and yet stay on his ranch in Lower Willow and work with his herds.

During his tenure at Beaver Creek, Conrad and his family occupied the two-room parsonage when he preached on Sundays. Sophie used the lean-to kitchen to prepare food for the family while Conrad tended to his Methodist flock in the front room.

In 1872 and 1873, Conrad withdrew his name from the Conference and chose to serve as the Assistant Pastor and lay minister at Beaver Creek. In those two years, he spent more time tending to his ranch and readying his cattle for market. By 1874, he was ready to accept another MEC charge.

Around that time, Conrad and Sophie decided their very tiny, cramped log cabin on the Lamar Moore Survey was too small for their growing family, which now numbered eight. They decided to build a new, larger house on the Thomas Osburn Survey, not far from their present home. After walking about the Osburn Survey several times, Conrad chose a site that was about 1,000 feet inside of the Survey's east boundary and about 700 feet north of the Lower Willow Road. Importantly, the building site was well above the flood plain of the Llano River but the river would be quite visible from the house. The new site was level and sparsely vegetated with a variety of cacti and small mesquite trees.

Since they had steadily accumulated money through the sale of cattle in 1869, 1870, 1871, and 1872, Conrad and Sophie decided that they would build a sturdy rock house, rather than another log structure. In Mason, he hired a mason, August Brockmann, to do the stonework for them (see Figure 11-1). They determined that the new house would be rectangular in shape but would have a full second story with a corrugated metal roof. The children would sleep in the upper area and gain access to it through an interior stairway. Most interestingly, the house would feature a well in the kitchen. On the inside, its floor would be composed of wooden planks and the inside walls would be fully plastered. In the 1870s, it would have been a very modern house that would have been much easier to live in than a standard log cabin of the time.

Figure 11-1 Ruins of the Pluenneke's Rock House

Near the end of 1872, the Pluennekes moved into their new home. [142] After living in the small log cabin for nearly 20 years, the new home seemed spacious. Sophie was very pleased to have the indoor well and not be forced to send Sophie, Henry, or Conrad Jr. to Willow Creek day after day to fetch pails of water. Even though the new house was more removed from her brothers, Sophie felt secure and content about life. Her husband was no longer required to travel regularly and his cattle ranch was earning them a handsome income. With more land, however, Conrad and his oldest sons spent more time tending to their cattle which were now spread over nearly 3,000 acres, an area that included the Leifeste and Lehmberg property as well as their own. Even though Conrad worked longs day tending to his cattle herd, Sophie was content knowing he would be home for supper.

After their new house was finished, the Pluennekes looked forward to a contented and rosy future. Conrad had the ministerial job that he had desired for so long. They owned several thousand acres of good ranch land and their cattle business was generating a steady stream of income. Their children were maturing and the youngest child was now 14 years of age. Life could not have been better for the Pluennekes in Mason County.

---

[142] Sometime later, the wooden annex was added to the original stone building.

Sadly, their placid life along the Llano River didn't last very long. The lawless period in Mason County, which began during the Civil War and which lasted throughout Reconstruction, brought a criminal element into the Llano River Valley seeking to make money through rustling cattle. They were drawn in by the rising price of cattle and a certain knowledge that in that open range era, local ranchers could not watch over and control their large herds all the time. The rustling began innocently enough when ranchers from neighboring counties began to range their cattle herds onto ranches in Mason County and allow them to graze among the local owner's herds. That mixing of herds caused some friction among cattlemen but the cattle were sorted by brands and order was reestablished. Branding laws and local conventions seemed to handle the problem. Trouble began when dishonest stockmen began to range their cattle westward onto settler's property and practiced shady methods such as *mavericking* and outright rustling to steal the cattle from them.

Many early settlers, mostly German immigrants, had moved into the country as early as 1854 and begun to develop ranches on land that had the most abundant water and the most abundant grasslands. Those were also areas where the out-of-county ranchers wanted to range their cattle. In their eyes, the German immigrants were *foreigners* who had no right to that prime land, even though they had bought and developed it. The stockmen were Texians and they felt emboldened to intimidate the *foreigners* by taking their cattle and forcing them off their land. In this case, some of the German settlers stood their ground, banded together, and fought back. What affected one of them, affected all of them. In the ensuing fight, they would adopt Texian methods.

As a result of the location of their house, the Pluennekes were much closer to the Lower Willow Road than it had been on the Lamar Moore Survey. The road was now about 600 feet south of their front door. As a consequence, they became aware of traffic on the road. In some cases, it was cattle herds that were being driven down the road to the Upper Road but in other cases, it was wagons or riders. Generally, the traffic was generated by neighbors but occasionally, it was other people who were moving cattle or heading towards Hedwig's Hill. Over the time that the Pluennekes had lived in Lower Willow, other ranchers had bought property around them and settled, people not named Leifeste or Lehmberg. In the open range era, their cattle also roamed the countryside. The intermingling of many herds made managing cattle more difficult.

In the early 1870s, cattlemen from neighboring counties (e.g., Burnet County) deliberately began to range their cattle westward onto the ranches of the German immigrant settlers in the Llano River Valley. Mixed in with those "non-resident stockmen," as Johnson (2006) referred to them, were a criminal element whose dual purposes were to intimidate the German immigrants in a bold attempt to drive them from their land and also to rustle their cattle.[143] In the open range, identifying and protecting one's cattle when herds became mixed was a difficult chore. The only solution was branding.

Because branding was the crucial and perhaps, only means to stop rustling, branding laws were enacted in Mason County that were meant to curb the practice. One such law required that stockmen who wanted to move cattle out of Mason County had to have the brands of their herds checked by a duly elected Brands Inspector. Dan Hoerster, a rancher of German descent, was elected to that post in 1872 and promptly became a hated man to the outlaw faction because he strictly enforced the law. When he spotted brands that had been altered or calves that had not been branded, he required the stockmen to compensate the owner. That practice led to heated arguments over ownership of some cattle.

Back in 1851 and again in 1854, Conrad Pluenneke had registered his brand in Gillespie County. When Mason County was established in 1858, those brands transferred to the new county. In Lower Willow, Conrad and his older sons, particularly Henry, carefully rounded up their cattle and branded or marked all of them with his registered symbols on a regular basis. All the ranchers in the area did likewise. Despite their efforts, cattle rustlers still managed to steal cattle from all of them. Since the livelihoods of the immigrant families were based largely on cattle sales, such stealing cut at the heart of their existence. They could not tolerate rustling and stay on their land. When rustling did occur on one of their ranches, the German ranchers banded togeth-

---

[143] Sonnichsen (1957) "The mere fact that Texas was a frontier state for so long accounts for much of the trouble. The roughest sort of people (mostly southerners with their own code of conduct) found refuge there in the early days and sometimes the only way the good settlers could deal with them was to resort to "folk justice."

er and pursued the outlaws but rarely caught them. The law, on their side, was equally ineffective against organized rustling.

It was well known that all of Mason County was patrolled by two lawmen, sheriff John Clark and his deputy John Wohrle. Elected in 1872 with a mandate to keep the peace in over 900 square miles of rugged frontier territory, sheriff Clark and his deputy had a daunting task. When rustling occurred in the backcountry, it often took a day or two to locate and inform the sheriff of the crime. By then, the outlaws had fled deeper into the frontier (Menard County or McCulloch County) and altered the brand on the stolen cattle. As beef prices climbed ever higher, rustling became an easy way to make money and not have to be concerned with raising the cattle. As a result, more and more rustlers moved into John Clark's jurisdiction and found many ways to steal cattle. Over time, some of the rustlers became known in Mason by name or by gang, although there was scant evidence on which to arrest or convict them. Occasionally, the sheriff was fortunate and managed to apprehend some in the act of rustling.

Sheriff Clark had many ardent supporters among the German immigrants who settled in the Llano River Valley. They often were part of the sheriff's posses and spent time tracking down known rustlers. On the rare occasion when rustlers were apprehended and tried, juries often found them innocent out of fear of retribution and the legal system set them free. Failure of the jury system frustrated the German ranchers even more. By 1874, the rustling epidemic had gone on for over four years and the German immigrant ranchers were frustrated and angry with the situation in Mason County. Some wrote to the Governor for help.

In early 1874, at the request of those citizens, Governor Coke sent a detail of Texas Rangers to Mason County to quell the rustling spree. Under the command of Lieutenant Dan W. Roberts, the unit showed its colors and patrolled around the county but in reality, it did little to end the rustling problem. Like sheriff Clark, their presence was too small to be effective in such a vast area. Even divided into several smaller units, they failed to find the rustlers. In the end, they too had little effect at ending the epidemic of rustling that plagued Mason County.

From the day of their arrival in Texas, many of the German immigrants had been reviled by some Americans but by not all. In 1874, they were being harassed yet again by some who wanted to steal their cattle and drive them from their land. It was too much! At that point, something in the collective mind of the German settlers changed. Being complacent and trying to stay removed from the fray had gotten them nowhere. A few of the German settlers decided to take matters into their own hands and fight back. Those men felt it was a matter of survival for their families and their chosen way of life.

Recognizing that sheriff Clark or Captain Robert's detail of Rangers were not effectively curbing the thievery, local ranchers who had been hit hard by rustlers, particularly many of Germanic heritage, began to organize into a Vigilance Committee. If local lawmen and the Texas Rangers could not stop the rustlers, they would solve the problem themselves by taking preemptive measures. They would identify the rustlers and apply what was then known as *frontier justice*. As Sonnichsen wrote in 1957, " they were German in language and custom but they were beginning to get the hang of one American custom: the use of rope, steel, and lead to maintain peace and property rights. As had been done to some of them by American Confederate soldiers during the Civil War era, they determined to find the rustlers and lynch them or shoot them on the spot without subjecting them to a public trial, which the Germans had come to realize would be futile in Mason County."

At various homes in the Llano River Valley, meetings were held to organize for vigilante action. Word of the meetings and who attended filtered throughout the community. German names such as Bader, Hoerster, Doell, Jordan, Keller, Kothman, Lehmberg, Leifeste, Pluenneke (Henry), and Oestreich were rumored to be part of what had come to be called the Hoo Doos, or in other terms, a Vigilance Committee. Sheriff Clark and deputy John Wohrle were also rumored to have ties to the group. [144] Many of those names were also stalwarts of the local Methodist churches and that troubled the Reverend Conrad Pluenneke. Lynching and executing people was not what Christ accepted as social justice, even though the outlaws might be thought to deserve such a fate. What distressed Conrad Pluenneke was that some of those names were of his own Beaver Creek congregation.

After Sunday services, he sought those members out and talked to them privately. Inwardly, he felt the same frustration and the same an-

---

[144] In the era of Reconstruction, it is highly likely that the German element helped get Clark elected.

ger that they did but he could not condone violence. He prayed ardently for direction and urged them to use lawful means instead of resorting to mob rule. He pointed out that the fifth Commandment was *Thou Shalt not Kill* and failure to follow that Commandment was a sin with very grave consequences. [145] Did they want to spend eternity in Hell as result of consciously deciding to lynch rustlers, who coincidentally also had souls?

Early in February of 1874, the sheriff managed to apprehend the Baccus gang, as they were known in the region, and put them in the Mason jail. They were six in number, five men and a boy, all led by Linge and Pete Baccus. The gang was composed of known rustlers and the word of their arrest spread quickly throughout the community. When members of the Vigilance Committee learned of their incarceration, about 40 of them assembled and rode into Mason. Wearing masks, they went to the home of deputy Wohrle and attempted to get the keys to the jail. Failing that, they rode to the jailhouse where they confronted sheriff Clark and Ranger Roberts, both of whom stepped aside in the face of superior numbers. The Vigilance Committee took the five men from the jail, but left the young boy behind. The vigilantes headed south from Mason and attempted to kill all of their captives. The Baccus brothers were lynched and another of the gang was shot to death before the sheriff tracked down the Vigilance Committee and interceded. While the vigilantes faded into the wilderness, two of the Baccus gang managed to escape. As a result of that incident, the masked Vigilance Committee members became known as the "Hoo Doos" or "the mob" in Mason County.

The action of the Hoo Doos, instead of quelling the rustling spree as they might have hoped to, ignited a major feud that lasted for years. For a few months, there was peace in the county but that all changed in May of 1874 when sheriff Clark sent deputy Wohrle to arrest Tim Williamson on charges of stealing cattle plus some other undefined tax issues. In the process of taking him back to jail in Mason, Pete Bader [146] and a few Vigilantes showed up. For some unknown reason, Wohrle shot Williamson's horse, putting him on foot. Bader proceeded

---

[145] Such a sin is akin to a mortal sin, which in Catholic terms, is one that is grave and consciously performed. Once performed, it destroys the relationship between God and man and results in damnation.

[146] Pete Bader was described as a "rough and tumble guy."

to run down and shoot the unarmed Williamson without any sign of mercy. Deputy Wohrle was either unable or unwilling to stop Bader.

In Blanco County, William Scott Cooley learned of Williamson's death. Cooley who was a friend and sort of ward of Williamsons, went berserk and vowed to exact revenge on whoever killed his friend. He rode to Mason and quietly poked around for several days, apparently intent on identifying who would pay for Williamson's death (Roberts, 1929). He tracked down Wohrle and systematically shot him and then scalped him. After killing the deputy, he displayed Wohrle's scalp in saloons and openly bragged about killing him. Shortly, a gang of violent desperadoes collected around Cooley and formed what became known as the Cooley Gang. They terrorized Mason County all summer. They killed people who Cooley believed had aided sheriff Clark or crossed them in some way. The local citizenry, unsure of who might be killed next, lived in fear and tried to stay out of public view.

Again, the local citizenry appealed to Governor Coke, asking for protection. He sent Major Jones with about 40 Texas Rangers to Mason County. After they arrived, they searched for Cooley with no success and received little support from the general community.

In early September, sheriff Clark learned that the Cooley gang was in Loyal Valley and constructed a ruse that managed to induce two members of the gang to ride into Mason. On the way, the sheriff and a posse of about 60 men ambushed the two, killing one but sparing the other. Later that month, the Cooley Gang killed the man who had summoned the gang members into that ambush.

On Monday September 28th, members of the Cooley Gang ambushed the Brands Inspector Dan Hoerster (age 32), Henry Pluenneke (age 23), and Peter Jordan (age 28) as they rode casually into Mason, killing Hoerster. Henry Pluenneke and Peter Jordan took cover and with rifle fire, managed to drive the ambushers away. Someone in Mason rode out to the Pluenneke ranch with some urgency and informed them of the event.

Upon being informed that his son, Henry Pluenneke, and his two friends had been involved in an ambush at Mason that was initiated by the Cooley gang, he inquired of his son's condition. He was told that Henry had survived unscratched. At that news, Reverend Conrad

Pluenneke first bowed his head and gave thanks to God for protecting Henry and then went purposefully into the house, donned his clerical garb, and saddled up Storm. At full gallop, he rode into Mason to comfort Henry and learn from him what had transpired. After hearing how the ambush had transpired, he and Henry rode out to the Hoerster family ranch to support the family and offer his condolences. At the Hoerster's house, they met a number of the other German ranchers, armed and angry at the turn of events. Predictably, the talk was about how to exact revenge on the Cooley gang.

As a Methodist minister, Conrad counseled calm before heated action but he was reminded by some present that in the Old Testament, God had unleashed the fury of his people to slay entire nations (e.g. the Hittites) on numerous occasions. Was it therefore not acceptable to God to slay the Cooley Gang? Conrad countered that the New Testament had supplanted the Old Testament and it presented a very different face of God, one that was more forgiving. It preached forgiveness but also held to the Commandments.

One of the men spoke directly to Reverend Pluenneke "You served in the Mexican-American War where you were required to shoot Mexican soldiers should they attack American fortresses that you helped defend. What is so different about taking up arms now and shooting criminals?"

Conrad countered "In Exodus 20:14, the Sixth Commandment is laid down: *Do not Kill.* That message is repeated 12 times in the New Testament. Deliberate killing or murder is a sin and brings with it the possibility of eternal damnation to Hell. My *Bible* does not include exceptions or conditions under which killing is permissible. The Commandment is absolute: those who kill will be damned to Hell. Do all of you assembled here wish to risk spending eternity in Hell? I don't!" That question gave pause to several men in the group, but shortly they went back to plotting revenge.

Conrad Pluenneke did not want to be part of that cabal so he and Henry made their exit from the Hoerster home. As the Reverend left the Hoerster ranch, he thought about the Hoo Doo War issue and knew he faced a moral dilemma. He had taken up arms against Mexico and while he did not actually kill anyone in his brief tour of duty, he would have done so to save his own life or those of his comrades. But that was before he found God! Yet, internally he felt the same hatred that the other German immigrants felt toward the Cooley Gang but he knew he had to find a way to get past that anger without killing any of them. On the other hand, a member of his family had been attacked by the Cooley Gang and he had to respond in some way: Either exact revenge or turn the other cheek. Oh, Lord, show me the way!

For the past two decades, Conrad Pluenneke had struggled mightily to maintain a close relationship with his God. When he had fallen short, he ardently and in his own words "cried hot tears" while desperately trying to regain favor with God. To exact revenge on the Cooley Gang would cause him to lose that connection to God, that closeness, permanently. He knew he was unwilling to risk that. Nothing in life was more important to him than God and serving Him. On the other hand, failing to avenge the ambushing of his son and the death of his friend, Dan Hoerster, might make him look weak in the eyes of some men of German heritage. While he cared deeply about the Methodist flock that he served and his other immigrant friends, it mattered more to him how God viewed him. God would understand if he took the moral high ground and condemned the ambush from the pulpit but refrained from taking up arms against the gang.

From those collected at the Hoerster ranch, a posse was quickly assembled and rode to Mason to take up pursuit of the gang. Some distance away from Mason, it managed to capture one of the gang. Mysteriously, that gang member never made it back to Mason.

Subsequently, Scott Cooley and some of his men rode over to Llano County and mistakenly killed Karl Bader (Peter Bader's brother), believing he was Peter Bader. Later, Cooley realized his mistake and killed Peter Bader as well, thus avenging Williamson's death, in his mind. In that same year, the Methodist church at Upper Willow was burned to the ground.

And so it went.[147] The feud was the stuff of Hollywood westerns and lasted for decades. The Hoo Doo Wars raged on for years but the Pluenneke family was not physically affected again. The war did, however, disrupt Conrad's vision of an idyllic existence at Lower Willow. Gone was the idea that he could just preach on Sunday, raise cat-

---

[147] In 1876, Cooley was allegedly poisoned in a Fredericksburg bar.

tle on the other six days, and exist in peace and harmony. Life in Mason County was very difficult and starkly real everyday. To exist in it, Conrad had to be constantly vigilant and active every day.

In 1874 and 1875, Conrad Pluenneke was assigned to the MEC branch of the Methodist church in Fredericksburg. Like Beaver Creek, a portion of the congregation who supported the Union became distraught with the MEC-S in 1871 and split away. Unlike Beaver Creek, the splitting faction left the church and began to meet separately in the Kneese's home on San Antonio Street. In a matter of years, land would be acquired on Edison Street and the Fredericksburg MEC would become the new Edison Street Methodist Church. Conrad would become its third minister, following Gustav Elley and Anton Ulrich in the post. Church records reveal that he performed many marriages, baptisms, and funerals during his tenure of two years. On May 15, 1873, he officiated the wedding of Johanna Kneese and Daniel Stiehl, son of his old friend and mentor from Fredericksburg, Heinrich Stiehl. The wedding ceremony gave them another chance to meet and talk about Methodism. Eight years later, Heinrich Stiehl would depart the Earth and go to be with his Maker.

In 1874, Conrad Pluenneke attended the organizational meeting of the South German Conference that was held at Industry on January 15th. Attending it meant another trip of over 400 miles in the dead of winter. At the meeting, Conrad became one of 13 charter members. At year's end, the South German conference would have 17 preachers, 7 local ministers, and 438 members plus 73 on trial. It had but 9 churches and combined assets of $13,440, roughly $1.70 per member.

From 1876 until 1878, the Texas Conference of the MEC assigned Conrad to the Beaver Creek community for a second stint as its pastor. During that time, more than 35 people joined the small rural congregation and it flourished under his guidance.

After that assignment, Conrad resigned himself to be a lay minister, assistant pastor, and church benefactor until he retired from active ministry in 1895. During that final decade, his health began to fail.

His ranch, now quite a bit larger at 4,148 acres, was managed by his four sons. In 1887, they fenced off the Thomas Osburn Survey with barbed wire, apparently closing off the Lower Willow Road for a time

(DeVos, 1986). After the ranch was fenced, his health began to deteriorate and he began to take life a little easier. In 1895, he retired from the active ministry and became content to just attend Methodist services at Beaver Creek. He spent much of each day in bed but occasionally, he would summon enough strength to get up and leave the house for walks about the Osburn Survey.

After he retired, Conrad Pluenneke would occasionally walk down a heavily used path from the house to a spot from which he could see the Llano River and its confluence with Willow Creek. *The Place*, as he referred to it, always brought him comfort and great peace of mind. At his place, he would sit atop a half-submerged granite boulder for an hour or so and just contemplate life. Over the years, he had gone to this place many times when he wanted to think clearly about a pressing issue or when he wanted to commune privately with his God. From his little perch, he would survey the Llano River and marvel at its beauty. It made him very proud to know that he owned a large stretch of land along such a magnificent river. Even in his advanced age, he frequently had to chide himself about being too proud of worldly things, such as the amount of land that he owned, and he often had to remind himself that his land was a gift from God, not an accomplishment of his own making. As he had ever since becoming a Methodist back in 1852, he still strived mightily to follow *The Discipline* every day and pride was a forbidden self-indulgence in the Methodist way of life.

In the spring of 1896, he made the trip down his dirt path to *The Place* one last time. Something inside him had informed him that his time on earth was coming to an end and he desperately wanted to go to his special place and take in the view of the Llano River once more. Racked by failing health and age, it took much effort for Conrad Pluenneke to walk the half-mile distance to his favorite spot, mount the granite boulder, and get comfortable but he managed to do so.

As he gazed out at the confluence, he recalled that day in his father's field in Germany when he had pondered his future and wondered about what he would accomplish in life. At the time, he had been a practicing Evangelical Lutheran but that had amounted to little more than going to church regularly and seeing his friends. He truly had not known God back then, not in the way he did now. In Texas, following the guidance of Heinrich Stiehl and then Charles Grote, he had become an ardent Methodist and risen through its ranks to become a highly respected Elder in the Methodist Episcopal Church. He had ridden the Llano River Valley circuit, had been a pastor at the Fredericksburg Methodist Church twice, and had been instrumental in establishing an enduring church at Beaver Creek. In 1842, he could not have imagined that he would be so involved in doing God's work in Texas.

The greatest dream of that young man standing in his father's field back in Germany was to shake off the last vestiges of feudalism that had held his family down by coming to possess a domain and along with it, the correlated wealth and prestige. In his 49 years in Texas, he had managed to do just that. At age 34, he had boldly bought the large Lamar Moore Survey for $600 [148] and then shared it with the Leifeste and Lehmberg families. Just three years later, he had bought part of the Isaac Hamilton survey on the Llano River that abutted the Lamar Moore Survey. After a successful cattle drive in 1869, he had acquired the Thomas Osburn survey, adding another 1,476 acres of land that straddled part of Willow Creek and abutted his Lamar Moore land on the west. Shortly thereafter, he built a substantial rock home on the Osburn Survey and moved his family there. In subsequent years, he had added thousands of additional acres to his holdings in Mason County. Those acquisitions allowed him to fulfill his life-long dream of owning a landed estate with the legal right to pass it to his progeny. In Heaven, his long-deceased ancestors must have smiled down on him. In Texas, the Pluennekes were no longer serfs.

While he was amassing land, he had also built a substantial cattle ranching business in Mason County. Starting with a few head of cattle in Fredericksburg, he had grown that herd to a number that ranged upward from 500 head. Over the years, he learned much about cattle ranching from the Kothmann brothers whom he admired.

While he mused about his life, Conrad also thought about his years back in Germany and wondered what his life would have been like had he stayed in Germany. He would have inherited the small family farm and led an agricultural life wringing out subsistence from the land. He and his wife would have been content but little more because they would have continued to live as poor subsistence farmers.

---

[148] Spending $600 in 1853 dollars is roughly the equivalent of spending roughly $229,000 in 2014. That land might sell for $6 million dollars today.

Those thoughts triggered him to remember his first wife. He had felt so fortunate when she agreed to marry him and it bothered him now that he could barely remember what she looked like. In his memory, he could still recall some of her mannerisms but her appearance had largely vanished. At times over the fifty or so years since her untimely death in Karlshafen, he had ruefully thought about her and wished that her fate had been different. He deeply regretted his role in uprooting her from Germany and taking her to the hellhole they called Karlshafen. It would be easy for him to shift the blame for her death onto the Adelsverein. After all, it was their incompetence that led to all the misery but in the end, it had been he, Conrad Pluenneke, who pushed the family to emigrate. Inwardly, he knew he was culpable and that still troubled him. Through God's grace, he had come to grips with that guilt and knew that he had been pardoned by the One that matters.

His thoughts then drifted to his late father, Johann Heinrich Conrad Pluenneke, and his early life in Klein-Lafferde. His father had taught him the value of hard work as well as thrift and those values had served him well in Texas. He had worked hard and he had wasted little. When his father died at Karlshafen, Conrad served in the U.S. Army in Mexico and had accomplished little in life up that point. He regretted that his father did not live long enough to see how successful he had become in Texas and how he had made their family dreams come true. He felt that his father, had he lived on, would have been very proud of him.

From his father, his thoughts roamed to his mother and two sisters who lived near Houston in Buckhorn. After Karlshafen, they had made a life there and that pleased him. His sister Conradina had married well and she had a family. His other sister Karoline had also married and she had a new family. He and the rest of his family had their differences over religion but those had been smoothed out over ensuing years.

He thought about Heinrich Stiehl and what a huge influence he had in those early years in Fredericksburg. He thought about his conversion at the camp meeting on Stiehl's land, about the missionary Heinrich Young, and about the guidance that Reverend Grote had given him afterwards. They changed his life.

And then his thoughts drifted back to the present. He thought fondly about Sophie and their children. When his first wife had died in

1846, he thought he would never find another woman that would make him as happy as she did but he was wrong. Marching off to war, he had become close friends with Heinrich Leifeste and through him, he had met Sophie Leifeste in Fredericksburg and came to love her dearly. She had joined him in Methodism and supported him as he rose through the ranks of that religion. While he rode the circuit, she selflessly managed the ranch and kept the family going, always content to exist in his large shadow. He hoped that over the years he had conveyed to her just how much he appreciated her and her support. She was his ideal mate. After he departed the Earth, he knew she would carry on as she always had and that gave him tremendous comfort.

As he looked back on the entirety of his life, he began to see a pattern emerge that had never been so apparent to him before. To clarify it, he took a scrap of paper from his coat pocket and with his stubby pencil, began to write down all the important people in his life. He began with his parents and then added his first wife, Heinrich Leifeste, Fritz Stein, John O. Meusebach, Emil Kriewitz, Sophie Leifeste, Heinrich Stiehl, C. A. Grote, Fritz Kothmann, Dietrich Kothmann, and a few others. He studied the list for a few minutes and then in a parallel column, began to add the significant events that had occurred in his life: emigration, the deaths at sea, his first wife's death, meeting Heinrich Leifeste, the war in Mexico, his work in the warehouse at Indian Point, acting as a scout for Kriewitz's outfit, meeting Sophie, becoming Methodist, serving in various capacities in the Methodist church, buying the Lamar Moore Survey, raising cattle, and so on. As he scanned the two columns, he could not help but see how key people had entered his life during critical times and had gently reoriented him to a different path, always toward a better place in life. When he had felt lost and without direction, he had begged for God to show him the way. At those points, key people had entered his life and like lamp holders, illuminated the path for him through life's many twists and turns. Looking back, he could clearly see the pattern of his life now, with its inherent guidance. It showed God to be like a master chess player, deftly moving his pawns here and there to accomplish a larger strategic plan. God had always had a plan for his life. He, as a mortal man, had only dimly glimpsed elements of that plan at intermediate junctures in his life. While Conrad had been busy accomplishing goals of his own, God had gently guided him to conduct His business in Mason County. Conrad Pluenneke had achieved his mortal goals but God also achieved far loftier goals through him.

As a result of his efforts, Conrad Pluenneke had reached many people in Mason County, brought many people to Christ, and had effectively spread the Word of God throughout central Texas. He had never been too busy to help people in need. As a role model, he had set the moral bar very high in his daily life. All the pain and angst that he had suffered through had a grander purpose: he saw that his work would live on in places like the Beaver Creek Methodist Church and its surrounding community.

Finally, he came around to contemplate his own mortality. Age and disease had robbed him of many of his personal talents to the point that he knew that the Grim Reaper was at his doorstep. Because of his deep and abiding faith in God and His promise of eternal life, he did not fear death. On some specific day soon, he knew that his human body would fail and that he, Reverend Conrad Pluenneke, would cease to exist in his earthly form. After death, he knew his body would be transformed to a spiritual state that would allow him to be with his Maker. What comforted him was the assurance that God had given him that on that fateful day he would be lifted to Heaven where he would see Christ and all the good people who passed before him.

He thought about being in Heaven, a place where all his aches and pains that were caused by age would cease to exist. At 78, it felt almost everything in his body hurt at some time or another. In his infirmity, relief from that pain sounded wonderful but he had felt he had a bit more to do for God before he departed the mortal world. Slowly, he came out of his reverie and slowly trudged back to the house where Sophie was waiting.

That spring, he became housebound so many of his old friends and church officials came to call on him and reminisce about old times. Among them were Elder Gustav Elley, Reverend Frederick Vordenbaumen, Reverend Anton Ulrich, and members of the Beaver Creek Church. At times, he knew those people but in the middle of conversations with them, his face would go blank and he would begin talking about events of which they had no knowledge.

In more lucid moments, he wondered aloud about old friends and acquaintances.

"What happened to Emil Kriewitz?", Conrad would muse.

Sophie quietly told him that Emil Kriewitz had settled in Castell, had been Postmaster until 1883, and then like him, had become a rancher. Upon hearing that, his mind would then dart to another dear friend.

"Where is my old friend Heinrich?" he would ask, referring to Heinrich Leifeste. To that question, Sophie would patiently answer "He's just across Willow Creek. He'll be here tomorrow."

"Ah!" Conrad would answer, "It will be good to see him again. It seems that I have known him all my life. Is he doing well?"

To that, Sophie would sigh, nod her head, and say, "My brother is well."

Then he would move to the next person. "Where is Charles Grote these days?"

"Reverend Grote", she explained, "retired here in Mason County in 1884 and went to be with our Lord in 1887."

"Good man," he would mumble. "Always right with the Lord."

The next day, he would ask about the same people again, not re-calling events from the previous day. Sophie, always the patient wife, would dutifully answer all his queries repeatedly. In a month or so, his queries became less frequent and he began to stare blankly into space for most of the day. Sophie, not in good health herself, fed him and cared for him as much as she could but his condition continued to de-teriorate. One by one, their children came and sat by his bedstead, hop-ing for signs of improvement but Conrad's health did not improve and the doctor from Mason gave them no room for optimism. "His condi-tions is one that is poorly understood and one for which there is no cure," the doctor said bluntly.

Sensing that his mortal time on Earth was elapsing, Conrad again struggled to recall the details of his life. Had he really crossed the At-lantic? Had he really gone off to war in Mexico with his friend, Hein-rich Leifeste? Had he really bought all that land on the Llano River? Had he risen to the status of Elder in the MEC? To him, it seemed as though he had done all of that but his memory was fuzzy. What had enabled him to do all those things?

In one of his rare moments of clarity, Conrad Pluenneke recalled a letter that had been sent to Wilhelm Nast that had been published in *Der Christliche Apologete* in 1849. It had been written by someone named Doering, another German immigrant who had also struggled to understand what had motivated him to leave the Fatherland and come to America. Doering [149] discovered that it had been the Finger of God that directed his life. Conrad smiled faintly and whispered to no one in particular "Yes, it was the finger of God that quietly showed me the way at each crucial step of my life. From the very beginning, He, the Almighty, chose me to be one of His own and has always had a plan for my life."

On May 13th of 1897, Conrad Pluenneke lay on his deathbed at their rock house on the Thomas Osburn Survey, surrounded by most of his children and grandchildren. Near the end of his life, he whispered aloud, "Tonight I will be with God" and smiled that faint smile for which he was known. At midday, he smiled broadly at a vision of a crooked finger beckoning him. Summoning the rest of his energy, he said a loud Amen to the vision that only he could see and followed that with "Lord, I will come." That night, Reverend Conrad Pluenneke died quietly at his home in Lower Willow.

Later that month, J. Ott wrote a eulogy about him: "(Near the end, someone) had to stay day and night with him. He carried his cross (faith) to the very end with a great commitment; as many times as I visited him, he was always thrilled when I read out loud from the *Bible* and when I prayed with him he closed with an audible AMEN. He still tried to comfort the mother (Sophie) who is now quite weak herself. At last, on May 13th, the wheels of life stopped. His son (John) arrived from New Orleans but was too late to see him alive. At the time of his homecoming, the District meeting was being held in Seguin. Brother Schreiber held the service of mourning and read Corinthians 15, 55-57. Brother Pluenneke left behind (his family) and an army of comrades-in-arms for God's service. Since I was personally acquainted with him, I must testify that his character these past 24 years had always been of the highest and work done with much love."

---

[149] Part of Doering's letter was quoted in the Prologue.

Chapter 14

EPILOGUE

Conrad Pluenneke was an extraordinary man, no question, and his life spanned an extraordinary era of Texas and Methodist history.

If one considers that the frontier era of Texas history lasted about 72 years, roughly from the founding of Austin's Colony in 1821 to 1893, the year that historians regard as the end of the American frontier, Conrad Pluenneke lived through 47 years of that span. He participated in the Mexican-American War, the settling of Fredericksburg, the settling of Mason County along the Llano River, and the era of trailing cattle to distant markets. He also lived through the Civil War Era, Reconstruction, and the Hoo Doo Wars of Mason County. Although he came to Texas on the heels of the Methodist split over slavery in 1844, he lived to witness the resurgence of the MEC in Texas which helped set the stage for the United Methodist Church in the 20th century.

Throughout his adult life, he was focused on the major goals of his life and controlled every detail. His distinctive signature on Methodist documents and on real estate documents reflect his controlled, precise nature. In his obituary published in the Mason County News, it was written that, "He was faithful to every duty in his life and every detail was attended to carefully and promptly." So true! In his biography, one can see that he constantly juggled his equally firm commitments to his Methodist faith, his family, his friends, and his cattle ranch. In each of those endeavors, he seems to have applied an almost laser-like attention to the job at hand. He worked diligently and efficiently at all of them every day of his life. Doing those four things concurrently, and with so much vigor, must have taken a toll on him. There is nothing in the record to suggest that he ever slackened his pace or took time off to just relax and enjoy life. To him and to many Methodists of his day, "Idle time was a tool of the Devil." Pleasure for him was in accomplishment. The more he accomplished, the happier he became.

If you were not a staunch Methodist and not overly concerned about human souls perishing in the depths of Hell, you might have had difficulty interacting with him, particularly in the early days of his ministry. He seemed to have had a serious, abrupt, and hortatory demeanor toward non-Methodists, as evidenced by the somewhat preachy tone of his letter to his cousin back in Germany and in his communications with Pluenneke relatives in Buckhorn. However, if you were of a Methodist persuasion, Conrad Pluenneke would have been someone you would have liked, someone you would have greatly admired, someone you would have trusted, and someone you would have readily followed. He would still have inquired about your soul upon every meeting but he would have been your friend.

He was enabled to accomplish all that he did because he had an extraordinarily strong and supportive wife, Sophie. Whether it was because he was riding the circuit, preaching as a pastor in another town, or attending mandatory Methodist Conferences far away from Mason County, he was away from home a lot for a frontier rancher who depended on cattle sales to earn a living. In his absence, she and their sons covered for him and thereby enabled to advance in Methodist circles. Sophie had to have been an extraordinarily strong and patient wife to cope with the life of a circuit riding Methodism minister. Her silent strength enabled him to accomplish much. In that frontier era, where women could not even vote, it is sad that so little was recorded about her life.

Figure 14-1 Sophie (nee Leifeste) Pluenneke

Sophie Leifeste followed her husband to Heaven early on the 9th of January in the following year, 1898. Both are buried side-by-side at the Lower Willow Cemetery near their home and beside the Llano River but always fondly remembered in Mason County

REFERENCES

Books

Barton, Barbara. *Pistol Packin Preachers*. Republic of Texas Press, Dallas TX 2005.

Bierschwale, Margaret. *A History of Mason County, Texas*. Premier Publishing, Mason TX 1998.

Biesele, Rudolph L. *The History of German Settlements in Texas 1831-1861*. Eakin Press, Austin TX 1930.

Biggers, Don H. *German Pioneers in Texas*. Eakin Publications, Austin TX 1925.

Bracht, Viktor. *Texas in 1848*. Naylor Printing Company, San Antonio TX 1930.

DeVos, Julius. *Conrad Pluenneke: Citizen*. Mason County Historical Book, Supplement I. Mason County Historical Commission, 1986,

Douglass, Paul F. PhD. *The Story of German Methodism*. The Methodist Book Concern, Cincinnati OH 1939.

Ernst, Friedrich. *Letter to Mr. Schwartz, Oldenburg, 1832*. Cited in Tiling, Moritz. *History of the German Element in Texas from 1820-1850*. 1913.

Fehrenbach, T. R. *Lone Star A History of Texas and the Texans*. Da Capo Press, Austin TX 1968.

Ferrell, Robert H. *Monterrey is Ours! The Mexican War Letters of Lieutenant Dana 1845-1847*. The University of Kentucky Press, Lexington KY 1990.

Feuge, Robert L. *Christoph Feuge, a German Pioneers Story*. Llumina Press, Coral Springs, FL 2009.

Garber, Paul N. *That Fighting Spirit of Methodism.* Piedmont Press, Greensboro NC 1928.

Geue, Chester and Geue, Ethel. *A New Land Beckoned.* Texian Press, Waco TX 1966.

Gravis, Peter W. *Twenty-five years on the Outer Row.* Cross Timbers Press, Brownwood TX 1966.

Hardt, William C. and Hardt, John Wesley. *Historical Atlas of Texas Methodism.* CrossHouse Publishing, Garland TX 2008.

Howe, Daniel W. *What Hath God Wrought - The Transformation of America 1815-1848.* Oxford University Press, Oxford (England) 2007.

Jeffrey, Julie Roy. *Frontier Women: The Trans-Mississippi West 1840-1880.* Hill and Wang Publishers, New York City, NY 1979.

Johnson, David. *The Mason County "Hoo Doo" War, 1874-1902.* University of North Texas Press, Denton TX 2006.

Johnston, William Preston. *The Life of General Albert Sidney Johnston.* D. Appleton and Company, New York City, NY 1878.

Jordan, Gilbert J. *Yesterday in the Texas Hill Country.* Texas A & M Press, College Station TX 1979.

John, I. G. *Handbook of Methodist Missions.* 1893.

Kearney, James C. *Nassau Plantation.* The University of North Texas Press, Denton TX 2010.

King, Irene M. *John O. Meusebach Colonizer in Texas.* University of Texas Press, Austin TX 1967.

Kleinecke, Charles W. *Jr. Fischer Miller and G.E.C. Forever.* Self published. Corsicana TX 2011.

Klose, Nelson. *A Concise Study Guide to the American Frontier.* University of Nebraska Press, Lincoln, NB 1964.

Kriewitz, Emil. *Recollections From Indian Times.* In Penniger, R. *Fredericksburg, Texas: The First Fifty Years.* Fredericksburg Publishing Company, Fredericksburg TX pages 48-49, 1896.

Outler, Albert C. *John Wesley.* Oxford University Press, New York City, New York 1964.

Morgenthaler, Jefferson *The German Settlement of the Texas Hill Country.* Mockingbird Books, Boerne TX 2007.

Nail, Olin W. *The First 100 Years, 1858-1958 The Southwest Conference of the Methodist Church.* Capitol Printing Company, Austin TX 1958.

Olmstead, Frederick Law. *A Journey Through Texas; or a Saddle-trip on the Southwestern Frontier.* Mason Brothers, New York City NY 1860.

Pioneers in God's Hills. von Boeckmann-Jones, Austin TX 1960.

Pool, William C. *A Historical Atlas of Texas.* The Encino Press, Austin TX 1975.

Raunick, Selma and Schade, Margaret. *The Kothmanns of Texas.* von Boeckmann-Jones Press, Austin TX 1931.

Roberts, D. W. Mrs. *Reminiscences of Six Years in Camp with Texas Rangers.* von Boeckmann-Jones Press, Austin TX 1928.

Roemer, Dr. Ferdinand. *Texas.* (translated by Oswald Mueller) Standard Printing Company, San Antonio TX 1935.

Roland, Charles P. *Albert Sidney Johnston: Soldier of Three Republics.* The University Press of Kentucky, Lexington KY 2001.

Seidman, Dov. *How: How we do Anything Means Everything.* John Wiley & Sons, Hoboken NJ 2007.

Shils, Edward. *Tradition.* University of Chicago Press, Chicago IL 1981.

Simms, Brendan. *The Struggle for Mastery in Germany, 1779-1850.* St. Martins's Press, New York City, NY 1998.

Sonnichsen, Charles L. *Ten Texas Feuds*. University of New Mexico Press, Albuquerque NM 1957.

Tennery, Thomas. *The Mexican War Diary of Thomas D. Tennery*, edited by D.E. Livingston-Little, University of Oklahoma Press, Norman OK 1970.

Tiling, Moritz *History of the German Element in Texas From 1820-1850*. Self Published, Houston TX 1913.

Wilson, James Q. *The Moral Sense*. Free Press Paperbacks. New York City, NY 1997.

Magazine Articles

Goodyer, Bronwen. *An Assistant Ship Surgeon's Account of Cholera at Sea*. Journal of Public Health, Volume 30, Number 3, 2008.

Hunter, J. Marvin. *Brief History of the Early Days in Mason County*. Frontier Times, 1928, Volume 6, numbers 2 and 4.

Passmore, Leonard. *Killing of Mr. and Mrs. Kensing*. in Frontier Times, 1924, Volume 1, number 8, pages 8-10.

Newspaper Articles

Kendall, George W. *Dispatches From the Mexican War, April 17 to August 25, 1846*. Published in the Daily Picayune, New Orleans, LA.

News About the Army of Occupation in The Civilian and Galveston Gazette, Volume 8, February 26, 1846.

Other Publications

Baulch, Joe. *The Dogs of War Unleashed: The Devil Concealed in Men Unchained*. West Texas Historical Association Yearbook, 2010.

Der Christliche Apologete. Nast, Wilhelm Editor. Cincinnati, OH

INDEX OF PROMINENT PEOPLE

APPENDIX

Appendix 1

Einwanderungs-Vertrag.

Zwischen dem Vereine zum Schutze deutscher Einwanderer in Texas, repräsentirt durch den zur Abschließung der Contrakte speciell beauftragten Direktor, Herrn Grafen Carl zu Castell, und in dessen Abwesenheit durch seinen mit Specialvollmacht versehenen Stellvertreter, Herrn Dr. jur. B. Hill, Sekretär des Vereins

Eines Theils

und dem

Herrn Conrad Plümnecke aus Kl. Lafferde.

Andern Theils

ist nachfolgender Vertrag verabredet und abgeschlossen worden.

§. 1.

Es verleiht der Verein zum Schutze deutscher Einwanderer in Texas dem Herrn

Conrad Plümnecke

nebst seiner Familie, bestehend aus *Zehn* Personen, welcher dies für sich, seine Familie, seine Erben und Rechtsinhaber in bester Form Rechtens annimmt, 320, sage dreihundert und zwanzig acres Landes, zu entnehmen von seinen Ländereien, gelegen in der jetzigen county San Antonio, Republik Texas, sowie jener Landstrich gegenwärtig daliegt, in dem Zustande, in welchem er sich derzeit befindet, und wie solche dem Einwanderer durch einen Agenten des Vereins an Ort und Stelle werden bezeichnet werden.

§. 2.

Es benutzt der Einwanderer den ihm überwiesenen Landstrich als Eigenthümer, ungefährdet in allen im Eigenthume liegenden Rechten, vom Tage der Besitz-Einweisung an gerechnet, ohne jedoch während einem Zeitraume von drei Jahren, von bezeichneter Epoche an gerechnet, diesen Landstrich ganz oder theilweise veräußern zu können.

§. 3.

Es findet dieser Uebertrag des Landes unter folgenden weiteren Bedingungen Statt. Es hat der Einwanderer

1) drei nacheinanderfolgende Jahre, vom Tage der Besitz-Einweisung an gerechnet, auf den bewilligten Ländereien zu verweilen;

2) in demselben Zeitabschnitt fünfzehn acres Land zu umzäunen und in Cultur zu erhalten;

3) ein Wohnhaus auf seinem Grund und Boden zu errichten;

4) sich dem vom Vereine entworfenen Colonisations-Plane und den gesetzlichen Bestimmungen des Landes im Allgemeinen zu unterwerfen.

Johann Heinrich Conrad Pluenneke's Contract (Page 1)

§. 4.

Die betreffenden Landes=Vermessungskosten fallen dem Einwanderer zur Last, der Verein aber legt dieselben vor: es haften für diesen Vorschuß sowohl, als alle andern dem Einwanderer durch den Verein etwa gemachten Vorschüsse, die umsonst bewilligten Ländereien und die darauf aufgeführten Gebäude und Vorrichtungen als Pfand, bis zur gänzlichen Abtragung der Schuld.

§. 5.

Gegenwärtiger provisorischer Erwerbstitel wird in Texas selbst durch eine von der teranischen Regierung ausgestellte, auf den Namen des Einwanderers lautende, definitive Eigenthums=Urkunde, umgetauscht, und zwar drei Jahre nach der Besitz=Einweisung, und wenn die oben festgesetzten Bedingungen von Seiten des Einwanderers erfüllt worden sind.

§. 6.

Bei nicht pünktlicher Erfüllung obiger Bedingungen durch den Einwanderer, verliert derselbe seine Rechte auf gegenwärtige Verleihung, und es fallen die auf den vom Vereine ihm verliehenen Ländereien aufgeführten Gebäulichkeiten, so wie die Ländereien selbst dem Vereine als Entschädigung anheim.

Gegenwärtiger Vertrag soll pflichtgemäß und treu von den Contrahenten in allen Punkten gehandhabt und beobachtet werden, was dieselben anmit durch eigenhändige Namensunterschrift geloben.

So geschehen Bremen, den 31 October 1845

Conrad Pluenneke

Im Namen und Auftrag der Direktion des Vereins zum Schutze deutscher Einwanderer in Texas.

Consulate of the Republic of Texas for the port of Bremen.

These are to certify, that appeared before me Mr. Conr. Pluenneke and made oath, that the whole content of the aforegoing agreement was well comprehended and consented by him, and both parties signed the same in my presence.

Done in Bremen, this 31st of October 1845.

Wm Kehrmann

Vice-Consul of the Republic of Texas

Pluenneke Contract (Page 2)
Appendix 2

Exit Log for the *brig Apollo*

Appendix 3

Private Conrad Pluenneke's Army Pension

<u>**Appendix**</u> 4

Influential 19th Century Methodist Ministers

Carl Biel

Charles A. Grote

John Devilbiss

Eduard Schneider

www.ingramcontent.com/pod-product-compliance
Lightning Source LLC
Chambersburg PA
CBHW070409290526
45791CB00005B/1688